Information Technology Management

C I *m* A

Published in association with
the Chartered Institute of
Management Accountants

C/R

Other titles in the CIMA series

Stage 1

Economics for Accountants
Keith West

Foundation Accounting
Mark Lee Inman

Quantitative Methods
Kevin Pardoe

Stage 2

Cost Accounting
Mark Lee Inman

Financial Accounting
Peter Taylor and Brian Underdown

Management in Practice
Cliff Bowman

Stage 3

Advanced Financial Accounting
Peter Taylor and Brian Underdown

Business Taxation
Neil Stein

Company Law
Julia Bailey and Iain McCullum

Management Accounting Techniques
David Benjamin and Colin Biggs

Stage 4

Control and Audit in Management Accounting
Jeff Coates, Ray Stacey and Colin Rickwood

Decision Making
Roland Fox, Alison Kennedy and Keith Sugden

Financial and Treasury Management
Paul Collier, Terry Cooke and John Glynn

Management Accounting: Strategic Planning and Marketing
Patrick McNamee

Information Technology Management

Stage 2

Second edition

K. N. Bhaskar and R. J. W. Housden

HEINEMANN PROFESSIONAL PUBLISHING

Heinemann Professional Publishing Ltd
Halley Court, Jordan Hill, Oxford OX2 8EJ

OXFORD   LONDON   MELBOURNE   AUCKLAND   SINGAPORE
IBADAN   NAIROBI   GABORONE   KINGSTON

First published as *Accounting Information Systems and Data Processing* 1985
Reprinted 1986, 1988
Second edition 1990

British Library Cataloguing in Publication Data
Bhaskar, Krish *1945*–
    Information technology management – 2nd ed.
    1. Management accounting. Applications of computer systems
    I. Title   II. Housden R. J. W.   III. Chartered Institute of
    Management Accountants   IV. Bhaskar, Krish *1945*–.
    Accounting information systems and data processing
    658.15110255

ISBN 0 434 90077 X

Photoset, printed and bound in Great Britain by
Redwood Press Limited, Melksham, Wiltshire

Contents

Preface		vii
Acknowledgements		ix

Part One Introduction — **1**

1 The management accountant and the computer-based information system — 3
2 An introduction to computers — 15

Part Two Computer Technology — **25**

3 Computer hardware — 27
4 Software and the principles of programming — 45
5 File organization and processing — 77
6 Data organization and management, databases — 96
7 On-line systems and networks — 126
8 Computer systems – control and security — 171

Part Three Systems Analysis and the Business Environment — **211**

9 Systems theory and control systems — 213
10 Systems analysis and design — 233
11 Business activities and organization — 272

Part Four Applications — **301**

12 Basic accounting systems — 303
13 Enhanced management accounting systems — 335
14 Financial models and spreadsheet applications — 364
15 Decision support systems — 388
16 Office automation — 420
17 MIS and management accounting, productivity and cost control — 434
18 Computer auditing — 451

Appendix: The audit process — 479
Glossary — 486
Index — 496

Preface

Our many years' teaching experience of undergraduate and postgraduate students of accountancy, computing and in particular computerized accountancy has both pointed up the need for such a book as this and contributed much to its production. We feel that the scope of the book is also enhanced by our combined knowledge of the modern business environment; it is built upon a broad understanding of computerized accountancy in the 'real world', based on a great deal of consultancy work for companies of all sizes. We hope this combination has given rise to a fruitful mix of the theoretical and the practical.

The book attempts to bring together an overview of the current state of the art in business computing and the development of management information systems, from the perspective of accountancy. We feel that it offers a full and highly comprehensive exposition of its field, seldom found elsewhere. We have tried wherever possible to illustrate the text with sample reports and figures and, of its kind, the book is particularly rich in practical examples based on accounting applications.

In examining computer applications, we incorporate the latest uses to which computers – large and small – are being put within the business environment, and we take a fresh look at computing as it relates to decision support systems and financial modelling. We also examine the present status of western technology and, in the final chapter, contrast this with the Japanese approach to a typical management accounting problem.

The structure of the book is in four basic parts: a brief introduction followed by sections on computer technology, systems analysis and the business environment and, finally, computer applications. The first parts are aimed at endowing the non-computer expert with the knowledge and understanding to tackle the applications section. The final parts deal in more general terms with computing as it relates to accountancy, and assume very little prior knowledge of accounting concepts, although students will normally be expected to have read such texts as C. T. Horngren *Cost Accounting: A Managerial Emphasis* (Prentice Hall International, 1977) and R. S. Kaplan *Advanced Management Accounting*

(Prentice Hall, 1982). For the computing novice, unfamiliar with the technical terms and jargon which necessarily occur throughout the book, a glossary is included at the end of the work.

The book is written primarily for the student of accounting who needs a thorough introduction to computing and data-processing applications. In addition, we feel that there is plenty of new material in the book – particularly in the final part – to interest even a fairly sophisticated student of computerized accountancy or management accounting. It is hoped that the reader of this book will acquire the kind of understanding of computer technology, as it applies to accounting, that will enable him to make personal use of the new technology.

Part 2 discusses the technical details of computers. There are two reasons why the management accountant should have a better understanding of computer technology. First, the computer is like any tool: the better one's understanding of how it works, the more effectively it can be used. Secondly, it is essential for the management accountant to communicate with computer personnel in the design, development, implementation and operation of a management information system, and to deal successfully with computer salesmen and sales engineers: the management accountant should be able to talk to and understand the computer scientist (the computer theorist), data processing staff (the computer practitioner) and salesmen from the computer industry.

Part 3 looks at the computer-related topic of analysing business systems and the steps involved in studying, designing and implementing a new information system. Although this section makes some use of theoretical concepts it is aimed at a practical level. A number of basic issues are identified that influence the choice of design alternatives.

Given an understanding of computer technology, business sytems and systems analysis, Part 4 considers various applications. This section consists of a number of chapters each dealing with a different management accounting topic. Chapter 12 deals with routine ledger accounting systems. Chapter 13 presents a wider set of management accounting activities and includes performance measurement, budgeting and variance reporting and investigation. Chapters 14 and 15 consider the decision support system areas. Chapter 16 describes the rapidly developing area of microcomputer applications, and Chapter 17, whilst highlighting some aspects of greater productivity and the control of data processing costs, also suggests some future trends. Chapter 18 deals with computer auditing.

Acknowledgements

We wish to thank Paul Gardner, Martyn Farnworth and Mark Barry for their help in various ways and at various stages in the production of this book, and Jane Housden, Pam Sinclair and Maureen Edmonds for many hours of typing and proof-reading. We should like also to acknowledge the parts played by many other individuals not mentioned here who have contributed directly and indirectly over the years, not least our families. Any errors or omissions, however, remain our own responsibility.

For the second edition we are indebted to the staff of the Computer Industry Research Unit for the help and assistance provided in the preparation of the revised manuscript. Their excellent technical and editorial contribution has been much appreciated. Special thanks to Peter Lambert who gathered together these contributions into the final draft.

Part One

Introduction

1 The management accountant and the computer-based information system

Accountants are providers of information for decision-makers inside and outside the firm. Management accountants are not so concerned with external users of accounting information. Their focus of attention and orientation is aimed at the provision of information to management. One of the explications of management accounting given in the CIMA Student's Guide is:

> '... the successful development and operation of every individual industrial and commercial enterprise is dependent on the soundness of the plans and the day-to-day decisions made by its management. The management of a company must always strive to achieve the most effective use of its human resources and of its material and financial assets. ... Success or failure depends ultimately on the quality of the decisions made by management, and this in turn depends on the ready availability of up-to-date significant data. The work of the cost and management accountant is vital in ensuring that management's objects are achieved.'

Notice the use of the terms *available, up-to-date*, and *significant* data. It is in these areas that computers can help the management accountant to be more effective in his or her work; and this should result in better managerial decisions. In the same booklet, another reference is made to the work of a management accountant:

> 'In general, the cost and management accountant's specialised knowledge and experience is directed to collecting, collating, interpreting, and communicating a wide range of information and advice regarding costs, cost trends, measurement of performance against standards, budgets, pricing, the effect of changes in volume of sales and production, and other matters needed for sound day-to-day control of the use of resources. Where necessary, he installs the accountancy systems to enable this to be done, possibly using computers.'

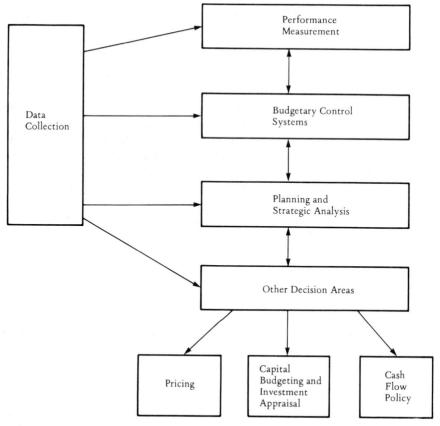

Figure 1.1   *The computer and the role of the management accountant*

Sometimes a management accountant may install and run a computer system. More often than not a management accountant will be involved with the design of and implementation of a computer-based system. Computers help in the collection and collation processes: in fact without computers the job of a management accountant would often regress to the job of a glorified data processor – a clerical role of extreme boredom. Besides data collection and collation, the computer can also be used in the presentation, and hence interpretation, of routine or *ad hoc* reports.

Role of the management accountant

The reader will already be aware that the role of the management accountant covers an extremely broad area with many problems of interpretation. Given the all-embracing definition of the provision of information for decision-making, can we be more specific, particularly with regard to the use of computers? In Figure 1.1, a schematic representation of the functions has been drawn. Starting with data collection, the functions include performance measurement, budgetary control systems, planning and strategic analysis, and other *decision support areas* such as pricing and capital budgeting.

Where can the computer aid the management accountant? The answer is in all the functions shown in Figure 1.1. Most business computer systems contain some form of an accounting system, but very few computer systems really cater for the full needs of the management accountant. However, this is changing with the development of sophisticated micro-based technology. Real world applications are now catching up with theoretical applications. In the early 1980s, users began to demand software which could integrate the main applications needed for data processing and analysis. For example, specialized software and integrated packages offering graphics, word processing, spreadsheet and database management facilities are now widely available.

The computer revolution

The technological revolution has meant that the physical size of computers has decreased, while performance, ability and capacity have dramatically increased. Microtechnology has now entered a new generation of development and can offer virtually all the resources necessary to run a modern business.

Although CIMA has been much concerned with computers and information processing, the accounting profession as a whole has tended to be slow in reacting to the technological revolution. Consequently, a new functional area (Data Processing/Management Services/Computing) has arisen in business, taking over a role more traditionally associated with the finance function. Either the accounting profession must react and utilize the new facilities or another group may take over functions formerly associated with the accountant. The management accountant and his orientation on information are particularly vulnerable. This, if nothing else, should provide both the student and the qualified practitioner with the motivation to learn and harness the possibilities created by the information and technological revolution now under way.

One question which has yet to be resolved is whether the computer specialist shall take over areas that were originally the province of the management accountant – remember that management accounting is a service function and must respond to the needs of its users. Many computer specialists, particularly the data processing specialist, would regard the collection, collation and dissemination of information as their province. Will the management accountant lose some of his functions? In some organizations, especially the larger company, the answer is yes. In smaller companies the answer is no: it will be the management accountant who will (and currently is) fulfilling the role of the DP specialist.

Our feelings about the future are that the growth of computing is such that the DP specialist simply cannot handle the volume of all requests from society for the collection, collation and dissemination of data on computer-based information systems. The DP specialist will increasingly be called upon to undertake complicated or tricky work connected with data processing. We believe that the lion's share of the routine business DP work will fall on the shoulders of the accountant – and in particular the management accountant.

Information systems

Many of the functions performed by a management accountant are part of the *management information system* (MIS). A MIS provides the information management needs to operate a business and to make decisions. The MIS can be manual, semi-computerized or fully computerized. *Data* representing information, are the input to the MIS and considered alone have no meaning. When suitably processed, output data are interpreted to derive *information* which will increase knowledge in a decision environment. The MIS hence uses raw data as an input and processes all data within an organization to provide management with the required information. One point of view is that the management accountant's focus of interest, whilst being wider than that of the financial accountant, is a sub-set of the MIS. Others would argue that *all* information is increasingly becoming the province of the management accountant.

Information demands

On the demand side there are several reasons to believe that, in the future, industry will need more and more data processing and greater calculating power of computers.

Firstly, the business environment is becoming increasingly complex in terms of such phenomena as inflation, the size of organizations, influence of government and international agencies, technological developments and opportunities, spread of world trade, international competition and so on. The modern manager has to consider many, many more factors than his predecessor of even a generation ago. His or her demand for information is correspondingly higher.

Secondly, management science has been developed as a means of helping the modern manager cope with the demands placed on him or her. A number of mathematical techniques of great potential aid to managers are now available (e.g. mathematical programming). These techniques have two factors in common: they use extremely complex and lengthy calculation processes and they provide good answers only when provided with sufficient, accurate data relevant to the problem. Hence, in this case there is a need both for calculating and for data processing power.

Thirdly, business is being inundated with demands for information from society in general and from its representatives (e.g. local and national governments, trade unions, creditors, customers). To meet this demand, industry needs extra information processing capacity, since clearly the requirements of these bodies and of management will not coincide.

For all these reasons the information processing and calculating requirements are likely to grow very substantially in the future. Developments on the supply side are likely to be such that increasingly this demand will be met by the use of computers.

Need for management information

Why is there this growing need for information?

The management process is sometimes defined as the process of planning, organizing, staffing and controlling. The performance of a business depends on how well these functions are being carried out. The fundamental assumption usually made is that better quality information helps management in the process of managing a business. Much of the management process involves making decisions; to make a good decision requires good information as to: (a) the internal or external events that led to the need for a decision to be made; and (b) the likely consequences of alternative decisions. Good information can lead to good decision-making which in turn leads to successful attainment of organizational goals. One way of explaining how better information leads to better decisions is that good information can reduce the element of uncertainty in decision-making and this implies that the consequences of alternative decisions can be more accurately predicted.

Are there any reasons why better information should lead to better decision-making and good managerial performance in meeting the objectives of the business or organization? The above explanations require further elaboration and this is given below.

1 Computers can provide a faster awareness of problems and opportunities by analysing current and historical internal and external data in order to detect opportunities and challenges.

2   Computers can help in the budgetary control process by quickly signalling out-of-control situations requiring corrective action when actual performance deviates from what was planned.

3   The computer can free the manager of clerical data-gathering tasks so that more attention may be given to analysis and planning.

4   By providing an extremely fast and powerful response, computers allow managers to consider a greater number of more complex problems which could not otherwise be considered since the information could not be produced or analysed in time to be of any value.

In summary, computers can help with furnishing the mass of information stored in an organization's MIS. Mere information is not enough: it must be presented in a suitable form to help management. By providing an extremely fast analytical ability, computers allow managers to consider a greater number of more complex problems. A smaller number of simpler problems could not have been considered without the aid of a computer since the information would not have been produced or analysed in time to be of any value. What is the effect of a strike? Which products do we drop during a temporary raw material shortage? These and other questions may require very fast response as would various government-initiated questions. For example the government may have been approached by a Japanese manufacturer and wishes an immediate response on the detailed effect of such a venture on your company.

What information is needed?

What information does management need to manage effectively? Although this question is examined in greater detail subsequently, one or two problems are highlighted here.

Managers are people and, unfortunately, no two people think in identical ways. Different managers view an organization in different ways; different managers may differ in their belief as to what information is relevant in analysing a problem and in decision-making.

Given this distinctive managerial perspective on relevance, time is often of the essence to management. Scarcity of information must be traded-off against the opposite situation of *information overload* – management, swamped with too much undigested information, will simply ignore it. Can some basic requirements be outlined? In theory, information should be:

1   *Accurate*. Facts and information should be correct. Sometimes the requirement for absolute accuracy is not important – a name or address spelt slightly incorrectly may not matter – at other times the accuracy must approach 100 per cent (e.g. account balances).

2 *Timely*. The characteristic of timeliness is important since it is of little consolation to the manager to know that although the information was accurate, it arrived too late to be of use. Questions such as the *response time* (the length of time the computer takes to respond to a user's request) of a computer-based information system to *ad hoc* queries and the delay in the preparation of routine or regular reports are an important consideration for the management accountant. Some information may be classified as 'time-critical'.

3 *Complete*. For managers to make a good decision, they require accurate, timely and complete information. All the necessary information is required otherwise a critical missing fact, vital to a decision, may result in a poor decision being made.

4 *Concise*. A computer-based information system stores vast quantities of facts and data. Managers cannot hope to extract the information required from mountains of printed material. What is required is concise summaries of the relevant data – charts, tables and financial reports may help – highlighting areas of exception to normal or planned activities.

5 *Relevant*. Information that does not lead to action or provide new knowledge or understanding is irrelevant.

One of the reasons for the growth of computer-based information systems is that traditional systems do not provide information with these five basic properties. A computer-based information system can be defined as a collection of inter-related computer-based processing procedures developed in an organization and integrated as necessary with other manual, mechanical, and/or electronic procedures for the purpose of providing accurate, timely, complete, concise and relevant information to aid decision-making and other managerial functions. Since management accounting is often defined as the provision of information for decision-making, we return to the concept that a computer is a tool allowing the management accountant to carry out his duties more effectively.

An additional complication in trying to define what information fulfils the above characteristics concerns (a) the organizational level of management and (b) their function. Managerial organizational levels are usually divided into three categories: top, middle and lower. Lower management are concerned with operating and detailed control considerations and as such mainly use detailed internal information. Top management, on the other hand, are more concerned with planning and policy-making and thus only need summarized internal information, but require detailed external and environmental information. The latter includes information about competitors, customers, suppliers, technology, government and the macro-economic environment. Some of this information would not lend itself readily to computer applications, although questions of, say, the effect of a strike by a supplier may be analysed using the computer system. Management in different functions will also require different information. Product planners will require marketing and cost information as well as much external information. Personnel management will require payroll, productivity and training information. Production management will require detailed stock, machine breakdown and productivity information. By and large the information required by management accountants pervades most managerial functions.

One of the principal lessons to be learnt is that the types of decision made by managers vary so enormously and the most fundamental requirement is that the MIS system must be sufficiently flexible to cope with the changing requests by management for information. This subject is returned to later in the book.

Information-processing activities

With the cost of information-processing technology falling, the power and facilities offered by computers increasing, the growing information needs of management can be satisfied. To understand how this may be achieved it is useful to distinguish different sets of activities. Figure 1.1 showed the roles of the management accountant but these roles can be re-classified into those applications involving routine reporting and those used for decision support areas.

Data processing

The routine reporting of performance measurement or actual versus budget figures are tasks involving *data processing* (DP). DP functions, and information processing in general, consist of three activities. These are input, manipulative and output activities as shown in Figure 1.2.

Input activities consist of organizing or capturing data in some form which is suitable for subsequent processing. Manipulative activities consist of up to four operations:

Classifying – identifying and arranging items with like characteristics;

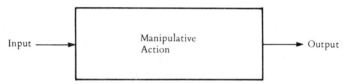

Figure 1.2   *Data processing activities*

Sorting – the arrangement of data in a predetermined sequence to facilitate processing;
Calculating – arithmetic manipulation of the data;
Summarizing – data must often be condensed, compressed or exceptions highlighted so that output reports may be of value by being concise and effective.

After input and manipulation of data, the final activity is output and interpretation of the results. The raw data having been captured and processed the results can be subject to a number of distinct operations including (a) *storage* (or filing) in a suitable place for future reference, (b) *retrieval* or recovery of filed data when required and (c) *reproduction* of the data as output reports. Finally the output is interpreted and the resulting information *communicated* to management. All these steps can be carried out manually. Historically, the candidates for aiding the input, manipulative and output DP functions have been:

Manual methods alone;
Manual methods with machine assistance;
Electro-mechanical means (i.e. the obsolete accounting machine);
Electronic methods.

The solution to most business information-processing requirements dictates a combination of processing techniques with computers carrying out large-volume tasks, whilst manual methods may be more economical for small-volume jobs.

The DP areas can thus help the management accountant in the following areas:

1 Data collection;
2 Conversion of the 'raw' data into more useful information, this process will involve the collation, summarization and analysis of the collected data;
3 The routine dissemination of the data and information to relevant responsibility centres and management;
4 The servicing of *ad hoc* requests for information; and
5 The routine reporting of actual versus budget figures and the provision of further information where variance investigation is required.

Although one reason has been highlighted for using computers in the DP area – the sheer inability of any other method to handle the workload – this is not the only reason. In addition, more businesses are becoming computerized and more functions within a business are also being transferred to electronic data processing techniques. Why?
The principal reasons are:

1   Difficulties in handling increased workloads created by
    (a) the increased demand for information already alluded to, and
    (b) the growth in size and complexity of activities of a firm;
2   Failure of manual methods to supply accurate information;
3   Failure to supply timely information;
4   Productivity or cost-cutting reasons.

This last factor must be further considered. Rising labour and labour support costs associated with non-computer operations have led management to consider the use of computers. The justification for switching to a computer is that, although the equipment costs a larger initial sum, it may (1) save on labour costs or (2) allow for more work without additional staff. Cost savings are, however, often illusory. Until recently, computing systems have not resulted in immediate labour savings – though a firm may be able to achieve these in the long run. This is because it is difficult to make labour redundant and because of the need to hire new specialist labour and retain some of the existing labour. However, in situations where the computer did not achieve cost savings, it could be justified on the grounds of providing more and better data plus the ability to handle increased volumes of data at little or no extra cost.

In increasingly competitive international and national markets it is important that the business community remains especially conscious of efficiency. Productivity comparisons, at all levels from top management downwards and continuing right down to the shop floor, are not favourable internationally – particularly with the Japanese and West Germans. Using somewhat simplified accounting procedures, a number of businesses have achieved substantial cost savings by the introduction of radical new computer technology and have, at the same time, provided an enhanced ability to provide better information to management. Productivity and potential cost savings resulting from increased mechanization through the use of the latest computing technology is a major focus of this book. In the tough competitive world today, the management accountant must be efficient *and* responsive to the needs of management.

Forward-looking information systems

Management accountants are not only responsible for providing reports about current and historical events; their functions also include planning, forecasting and decision-making. Increasingly computer applications are being used to assist the management accountant in performing these functions. Indeed a new 'buzzword' has been used to describe the use of computer applications by accountants – 'financial modelling'. The arguments for financial modelling include:

1 *Speed*: the computer can quickly calculate the forecasts or plans.
2 The ability to *redo* the plans or forecasts with changed assumptions or data.
3 The ability to incorporate *increased complexity* in the financial model which would be impractical in a manual calculation.

Financial modelling is a significant growth area for management accountants. Bert Gardner (FCMA), Financial Director of Yorkshire Imperial Plastics believes that by the year 2000, every management accountant will be heavily involved in using the computer for planning purposes. The computer must not just be regarded as a tool for helping process routine information. Whatever work the management accountant undertakes, the computer may be able to help and provide a flexible, powerful and effective tool.

The processes of longer run planning and short-term budgeting are important. Both require the specification of goals and objectives, the establishment of the budgets or plans that serve as the basis for control, and the revision of those plans as a result of changing conditions. Specifically, the planning process may be broken into the following steps:

1 Identify the problem or opportunity;
2 Gather and analyse relevant facts;
3 Determine suitable alternatives;
4 Evaluate and select the most appropriate alternative,
5 Implement, control and revise decisions.

The computer can help in each of these steps. By providing data or analysing existing data in new ways, new problems may be identified. For example, suppose sales of product Y are declining in region X. The next step is to analyse all relevant facts. One might look to see if there has been adequate sales support, problems with customers and so on. Alternatively, the computer may be helping to forecast sales, identify a new opportunity (e.g. market for product Z is expanding very fast).

By using financial modelling, linear programming, network analysis and other operations research techniques, the management accountant can search for, evaluate and successively refine suitable alternatives. Sometimes, the computer may be used very much as a calculator (e.g. discounted cash flow calculations) and at other times more complex financial and/or economic computer models may be built to test the effects of alternative pricing strategies. Finally when decisions have been made, the computer can help to split the global decision into a number of subordinate plans required to implement those decisions.

Within the context of budgeting, the computer can be helpful in aggregating detailed operational budgets at the cost or profit centre level. The computer also facilitates the process of experimenting with and refining the initial 'first-guess' budgets of those centres.

Conclusion

This chapter has examined the role of the management accountant and the use to which he or she can put computers in an information system. Some of the functions of a management accountant are of a routine nature and this was more or less covered by the computing concept of *data processing*. The remaining functions were more concerned with providing information for management decisions and indeed assisting with the decision-making process – these areas being described as *decision support systems*. Naturally, the management accountant has many functions which do not involve the computer (e.g. cost allocation schemes, the negotiation and creation of participative budgets and so on). But the computer is an extremely effective and powerful tool which can help the management accountant in many areas.

The concept of an information system and, in particular, a MIS was introduced. The demand for information is increasing due to (1) demands by management faced with an increasingly complex business environment and aggressive competitive market place and (2) requirements by external sources such as local and central government agencies. At the same time a technological revolution has occurred on the data-processing side and it is now possible to meet the increased demands for information through cheaper and more powerful computers and related equipment.

Earlier in the chapter, we also discussed the nature of information and how this might help management make better decisions and meet their firm's objectives. Although this topic will be returned to later in the book, it was noted that information should be accurate, timely, complete, concise and relevant. Too much information, leading to *information overload*, could be as bad as too little.

One of the surprising features of computer-based information systems is that technological progress seems to be occurring at such a pace that the full facilities available on modern computing systems are not utilized. It is tempting simply to do what we have done before. Innovation and new techniques always create unforeseen problems and there is, in any case, a learning cost associated with any form of change. One of the objectives of this book is to make the reader aware of what may be achieved using current technology. However an analogy can be drawn between the use of a computer and the use of any other tool: it is too easy to be carried away by the aesthetic value of the tool itself whilst forgetting the primary aim – the use to which the tool has to be put.

2 An introduction to computers

In this chapter we discuss the basic constituents of a computer. The material presented is fundamental and lays the foundations for later chapters. Most readers will have had some exposure to computing and will wish to decide which of the later sections are relevant to their particular interests and experience. A comprehensive guide to the remainder of the book is included in the Preface.

Computer systems

Computer systems are composed of two principal ingredients:

1 *Hardware*. Hardware is the generic term for equipment, circuits and machinery which come in boxes or containers; that is, physical objects that can be seen and touched.
2 *Software*. Once the hardware has been installed it is nothing more than an assembly of circuits and components which is quite useless without instructions for its use. Software are the instructions, represented or stored electronically in the machine itself, to control and co-ordinate the operations of the components in the system. The instructions endow the machinery with the ability to process data. Different instruction sequences are required for different data-processing activities. The activity of designing, implementing and maintaining software is called programming and is usually undertaken by specialists.

The management accountant must remember that apart from hardware and software, there is another vital ingredient to any information processing system – man. For men must program the computer to perform the data processing, men must input the raw data to be processed and receive output from the system if it is to operate successfully.

In the previous chapter, an information-processing system was defined as having an input, processing capability and an output. Similarly, computers have all three of these attributes plus the unique and infallible ability to remember or store representations of facts and information. This additional attribute is particularly important as we shall find it convenient to think of a computer as a data storage and processing machine. Figure 2.1 shows a diagrammatic representation of a simple computer. In this instance, data are input via a Visual Display Unit (VDU). VDU is used as a generic term for a combined keyboard and television-type screen (also known as a monitor or terminal). Such an arrangement in modern networked microcomputer systems would be known as a 'workstation'. Data can be output either onto the VDU or onto a *printer*: this may be a device similar to a typewriter without a keyboard (usually it can print at higher speeds than a typewriter).

The *store* is composed of two parts. First, a *primary* (main or immediate access) store is used as a working storage area with very high speeds of access and data transfer. *Secondary* (or *backing*) store is used for longer term storage to file data away – the storage medium is usually disk (similar to a series of gramophone records one on top of the other) or magnetic tape (similar to reel-to-reel tape used in tape recorders). Recent developments in laser technology suggest that laser disks may play an increasingly important part as a secondary storage medium.

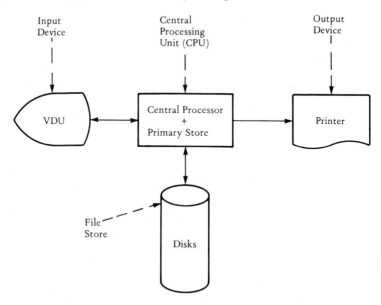

Figure 2.1   *Diagrammatic representation of a computer system in its simplest form*

The actual processing is carried out by what can only be described as the nucleus of the computer – the processor. This unit actually interprets the stored instructions, performs all the calculations, controls the transfer of data between units and co-ordinates the operation of all the units. This coupled with the primary store is called the central processing unit (*CPU*). The backing/secondary/auxiliary store is often described as the filestore. Let us recap:

Input device	a means of input to the computer (nowadays this is usually a keyboard terminal e.g. teletype or VDU);
Central processing unit	a unit which acts as a short-term store, a number-cruncher and a means of organizing and controlling all the parts of a computer;
File store or secondary store or backing store	a means (or series of devices) whereby substantial amounts of data organized as files can be stored for relatively long periods of time (usually stored on magnetic tapes or disks);
Output device	an output device for transferring information from the *processing unit* or *file store* to humans who can then read (or hear) the information for themselves (usually a VDU, teletype or printer).

Diagrammatically, these four constituent components are often represented by the symbols used in Figure 2.1 (we have assumed an input device of one VDU (Visual Display Unit) and an output device of one line printer).

Basically, Figure 2.1 represents the totality of a computer system. Data about transactions and events is input to the system via the VDU or input device and is processed by the processing unit which stores the data in the file store. Details of all ledgers for example will be maintained in the file store. Reports will be prepared on the output device and may be of two forms – some reports will be a summary or a detailed description of the files held in the filestore; other reports will be a list or a summary of the data contained in a particular file, for example a detailed record of transactions as they were input.

Two types of input to the computer must be distinguished. First there is the input of raw data to be stored or processed: transaction details or other data about the occurrence of an event. How does the computer know what processing is required? Instructions must be supplied to the computer about its own internal organization and about tasks and procedures to be performed. For example, before a transaction can be entered into a computer, the computer must be told to ready itself to accept a transaction. The instructions, like data, are input via the VDU. They may be executed immediately or stored for later execution. We call this type of input *commands*, which must be distinguished from the former type of input which can be called *data entry*.

A command to initiate the preparation of a particular report may nevertheless require some data entry such as, for example, the date, the period which the report is to span, the number of copies of the report and so on. Other commands would include a start-up or close-down procedure, the running of various data entry procedures, the printing of various reports and the updating of a file with other data stored in the file store. This last point requires further elaboration.

A sales ledger for example may be one of several files contained in the file store of a computer system. Data about sales transactions may not be input directly to the sales ledger. Instead the data entry function may first input the data on to a temporary transactions file. At a suitable time when the input data has been validated or checked the data from the temporary file may be used to update the sales ledger file.

It is convenient to introduce a number of other terms as this stage. An *on-line* system means that the data are input directly to the system. A VDU directly connected to a computer is *on-line*. A cash till in which the transactions are recorded onto a cassette tape which is subsequently input to the computer is said to be *off-line*. A *real-time* computer system is one in which a computer system controls an environment by receiving data, processing them, and taking action or returning results sufficiently quickly to affect the functioning of the environment at that time. Most VDUs are used on-line and in real-time – data are input to the computer and if possible checked immediately; if an error in the data is detected (e.g. an invalid date) then the computer will tell the person inputting the data by responding with an appropriate error message (usually within 2 or 3 seconds). A terminal or VDU which is on-line/real-time is usually said to be *interactive*. The terminal operator is in direct communication with the computer and *interacts* with the computer. This dialogue with the computer is sometimes referred to as a *conversational mode* of communication with a computer.

An alternative to interactive mode of operation is sometimes referred to as *batch* mode. The reader will be familiar with batching procedures which occur outside a computer system. For example invoices may be held, not dealt with immediately, and a monthly 'batch' of all invoices input to the system. It may be more efficient to batch operations or simply impossible to perform them in real-time in which case they must be queued and performed later. Similarly, in a computer it may be inconvenient or even impossible to respond to a request in real-time or interactively. A series of commands may then be stored as a particular task to be performed later. The tasks may be queued and the computer may work through them systematically, storing the results of these tasks in files. The *batch mode* of operation, in contrast to the interactive mode, would be the sort of operation whereby you leave the computer with a sequence of requests to be serviced sometime under the control of a batch control system leaving the operator free to go and do something else. Batch systems may operate at night when there is no operator in attendance.

Although it is possible for a computer to have many VDUs on-line simultaneously, for the moment we will assume that there is only one VDU and one line printer. How can the computer interact with a user at a VDU, service the line printer, examine a file from disk and look after its internal administration? First the computer has great speed. While it may take a human several seconds to think of an appropriate response to a VDU prompt, the computer will respond to a user's inquiry within a fraction of a second (if it has nothing else to do). Second, most file stores (such as disks) and most printers have some degree of autonomy and intelligence. What the processing unit does is to parcel up a sequence of instructions and delegate them to the local intelligence attached to a file store or line printer. Thirdly, sometimes the requests for attention by the processing unit are so great that they must be queued. Queues are built up both in the processing unit (usually a short note of what is to be done) and in the file store (the full details of all demands for attention). Some demands for attention are more urgent than others, for example a request from an on-line VDU. In order to stop the processing unit doing whatever it was doing and service this priority demand for service, the processing unit comes equipped with an *interrupt* feature. The computer can be set up so that certain demands with higher priority will interrupt what it is doing and jump in front of a queue of less important requests. When this high priority demand has been serviced the computer will resume where it left off.

One final piece of information is required at this stage to enable us to understand a simple computerized system. When something is to be printed, the computer may actually print whatever is to be printed as it is generated, that is as it is processing the input data or the file. It is however much more likely that the computer will form a temporary file, in the file store, of the data that is to be printed and will then transfer that data to the line printer when it has completed all the processing (in this way the processing unit has parcelled the instruction nicely and can simply say to the local intelligence in charge of the line printer: 'print this file please'). Sometimes, there are several files to be printed, in which case a queue of files to be printed will be formed by the computer and stored in the file store. (This process is called *spooling* and is not available on some of the smaller micro-computers.)

The current computer range

In the previous chapter, a glimpse of part of a computer-based information system was given. Processing methods were also divided into four types: manual, machine-assisted, electro-mechanical and electronic. An example of machine-assisted processing was the use of the accounting machine which contained a typewriter, and adding *counters* or *registers*, to print the accumulated totals for different classifications. More recent accounting machines have much larger data storage capabilities and have the processing features of a computer (i.e. like a sophisticated calculator) but do not really have a file store – all information is contained on ledger cards with typed information. This type of accounting machine couples type-writing and form-handling ability with the features normally associated with a programmable calculator. Electro-mechanical systems offer similar accounting functions but store data in a machine-readable form, for example, the visible-record computer (VRC) stores data in magnetic as well as printed form. The VRC could read from and write to this magnetic storage. The VRC began to provide the kinds of facility that are expected of modern electronic processing systems. That is, to manipulate, store, retrieve and reproduce data. Electro-mechanical processing systems were made obsolete by the development of the electronic computer.

Development of electronic computers

The first type of computer to be used widely – termed the first generation machines – were mainly designed for scientific use in the period 1954 to 1960. They were large and unwieldy, relying on vacuum tubes for main memory and handling a single program at a time. The progenitor of this generation was UNIVAC 1, built by Remington Rand. The second generation machines appeared around 1960 and were more versatile, using transistors instead of vacuum tubes and also employing disk storage. It was during this second stage that high level languages like COBOL and Fortran were developed. The third generation of computers was announced in the mid-1960s and included IBM's System 360 and ICL's 1900 range. They combined the speed necessary for scientific applications with the high input/output and file-processing capability required for business use. This generation of machine was faster, cheaper and more flexible in its application. This was achieved through the use of (1) *integrated circuits* (several circuit elements in one monolithic chip); (2) *modularity* (building block principle of constructing a computer to a required specification); (3) *multi-access* (the means whereby several input and output devices could be connected on-line/real-time simultaneously); and (4) *multi-programming* (doing several distinct jobs at the same time).

During the early 1970s, most manufacturers brought out new ranges of computers which were basically more powerful, faster, more sophisticated and could handle a larger throughput of data and larger file stores – usually provided at a cheaper real cost. Sometimes these machines are referred to as *fourth generation* computers. However, the early 1970s also saw another revolution.

Computer manufacturers like IBM, ICL, Burroughs, Corporation, Honeywell, Sperry-Univac and Control Data Corporation were mainly in the third/fourth generation computing area. (NCR was an exception in that it covered the computer, accounting machine and VRC market.) However, new names such as Digital Equipment Corporation, Data General, Hewlett-Packard, Perkins-Elmer (Interdata), Harris, and Prime began to be known as major manufacturers of a new type of computer – the *mini*computer.

From the mid-1970s on another set of new names entered the computer market. For example, names such as Intel, Zilog, Motorola, Commodore, Texas Instruments, and ITT became well known as manufacturers of *micro*processors.

From the early 1980s onwards we have witnessed the growth of a fifth generation of computers, characterized, in particular, by developments in the speed, power and general capability of the micro or personal computer, now an essential business tool. In mid-1987 a new generation of PCs appeared with a greatly improved overall performance.

Computer sizes

The development of electronic computers has seen both increasing complexity and a reduction in the size of the equipment. We can distinguish between a number of computer size categories: mainframes, minicomputers and microprocessors.

Medium computers or *mainframes* were and still are very refined fourth generation machines. Their current cost is from £150,000 to over £5 million. Obviously, the distinction between the categories is difficult to define and will become increasingly less distinct. A final category is the *very large system* (VLS) which is very expensive and is either very fast or has special capabilities. Most *mainframes* are now *fourth generation* machines by virtue of the fact that they utilize advanced technology which has improved upon the performance and size of the third generation machines.

Table 2.1 shows how the technology of the machines has changed over successive generations. The integrated circuit has been even further reduced through *large-scale integration* (LSI) of circuits. With better technology, the size required to house a given computer power has also fallen. Circuit miniaturization, because of the shorter distances for electric pulses to travel, has also brought increased speed of operation. Early machines with speeds measured in *milliseconds* (one thousandth of a second) were replaced by second generation machines with internal operating speeds of *microseconds* (one millionth of a second). Current

Table 2.1   Differences between generations of computers

Generation of computer	1	2	3	4	5
Approximate time	1955	1964	1970	1975	1988+
Technology	Valves and tubes	Transistors	Integrated circuits (IC)	Large-scale integration (LSI)	Large-scale integration of existing LSIs
Speed* Time taken to execute an instruction in the CPU	333 microseconds	10 microseconds	100 nanoseconds	30 nanoseconds	5 nanoseconds
Maximum memory in bytes (or characters)	20,000	128,000	1 million	10 million	Virtually unlimited
Reliability Mean time between failures of CPU	Hours	Days to weeks	Weeks to months	Months	?

*A microsecond = 1/1,000,000 of a second; a nanosecond = 1/1,000,000,000 of a second.

computers, including some microcomputers, have operation speeds of a few *nanoseconds* (one US billionth of a second).

Minicomputers were very much cheaper third or fourth generation machines having similar features to the next category of computers, but with less sophisticated file-handling capabilities. In 1975, the cost of a third or fourth generation machine from IBM (System 370) or ICL (ICL 1900) ran to over £200,000 for a small system. A small minicomputer could be bought for around £50,000 with the same number-crunching ability though a reduced file-processing capability. (The current cost for a typical minicomputer system is £10,000–£150,000.)

The typical microprocessor system is made on a single tiny chip of silicon and is combined with other elements that provide input/output connections and file store to provide a general purpose system which can perform some of the same (or similar) operations as much larger machines. This is the age of the microprocessor. Even the lowest-priced business computing system, costing as little as £2,000, is as powerful as the mainframe computers of the 1970s. A number of widely separated autonomous microcomputers can be connected together by data communication lines to form a networked computing system of which the total capacity is more than sufficient to meet most business needs. Hardware developments have progressed ahead of software. The advanced microprocessor-based computers, sometimes known as workstations, are as powerful as some mainframe computers of the 1970s. Our inability to produce sufficient quality software to match the potential of the existing hardware will be the main constraint on future developments.

Guide to current systems

Below is a table summarizing some of the current systems available from three major suppliers. Distinctions are made between the smaller (PC) and larger (workstation) microprocessor-based computers and between the larger and smaller mainframes.

Table 2.2   **Guide to current systems, circa 1990**

Size	*Range*	*ICL*	*IBM*	*DEC*	*Price guide for a typical configuration*
					£000
MICRO PROCESSOR	PCs	QUATTRO VIENNA	PS/2	DECmate	<5
	Workstations	DRS (UNIX) (AIX)	RT RIOS	VAX Station	<25
MINI	Small	DRS Series 300 (UNIX) [Other: System 25]	RT RIOS (AIX) small AS/400s (OS/400)	Micro VAX (VMS)	10–150
MAINFRAME	Medium	DRS Series 400/500 (UNIX)	AS 400 (OS 400)	Large Micro VAX Small VAX 6000 (VMS)	100–500
	Large	Series 39 ESSEX	3090s (MVS or VM)	Large VAX 6000 (VMS)	300–2,000

Part One: Further reading

Amey, L. R. and Eggington, D. A. *Management Accounting: A Conceptual Approach* (Longman, 1973)

Bodnar, G. H. *Accounting Information Systems* (Allyn and Bacon, 1980)

Cushing, J. R. and Davis, B. E. *Accounting Information Systems: A Book of Readings with Cases* (Addison-Wesley, 1980)

Dearden, J. *Cost Accounting and Financial Control Systems* (Addison-Wesley, 1973)

Fanning, D. (ed.) *Handbook of Management Accounting* (Gower, 1983)

Hicks, J. O. and Leininger, W. E. *Accounting Information Systems* (West Publishing, 1981)

Horngren, C. T. *Cost Accounting: A Managerial Emphasis* (Prentice-Hall, 1977)

Hunt, R. and Shelley, J. *Computers and Common Sense* (Prentice-Hall, 3rd edn. 1983)

Kaplan, R. S. *Advanced Management Accounting* (Prentice-Hall, 1982)

Morse, W. J. *Cost Accounting: Processing, Evaluating, and Using Cost Data* (Addison-Wesley, 1979)

Oliver, D. H. and Chapman, R. J. *Data Processing: An Instructional Manual for Business and Accountancy Students* (DP Publications, 1979)

Page, J. and Hooper, P. *Accounting and Information Systems* (Prentice-Hall International, 1979)

Sanders, D. H. *Computers in Business: An Introduction* (McGraw-Hill Kogakusha, 1979)

Part Two

Computer Technology

3 Computer hardware

In Chapter 2 a distinction was made between *hardware* (equipment) and *software* (the instructions that control and perform useful operations). The instructions that run a computer form something known as a *computer program* (henceforth program) and are stored in the primary store of the computer. Although this chapter concentrates on hardware, reference will be made from time to time to the place of programs within the overall structure (or architecture) of the computer.

At this point the management accounting student may throw up his hands in horror at the terminology. Yet it is vitally important for all potential management accountants and practitioners to become familiar with computer jargon.

There are two distinct types of computers: *digital* and *analog* computers. Hybrid computers combine some of the features of both digital and analog machines. Analog computers have very few applications in the business world so we shall not consider them. Digital computers represent numbers and other data as electrical pulses and by the states of magnetic devices, which allow a numerical representation in binary coded form.

Central processing unit

In Chapter 2 we outlined the basic ingredients of a computer system: input and output media, central processing unit and filestore. To begin with it must be pointed out that all the peripherals (e.g. input/output devices) usually have *controllers* which can carry out a certain amount of servicing of requests by these relatively slow devices independently of the CPU. Remember that to the CPU one millionth of a second may seem a long time whilst a printer may only output one or two characters every one thousandth of a second. Whilst waiting for a human to reply to a question, which can take several seconds, the 'opportunity cost' to the central processor could be millions of arithmetic calculations. Similarly, access times to filestore are slow and once again disks usually have associated controllers to carry out certain specified tasks without CPU intervention.

The CPU is an important piece of equipment because it is the 'heart and brain' of a computer system. In Figure 3.1 the CPU is expanded to show:

(a) primary storage (or memory);
(b) the control unit;
(c) the arithmetic and logic unit;
(d) input and output storage areas (buffers).

Instructions are transferred (copied) one at a time from the main store to an instruction register in the control unit, where they are decoded and executed. The control unit sends appropriate signals to activate other units. Each peripheral unit and its controller has its own *interface* (i.e. communication channel) to the CPU's control unit.

The primary storage area will actually be subdivided into four conceptual areas (but these are not fixed by built-in physical boundaries). Three of the four storage areas are used for *data storage* purposes: an *input storage* area to receive data from input media, an *output storage* section containing processed information that is awaiting an output operation, and a *working storage* area that contains data being processed as well as intermediate results of processing (the processing being under the control of a pro-

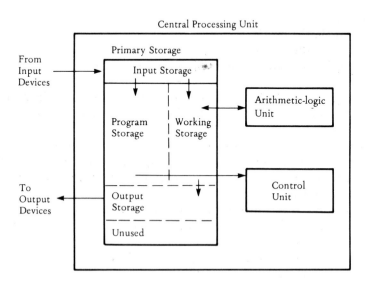

Figure 3.1   *Ingredients of a CPU*

gram). The fourth area of primary storage is the program storage area containing the processing instructions.

Input data will be transferred from an input device to the input storage area until needed. When some actual processing is desired, data are transferred to the arithmetic-logic unit and processed. Intermediate results, generated in the arithmetic-logic unit, are temporarily placed in a designated working storage until needed subsequently. (Data may move between the working storage area and the arithmetic-logic unit a number of times.) The final results are transferred through the output storage area to an output device.

The order in which the instructions contained in a program are obeyed is generally determined by the order in which they are input and stored in the program storage area. Each instruction in turn is copied from the program storage area to the control unit where it is decoded and executed, then the cycle is repeated for the next instruction in sequence.

The primary storage area consists of a number of storage locations each of which can be separately *addressed*. There is a distinction between the address number and the content of a particular storage location. This concept can best be illustrated by a simple example using a model computer. Suppose the following data have been input for a particular employee: he worked 36 hours for £4.21 an hour; the tax structure is such that he must pay tax at 25% on the total gross amount. This data will form an input record of payroll data. The steps involved are as follows:

1   Read the employee's payroll data into primary storage ready for processing;
2   Calculate total earnings;
3   Calculate the tax deduction;
4   Calculate the take-home pay;
5   Print a cheque for the amount of take-home pay.

This sequence, which has to be repeated for each employee on the payroll, is not in a form suitable for direct interpretation and execution by a computer. It is the job of a programmer to construct an equivalent sequence of machine instructions to perform these operations and to repeat them for each employee. However, it is convenient for the present to assume a fairly high level of instructions for our model computer as shown in Figure 3.2.

We assume that the primary storage area of this computer has 24 locations divided between program and data storage areas as follows:

Input storage: locations 01, 02, 03 and 04;
Working storage: location 05;
Program storage: locations 07 to 17;

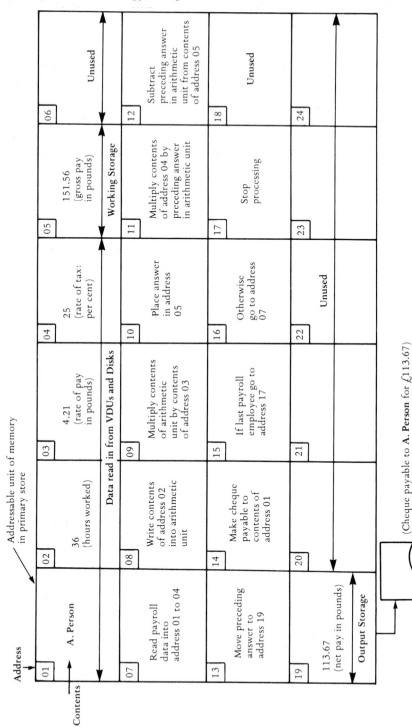

Figure 3.2   *Storage areas in CPU memory*

Output storage: location 19;
Unused storage: locations 06, 18 and 20 to 24.

First, the program of instructions must be input to the program storage area, locations 07 to 17. Then, the computer operating under the control of this stored program commences execution. The first instruction, stored at location 07, is copied to the control unit, decoded and executed, causing the payroll data to be read from the input device and stored in locations 01 to 04. Each of the succeeding instructions in turn is fetched, decoded and executed until the computer is directed by a specific instruction, such as those at locations 15 and 16, to do otherwise. As the instructions are carried out, an intermediate result (gross pay, which we require to be kept) is placed in a working storage area, location 05. Finally, the instruction at location 14 causes a cheque to be printed on special stationery (or possibly held in a *spooled* file*) using the output data assigned to the output storage area, location 19, by the previous instruction. The whole sequence of instructions from location 7 to 14 is repeated while there are more employees to be dealt with and then the processing stops.

Architecture of memory

All information in the store is represented in binary form. A basic unit is the binary digit or BIT – equivalent to whether a device is on or off (representing one or zero). A BYTE is 8 bits (i.e. a collection of eight zeros and ones) and is usually coded to represent a character (e.g. A–Z, 0–9, £, *, ≠ etc.). A *byte* and a character are terms often used interchangeably.

The storage capacity of each unit of addressable memory is something that is fundamental (being built-in) to the machine. In some machines the addressable unit is a single character whereas other machines are designed to store a fixed number of characters at each address and the computer treats this fixed-length collection of characters (which could either represent data or an instruction) as a *word*. Character- or byte-addressable machines are said to be variable word-length machines. Clearly, the longer the word-length the more data that can be held in a single word and, in particular, the bigger the range of numbers that can be represented in and processed as a single word. This facilitates efficient arithmetic processing of numerical data. In a fixed word-length machine, no matter how little data there is in a word, the whole of the contents of any storage location must be accessed and processed as a single indivisible unit. A variable word-length machine allows more efficient use of storage, but arithmetic on multiple bytes of data cannot be performed in a single operation.

*i.e. a file created temporarily which will then enter a queue of files waiting to be printed.

In order to combine the storage efficiency of a variable-length word machine and the processing efficiency of the fixed-length word, many manufacturers offer an architecture that can be operated with both variable- and fixed-length words. On byte-addressable machines, bytes can usually be grouped together and operated on as a single fixed unit as follows:

Half word   = 2 bytes;
Word   = 4 bytes;
Double word = 8 bytes.

Thus, many computers have (a) a built-in instruction to operate on variable-length words (with the instruction itself specifying the number of characters in the word) – especially useful for storing names or any other string of characters, and (b) additional *sets* of instructions which operate automatically on fixed sets of data – especially useful for arithmetic and scientific uses.

There is another factor yet to be considered. The control unit can access data at any address in memory but it is critically dependent in its addressing ability on the size of the fixed length words: the smaller the size the smaller the maximum address that can be stored. For example an 8-bit representation of an address limits the range of directly adressable store to $2^8 = 256$ words. A 16-bit address gives direct access to about 64,000 words* (64K words to use the common terminology, or 128K bytes – 2 bytes to a 16-bit word). By means of sophisticated hardware and software routines it is possible to indirectly address storage outside these limits but at some cost to performance. Using such techniques an 8-bit microprocessor might address about 64K bytes of store and a 16-bit machine more than 64K words. Machines with 32-bit words can address very large amounts of memory.

What this means is that some smaller machines – with small fixed length word addressing – are unable to (1) store a large number of instructions or (2) to hold much data in primary store. In certain business applications this may not matter; in others it will. Typically, the size limitations shown in Table 3.1 obtain.

The rapid development of microcomputer hardware means that the

Table 3.1

8-bit microcomputer (e.g. ZILOG Z80A)	64K bytes
16-bit microcomputer (e.g. INTEL 8086)	up to 1 megabyte
32-bit microcomputer (e.g. INTEL 80386)	16+ megabytes
Medium 16-bit minicomputer (e.g. PDP-11/44)	up to 2 megabytes
Mainframe (e.g. IBM AS/400)	4-96 megabytes

*The precise number is actually $2^{16} = 65,536$.
Memory is usually added on in increments of 16,384 (= 16K), 32,768 (= 32K), 65,536 (= 64K), 131,072 (= 128K), 262,144 (= 256K), 524,288 (= 512K or 1/2 megabyte), 1,048,576 (= 1 megabyte), 2,097,152 (= 2 megabytes).

availability of *total* primary or random access memory (RAM) is becoming less of a problem. For example, 8-bit microcomputers are now obsolete and the minimum RAM of commercial microcomputers is now 640K bytes. However, there is still the problem of *available* primary memory. Modern software makes considerable demands on primary memory, for example, Lotus 1-2-3 requires a minimum of 640K primary memory. Some of the total primary memory will be used by the operating system of the computer and the amount of available memory can be reduced further if the user has 'Terminate and Stay Resident' (TSR) programs. These programs, for example Sidekick, can be used while another application is already in use, without having to quit out of the application. In order to do this they have to be stored in primary memory. Another way in which available primary memory can be reduced is by installing a cache memory. This is part of primary memory allocated as a data store for very frequently used data or instructions. The reason for using a cache memory is that accessing information from secondary, or Read Only Memory (ROM) is relatively slow.

A feature of most modern computers is read-only memory (ROM). This is used to hold *microprograms* and firmware, very low-level machine instructions, that need to be permanently available in the store. The contents of ROM can be read and executed but not overwritten. Programmable read-only memory (PROM) is similar to ROM but can be reprogrammed by specialists using appropriate equipment. The uses of microprograms held in ROM are two-fold. First a CPU can be made to behave and function differently by changing the microprogramming. Instruction sets made available to the user may be implemented as microroutines which enable the machine to perform particular kinds of operations, possibly making it more suitable for either business or scientific applications. Secondly, the efficiency of a machine can be increased by microprogramming certain specialized tasks for which electronic circuits, designed to perform these dedicated tasks (sometimes called hardwired instructions) are not supplied because of their expense.

Types of memory

Apart from valves, which became obsolete in the early 1960s, magnetic core storage technology first dominated memory. Cores are tiny rings which can be magnetized in either of two directions (thus representing the value 0 or 1). Although core storage has the asset that it is non-volatile (i.e. when the electricity is switched off it retains its state), semiconductor storage is now universal. Semiconductor memory consists of integrated circuits. The more expensive semiconductors (bipolar semiconductor memory) are used in cache and arithmetic logic units where speed is of the utmost importance. Metal-oxide semiconductor (MOS) memory is slower and cheaper and is generally used for main memory. The semiconductor memory is volatile and therefore many larger systems would cover themselves against power failure by having a backup power supply system. Semiconductor memory is cheaper, more compact and can be faster than core memory.

To those interested the operation of a semiconductor chip is as follows. There will be a block of transistors (say a grid of 64 bits). Transistors act as switching devices allowing each grid point to be either charged (one) or not charged (zero). At each mesh point on the grid is a tiny capacitor capable of holding the charge which is periodically refreshed, since the capacitor tends to lose its charge. To charge a particular capacitor, the row and column numbers must be calculated and the correct transistor switches turned on, thereby charging the relevant capacitor, which is then sensed as on, representing a 'one'.

File store

The reader may wonder at the moment why, if such large amounts of random access memory are available with semiconductors, there is a need for other types of memory – file store (or *backing store* or auxiliary store). The answer is cost.

Magnetic disk storage

By far the most common medium of secondary storage is now the magnetic disk. This has approximately 200 concentric 'tracks' on each of which information can be recorded and sensed magnetically by means of a read/write head. Each track is normally sub-divided into 'sectors' which can be individually addressed. The number of sectors will be between two and sixteen, and a sector will typically contain 500–4,000 characters of data.

Very frequently, a set of disks will be mounted together on a common axis to form a disk pack (Figure 3.3). If there are six disks, this gives ten usable surfaces (all except the two outer-most), each of which has its own access head. An important feature of multiple disk packs of this type is that the heads move across the tracks together, rather like the teeth of a large comb being slipped between the disk surfaces. Consequently, the tracks which can be accessed at any one time all lie in the same radial position relative to the central axis. This gives rise to the important concept of a *cylinder* or *seek area* of data, i.e. all the data which can be accessed without further movement of the read/write heads.

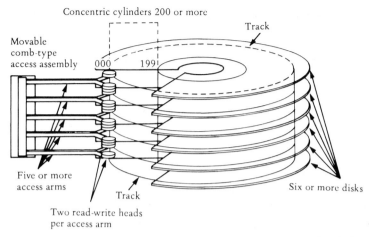

Concentric cylinders 200 or more

Track

Movable
comb-type
access assembly   000   199

Track

Five or more
access arms

Six or more disks

Track

Two read-write heads
per access arm

Figure 3.3   *Schematic diagram of a replaceable disk unit showing the concept of a cylinder of data*

When data which uses magnetic disks is to be read or written, two operations are involved: positioning of the heads at the appropriate point of storage, and transfer of the data to or from the main memory. The time needed for these operations is known as *access time* and *transmission time* respectively.

The access time itself has two components, namely the *seek time* needed to move the access heads to the correct cylinder position, and the *latency* or rotational delay which occurs while the beginning of the required sector rotates to the read position. An average seek time could be 50–100 milliseconds, but the latency is only about 10 milliseconds. There is thus a considerable advantage in speed if data can be accessed without the need to move the head assembly. For this reason a file of data will, so far as possible, be placed on a set of tracks with a common radius – forming a 'cylinder' of data – rather than across all the tracks of a single disk.

Where this is not practical, for example when a file is larger than the capacity of a single cylinder, or when using a single disk device such as a cartridge disk (a small one disk pack) the aim should always be to minimize head movement by steady progression of the data from one track to an adjacent track.

The great merit of replaceable disk packs (and exchangeable cartridge disks) as opposed to fixed disks, is that as their names imply, one set of data can be physically removed from the disk drive and replaced by another. Thus although there is a limit to the storage capacity of the disk unit which is mounted on the drive at any one time (i.e. the volume of data which is currently on-line), any number of other units can be kept available, ready to be mounted on the drive when necessary. In particular, individual users can be supplied with their own private data storage media which they can buy at minimal cost (about £50 for a 45M byte cartridge disk, the most common user storage unit, or about £350 for a 67M or £900 for a 300M byte disk pack).

For some applications a computer system may include a 'fixed-head' disk drive. This is a device in which the disk unit is permanently attached to its drive, and there is a separate access head for each track. This means that the access time depends solely on the latency involved. Since these devices are faster in operation than de-mountable disks, but have a limited storage capacity, they are most frequently used to hold system software rather than users' data. However, some manufacturers are tending to use fixed, or hard, disks more and more because of their greater reliability.

Another type of disk which is especially useful on the cheaper-priced systems is the interchangeable *'floppy disk'* (or *diskette*). This is an inexpensive and low-capacity online storage device. The development of the floppy disk has occurred in a similar way to the development of the computer, with a reduction in size coupled with improved performance. The first commercial floppy disks were eight inches in diameter and are used with minicomputers. For microcomputers floppy disks usually come in two sizes (5.25 and 3.5 in) and the storage capacity of the disk will vary between 160K bytes and 2000K (2M bytes). Since the mid-1980s, the 3.5 in mini-floppy has grown in popularity because it generally has a larger storage capacity and is more robust due to the fact that the outer

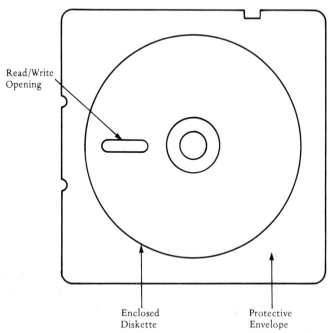

Figure 3.4 *Visual impression of a floppy disk*

protective envelope is made of hard plastic. A visual impression of a floppy disk is given in Figure 3.4. The capacity of floppy disks depends on how closely the magnetic grooves, which record the information, are packed together. This is the density of the disk and can be single, double, or quadruple. In order to use a floppy disk, a computer must have the correct disk drive and be able to read the particular disks. Some computers will not read disks which have been configured at higher densities.

A final type of device is the IBM Mass Storage System which arranges tube-shaped cartridges in honeycomb storage compartments. Designed to hold several thousand megabytes of information, the actual cost of the device is high but the cost per byte is low. (Each cartridge can contain 50 megabytes and the capacity of the system is 472,000 megabytes.)

In general, for each disk there is an interface through which it is connected to the CPU and there is a need for additional electronic components to control the device; this is called a *controller*. Sometimes several disk devices may be looked after by the same controller. Several disk drives can share one communications path (known as a *channel*) between the CPU and the relevant controller. However, if the disk drives are being used simultaneously, then there may be contention for channel space. In this event, it may be appropriate to have more than one channel. In Chapter 8 the use of multiple channels is advocated for security reasons.

Magnetic tape storage

The increase in the availability, capacity and performance/cost ratio of disk storage has tended to eclipse magnetic tape as a mass storage medium for on-line systems. However, magnetic tape systems can still be found on some mainframe and minicomputer systems and for off-line backup storage for microcomputers. Tape-streaming, as this form of backup is sometimes called, allows all the data from a fixed disk to be stored on to magnetic data cartridges. It is important that this is done frequently in order to protect valuable data from being lost as a result of some disaster occurring with the microcomputer.

Operationally, the fundamental point is that tape can only be used in a serial or sequential manner. New data can be appended to existing blocks, but it cannot be inserted, even if the new data is to replace a block of the same size. This is because the tape cannot be stopped sufficiently accurately as it is wound backwards or forwards. Consequently, when a file held on magnetic tape has to be updated, the only way is to write a completely new tape, copying or modifying each block from the old tape in turn.

Magnetic drums

Magnetic drums are very much like fixed-head disks: they consist of a cylinder with a magnetized surface rotating on its axis. There is usually a fixed read/write head on each track. Magnetic drums are fixed like fixed disks – remaining permanently in their cabinet. Drums are often used as a backing store on mainframe computers but are rarely a feature of modern computer systems which rely upon semiconductor memory for primary storage and fixed disks for secondary storage.

Optical storage

Another storage medium, offering a capacity far in excess of the traditional magnetic disk, is the video or optical disk. The first optical disks have very high storage capacities measured in gigabytes (1000 megabytes) but unlike magnetic media cannot be overwritten when data changes. These WORM (Write-Once-Read-Many) disks have found applications such as 'videobooks' and archiving visual material. However, the first optical disk drives which are capable of being overwritten are now becoming available, for example, the Viglen III/386-25 uses a Ricoh 600M bytes optical disk drive as well as traditional fixed and floppy disks. The technology, however, is relatively new and has yet to establish itself as a form of mass storage.

Middle memory

Replaceable disk packs are cheap but relatively slow units; they come in relatively fixed amounts of storage (e.g. 100 megabytes) and suffer from inherent reliability problems caused by the moving mechanical parts and rotating disks. Semiconductor and core memory have no mechanical parts and are more reliable as well as being fast but are relatively expensive – one megabyte of memory usually costing between 20 to 200 megabytes worth of disk memory (excluding the cost of controllers and channels). Fixed disks (with a read/write head on each track*) and drums are faster than disks with replaceable packs but slower than the speeds obtained by semiconductor memory. Fixed disks and drums, however, suffer from the same disadvantage of using mechanical components with a lower reliability than solid-state electronic chips.

   Bubble memory is seen as a middle ground being slower and potentially much cheaper than semiconductor memory, though because of its solid-state construction more reliable than disks. The word bubble arises out of the concept of an 'on' circuit being represented as a positively

*Some fixed disks are relatively large (i.e. several hundred megabytes) and are relatively slow.

charged island in a sea of negatively charged magnetic film. Bubble memory is composed of a number of locations – each location holding a number of possible bubble sites – called minor loops. A number of minor loops are attached to a major loop which contains the necessary transfer sites (between major and minor loops) and read/write/erase stations. As with core storage, magnetic bubble is non-volatile (i.e. you don't lose data when the power supply is turned off).

Bubble memory is not the only possibility. One volatile storage technique is known as a charge-coupled device system. This is a compact form of semiconductor memory produced on a chip and is therefore faster than bubble memory.

In the long run one would expect a typical mainframe computer system to contain the following storage devices.

1 *Buffer/cache memory*, up to 128K bytes of extremely fast memory to hold program instructions and a certain amount of data.
2 *Main memory*, 1 to 16 megabytes of semiconductor memory containing the remaining program instructions and program data.
3 *Current or middle memory*, 2 to 100 + megabytes of bubble or other memory containing all the latest on-line files (for small to medium businesses).
4 *Secondary storage*, probably disks where low usage on-line files are kept and current memory is routinely copied to.
5 *Tertiary storage*, large businesses with large data requirements could not efficiently use disks for on-line data files (the files being too big); mass storage devices (or their equivalent) being the most efficient way of holding several thousand megabytes of information.

Input and output devices

Finally, in this chapter, a brief description of some common input and output devices is provided. Some, like punched cards, magnetic tape and paper tape, can be considered as examples of both input and output media.

Punched cards and paper tape

Punched cards and paper tape are now virtually obsolete as input media. The kimball tag is an example of a small punched card which may still be used by some retail stores to record sales information.

Magnetic Tape

Magnetic tape in the form of cartridge, cassette or standard reeltape is a popular form of input and output. It has a fast transfer rate and can be

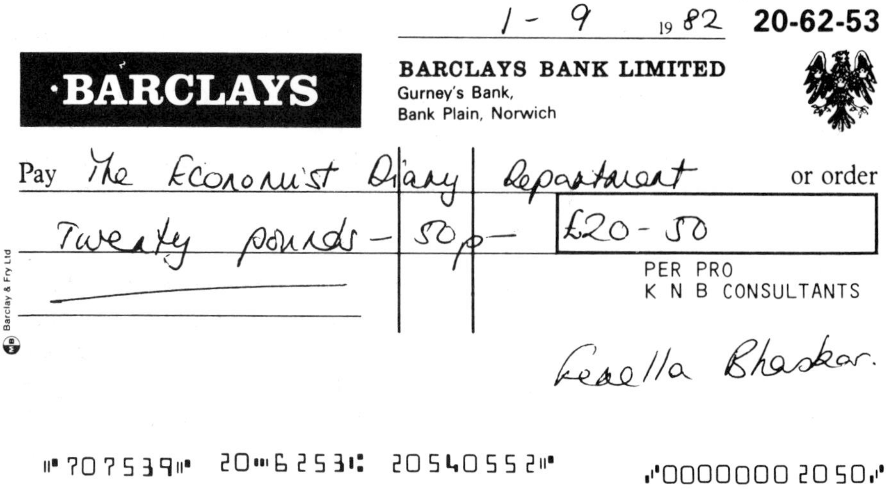

Figure 3.5   The MICR characters are shown on the bottom. The amount is keyed in by the bank

collected off-line by *magnetic tape encoders* or *key to tape* units, or as a by-product to the operation of a cash till – we shall return to these concepts.

Magnetic ink character recognition (MICR)

MICR is widely used by banks and on postal orders and luncheon vouchers as a means of processing large volumes of data. Figure 3.5 shows a cheque with the amount of the item filled in. Similar to punched cards, a certain amount of pre-sorting (by mechanical sorters) as well as encoding (the variable items) is performed. Fast document readers (100–2,000+ documents per minute) are used to read the encoded source documents. Only a limited number of characters can be used (up to 14). The characters are human-readable in ink which contains ferrous oxide and is magnetized. Unlike punched cards, cheques or other documents folded/smeared/stamped/written on/ crumpled can all be read with a high degree of accuracy. The disadvantage of MICR is that MICR calls for precise positioning, a high level of print quality control, and limits the input to one line of characters in a pre-determined position. For banking the system works, but its general lack of flexibility makes MICR a poor choice for most businesses.

Optical mark or character recognitions (OMR or OCR)

OMR is a device which can read small horizontal marks on documents and is useful for pre-printed order forms or mark sheets (see Figure 3.6(a)). OCR is similar to MICR in that certain pre-printed characters can be read by a document reader. OMR accepts marks made by humans whilst OCR is more useful for machine-generated documents (e.g. remittance advice accompanying a statement – sometimes called *turnaround accounting*). OMR has run into problems because of the limited alphabetic data and other documents have been found difficult to read and/or understand. Both systems are relatively inflexible and require expensive and sometimes sensitive machinery.

Bar coding is one device that is used heavily either by direct printing on a product, a badge attached to the product or on tag. Figure 3.6(b) shows the Universal Product Code (UPC) but there is also an EC equivalent. These codes can be automatically read-in by point-of-sale equipment and we shall return to these later. Of all the categories, bar coding coupled with automatic data capture (e.g. at a cash till in a retail store) is the system with the most growth potential. OMC and OCR have had some but limited growth.

The keyboard

The keyboard is the most frequently used form of input. Generally it relies on the standard QWERTY design used on most typewriters. It can be used for entering instructions and data directly to the computer and for inputting data to magnetic disk or tape.

The mouse

The mouse is a small, round device with a ball set into its base, which when moved on a flat surface, registers a corresponding movement of the screen cursor. As an input device, it avoids the need to use cursor keys.

Badge readers

A badge reader describes any plastic card (similar to a credit card) containing data which is magnetic, optical or represented by punched holes. Badge readers usually authorize access to a system, e.g. a bank cashpoint card. Another example is a phonecard as used with a British Telecom public telephone.

Terminals

VDUs with 24 lines and 80 columns of information, manipulated by a keyboard, seem to be the most popular form of output device. The VDU can either work in page mode (a full screen at a time) or scrolling mode

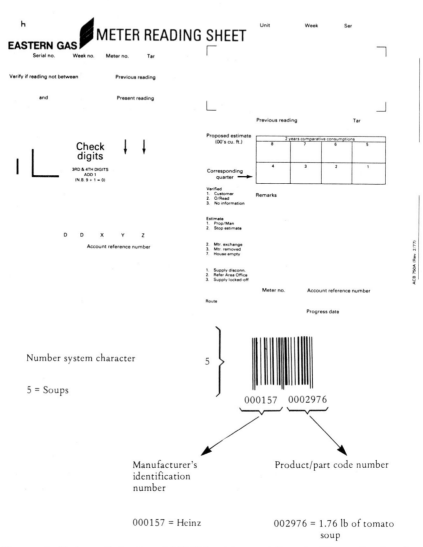

Figure 3.6   *Various optical systems: (a) OMR input document. Example of the use of mark reading techniques for collecting meter readings (based on an example developed by the Eastern Gas Board and published with their permission), (b) Universal Product Codes*

(when the display moves up a line at a time). Table 3.2 gives a number of further features of VDUs.

Table 3.2 **Further features of VDUs** After Clifton (1978)

(a) *Entry form*. This is a changeable electronic or optical display of a document outline. The keyed input data and computed entries are displayed within the outline as though they are being entered manually. This method enables the operator to always have a clear picture of the point reached in the work.

(b) *Double brightness*. This differentiates foreground from background data in order to emphasize the characters keyed-in as against annotations and data retrieved from storage.

(c) *A microprocessor*. This is built into the VDU to give it computing power, thus enabling it to act as an independent processor capable of editing its input and, in some cases, storing it on built-in magnetic tape cassettes.

(d) *A light pen*. This consists of a length of optic fibres that transmit light from the screen to a photocell. By pointing the light pen at the screen and simultaneously pressing a switch, a character can be pinpointed in much the same way as when using a cursor. In some models, the light pen projects a small spot of light onto the screen to facilitate positioning it.

(e) *A blinking cursor and blinking fields*. These are intended to draw the operator's notice to data items needing attention.

(f) *Split screens*. Two separate displays can be viewed side-by-side at the same time. For instance, a list retrieved from the computer's database at one side, and a list being selected from it at the other.

(g) *Movable and unpluggable keyboards*. These enable different sets of keys to be used according to the job in hand. Another method is to redesignate the keys by program and to use a mask or displayed keyboard to show the meanings of the keys.

(h) *Non-displayed input*. This eliminates unauthorized viewing of confidential data such as an identification code or security key.

(i) *Inverse video*. The characters appear as black on white, i.e. dull dots on a bright background. This feature is useful for emphasizing headings but does not have great advantage for business usage.

(j) *Protected fields*. Most VDUs have some form of intelligence and can be programmed to accept only certain types of data in certain fields on the screen.

(k) *Special program control buttons*. Some VDUs have special program control buttons which when depressed trigger a program to branch in a certain direction.

(l) *Hardcopy device*. Most VDUs allow the attachment of a hardcopy device.

One feature missing from the table is the capacity to display colour and graphics. There are also certain disadvantages with a VDU. Firstly, they can only display a limited amount of data at one time. Twenty-four lines by 80 columns is approximately equivalent to the text on a third of an A4 sheet of typing. A4 displays do exist but they are relatively expensive and generally used for specialist applications, such as desktop publishing. Secondly, VDUs are not generally portable and so you can't take the information away from the terminal. So the production of a paper, or hard, copy is an essential form of output.

Printers

Printers are responsible for supplying a hard (printed) copy of data. They may use either continuous paper which is fed through the printer by tractor feeds or friction, or single sheets which are delivered by a sheet feeder or hopper. There are many different types of printer, ranging from those which are slow and relatively simple to those which are fast and extremely sophisticated. At the bottom end of the range are the single character printers which perform like a typewriter, printing one character at a time. These are known as impact printers, i.e. printers where there is physical impact between the printing head and the paper. The daisy-wheel printer is an example of a more complex and higher quality impact printing device, operating at between 25 and 40 characters per second. As the name suggests, this employs a wheel with spokes radiating from a central hub. The type is located at the end of the spokes. A third example of an impact printing device is the line printer. This produces a complete line at a time using either a chain or a drum and can be found where a higher volume of printing is required.

The more advanced and expensive printing devices are non-impact and capable of producing 20,000+ lines a minute. They may use thermal, xerographic, ink jet or laser technology. Thermal printers use chemically impregnated or aluminiumized paper which is then carefully burned away to reveal characters stored on the backing paper. Xerographic printers utilize the technique of xerography, a dry copying process where the image to be copied is projected on to a plate, resulting in an electro-static charge which is retained where the image is black. Resinous powder is then applied to the plate, adhering to those areas which have remained uncharged. Ink jet printers form characters by spraying ink through very fine nozzles, while laser printers use a laser beam to produce characters on a light-sensitive drum.

Audio devices

Up to now, no mention has been made of audio input or output. With *Audio-response* devices, despite some fairly thorny problems of ambiguity and interpretation, some development work has been undertaken. Audio input must usually be matched against a library of words tuned to an individual person's dialect and voice pattern. Usually it must be a simple one or two word phrase. Audio output is easier since each word can be given a code and a number of standard sentence structures stored. It is unlikely that voice communication will surplant the VDU as a general I/O (input/output device), though audio-responses will play their role in certain well-defined situations. Modern cars give audio warnings of 'seat belts not secured' and various failure situations.

The speech synthesizer is now a familiar example of audio output. Using what is known as analysis technique, synthesizers can interpret messages by comparing them with words stored in digitized form in memory, and thus give appropriate responses.

4 Software and the principles of programming

One of the features of a digital computer that distinguishes it from other less sophisticated accounting and data-processing machines is its ability to store and execute a program of instructions without human intervention. Modern hardware is capable of performing more than 2 million multiplications per second, line printers can operate at over 1,000 lines per minute and output of data from primary store to magnetic tapes and disks is many 100 times faster. By comparison, any communication with and response from a human operator is so slow, at best a few seconds to type in the next command, or possibly minutes to find and mount a specified tape or disk, that for effective use of the hardware it is of fundamental importance to minimize and, if possible, to eliminate altogether the need for operator intervention. Programs of instructions must be prepared in advance, input and stored and then executed without further intervention. The collection of programs needed to control the operation of the computer and enable it to process data and solve problems is called software. Sometimes, the term software is used to refer to all non-hardware elements of computer systems. These include not only the instruction programs but also the documentation describing the programs, programming language manuals, specifications of the standards and techniques used in software development, operating manuals and the training of personnel.

It is very important to distinguish between the costs of hardware and software. Whereas hardware costs have fallen with the development of integrated circuits and the silicon chip, software costs have continued to rise over time. Software development is dependent on humans designing, writing and documenting the necessary programs; it is a time-consuming and therefore costly process. On large mainframe computer systems, the total cost of bought-in software, systems development and

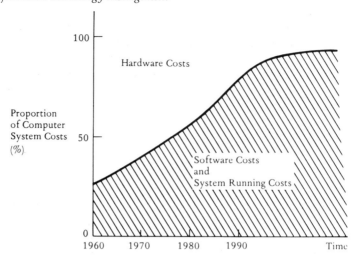

Figure 4.1   *Trends in mainframe system costs*

personnel far exceeds the hardware costs (see Figure 4.1). An important part of the running costs is the cost of training computer personnel in the techniques of computer-based information systems.

However, for smaller installations both the hardware and the software costs have fallen. The reason for this is that the fixed development costs can usually be spread over many more units (i.e. economies of scale). A small accounting package (including documentation) might take about 4 man-years to produce. If this cost is spread over only 10 installations then the cost to each is likely to be around £10,000, including an allowance for supporting overheads. The cheaper microprocessor systems are selling in greater numbers. With sales of, say, 1,000 systems then the cost of a small accounting system could be reduced to around £100 for each installation. Interestingly enough, at the time of writing, prices for accounting systems range from £100 for a modified U.S.-produced package to run on a microcomputer, to several million pounds for a bespoke system implemented for a large mainframe computer system. Accounting packages for minicomputers cost anything up to £25,000.

In terms of the tremendous advances in hardware, software development lags a long way behind. To some extent this is to be expected; software can only utilize new hardware once that hardware is available for use. Nevertheless, the full potential of existing hardware has never been realized. Much research has been directed towards the design of software development aids whose use will flatten the rising curve in Figure 4.1.

In order to understand a complete computer system it is necessary to build up a picture of all types of software. These fall into three broad categories:

1 *Operating systems* – a collection of programs and routines necessary to run the computer system and provide a number of service functions;
2 *Programming language translation software* – programs which accept instructions expressed in the user's programming language and translate them into machine instructions that can be understood and executed by the processor;
3 *Applications software* – programs written to solve user problems or for processing particular types of data.

Operating systems

The first generation computers were regarded as very powerful calculators used largely to solve scientific and mathematical problems – those involving calculations too lengthy or complex for manual solution. The solutions usually required very little input and output of data. Often the programmer was a highly skilled scientist, operating the machine himself, setting it up to load and run his programs, modifying the program and rerunning until the desired results were obtained. Between successive runs the computer would be idle and doing no useful work. This method of operation was grossly inefficient. The computer was simply an expensive tool designed to save the scientist's time.

In the mid-1950s some second generation computers began to incorporate operating systems to provide an interface between application programs and hardware, especially for input/output. These machines were more suitable for business purposes and were used to perform a wide range of business functions such as the payroll, maintenance of inventory records and processing accounting records. Although the computer operator was still a specialist, many of the functions that he needed to perform were routine and could be controlled by special programs. These programs, designed primarily to minimize the set up time before each job and to eliminate the need for operator intervention between jobs, were the first operating systems.

With the arrival of the third generation machines, operating systems had become commonplace. Since computers were now being used by an increasing number of people for business purposes, it was important for them to have a less obviously scientific and specialist application.

By supervising the program and controlling the input and output functions of each program, operating systems are able to minimize the need for human involvement. This controlling function ensures that computer time is used both efficiently and effectively. In summary, the following tasks are basic to most operating systems:

1 Provision of a user interface which allows the operator to communicate with and relay instructions to the computer.

2   Allocation of primary memory space for programs.
3   Supervision of input and output devices.
4   Transferral of data and programs to and from secondary store.
5   Running and monitoring of programs.

Where a computer system allows for multiprogramming, multi-access and multitasking, the operating system will take charge of even more processing details.

One disadvantage at the moment is the number and variety of operating systems. This lack of standardization considerably reduces the portability of the program software. Until fairly recently, CP/M was an extremely popular system but it has since been eclipsed by MS-DOS and its derivatives, which are used extensively as an industry standard. The minicomputer and mainframe environments are more uniform, with the UNIX operating system predominating. Although UNIX is very nearly 20 years old, it has proved remarkably resilient and adaptable, with many new features having been incorporated over the years.

Looking to the near future, we can expect OS/2, the latest development in operating systems, to herald some notable changes and shape the next computer generation. In marked contrast to the present generation of microcomputer operating systems (e.g. MS-DOS and UNIX), OS/2 has been specifically designed from the ground up to meet the needs of the end user and can therefore be described as the first complete operating system. Two main advantages are a memory capacity well above the 640K limit imposed by MS-DOS and the ability to perform multiple tasks (see page 52). This will afford users greater integration, larger programs and addressability, and easy access to data. Other features include windowing, transparent networking, graphical menu and icon display interfaces, and mainframe connectivity.

Multiprocessing

To justify the use of the computer on strict financial terms it is essential to make full use of the most expensive hardware components. One of the most significant developments in this direction is the facility for *multiprogramming*. When the CPU is idle, awaiting the completion of an input or output operation before processing can continue, one might ask what else it could be doing. If other programs were present in the store then, when no further progress can be made on one program, control might be switched to another program until such time as execution of the first program can be resumed. The interleaved execution of two or more independent programs by the same processor is called multiprogramming.

To illustrate the benefit of multiprogramming, suppose that two user programs are held in store, one of which is the data validation program with the input, processing and output pattern shown in Figure 4.2, and the other is a long calculation which uses the arithmetic unit for a long

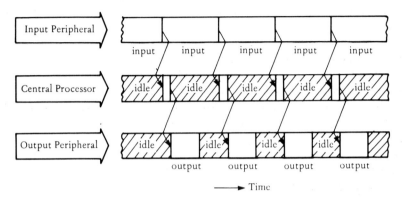

Figure 4.2   *Overlap of input, processing and output*

time without input and output. We arrange that this second program uses the CPU while the data validation program is waiting for input or output. The result is shown in Figure 4.3; the first program is running as fast as if the second did not exist and the second is held up for only a small amount of time while the first uses the CPU. With this combination of programs the CPU is working continuously.

Often, the impression gained by the users of a multiprogramming system is that their programs are being executed simultaneously. This is not so. Only one program at a time can be executed, control being

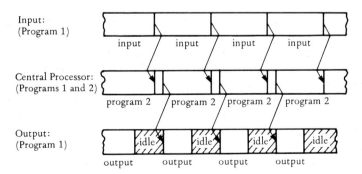

Figure 4.3   *Sharing of CPU time between two programs*

switched from one program to another whenever necessary to achieve acceptable levels of throughput and turnaround.

Another important concept in computing is *multiprocessing*. A multiprocessing system is an interconnected configuration of multiple CPUs with the ability to *simultaneously* execute several programs. Each processor is allocated to one and only one program at any one time. The reader should understand the distinction between multiprogramming and multiprocessing. Almost all medium to large modern computer systems offer multiprogramming facilities. Multiprocessing on the other hand is less well developed.

The development of multiprogramming has introduced much complexity to operating systems. Each program in the computer needs input and output. It is unlikely that there will be sufficient physical units for input and output to be directly from and to the input and output devices available. All input and output must be spooled. Instead of using small satellite computers to perform the spooling it was soon realized that the spooling programs are just two examples of service functions that can be interleaved with the execution of the various user programs on a multiprogramming system. The management of the execution of several programs is a complicated task. The operating system must keep track of all the programs in the system and the status of each – whether it is currently being executed, or idle and awaiting the completion of an input or output operation, or ready to resume as soon as the processor becomes free. There may be more than one program ready to be resumed; this introduces problems of conflicts and priorities.

The computer must be able to detect when a peripheral transfer is completed and then to update the status of the program that initiated the transfer. There must be some mechanism for breaking into the normal sequence of instructions executed by the CPU and not automatically fetching the next instruction in sequence. We call this an *interrupt*. The mechanism by which interrupts are made varies from computer to computer, but essentially it is as follows.

Within the CPU are two special registers called the *interrupt bit* and the *interrupt mask*, both of which are normally set to zero. The interrupt bit is used as a signal to the control unit to break into the current sequence of instructions. The interrupt mask indicates the reason for the interrupt. Interrupts can occur for many different reasons. They can signal the completion of an input operation, or an output operation, or the occurrence of an error such as an attempt to divide by zero,* or that the total execution time allocated to the current program has been exceeded, or that the operator wishes to suspend or abandon execution of the current program and so on. Each kind of interrupt causes its particular bit

---

*Division by zero gives an infinite result which cannot be represented in the finite store of a computer.

in the interrupt mask to be set to 1 and whenever any bit in the mask is set this automatically causes the interrupt bit to be set as a signal to control.

In the previous chapter we referred briefly to the basic cycle of operations performed by the central processor:

fetch next instruction.
decode instruction.
execute instruction.

In practice things are slightly more complicated. This sequence of operations has to be extended to include inspection of the interrupt bit each time before fetching the next instruction. We have:

test interrupt bit.
   if an interrupt has occurred
   then suspend execution of the current
      sequence of instructions;
      store all information necessary for
      the current program to be resumed later;
      clear the interrupt bit;
      commence execution of the interrupt
      service procedure where the mask will
      be inspected and appropriate action taken
   otherwise continue with the current sequence
fetch next instruction
decode instruction
execute instruction

Figure 4.4 gives a very simple view of the operation of the *supervisor* program which is the part of the operating system concerned with the overall supervision of multiprogramming.

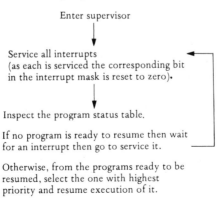

Enter supervisor

Service all interrupts
(as each is serviced the corresponding bit
in the interrupt mask is reset to zero).

Inspect the program status table.

If no program is ready to resume then wait
for an interrupt then go to service it.

Otherwise, from the programs ready to be
resumed, select the one with highest
priority and resume execution of it.

Figure 4.4 *Overall control of multiprogramming*

Multitasking

Multitasking describes the computer's ability to perform a number of tasks simultaneously. Although this has been a feature of mainframe and minicomputers for some time, it has only recently been demanded of, and applied to, smaller computer systems where there is a strong desire for greater flexibility and productivity. Multitasking is now so popular that almost every modern microcomputer has either an operating system or a custom program which provides it in some form.

At its most basic, multitasking operates serially; that is, it stops one task temporarily while another is performed (known as context switching). Ideally, an efficient multitasking system should be able to perform numerous services, the most important being resource management and interprocess communication. The former divides the computer's time, memory and peripherals among competing activities. The latter allows for the coordination of these activities by sharing information. By these criteria, serial multitasking is not the most efficient system. Although it can increase productivity and flexibility it does not make the most efficient use of the computer's time and power. True multitasking must rely on the efficient division of CPU time and the utilization of all the computer's power.

As an example of a modern multitasking operating system, let us look at OS/2. Developed jointly by Microsoft and IBM, OS/2 is a truly advanced system providing a vast range of application services. Its multitasking capability ensures that a program can be divided into discrete tasks that can be performed concurrently for different sets of data. For example, suppose that a spreadsheet program can be divided into three stages or tasks: Task 1 for data entry, Task 2 for calculation, and Task 3 for printing. Using OS/2, the tasks can be executed in the following way:

Period	Task 1	Task 2	Task 3
1	Data entry A		
2	Data entry B	Recalculate A	
3	Data entry C	Recalculate B	Print A
4		Recalculate C	Print B
5			Print C

Figure 4.5   *Multitasking capability of OS/2*

Timesharing

If the principal objective is to maximize CPU throughput then execution of a program once started should be allowed to continue until either the program is completed or the program initiates an input or output operation and cannot proceed until that operation is complete. Some interruptions are unavoidable, for example, events such as the completion of

input, or output, of a block of data for another program, operator intervention or the occurrence of an error. Any of these might cause the
supervisor program to be entered and control switched to another program. When several on-line terminal users are attempting to run programs simultaneously it is necessary to ensure that each is allocated a
reasonable share of the CPU time so that they receive responses to their
commands on an acceptable timescale, say 2 or 3 seconds rather than
minutes. This can be arranged by interrupting the execution of the current program after a fixed time interval, if it has not already been inter-
rupted by some other event, and switching control to another program.
Suitable organization of the queue of programs ready to resume execution
will ensure that each gets a fair share of CPU time. This *timesharing* of the
CPU between programs of several on-line terminal users can give each
user the impression that he has the whole machine to himself so long as
the system is not overloaded.

In the early 1980s a minicomputer system such as a VAX 11/780 with $3^{1}/_{4}$
megabytes (mega = 1 million) of primary store and 512 megabytes of disk
storage cost about £200,000 and was capable of supporting up to 64
on-line terminals provided they were not all running processor-bound
jobs and they included a significant number of users requiring a relatively
high level of input or output but little processing. A smaller system such
as a PDP 11 or Systime 3000/5000, with 160K bytes of primary store and
2×32 megabyte disks, costing about £35,000 and running a timesharing
operating system (such as RSTS/E) could support eight terminals and a
couple of printers. These prices do not include the cost of communications equipment and terminals.

Virtual storage

We have happily assumed that multiprocessing is the answer to the
problem of making the best use of expensive hardware but the need to
hold several programs in the primary store at the same time raises another
problem. The amount of primary storage is not unlimited and if it is to be
divided between several programs, each written on the assumption that
the user has access to the whole of the available store, we are faced with a
storage management problem. This is another major function of the
operating system. Clearly, it is only necessary to ensure that the program
currently being executed is in the primary store. Other programs could
temporarily be kept in on-line (secondary) storage and retrieved when
required. We can go further than this. Each program can be divided into a
number of small sequences of instructions stored in *pages*. Only those
pages actually required at any one time in the processing need be in the

primary store. The remaining pages may be kept in on-line storage until required. This facility can give each user the impression that there is unlimited primary storage. The pages actually held in primary store are said to be in *real memory*. The other pages which are currently inactive and not required, and are held on a secondary storage device, are said to be in *virtual memory*. Normally, a few pages from one or more programs will be held in real memory. Whenever control is transferred to another page of the current program or a page of another program the operating system must first check to see if the required page is already in real memory and if not it must retrieve the page from virtual memory, copying it into real memory in place of one of the pages which is for the time being no longer required. The operating system has to keep track of each page of every program in the system, to protect the pages of one program from access or violation by another program, and to ensure that pages are retrieved and made available in the real memory when required during processing. This virtual storage management is a complicated task.

Communication with the operating system

A sophisticated, modern operating system performs many of the functions previously carried out by the human operator. There are some tasks it cannot perform of course such as loading cards in a card reader and paper in a printer or mounting magnetic tapes and exchangeable disk packs. However, once a program has been loaded along with other programs, the software modules, which together make up the operating system, schedule the execution of programs, allocate input and output devices, allocate and manage storage needed by each program, organize queues and spooling, and service interrupts. In some of these tasks the operating system can be assisted by information provided by the user. For instance, where a job consists of several programs to be run one after the other, the output from one being the input data for the next it is necessary for the user to specify the order in which the programs must be run. It is also helpful if some indication of storage requirements, CPU time and volume of input and output records can be given. This information can be useful in determining the order in which to start various jobs, the appropriate mix of jobs and the relative priorities of jobs. High priority would normally be given to a job with large volumes of input and output but a user may wish to pay for a high priority on a job in order to get an 'express' service. The mechanism for communication between the user and the operating system is the job control language or commands.

The sort of written instructions which might be given to a human operator are the following.

My program is called MYPROG. It is written in the programming language BASIC and is held in a file called A240.MYPROG. Translate the program into machine instructions using the BASIC compiler. If syntax errors are found in the program then abandon the job otherwise store the machine instructions in a file called A240.MYOBJ. Now load and run the compiled program for me. The loaded program will not exceed 15,000 words in store. The input data for the program are held in a file called A240.MYDATA. Output should be sent to a file called A240.MYRESULTS. The execution time of the program should not exceed 5 seconds of CPU time. Since the program involves mainly calculation and little input and output, priority 8 should be adequate. Finally, print the contents of the data file and the results file on the line printer.

The details of job control languages vary from one computer to another and we shall not attempt to categorize them here. It is sufficient to give the equivalent of the above instructions in a hypothetical language which illustrates the facilities normally available.

```
JOB A240.MYJOB,////
LOAD #BASIC
INPUT A240.MYPROG
OUTPUT A240.MYOBJ
ENTER #BASIC
IF ERROR, ENDJOB
STORE 15000
LOAD MYOBJ
INPUT A240.MYDATA, 200 LINES
OUTPUT A240.MYRESULTS, 150 LINES
TIME 5 SECS
PRIORITY 8
ENTER MYOBJ
IF ERROR, ENDJOB
LIST A240.MYDATA, *LP1
LIST A240.MYRESULTS, *LP1
ERASE A240.MYRESULTS
ENDJOB
////
```

The preparation of job control commands for each job can be quite tedious. It is common to provide within the operating system a number of standard job descriptions with various default limits for storage requirements, input and output volumes and job time. The user then simply chooses the appropriate description for his job. For example he might simply write.

```
JOB A240.MYJOB (JOB CLASS C),////
BASIC SOURCE A240.MYPROG, DATA A240.MYDATA,
RESULTS A240.MYRESULTS
ENDJOB
////
```

where job class C imposes limits on time etc. appropriate for this job.

Service functions

In addition to facilities for controlling the operation of a computer system, the operating system also includes a number of service routines. These are programs and procedures required by many users and not just by one or two programs. Examples are procedures for file creation and maintenance, and programming language translation. All users need to create files containing programs or data and to modify or correct the contents of files. Inevitably, when typing large volumes of data or programs the user makes errors which must be corrected before the file is used. It would be possible for each user to write his own text-editing program receiving data containing errors, to modify the text line by line, and to output corrected text. This facility is required so often that a text editor is always provided as one of the service functions in an operating system. As with job control languages, the details of text editors vary from one system to another and some large systems include several text editors offering slightly different facilities. Some editors are line-oriented, others are context editors and some provide facilities for both context editing and line-by-line editing. Many of the text-editing instructions refer to the old draft of the file; this must be available for inspection during the editing process. Figure 4.6 represents the information flow.

The editing facilities typically include the following commands:
Deletion of a range of lines:
   e.g. DELETE 110:160
to delete lines numbered 110 to 160 inclusive;

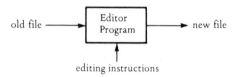

Figure 4.6   *Information flow during editing*

Insertion of additional lines:

    e.g. INSERT 110,6

    to insert 6 lines the first being immediately after line 110;

    the text to be inserted follows this command;

Print or display a range of lines:

    e.g. PRINT 200:250

Change part of a line:

    e.g. SUBSTITUTE /*oldstring*/*newstring*/

    to replace an occurrence of the string of characters specified as

    oldstring by the *newstring*;

Find the next line containing a specified string of characters:

    e.g. FIND /*string*/

and of course a command to terminate editing:

    END

These are but a few of the standard facilities that are always provided in some form or other.

Computer administrator's view of operating systems

So far we have presented a user's view of operating system software: what the system can do for him, how he communicates with it and the service programs and routines available for his use. This is fine in a simple, single user system but when the computing resources are shared between two or more competing users it is also necessary to ensure that each is allocated a fair share of the resources. It is the computer administrator's job to allocate and control the use of the resources. This is another area in which the operating system can provide assistance. Each user, or group of users, will normally be given a daily, weekly or monthly ration of the resources available. The computer monitors each job as it runs on the machine, logging such things as number of input and output records, amount of primary store used and the time for which the CPU is actively engaged in executing the job. The number of disk transfers can be recorded as can the number of pages 'turned' in a virtual storage system. These are all resources and facilities for which a user can be charged. The management software module of the operating system deals with the accounting and when a user's allocation has been exhausted his job may be terminated and further jobs charged to the same account may not be started. Such measures may be necessary to ration and control the resources allocated to programmers for program development. In an on-line environment, some control is necessary to prevent a few users from monopolizing the facilities to the detriment of other users. Access to files must be restricted to authorized users. Who is allowed to use the resources and for how long may depend on the time of day and on other work currently running on the machine. The computer will generally

produce a summary of the users and the resources used in each accounting period.

Programming languages and translators

We have made several references to machine instructions, machine
languages and programming languages. It is important to realize that
each computer has its own set of instructions expressed in a binary form
which can be decoded and executed by the central processor. The precise
form of these instructions differs from one type of computer to another.
Instructions expressed in any form other than the code for a particular
machine must be translated into the required code before they can be
understood and executed. Even a simple logical operation such as

LET C = A + B,

meaning
    take the value currently assigned to A; add to it the current value of B
    and assign the result to C
can appear quite complicated when expressed in binary machine instructions. In symbolic form it might be expressed as follows:

LOAD   3   A Load register 3 with the value of A
ADD   3   B Add to register 3 the value of B
STORE   3   C Assign the value in register 3 to C

where register 3 is one of a small number of registers (called accumu-
lators) in the CPU in which arithmetic operations can be performed. In
actual machine code the storage locations with symbolic names A, B and

Symbolic Form	Operation Code	Accumulator Register (3 in this case)	Index Register	Operand Address
LOAD 3 A	0001	011	000	001100
ADD 3 B	0101	011	000	001101
STORE 3 C	0010	011	000	001110

Figure 4.7   *Machine instructions for adding two numbers*

C must be expressed as actual binary addresses and the operations LOAD, ADD and STORE must be written as binary operation codes for the particular computer. The form of the machine code equivalent of

LET $C = A + B$

might be as illustrated in Figure 4.7. We have assumed a 16-bit instruction word. The index register, also in the CPU and normally used to modify the address part of an instruction, is not used in this example.

Machine code programming has obvious drawbacks, not least of which is tedium. The attention to detail necessary in constructing a sequence of instructions of any significant length inevitably leads to errors which are not easy to detect and correct. In the very early days of computing all programs were written in this form and programming was a skill at which only a few were proficient. It was not long before symbolic forms of instructions were introduced with mnemonic operation codes and symbolic address parts, for example

ADD 3 B

in place of

0101 011 000 001101

where 0101 is the code for the addition operation represented by the mnemonic ADD and 001101 is the binary address of the storage location referred to as B. Programs were developed to assemble the machine code equivalents of symbolic instructions and these assembler programs relieved the programmer of the chores of detailed storage allocation and management. Instead of thinking in binary he could work at a level slightly removed from the machine. For the most part assembler language instructions are in one to one correspondence to machine instructions with only a few *macro* instructions translating into two or more machine instructions. Assembler languages reflect the architecture of the particular machines for which they are designed and are a long way removed from the problem-orientated languages in which the user normally expresses his problem.

At the other end of the spectrum we have the so-called high-level or problem-orientated languages which include

Table 4.1   Examples of programming languages

COBOL	(Common Business Orientated Language) is a frequently used language which has maintained its popularity over a good many years. It has numerous commercial and business applications due to its data processing and file handling facilities.

FORTRAN	(FORmula TRANslation) is another language which remains popular despite its age. It is used mainly for scientific and engineering and research purposes.
ALGOL	(ALGOrithmic Language) was the first of the algorithmic languages and was used for mathematical applications
BASIC	(Beginners All-purpose Symbolic Instruction Code) was developed as an introductory language to programming. It is now one of the most widely used languages and has the virtue of being easy to use but offers little support for the principles of software engineering.
PROLOG	This is a language which can make logical deductions from data premises and is a widely used non-procedural language.
C	This is a widely used high level language designed for system programming. It is often used for software development in a Unix environment.
PASCAL	This is a derivative of ALGOL developed in the late sixties. It is a structured language with algorithmic features.
ADA	A modern programming language supported by the US DOD incorporating many Pascal-like features plus facilities for real-time control, multitasking. Suitable as a general purpose design language with a strong support for good software engineering.

FORTRAN and COBOL are two of the most important languages since they are so widely used. FORTRAN, as the name suggests, was originally designed for scientific and mathematical use. It was first introduced in the late fifties and was the first generally available problem-orientated language. Since its introduction probably more than 100,000 man-years of programming effort have been put into development of the language itself and enhancements to internationally accepted standards. This is a significant investment. The chief advantage of the language today is its availability on a wide range of computers together with extensive libraries of scientific subroutines to perform many standard tasks. FORTRAN is not ideal for the processing of large volumes of input and output of alphanumeric records such as are normally the subject of business and commercial data processing. FORTRAN 77, the latest agreed standard, provides facilities for handling character data as well as numerical data and has much improved facilities for file processing, but it is still basically a language for engineering, scientific and mathematical applications.

On the other hand COBOL, originally developed for use by the American Army, was specifically designed for file handling and since more than 50 per cent of all computer applications are in business – the processing of files, records and fields – COBOL has become widely accepted as the major programming language for business applications.

ALGOL is not so popular. It was designed primarily for scientific applications, builds on the experience gained with FORTRAN, overcomes many of the deficiencies of FORTRAN but like FORTRAN is not ideal for business computing.

PL/1 represents an attempt by IBM to design a truly general purpose language suitable for both scientific and business use. It combines many of the features of FORTRAN, ALGOL and COBOL but is not so widely implemented as FORTRAN and COBOL.

PASCAL is one of the most recent of the ALGOL family. It was designed as a simple language providing the best features of ALGOL in a form which can be implemented efficiently. Facilities for character handling, records and simple file processing are provided. Although derived from a family of languages originally designed for scientific applications, PASCAL has become very popular simply because it can be implemented on small machines. It is already available on most microprocessor systems.

The distinguishing feature of BASIC is that it is more than a programming language; it is a complete programming system designed specifically for on-line use. It is in itself an operating system providing all the necessary commands for file creation, editing and running of programs. The language is also very easy to learn. Like FORTRAN it is a living language in that it has developed significantly since it was first introduced. It is widely available on small computer systems and has become popular both for numerical data processing and simple business data processing.

We do not propose to give detailed descriptions of any of the languages mentioned above. The reader who wishes to study a particular language in sufficient depth to write his own programs is referred to one of the specialist programming language texts listed in the bibliography at the end of this section. Instead we shall illustrate some of the principal features of FORTRAN, BASIC and PASCAL with reference to a Discounted Cash Flow problem. This is followed by an example program in COBOL.

Case studies

First we illustrate some features of BASIC, FORTRAN and PASCAL with reference to a discounted cash flow problem.

In the usual notation, if

C_t = cash flow at time t,

r = interest or discount rate, and

I = initial capital cost,

then the net present value after n years is given by the formula

$$NPV = \sum_{t=1}^{n} \frac{C_t}{(I + r)^t} - I.$$

The values to be supplied as input to the program are

n, the number of years,

c, the vector of cash flows for the n years,

r and I.

The output required is the net present value (*NPV*) after *n* years. It is also good practice to print the input data as a check that correct values have been input and used in the computation.

Before the solution can be coded in any particular programming language we must devise an algorithm for the computation required to evalute *NPV*.

We approach this in a top-down way. That is we identify the principal steps involved and then refine each step until the algorithm is in a form suitable for coding in the chosen language. In other words we plan the solution in some detail before we concern ourselves with the details of the programming language. However, in planning the solution we may be influenced by the nature of the particular facilities provided by the programming language.

The first outline solution may be expressed either as a flowchart or in simple English as shown in Figure 4.8.

The input and output operations represented in boxes 1 and 3 of the flowchart are already in a form suitable for coding. The only detail of

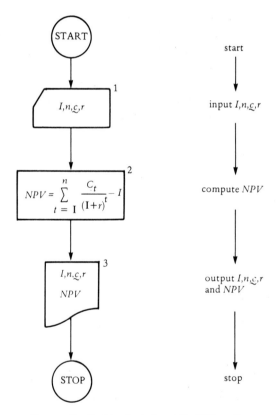

Figure 4.8 *First-level solution of the DCF problem*

particular interest at this stage is how we input the n cash flow values C_1 to C_n. This will depend on the language chosen. In BASIC and PASCAL, once the value of n has been input, an instruction to input a cash flow value is executed n times in a *loop*. In FORTRAN there exists a special form of the input statement with an implied loop designed specifically for this kind of input. Apart from this the differences in the code, as shown in Figure 4.9, are largely a matter of syntax. It is worth noting the line numbers associated with BASIC. These facilitate editing of the program file.

The output statements are very similar but with the transfer of an additional value, *NPV*.

Now we come to the heart of the problem: refining step 2 for the computation of *NPV*. If we know *NPV* after *j*–I years then the value after *j* years is given by

$$NPV_j = NPV_{j-1} + C_j / (I + r)^j.$$

This suggests that we start with an initial value $NPV_0 = -I$ and perform the computation of NPV_j from NPV_{j-1} n times with j taking values from 1 to n. The detailed code is given in Figure 4.10. (The efficiency of this code could be improved but at this stage we are more concerned with clarity than efficiency of execution.) Again the differences between BASIC, PASCAL and FORTRAN appear to be only a matter of syntax. However, there are fundamental differences between the three languages that are

(a) BASIC

```
110   INPUT 'INITIAL INVESTMENT';  I
120   INPUT 'NO. OF YEARS';  N
130   FOR J=1 TO N            ⎤ loop to input
140   INPUT C(J)              ⎥ cash flow values
150   NEXT J                  ⎦
160   INPUT 'INTEREST RATE';  R
```

(b) PASCAL

```
read (I,N);
for J := 1 to N do read (C[J]);
read (R)
```

(c) FORTRAN

```
      READ (5,100) I, N
100   FORMAT ('INITIAL INVESTMENT', F10.2/
    1              'NO. OF YEARS', I5)

      READ (5,101) (C(J), J=1,N)    ⎤ implied loop to
101   FORMAT (5F 10.2)              ⎦ input cash flow values
      READ (5,102) R
102   FORMAT ('INTEREST RATE', F10.2)
```

Figure 4.9 *Instructions for input of data to DCF program*

(a)   BASIC

```
180   LET P = −I
190   FOR J = 1 TO N
200   LET P = P + C(J)/(1+R)**J
210   NEXT J
```

(b)   PASCAL

```
NPV : = −I;
for J : = 1 to N do NPV : = NPV + C[J] /(1+R)↑J
```

(c)   FORTRAN

```
      NPV = −I
      DO 10 J = 1,N
10    NPV = NPV + C(J)/(1.+R)**J
```

Figure 4.10   *Instructions for computation of NPV after n years*

not evident from what we have done so far. One of these is the convention for choosing and introducing (declaring) symbolic names (identifiers) for the numerical values (variables) used.

In this respect, BASIC is the simplest and least flexible. Identifiers consist of a single letter or a letter followed by an integer subscript and generally need no introduction although the dimension of a subscripted variable such as our cash flow values $C(1)$ to $C(N)$ should be declared. For example DIM C(20) tells the BASIC system that we shall use up to 20 numerical values $C(1)$ to $C(20)$. Most versions of BASIC provide for integer variables, i.e. numerical values having no fractional part such as the J used for counting in the loops of Figures 4.9 and 4.10. An integer variable identifier is followed by a % symbol, e.g. J%. Names of character string variables are followed by $. Some recent implementations of BASIC allow long variable names such as CAPINV for capital investment and NPV.

FORTRAN has long variable names, restricted to 6 characters in the standard form but most implementations allow more. Generally, a FORTRAN variable consists of a letter optionally followed by any combination of letters and the digits 0 to 9. By default an initial letter in the range I to N denotes an integer variable; other initial letters denote general (called REAL) number variables. This default can be overridden by explicit declaration statements such as

INTEGER J
REAL I, R, NPV, C(20)

FORTRAN also provides variables of type LOGICAL (for example, to store the results of conditions: TRUE or FALSE), COMPLEX (for certain mathematical computations) and CHARACTER (to hold a character; FORTRAN 77 only) but character strings, of variable length, are not available.

Pascal identifiers have a similar form to FORTRAN identifiers but must all be explicitly declared at the beginning of the program. The data types available are integer, real, char, boolean (i.e. logical), arrays of any of these types and record structures. This last facility is essential for most business data processing. Strings, as provided by BASIC, are not available in PASCAL.

A complete BASIC program for the DCF calculation is given in Figure 4.11.

Much more important differences are in the control structures offered by each language, i.e. facilities for conditional execution and repeated execution of groups of instructions. The sort of facilities one might look for are instructions such as

if some condition *then* do something

or more generally

if condition *then* do this *else* do that

or even

if condition/1 *then* action/1
else if condition/2 *then* action/2
else if condition/3. . . .

. . . .
else if . . . . action/*n*

```
100   DIM C(20)
110   REM *** INPUT DATA VALUES ***
120   INPUT 'INITIAL INVESTMENT';  I
130   INPUT 'NO. OF YEARS';  N%
140   INPUT 'CASH FLOW VALUES'
150   FOR J% = 1 TO N%
160   INPUT C(J%)
170   NEXT J%
180   INPUT 'INTEREST RATE';  R
190   REM *** COMPUTE NET PRESENT VALUE, P, AFTER N YEARS ***
200   LET P = −I
210   FOR J% = 1 TO N%
220   LET P = P + C(J%)/(1+R)**J%
230   NEXT J%
240   REM *** OUTPUT RESULTS ***
250   PRINT 'INITIAL INVESTMENT';  I
260   PRINT 'INTEREST RATE';  R
270   PRINT 'CASH FLOW VALUES'
280   FOR J% = 1 TO N%
290   PRINT C(J%)
300   NEXT J%
310   PRINT 'NET PRESENT VALUE AFTER';  N%;  'YEARS =';  P
320   END
```

Figure 4.11 *Complete BASIC program for DCF calculation*

(a)   Unstructured BASIC

```
5000      IF SALES > 1000 THEN 5100
5010      DISCOUNT = 0
5020      VALUE = PRICE * SALES
5030      GOTO 5200
5100      VALUE = PRICE * SALES * 0.95
5110      DISCOUNT = 0.05 * PRICE * SALES
5200      PRINT . . . .
```

(b)   Structured BASIC

```
5000      IF SALES > 1000 THEN VALUE = PRICE * SALES * 0.95
                             DISCOUNT    = 0.05 * PRICE * SALES
                   ELSE DISCOUNT   = 0
                             VALUE       = PRICE * SALES
5010      PRINT . . . .
```

Figure 4.12   (a) *unstructured BASIC, (b) structured BASIC*

Control structures for repetition of instructions can take a variety of forms. We have already met the *for . . . do* instruction for executing a sequence a specified number of times.

The general form allows a control variable to take some initial value and be incremented or decremented by another specified value each time the loop is executed until a specified final value is reached. In FORTRAN the incremental step value must be positive. In PASCAL the step must be either + 1 or − 1. There are other differences which we shall not go into here.

Other structures for repetition of statements include

while some condition *do* something

and   *repeat* some action *until* some condition.

The original versions of BASIC and FORTRAN offered virtually no sophisticated control structures. FORTRAN 77 offers the BLOCK IF i.e. IF . . . THEN . . . ELSE. . . . Structured BASIC and PASCAL offer most of the facilities mentioned above. The chief advantage of well structured code is its readability and hence the ease with which it can be constructed and, if necessary, modified. Figure 4.12 illustrates this with a section of code written in both structured and unstructured BASIC with long variable names.

Subprograms

Applications programmers often find that certain processing tasks need to be performed in more than one of their applications or at several different points in one program. For example, it is often necessary to sort a file of records into order on some field such as customer order number or date order. Instead of rewriting subroutines to perform such tasks every time they are required it is much more efficient in terms of programming effort to implement a general sorting subroutine which can be applied to different files of records and make it available, as a library routine, to any program that needs it. The concept of subroutines, or subprograms, can also be applied to break a large program down into a number of simpler subprograms each of which can be developed and tested independently of the others. A subroutine generally receives input, in the form of parameters, from the primary program or other subroutine that activates it. For example, suppose A denotes a vector of N numerical values properly sorted into ascending numerical order (we shall refer to the list of values $\{A_k : K = 1 \text{ to } N\}$), and let INSERT be the name of a subroutine with parameters $(X,N,\{A_k : K = 1 \text{ to } N\})$ which inserts a value X into the sorted list A, increases N by 1 and returns the increased list in the same vector A. In a FORTRAN-like language the subroutine is invoked from the main program by means of a CALL instruction

CALL INSERT (X,N,A)

The same subroutine could be called from another point in the program with parameter values (Y,L,B) to insert a value Y in a sorted list $\{B_k : K = 1 \text{ to } L\}$ by the instruction

CALL INSERT (Y,L,B)

The flow of control in these two calls is illustrated in Figure 4.13. Note that

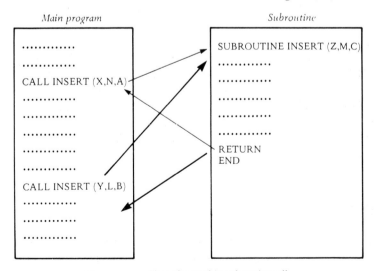

Figure 4.13   *Flow of control in subroutine calls*

before transferring control to the subroutine the computer must remember the point in the calling routine to which control is to be returned after completion of the insertion.

Subroutines are only one kind of program segment. Another concept is that of a function, for example the square root function SQRT(X), and trigonometric functions SIN(X), COS(X). Such functions are required in many mathematical computations and all scientific programming languages offer an extensive range of mathematical functions. The function will normally have one or more parameters and is invoked when encountered during the evaluation of any expression in which it occurs. For example, in FORTRAN we might write

$$ROOT1 = (-B + SQRT(B*B-4.*A*C))/2.*A)$$
and $$AREA = SQRT (S*(S-A)*(S-B)*(S-C)).$$

The actual mechanism for input of parameter values to subprograms and output of results from subprograms varies from one language to another. We shall not consider the details of parameter passing.

BASIC does not offer subprogram facilities in the general sense but a number of built-in mathematical and string-processing functions are available. FORTRAN supports independently compiled subprograms, both functions and subroutines, and most implementations offer extensive libraries of predefined subprograms. FORTRAN subprograms cannot be invoked recursively, i.e. a routine cannot call itself, but that is not a serious limitation for most applications.

We have mentioned but a few of the distinguishing features of BASIC, FORTRAN and PASCAL. Another important respect in which they differ is in the facilities for clear and tidy formatting of printed output. It is not possible to give a full appreciation of these features in the short space available nor will the reader need to know all of these languages in detail. For a more detailed study he is referred to the specialist programming language texts listed in the bibliography.

COBOL

To conclude this section on programming languages we consider an application program written in COBOL. Our example in Figure 4.14 involves selective printing of payroll records. It is intended to give a feeling for what a COBOL program looks like and not to be studied in detail.

Without dwelling on details, let us describe what the program does. At the first level three subroutines are defined:

```
PROCEDURE DIVISION.
PROGRAM-CONTROL.
      PERFORM START-RUN.
      PERFORM READ-SELECT-PRINT
            UNTIL FILE-END = "YES".
      PERFORM FINISH-RUN.
      STOP "END OF PROGRAM PAY-2".
*
START-RUN.
      OPEN INPUT PAYROLL-FILE
            OUTPUT PAY-REPORT-2.
      ACCEPT RUN-DATE FROM DATE.
      WRITE HEADING-LINE FROM REPORT-TITLE AFTER PAGE.
      MOVE "NO" TO FILE-END.
      READ PAYROLL-FILE
            AT END MOVE "YES" TO FILE-END.
*
READ-SELECT-PRINT.
      IF DEPT IN PAY-RECORD = "SALES"
            IF DOB-YEAR + 50 > RUN-YEAR
                  PERFORM PRINT-DETAIL
            ELSE
                  IF DOB-YEAR + 50 = RUN-YEAR
                        IF DOB-MONTH > RUN-MONTH
                              PERFORM PRINT-DETAIL
                        ELSE
                              IF DOB-MONTH = RUN-MONTH AND
                                    DOB-DAY NOT < RUN-DAY
                                    PERFORM PRINT-DETAIL.
      READ PAYROLL-FILE
            AT END MOVE "YES" TO FILE-END.
*
PRINT-DETAIL.
      MOVE SPACES TO OUT-RECORD.
      MOVE CORRESPONDING PAY-RECORD TO OUT-RECORD.
      WRITE OUT-RECORD AFTER 1.
*
FINISH-RUN
      CLOSE PAYROLL-FILE
            PAY-REPORT-2.
```

Figure 4.14   *Procedure division of COBOL program for selective output of pay records*

START-RUN   opens the file PAYROLL-FILE for input and
                              the file PAY-REPORT-2 for output, initializes
                              the variables RUN-DATE and FILE-END,
                              outputs a heading for the output and reads the
                              first record from the input file.

READ-SELECT-PRINT   is the heart of the program.
                              The current input record is tested to see if the
                              employee is in the SALES department and
                              over 50 years of age on the day of the run. If so,
                              a further subroutine, PRINT-DETAIL, is per-
                              formed to copy data from this record to an
                              output record which is then printed. The next
                              payroll record is then read.

FINISH-RUN   Simply closes the PAYROLL-FILE and the
                           output file PAY-REPORT-2.

The program commences by performing START-RUN. Then the subroutine READ-SELECT-PRINT is performed repeatedly (i.e. for each
input record) until the end of the input file is reached. Finally FINISH-
RUN is performed and the program terminates.

Nothing further can be deduced about what the program does without
more information concerning the data involved in the processing. In
particular, the precise action of the MOVE CORRESPONDING instruc-

```
DATA DIVISION.
FILE SECTION.
FD   PAYROLL-FILE          BLOCK 2048 CHARACTERS
                           LABEL RECORDS STANDARD
                           VALUE OF FILE-ID "PAYROLL-FILE".
01   PAY-RECORD.
     02   SURNAME               PIC X(20).
     02   INITIALS              PIC X(4).
     02   DATE-OF-BIRTH.
          03   DOB-DAY          PIC 99.
          03   DOB-MONTH        PIC 99.
          03   DOB-YEAR         PIC 99.
     02   DEPT                  PIC X(6).
     02   TAX-CODE              PIC X(4).
     02   PAY-AND-ALLOWANCES.
          03   SALARY           PIC 9(4)V99.
          03   NON-TAXABLE-PAY  PIC 9(4)V99.
     02   GROSS.
          03   GROSS-PAY-TO-DATE   PIC 9(4)V99.
          03   GROSS-TAX-TO-DATE   PIC 9(4)V99
          03   GROSS-PENSION-TO-DATE
                                PIC 9(4)V99.

FD   PAY-REPORT-2          LABEL RECORDS OMITTED
01   OUT-RECORD.
     02   FILLER                PIC XX.
     02   SURNAME               PIC X(20).
     02   FILLER                PIC XX.
     02   INITIALS              PIC X(4).
     02   FILLER                PIC XX.
     02   DEPT                  PIC X(6).
     02   FILLER                PIC X(8).
     02   GROSS.
          03   GROSS-PAY-TO-DATE   PIC Z(3)9.99.
01   HEADING-LINE              PIC X(100).

WORKING-STORAGE SECTION.

01   REPORT-TITLE              PIC X(56) VALUE
     " SURNAME          INIT   DEPT    GROSS PAY TO DATE".
01   FILE-END                  PIC X(3).
01   RUN-DATE.
     02   RUN-YEAR             PIC 99.
     02   RUN-MONTH            PIC 99.
     02   RUN-DAY              PIC 99.
```

Figure 4.15   Data division of COBOL program for selective output of pay records

tion, in the sub-routine PRINT-DETAIL, depends on the details of the data records predefined in the Data Division of the program. These are shown in Figure 4.15.

With these definitions the effect of

MOVE CORRESPONDING PAY-RECORD TO OUT-RECORD

is to transfer data as shown by the arrows in Figure 4.16.

For further details of COBOL the reader is referred to A. Parkin, *COBOL for Students* (Arnold, 1982).

Programming language translators, both low-level assemblers and compilers for high-level, problem-orientated languages are essential service programs in any operating system. Rarely, if ever, are programs written in machine code. Occasionally, experienced programmers may 'patch' a faulty program in machine code as an emergency measure and to avoid recompiling the whole of the original program but this is not a recommended practice.

It is important to appreciate that the user's application program, called a *source* program, is data to be input to the translator program. The output from the translator is another program, functionally equivalent to the source program but in machine instructions which the CPU can decode and execute. This machine code program is called an *object program*. The translation process is depicted in Figure 4.17.

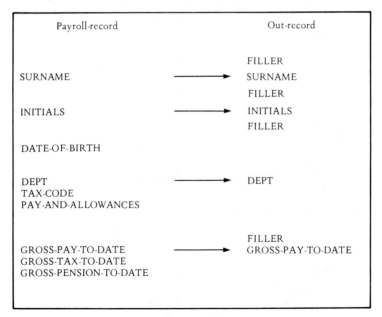

Figure 4.16

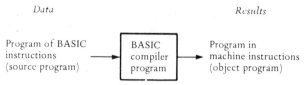

Figure 4.17   *Translation from BASIC source code to object code*

Very rarely does a user write an error-free program at the first attempt. Language translator programs always include routines to check the validity of input source code as far as possible and to report any errors as fully as possible. Syntax errors, i.e. grammatical errors in the use of the language, are relatively easy to detect. Some semantic checks can be performed but the translator program cannot check for logical errors in the design of the source program. These usually become apparent only when the generated object code is executed and produces incorrect results. Here again, the system may provide some aids to detecting the cause of the errors (we call these *debugging* aids – i.e. aids to getting the bugs out of a program). The run-time debugging aids often include post-mortem facilities such as a full print-out of the values of all or selected variables at the point at which the error is detected, and a trace of the results of operations preceding the occurrence of the error. The inclusion of such facilities involves a considerable overhead in terms of size of the compiled object program and in the execution time of the program. For efficiency, the inclusion of diagnostic facilities is usually an option used only during the development stage of a program. Once a program is thought to be free from error it can be recompiled without diagnostic facilities.

Fourth generation languages (4GLs)

Moving strongly in the direction of user-orientated and non-specialist programming languages we have what are known as fourth-generation languages (4GLs). These are very high level and are distinguished by their power relative to COBOL (one 4GL command could be equivalent to 100 COBOL instructions). In comparison with procedural languages, fourth generation languages differ in the following ways:

1   They are easier to learn and use.
2   Screen design features allow for quick and simple responses.
3   Provision is made for report writing.
4   The translation software handles the processing logic so that the programmer is not required to specify how tasks should be performed.

The aim of fourth generation languages is to allow the user to program easily and efficiently. Users specify their requirements while the computer creates the instructions necessary to execute them. The use of fourth generation languages has led to the development of new design techniques. A good example would be prototyping, a technique which allows the user to see precisely what will be available in the final program and thus make specification adjustments where necessary. Generally this will take one or two forms. In the first, a simple system is designed containing only the basic functions required by the users. However, it has enough to be serviceable and by using the prototype it is possible to discover what other functions should be added and what modifications should be made to improve its effectiveness. This approach is very useful when developing decision support systems.

The second method simulates the functions of the system during an initial design stage. Simulation will give some indication of how easy the system is and what features need to be expanded or refined. On this exploratory basis a final system can be built. This type of prototyping is often used to implement transaction systems, which usually need to be implemented with all the functions operating from the beginning.

Spreadsheets

For the management accountant, one of the most important areas of development of user-orientated languages is that of spreadsheets. The basic concept of a spreadsheet can be considered in terms of someone having a very large piece of paper that can be easily written to and erased from. The piece of paper can carry out calculations and draw diagrams.

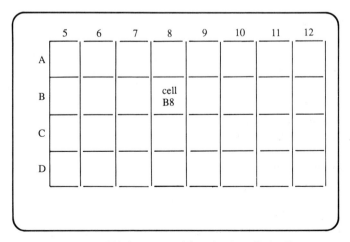

Figure 4.18   *Window on spreadsheet showing cells A5–D12*

This means that routine management reports can be produced quickly and easily.

The information on our piece of paper, our spreadsheet, is split up into a number of pigeon holes or 'cells'. These cells form a grid. Each cell has its own address which is usually a pair of coordinates. In order to handle the large amounts of data that even a small company generates, the spreadsheet grid is potentially very large. When implemented on a computer only a small part of the grid can be shown on the computer screen at any one time. The diagram (Figure 4.18) shows a computer screen of a spreadsheet. The area shown on the screen is known as a window. The other cells, for example A1–C4 cannot be seen by the user, unless the window is moved over the relevant area of the spreadsheet. Movement around the spreadsheet is usually by using the address of a particular cell to be viewed, although other methods of movement are often also provided, for example, finding a particular value in a cell.

So, at any one time, the user is viewing a window showing part of the spreadsheet, and will also be able to write to, erase or modify a cell. The cell on which the user is currently working is marked or highlighted in some way.

Now we have described the appearance of a basic spreadsheet, let's examine what it can do and what can be put into it. A cell can be used to store three types of information: text, numeric data and formulae. Text can be entered into a spreadsheet to provide headings, notes and information. This makes it clear to the user what the spreadsheet contains and does. Without it the spreadsheet would be an incomprehensible load of figures. Numerical data is used in calculations. The calculations themselves are stored in cells as formulae, although the user will usually see the result of the formulae in the cell. The formulae use the addresses of the cells to identify the data to use in the calculation. A sum to add up a row of figures would look something like: SUM(A1–A12). If the value of a cell changes the result of the formula will also change. Some spreadsheets require the user to instruct the computer to recalculate formulae. Others will do it automatically. More advanced spreadsheets also provide the user with other facilities, including graphical presentation of data, and programming capabilities to allow users to develop advanced facilities.

At a simple level the spreadsheet can be seen as an electronic ledger, taking in income and expenditure figures, calculating totals and working out basic management statistics (profit margins, liquidity ratios, etc.). Beyond that, by introducing forecasts and projections into the spreadsheet it can become a valuable tool in planning growth and expenditure.

Conclusion

As programming languages have progressed, we can see that they have become more clearly user- and problem-oriented. The path of development began with machine languages designed for specific computers; it moved through assembly languages, using symbolic code, and then to high level languages using a problem based syntax. Finally, we have the fourth generation non-procedural languages which allow the user to define the task while the computer looks after the processing details. As a basic guide, the merits of a programming language can be assessed according to the following criteria:

1   Ease of use;
2   Portability;
3   Flexibility;
4   Level of control structure;
5   Facilitation of good software engineering practice;
6   Non-procedural capability.

Ease of use is coterminous with user friendliness. A programming language is easy to use when it can be learned quickly and applied by non-specialist users. Simple commands such as STORE and SORT, common to high level and fourth generation languages, will define the level of programming ease.

Portability is a highly desirable feature allowing a program to be developed with a standardized application for different computers or different operating systems. If a programming language is portable it will employ a source code which can be used in a range of computer environments.

Flexibility describes the degree to which a programming language can be extended by means of user defined facilities and the ease with which it can be applied. An example of such flexibility is the facility to define new data types and operations on those types.

The level of control structure in a program design will determine its susceptibility to errors and the development time required to design and implement programs. A good example of a clearly defined control structure can be found in PASCAL.

Finally, non-procedural capability is a feature which allows a programmer simply to outline the processing to be carried out, while the processing procedure and details are handled by the translation software. This is characteristic of the fourth generation languages and makes it much easier to develop applications software.

One interesting development which has resulted from the growth and increasing application of microcomputers is the appearance of generic packages. These have been designed for certain broad-based functions such as word-processing, database management, spreadsheets and desktop publishing. Many incorporate their own programming languages –

for example, LOTUS 1-2-3, dBASE III+ and the new dBASE IV. LOTUS 1-2-3 is a widely used spreadsheet application possessing command structures or macros which provide a programming capability. dBASE III+ and dBASE IV are database management systems which also offer a powerful programming language.

The growth of the micro in recent years has prompted the idea that the non-specialist can develop applications on the computer without learning a conventional programming language. This has been made possible by the development of non-procedural techniques. Common to many of the database packages now available are support facilities which obviate traditional and more demanding programming techniques. With the needs of the end user in mind, several types of application software have been developed to reduce the time spent on conventional programming. Familiar examples include query languages, report generators and code compilers (these will be discussed more fully in Chapter 6).

5 File organization and processing

The volume of data involved in a business is very considerable and hence the efficient storage, retrieval and processing of files of data is of major importance. In Chapter 3, we described the principal features of a number of magnetic storage devices and commented on their suitability for storage of files. In this chapter we shall consider the structure and organization of files of data and factors affecting the choice of storage media for files.

Records, fields and files

The basic building block of computer data is the character. Single characters rarely represent useful information on their own but several are grouped together as a single logical piece of information to form a *field* such as a customer name, an order number, or a description of a product. Fields may be of any length and the characters within a field are read and processed as a single unit of information. Even fields are rarely useful on their own and most data-processing problems require that a number of related fields be grouped and processed together as a *record*. A simple record appertaining to a customer order might have the following fields:

Customer number,
Order number,
Date of order,
Salesman,
Product code,
Quantity ordered,
Sales value.

There could be one such record for each item sold over a period of time.

An organized collection of records is called a *file*. The set of integrated files in a data-processing system is called the *database*.

Files of data normally consist of between 100 and 100,000 records and are therefore too large to be held in the primary store of the computer all at once. They require the use of auxiliary memory such as magnetic tape or some form of fixed or exchangeable disk unit. More advanced developments such as magnetic bubble memories are also becoming more feasible for file storage.

Each of the records in a file is discrete and is labelled or identified by a key field. In our example above, the most likely fields to be used as keys are the customer number, the date and the product code. The choice of key field depends upon the processing involved. For example, we may be interested in all orders placed by a particular customer over a given period of time. On another run we may wish to analyse sales by product code. Whatever processing is required it is often convenient to begin by re-arranging the records in the file in appropriate order of the chosen key field or fields.

All the records in a file are usually of the same type; that is they contain similar fields. In our example, each record has seven fields of fixed length. Occasionally, it may be convenient to use records of variable length: either variable length fields such as customer name and address fields, or variable numbers of fields for example, one record could represent several different products ordered at the same time by a customer. In such cases it is necessary to include in the record some means of identifying the end of each field of information and the end of the record.

The subfields of an address field (street name, town, county and postal code) would each be delimited by an end of field symbol which is used to facilitate printing of the address in a suitable format. When a record consists of variable numbers of fields we might include an additional field specifying either the total number of fields or the overall length of the record; alternatively, the end of the record might be marked by a special symbol which we recognize as an end of record marker. It is usual to employ fixed-length fields and records, whenever it is convenient to do so, in order to simplify procedures for access to and processing of data. For example, although descriptions of products may be of variable length, the variations may not be sufficient to justify the considerable overheads of processing variable-length fields; a fixed-field length, sufficient to store the longest description is preferable.

Classification of files

Files can be classified in a number of ways:

> *Status* – permanent or temporary;
> *Contents* – data or program, binary or alphanumeric, mainfile or overflow-file;
> *Role* – for input, or output, or both;
> *Structure and organization of contents;*
> *Size;*
> *Frequency of access;*
> *Volatility* (frequency of modification);
> *Speed of access required* – real-time use or batch;
> *Security and protection required.*

These characteristics and the nature of the processing involved are significant factors in determining the storage medium to be employed.

Every record in the file must be held in a form that enables it to be accessed and processed efficiently by the computer, and with some degree of immediacy in a real-time system. There must also be protection from accidental or deliberate corruption of data.

Temporary and permanent files

Before we go into the details of file organization and processing it is worth distinguishing between temporary files and permanent files with a few examples.

An inventory master file might show the stock-in-hand of all the products, components and raw materials involved in a business. This master file is a permanent file, although the details of stock levels are continually being updated. Transactions, that is additions to and deletions from inventory, are used to update the master file. It is not always convenient or efficient to update the master file everytime a transaction occurs but may be more convenient to collect together a batch of transactions over a period of time, file them on a transaction file, and then process the whole batch of filed transactions to update the master file at regular intervals. The transactions file is a temporary file, which once the updating has been carried out, is of less value and can eventually be deleted. Legal and tax requirements are an important determinant of when temporary files may be deleted.

Another example of a permanent master file is the list of pending customers' orders in a business. New orders and shipment records are the transactions used to update this master file. Again, the transactions file is a temporary file.

Accounting records provide a further example. The master file would hold beginning of period balances. A temporary transactions file would hold records of receipts and expenditures during the period and this is used to update the master file at the end of the period.

These few examples are sufficient to highlight some of the common characteristics of many master files. The first is the question of timing. In many applications, it is not essential to update the master file as each transaction occurs but is quite acceptable and much more efficient to batch the transactions and update many master file records on one run. A bank might update its file of current balances on customer accounts at the end of each day. Payroll is usually computed, updating records of gross pay to date, total tax deducted to date, and pension contributions to date either weekly or monthly. Accounting records might be updated on a monthly cycle. Inventory might also be updated on a regular basis with a period determined by the company, but this is one example where there might be some advantage in updating the master file in real-time rather than in batch mode.

Another characteristic of this mode of updating is the high percentage of records updated on each batch-processing run. If we can afford to wait until sufficient transactions can be processed in one update run then updating can be much less expensive.

Updating master files

One of the most common business applications of the computer is the updating of master files. The updating required may be insertion of new records in the file, deletion of specified existing records, or perhaps changing the values of one or more fields in existing records. If the master file is stored on magnetic tape, then it is impractical to update it by overwriting existing field values, moving records to make room for new records, or to close up gaps left by deleted records. In practice, no attempt is made to alter the data on a magnetic tape file once it is written. Updates are always performed by creating a new master file incorporating all the amendments required. Figure 5.1 depicts the process involved. The broken line indicates that on the next updating run the new master file from this run becomes the input master file and yet another new generation of the master file is created. We often refer to the old master file and the master file as *father* and *son*. After the second update we have grandfather, father and son, and so on. One important advantage of retaining several generations along with their corresponding transactions files is that in the event of a file becoming corrupted as a result of computer malfunction, or for any other reason, the updating program can be run again and the new master file recreated. Modern hardware is very re-

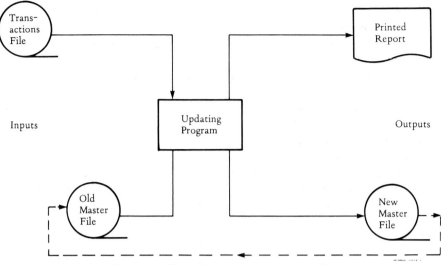

Figure 5.1 *Upgrading a magnetic tape master file*

liable, nevertheless it would be foolish to assume that nothing can go wrong and it is usual to keep at least the grandfather and the father files as well as the newly created son at any stage.

File organization

The nature and efficiency of algorithms for processing files of data is highly dependent on the organization of the data records in the file. We identify four basic types of file organization:

Serial,
Sequential,
Random, and
Indexed Sequential.

Only the first two methods of organization are possible on magnetic tape files, but any of the four can be used for files stored on disks and other direct-access storage media.

Serial files

A serial file is one in which the records are stored simply in adjacent locations as they occur. There is no attempt to arrange them in any particular order or in particular locations in the storage medium. Typically, a series of transactions, when input and stored on magnetic tape, would form a serial file. It is not possible to access isolated records in a serial file without first reading all the preceding records, that is the records can only be accessed in serial mode, starting with the first record in the file and proceeding through each record to the end of the file or until the required record is found. Since there is no semblance of order in a serial file, to locate any particular record in a file of n records involves examination of an average of $n/2$ records before the required record is found and all n records must be inspected before we can deduce that the required record is not in the file. The process of updating a master file stored serially can be very inefficient. It is almost always better to maintain the master file with the records arranged in logical sequence of key fields and to sort the batch of amendments into corresponding order before the master file update run.

Sequential files

The best-known file organization is the sequential method in which records are stored in position relative to other records in order of some chosen key field. Any particular record in the file is located simply by starting at the beginning of the file and comparing the value of the key field of each successive record with the desired key until a match is found. Efficient processing of a batch of input transactions therefore requires that the transactions are first sorted into the same sequence as the master file. The systems flowchart for the sequential master file update problem is shown in Figure 5.2. Sequential file organization is ideal for batch processing where transactions can be accumulated, sorted and then processed efficiently against the master file. Sequential files can also be stored on the least expensive storage medium, namely magnetic tape, which is only suitable for serial or sequential file processing.

The basic algorithm for processing a batch of transactions against a sequential master file has much in common with the simple process of merging two sequential files. We use the following notation:

R_M – the current record from the old master file;
R_T – the current record from the transactions file;
KEY– the key field of a record.

Thus, KEY(R_T) denotes the key field of the current transactions file record. We identify three kinds of updating:

Insertion of a new record (the transaction record) in the master file;
Deletion of the current master file record:
Alteration of the current master file record.

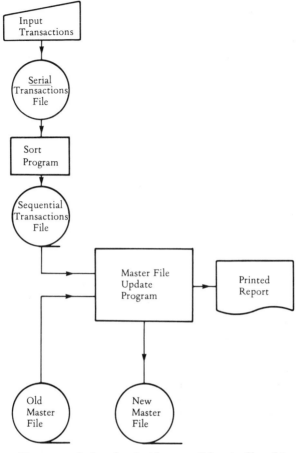

Figure 5.2 *Systems flowchart for sequential master file update*

The file updating actions are summarized in Figure 5.3.

Processing commences with the first record from each of the master file and the transactions file. The key fields are compared. While $KEY(R_M) < KEY(R_T)$, the next file position for an update has not been reached; the current R_M is written to the new master file without alteration and the next R_M is input from the old master file ready for inspection. When $KEY(R_M) \geqslant KEY(R_T)$, the current transaction record is processed (an insertion performed by writing the new record to the new master file) and the next transaction record is input ready for processing. If $KEY(R_M) = KEY(R_T)$ then the specified update may be a deletion, which is performed simply by reading the next record from the old master file, or it is an amendment to the current master record. In either case, when the update has been performed, the next R_T is then input ready for processing. This cycle continues until either the end of the old master file is

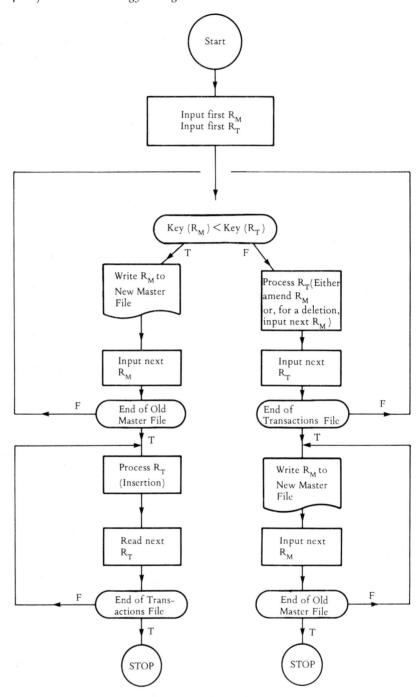

Figure 5.3   *Algorithm for processing a transactions file against a sequential master file*

reached, in which case any remaining transactions must be insertions at the end of the master file, or the transactions file is exhausted and any remaining master file records are input and written to the new master file without amendment.

Sorting

Sequential file processing requires that all files be sorted. Algorithms for sorting are of two types:

1 Internal sorts that are used when the primary store is large enough to hold the entire file of records to be stored;
2 External sorts that are used when the file to be sorted is too large to be held in the primary store all at once.

Almost all data files in a business are too large to be sorted by internal sorting techniques, so we shall concentrate on external sorting. It may seem improbable that a file of data records can be sorted into key sequence while most of the records are held on magnetic tape but it can be done if we use several magnetic tapes. The basis of the procedure for doing this is as follows. Suppose we have two sequences of records, each of which is already in the required order, and that the two sequences are stored on two magnetic tapes A and B, then it is possible to merge the two sequences to form a single ordered sequence, on a third magnetic tape, C. The algorithm for this is given in Figure 5.4.

External sorting algorithms for magnetic tape files consist of repeated merging of ordered subsequences by copying records from two input tapes to an output tape.

The classical example is the four-tape sort in which we use four magnetic tapes: A, B, C and D, say. Suppose that, initially, we have a serial file on tape A, i.e. a file of unsorted records in random order. To fix ideas, suppose the records on tape A have key field values as follows:
324, 361, 338, 303, 348, 388, 334, 327, 380, 333, 390, 378, 355, 387), . . .
These might be customer numbers, for example. We can divide the unsorted file into a number of ordered subsequences. (For simplicity, only the key fields are shown.)
(324, 361), (338), (303, 348, 388), (334), (327, 380), (333, 390), (378), (355, 387), . . .
The first stage is to copy alternate subsequences to two output tapes C and D as follows:

Tape A:	(324,361), (338), (303,348,388), (334), (327,380), (333,390), (378), (355,387), . . .	Input
Tape B:	Unused	
Tape C:	(324,361), (303,348,388), (327,380), (378), . . .	Output
Tape D:	(338), (334), (333,390) (355,387), . . .	Output

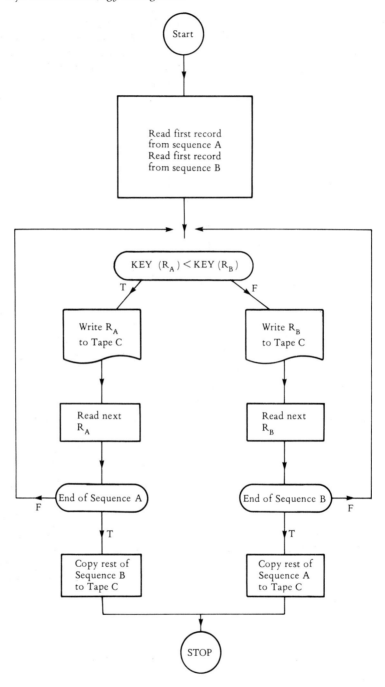

Figure 5.4   *Algorithm to merge two sorted sequences of records*

In the second stage tapes C and D become input tapes and A and B are output tapes. The first subsequence on tape C is merged with the first subsequence on tape D and the result written to tape A. Then the second subsequences from C and D are merged and written to tape B. The third subsequences are merged and written to tape A, and so on until the last subsequences have been merged, or if an odd subsequence remains it is simply copied with no merging.

Tape C:	(324,361), (303,348,388), (337,380) (378), . . .	Input
Tape D:	(338), (334), (333,390), (355,387), . . .	Input
Tape A:	(324,338,361), (327,333,380,390), . . .	Output
Tape B:	(303,334,348,388), (355,378,387), . . .	Output

The roles of tapes A and B, and C and D are then interchanged; A and B become input tapes, and C and D output tapes. The merging of successive sequences is repeated giving the following results:

Tape A:	(324,338,361), (327,333,380,390), . . .	Input
Tape B:	(303,334,348,388), (355,378,387), . . .	Input
Tape C:	(303,324,334,338,348,361,388), . . .	Output
Tape D:	(327,333,355,378,380,387,390), . . .	Output

The input and output tapes are interchanged and the merge repeated until eventually all the records are on one tape. They are then in ordered sequence of key fields.

In the worst possible situation the initial sequences are all of length one, i.e. the records are in reverse order. In practice this is most unlikely, but assuming the worst case, then if there are n records to be sorted we start with n subsequences. Each merge halves (or if n is odd, almost halves) the number of subsequences. It follows that the maximum number of times each record is copied from one tape to another in this sorting procedure is m where $2^m = n$, i.e. $m = \log_2 n$, and m is rounded up to the nearest integer above.

The sorting method we have described is the classical four-tape sort. There are variations and improvements on this but we shall not go into them here. Sorting is one of the fundamental operations in any business data-processing system and sorting procedures are normally provided within the range of software associated with the computer operating system.

Direct access techniques

Batch processing of sequential files is not always appropriate. For example, if you wish to make an airline reservation you will not be prepared to wait until shortly before the flight for confirmation of your booking. Similarly, a bank could not justify daily batch processing of deposits and withdrawals against current accounts, most of which would be inactive on all but a few days each month. Nor could the bank delay the updating of current accounts until the end of each month, for some accounts could then be considerably overdrawn for some time before any illegal transactions were detected. We need some form of file storage and organization that will allow rapid access to and amendment of selected records at a reasonable cost. Magnetic tape is essentially a serial storage medium. It is not possible to access the 400th record for example, without first reading the preceding 399 records on the tape. Serial file processing is not suitable when results are wanted quickly, when the hit-rate is low, i.e. when only a small percentage of the records are updated on any run, nor when the nature of the data is such that no suitable sorting order exists (for example, there is no obvious sorting order for a file of finger-print records so that a given print can easily be looked up). We need a storage medium that allows direct access, or almost direct access to any specified record in the file.

The telephone directory is a good example of a file of records which are accessed directly or almost directly. Although the entries for telephone subscribers are stored in alphabetical order, by name (a sequential file), when we want to look up a telephone number we do not start at the first name beginning with A and work our way through the directory until the required name is found. We commence our search at some point in the file near to where we expect to find the required entry. The technique used requires the records to be in sequence, but only a subset of the records are actually scanned.

Primary store allows direct access to any record, field or even character but the high cost of primary store prohibits its use for storage of large files of data. In Chapter 3 we described a number of secondary storage devices including magnetic drums and fixed and exchangeable disks, on which each storage location can be individually addressed and accessed. We shall now consider methods for organizing files on direct-access devices.

Random files

First let us deal with the logical concept of a bucket. A bucket is a logical unit of data that can be transferred between the primary store and the disk with a single program instruction. We need not concern ourselves with the physical layout of a bucket in relation to blocks, bands and cylinders of data on the disk. A bucket may consist of one or more blocks; its size is usually determined by the amount of primary store available to accommodate the bucket of data. Records may be stored one to a bucket but they can be stored several to a bucket depending on the size of bucket and the record length.

Serial and sequential organization and the batch processing technique already described for magnetic tape files can of course be used on direct-access devices, but with some loss of efficiency. Earlier, we identified two other methods, namely indexed sequential and random methods of organization which are suitable only for direct-access devices; they cannot be used on magnetic tapes.

Random file organization allows any record in the file to be retrieved by a single (direct) access to the file. Other records do not have to be examined as is the case with sequential files. The key field of the record is used to determine the location at which the record is to be stored and from which it is to be retrieved when required. There are three principal methods of determining the address of a record from its key.

1 If the number of physical addresses allocated to the file is roughly equal to the range of the keys then each key value maps directly into an actual bucket address. Thus, if the key values range from 0 to 1,000, then the record with key value 756 will be stored in bucket 756. There are a number of obvious variations and extensions to this simple mapping. A direct mapping is sometimes difficult to achieve; if the keys are not sequential then many storage locations may never be used.

2 Another method is to derive the physical address of the record from an index or dictionary in which each record has a unique entry. While the file is being processed the index is held in primary store and can be searched efficiently to find the disk address of the record with the given key. There is an overhead in constructing, maintaining and searching the index but this additional CPU activity may be justified by the time saved in making only one disk access to retrieve or store each record. The method is suitable for relatively small files, but for large files the size of the index can be untenable.

3 The third approach is by calculations on the key value to produce a bucket address. This usually involves 'hashing' or 'randomizing' techniques designed to distribute the records as evenly as possible over the range of buckets allocated to the file. However sophisticated these techniques, there remains the major problem of some buckets never being used whilst duplicates may be produced for others. Various overflow techniques have been developed to cope with the duplicates problem.

It is important to minimize the number of 'collisions' that occur, i.e. if $h(K)$ is the *hash function* determining the *home bucket* of the record with key value K we must minimize the number of times that

$$h(K_1) = h(K_2) \text{ for } K_1 \neq K_2.$$

**Table 5.1   Examples of the operation of four hash functions on a set of customers'
numbers**

Customer number	Hash functions			
	Cut key	Folded key	Mid square	Residue modulo 131
371983	83	(2)11	13	74
476295	95	(1)68	69	(1)10
310023	23	54	42	77
164908	08	(1)18	46	(1)10
237171	71	(1)11	00	61
409638	38	(1)47	32	1
143195	95	(1)22	48	12
302108	08	50	92	22

We will first consider some possible hash functions and then return to
the problem of collisions. The reader who is not interested in the details of
hashing and overflow techniques may wish to omit this section and turn
to the section on indexed sequential files on p. 91.

Suppose the file storage area consists of 100 buckets of a suitable size
and that there are less than 100 customer records to be stored. Suppose
also that the code numbers shown in Table 5.1 are the customer numbers.

One method is to cut two digits from the key and use these to give a
bucket address in the range 0 to 99. We could use the last two digits as
shown in Table 5.1 or any other pair of digits. In this example, two distinct
keys transform to address 08 and another two to 95. One disadvantage of
the simple key cutting approach is that not all the information in the key is
utilized. Another approach is to fold the key, sum the digit pairs and take
the two least significant digits of the sum. Thus,

$$371983 \longrightarrow \begin{array}{r} 37 \\ 91 \\ \underline{83} \\ \underline{211} \end{array} \longrightarrow 11$$

This method gives one duplicate for the given data but it uses all the digits
in each key and in principle it is better than simple cutting.

A third method is the mid-square method. The key is squared and two
middle digits taken from the result. Again this uses all the data to determine the bucket address:

$$371983 \times 371983 = 1383\ 7(13)52289 \rightarrow 13.$$

One very popular, simple and effective method is the residue method.
The address is obtained from the remainder left when the key is divided
by a suitable divisor. It can be shown that the division should be a prime
number or a number with no prime factors less than 20 in order to
minimize the number of collisions.

A hashing technique is said to be 'good' if it is simple to use and is likely to distribute a given set of keys uniformly over the possible bucket or location addresses. The arithmetic presents no problem to the computer. However carefully we choose the hashing function, some collisions are inevitable. It is therefore important to have efficient techniques for dealing with overflow records, i.e. records whose home bucket has already been allocated to another record. One of the simplest algorithms for locating an overflow record is to store it in the nearest free location to its home bucket. To retrieve the record when we find it is not in its home bucket we search the neighbouring buckets until the sought record is found. This can involve many additional disk accesses.

Thus when two or more records have the same home bucket, H, the second will be located in the first free bucket in the set

$$H \pm i, i = 1, 2, 3, \ldots$$

and successive records with home bucket H will be located in the next available bucket in the same set. This method, known as *progressive linear overflow*, suffers from clustering. First the set of overflow locations associated with H is superimposed on the set associated with $H - 1, H + 1$, etc. Secondly, all records with home bucket H have the same set of overflow locations. The second problem can be overcome by applying a second hashing function whenever a collision occurs. The first can be overcome using a quadratic overflow method: if the overflow set is $H + xi + \beta i^2, i = 1, 2, 3, \ldots$, where x and β are integer constants, then the overflow set for H is

$$H, \quad H + x + \beta, \quad H + 2x + 4\beta, \quad H + 3x + 9\beta, \ldots,$$

whereas the set for $H + x + \beta$ is

$$H + x + \beta, \quad H + 2x + 2\beta, \quad H + 3x + 5\beta, \quad H + 4x + 10\beta, \ldots$$

The overheads of maintaining and searching indexes or of applying complex formulae for address calculations and handling any resulting overflows can be very significant and partly offset the advantages of rapid retrieval of selected individual records. The programming of these techniques is also more complicated.

Indexed sequential files

One disadvantage of a random file organization is that it cannot be accessed in any other way as the records are not held in any particular sequence and are not necessarily in continuous locations.

An indexed sequential file is a compromise between sequential organization and random organization. The records are stored in order of key values so that sequential processing is possible but an ordered index is also maintained to facilitate efficient access by key value to selected individual records. To access one particular record directly, the sought key is located in the index either by a hashing technique or by a (binary) search (see Shave and Bhaskar, 1981) and then the record is accessed directly, or almost directly. We have already noted that maintenance of a large index with an entry for each record in the file may be unacceptable. An indexed sequential file often has a partial index, containing an entry for the highest (or lowest) key value in each bucket. This significantly reduces the size of the index but requires a little additional programming so that a key value can be 'bracketed' between two entries K_1 and K_2 in the index.

A further improvement for large files is the establishment of a multi-level index. At the highest level, a small master index is held in primary store. This contains references to sub-indexes held in the auxiliary store. These in turn contain references to further sub-indexes or to actual records. Searching a multilevel index involves one access to auxiliary store for each level but each sub-index is designed to be sufficiently small to be held in the primary store all at once so that it can be searched efficiently and the number of auxiliary store accesses minimized.

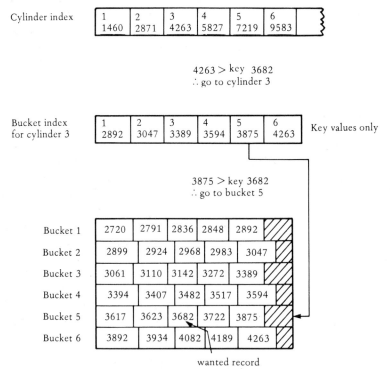

Figure 5.5   *Procedure for locating the record with key 3682*

One possible organization of sub-indexes is in terms of cylinder address (seek area) and bucket address. The procedure involved in locating a record is shown diagrammatically in Figure 5.5 in which it is required to find the record with key value 3682.

First, the cylinder index is searched for a key value greater than the wanted key (4263 > key 3682 so the wanted record is in cylinder 3). Then the bucket index for the home cylinder is searched (3875 > key 3682 so the record is in bucket 5). Finally, bucket 5 of cylinder 3 is input and searched for the wanted record. If the records were stored only one to a bucket then of course the final search would become a direct access to the wanted record but the bucket indexes would thus contain an entry for each record in the file. Partial indexing is commonly used.

Since indexed sequential files are held on direct access devices, updating can be in place, i.e. an existing record can be updated by reading, amending and writing it back in the same location. Records for insertion can be placed in overflow areas to which an index entry refers, whilst records which are deleted create gaps. The file must be re-organized from time to time to remove the gaps and to incorporate inserted records in the proper sequence. Indexed sequential files are simple to use and widely used since they combine the best features of sequential and direct access organization. The price paid for these advantages includes extra storage space required for indexes and overflow areas, and extra processing time for searching indexes and for the regular re-organizations. Manufacturer's software is available for creating and maintaining the indexes.

Security of direct access files

One of the nightmares of a data manager is the permanent loss of essential data. No system is infallible and it is important to establish procedures for recreating records or even whole files that may become corrupted. This is particularly important for master files which may have been updated and amended many times since their original creation. For sequential files held on magnetic tape, updating is by copying an old master and creating a new master. Two or three generations are retained for security. On direct-access devices, records are usually updated and written back in the same location without moving other records. The grandfather, father, son technique cannot be applied. On-line updating in real-time can present serious problems if anything goes wrong. The ways in which data can be lost from direct access master files include the following:

Incorrect transaction data is used to update a master file;
A software or operational error results in accidental overwriting of data;

Physical or electrical damage to a disk may make it unreadable, e.g. a disk head crash could damage the disk surface.

To guard against such loss it is necessary to 'dump' copies of master files onto other disks or magnetic tapes at regular intervals. These copies provide a starting point for recreating a file. If the system also keeps a record of all amendments performed, e.g. a copy of the original record and the update then it may be possible to automate the recreation of the file.

In a simple on-line order processing system the master file used may be

an order file,
a product file, and
a customer file.

These files are directly accessed and updated during order processing by overwriting selected fields and records. To permit reconstruction they must be dumped periodically. The input transactions used since the last

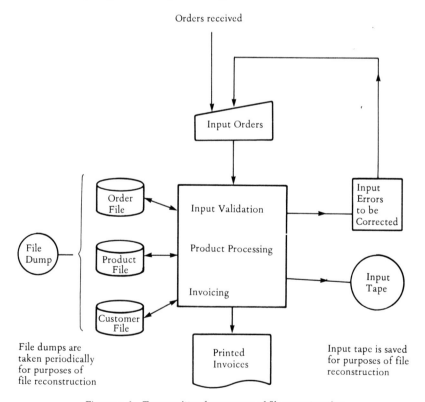

Figure 5.6   *Tapes written for purposes of file reconstruction*

file dump (records of orders received) must be retained. Then, if necessary, the master files can be reconstructed by a program that uses the last file dump and the input transaction tapes. Any corrections that may have been made to individual records following validation of the input must also be recorded on the input transaction tapes so that they too can be reconstructed automatically. Figure 5.6 shows the tapes in question.

Another safeguard is to delay actual deletions and to simply flag a record as deleted. On a re-organization run, any records flagged for deletion before some specified date may then be permanently removed. As a matter of principle, a printed record should be produced of any data to be erased from a file then any damage caused by accidental or premature erasure can be repaired.

6 Data organization and management, databases

In the previous chapter we described some of the most important, and commonly used, methods of file organization. We noted that magnetic tape files can only be accessed and processed sequentially and are suitable only for batch-processing, whereas indexed sequential and random files stored on direct-access devices are more suitable for on-line and real-time processing of selected individual records.

File design and management is a complex and specialized task. The choice of file organization can vitally affect the economics of a system and can influence the capabilities, flexibility and utility expected by the user. None of the organizations considered so far overcomes all of the problems encountered in a typical data-processing environment. One problem is that any one item of data may be required in a number of different applications and by different departments in an organization. The same file organization is unlikely to be equally acceptable in every case. Different access requirements may affect the mode of storage needed. One department may require direct on-line access to the data, while for another sequential files for batch processing might be more appropriate. Different keys may be applied by different user departments. For instance, product code is likely to be the key field in a stock report but when the product is received from a supplier or delivered to a customer, the supplier code and customer code are more important. This leads the different departments to create and maintain their own (duplicate) copies of the same data. Unnecessary additional copies waste storage space and create problems of compatibility between several different representations of the same object. Updates performed on one version have to be applied to all other versions to ensure that they are representations of the same data.

One answer to the problem of making the same data available in different forms for different users is to restructure (e.g. re-order) the data on the required key whenever necessary, but re-sorting is time-consuming and expensive and can only be justified in a batch-processing environment; it is the only answer for sequential magnetic tape files.

Another approach with indexed files, held on direct-access devices, is to maintain a different index for each user group or application. Whilst the actual data items are held only once, the indexes require a significant amount of storage space and the overheads of maintaining multiple indexes may be unacceptable.

List structures

An alternative to sequential, indexed sequential and random organizations is the list or chain organization. This is particularly useful where relationships between records need to be exploited. The basic concept of a list of records is that related records are chained together by pointers to form a linked list. The logical organization is completely divorced from the physical organization, that is successive records in a list are not necessarily held in contiguous storage areas on the storage device. The pointer is anything that allows the 'next' record to be located. For example, it could be the disk address of the next record. In a simple list organization, the first record points to the second record in the logical sequence, the second points to the third and so on to the end of the logical chain. The last record in the sequence stores an end-of-chain marker. Figure 6.1 shows a simple list of customer records chained together in order of customer number. Record insertion and deletion involves revision of pointers as well as processing the records themselves. If backward as well as forward pointers are stored such changes are more straightforward and the list can be searched in either direction.

Multiple lists of the same data simply involve the storage of more pointer chains within the records. For example, the chain demonstrated in Figure 6.1 makes the records available in order of customer numbers: 3142, 3491, 3507, 3618,-----, 4925; the structure demonstrated in Figure 6.2 preserves this order (pointer chain 1) but also allows access, via pointer chain 2, in the order 3142, 3507, 4925, 3491, 3618,-----.

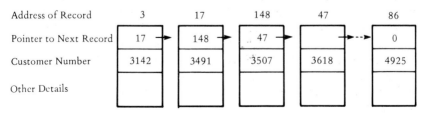

Address of Record	3	17	148	47	86
Pointer to Next Record	17	148	47		0
Customer Number	3142	3491	3507	3618	4925
Other Details					

Figure 6.1   *Simple list structure*

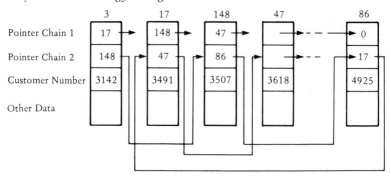

Figure 6.2   *Multiple list structure*

Tree structures

Using the concept of a pointer we can represent relationships of a hierarchical nature. Perhaps the most natural of all the non-linear structures is
the tree structure. Each record in a tree-structured file has a *parent–child*

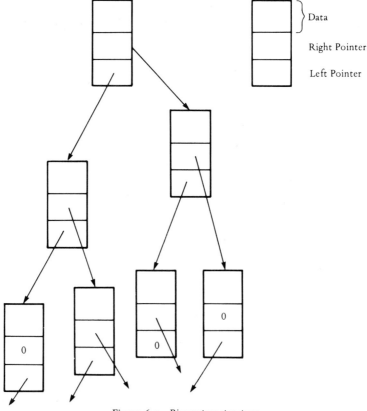

Figure 6.3   *Binary tree structure*

relationship with records at its immediate subordinate level. Each record has a unique parent and at the highest level in the hierarchy is a unique *root* node. In general, a record may have any number (zero or more) of children, but without loss of generality we can consider only binary trees, that is trees in which no record has more than two immediate subordinates. Any general tree can be represented as a binary tree. In a binary tree-structured file each record has two pointer fields, one pointing to a 'left' subtree and one to a 'right' subtree. Such a binary tree structure is demonstrated in Figure 6.3. Again, an end-of-chain symbol (e.g. a zero disk address) is used to indicate the end of a branch. Figure 6.4 shows the representation of a general tree structure as a binary tree.

Ring structures

Another simple structure which can be used to build more complex hierarchical structures is the ring structure. Generally, a ring structure is a list structure having both forward and backward pointers. The first record may be an index record, specifying the nature of the data in the ring, and the last record, instead of having an end-of-chain symbol, points back to

(a) *General tree structure*

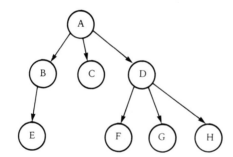

(b) *Binary tree representation*

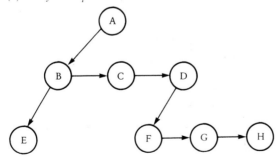

Figure 6.4 *Representation of a general tree as a binary tree: (a) General tree structure, (b) Binary tree representation*

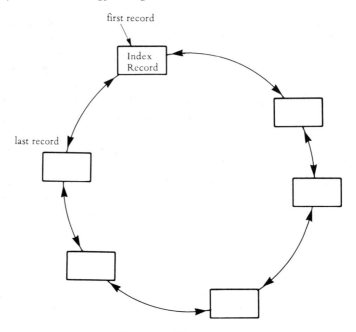

first record

Index
Record

last record

Figure 6.5   *Ring structure*

the first record so forming a ring. Figure 6.5 shows a simple ring structure. Any record may be on more than one ring, i.e. it may have more than one pointer chain passing through it. Figure 6.6 shows a representation of our general tree structure from Figure 6.4(a) using rings. In this structure, we have used three pointer fields in each record: forward and backward pointers connecting the record to other members of the same filial set (these form a ring) and a pointer to the ring formed by the children of the record. Starting from any record in the file it is possible to move either forwards or backwards around the ring and to move up or down the hierarchy as required through index records.

Network or plex structures

If any record in a data structure has more than one parent then the tree structure is clearly inappropriate. The data structure is then described as a *network* or a *plex* structure. In a plex structure any record may be connected to any other record in the file.

The possibilities are endless and as the data structures employed become more complex, in order to provide more flexibility of use, so do the routines required to access them.

A major disadvantage of all the approaches to data organization considered so far is that any attempts to make the same data available to multiple users engaged in widely different applications necessarily complicates the organization and data structures employed. Each user must be familiar with the actual physical storage structures and makes use of them within his application program. All of the requirements of the users must be provided for at the time the physical storage structure is designed. It is very difficult to build in sufficient flexibility to allow for particular applications which are not anticipated at the design stage. Later modifications to data storage structures to accommodate new applications may impair existing applications programs and changes in any application program may impair the data structure for that particular application. We need to separate the definitions of data and of physical data storage structures from the user's view of the data. The concept of data independence is central to the *database* approach.

Objectives of a database

The essential feature of a database approach is that data is regarded as a central resource of a company or organization. The intention is that data, like buildings, equipment, personnel or capital of the business, should be owned and maintained for the use and benefit of the business as a whole.

Four major objectives of database management have been identified (Everest, 1974):

1   *The database should be shared*; in other words, different users with different applications should be capable of accessing the same actual data at the same time. This reduces the need for duplicate copies of the data and saves storage space. It also ensures that the latest updates are available to all users of the data and that different incompatible versions do not evolve.
2   A second major objective is the *integrity of the database*. In a shared-data environment, this objective is fundamental since multiple users have access to the same data. No one user can be allowed to make alterations to the data which would impair other applications.
3   The database management system must be *responsive to an environment of diverse users*, having diverse needs and requiring diverse modes of access.
4   A fourth and very important objective is *evolvability*, which is the ability of the database management system to develop and meet the needs of future applications which could not be anticipated at the initial design stage.

For an MIS to have long-term survival within a computerized data-processing environment, it must possess all of the attributes listed in

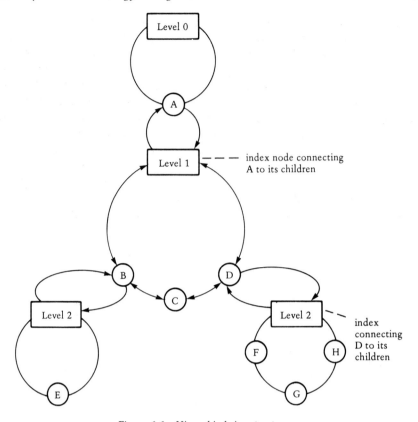

Figure 6.6   *Hierarchical ring structure*

these four objectives. To achieve them the data must be defined and exist *independently* of the application programs that use it.

Data independence has two major elements (Everest, 1974). First, there is the separation of the logical definition of data in the database from the physical representation and storage of the data on the hardware disks etc. supporting the database. This is the physical independence of data. Secondly, there is the program data independence by which we mean the separation of the logical definition of data as viewed by the user in his application program from the logical definition of the data in the database. This yields three different conceptual levels or views of the data as shown in Figure 6.7. The user need not concern himself with the physical representation or the detailed file structures. His view of the data, as defined in his program, is mapped into the logical definition of data (usually a subset of the data) in the database which in turn is mapped into the physical representation by the database management routines designed for this purpose.

At the centre of this model of a database system is the conceptual schema, which is an application-independent and storage-independent description of the data. The internal schema is a description of how the data is actually stored. An external schema is a view of the data as seen by one user or group of users. There may be several external schemas each relating to different and possibly intersecting subsets of the data defined in the conceptual schema. Figure 6.8 shows a schema for a purchasing system with two different subschemas used in two different application programs. The solid lines between blocks represent direct relationships between the entities. The PURCHASE ORDER record is connected to the PURCHASE ITEM records of which that purchase order is composed. The SUPPLIER record is connected to QUOTATION records for the parts that can be provided by that SUPPLIER. The dashed lines show cross-references. For example, the part name and part description are not stored in the PURCHASE ITEM records nor in the QUOTATION records.

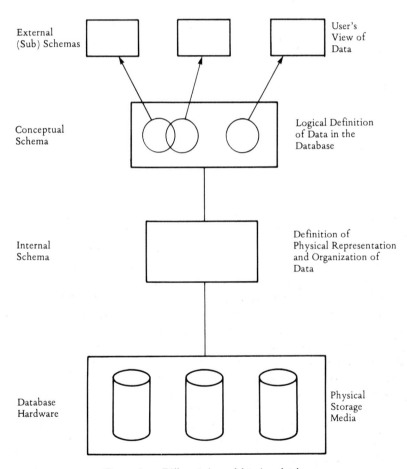

Figure 6.7 *Different views of data in a database*

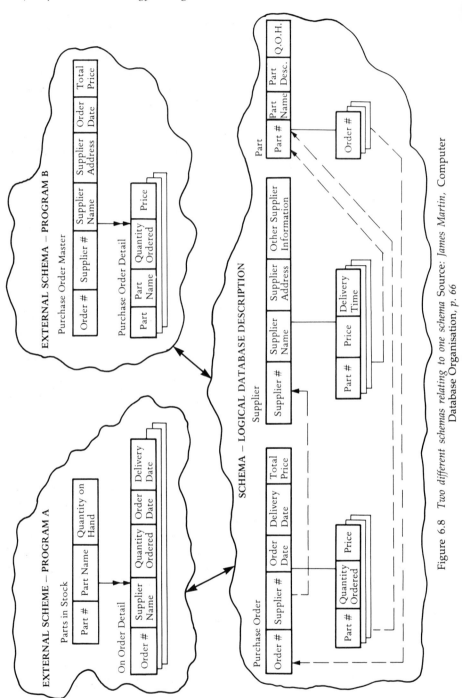

Figure 6.8 *Two different schemas relating to one schema* Source: *James Martin, Computer Database Organisation, p. 66*

These details are stored in the PART record. The cross-references enable such information to be retrieved more quickly but they are not essential. No information is lost if the cross-references are removed. On the other hand, the connections represented by solid lines are an essential part of the data, for example, the details of an order are available only through the direct connection between a PURCHASE ORDER record and its PURCHASE ITEMS.

It is difficult to give a good practical definition of a conceptual schema. Three different types of model have been used in existing database management systems:

Network models;
Hierarchical models; and
Relational models.

As their names suggest, these systems employ network structures, hierarchical (tree) structures and relations in their definitions of data. All of them generate system definitions which fall somewhere between the conceptual schema and the internal schema levels and consequently each system imposes some restrictions on the data structures and data transformations that can be defined.

We shall not describe any particular manufacturer's database system in detail, but a brief description will be given of each of the three approaches with examples to illustrate their principal features. First we shall look in more detail at the problem of data independence.

Data analysis

To achieve genuine data independence when a database is created the first and most important step is a thorough analysis of the data resources of the organization. This includes the identification of data, where it originates, how it is used and when it is needed. Where the same data is used in more than one application, any differences in terminology and representation must be reconciled. The volumes and frequencies of data should be determined (e.g. 3,000 stock issues a week).

Entity analysis

We refer to all items about which information is stored as *entities*. Some examples of entities are employee, job title, part, supplier, customer account, invoice, spending authority, an event or an abstract concept. An entity may have various *attributes* such as colour, name, size and price, which we may wish to record. An application programmer may wish to maintain a *record* about each entity; the *fields* of the record represent attributes of the entity. In addition to entities and attributes there exist *relationships* between pairs of entity types. These relationships are as important as the actual values of data items and must be represented in some form in the database. A relationship may take many forms, for example ownership, propinquity, sequence, similarity. More than one relationship type may exist between two entity types, e.g. for entity types House and Person we can identify an ownership relationship and an occupancy relationship. A relationship may involve two entities of the same type, e.g. the relationship sibling between two entities of type Person. Each relationship has a degree which may be one to one (1:1), one to many (1:n), in either direction, or many to many (m:n).

The data analysis function involves the identification, definition and description of all entity types, attribute types and relationship types occurring in an organization.

The objects and concepts of a system do not fall irrevocably into one of the three categories entity, attribute or relationship type. A classic example is provided by data which refers to marriages. The concept of marriage could be regarded as an entity type with attributes such as date, place, name of bride and name of bridegroom. Alternatively, marriage could be an attribute type, a status associated with the entity type Person. Marriage can also be regarded as a relationship type connecting instances of entity types Man and Woman. One of the tasks of the data analyst is to decide which of these viewpoints is the most appropriate within the system he is considering. An entity type probably provides the most flexible form of definition suitable for all applications of the system.

To illustrate the concepts of entity type, attribute type and relationship we shall consider a simple purchasing system and show how a model of the system is constructed. First we identify the entity types of the system and the associated attribute types. These include the following.

Entity type	Attribute types
Supplier	Supplier #, Name, Address, other details.
Part	Part #, Name, Description, Quantity on hand.
Purchase order	Order #, Order date, Delivery date, Order value, Date of payment
Purchase item	Part #, Quantity ordered, Price
Return	Date, Quantity returned
Payment	Date, Payment amount, Discount

Not all of the information required is available in these entity and attribute types. We must also identify relationships between pairs of entity types. For example, an order is composed of purchase items and is placed with a supplier. Relationships such as those between SUPPLIER and ORDER, ORDER and PURCHASE ITEM must be identified and represented in our model of the purchasing system. The relationships include the following

Relationship type	*Degree*	*Assumptions*
Supplier–Order	1:*n*	Several orders may be placed with the same supplier but no order is related to more than one supplier.
Order–Purchase Item	1:*n*	An order may be composed of several items.
Supplier–Payment	1:*n*	Several payments may be made to a supplier. Each payment is to only one supplier.
Payment–Order	1:*n*	A single payment may relate to several orders.
Supplier–Return	1:*n*	There may be several returns to the same supplier but no single return involves more than one supplier.
Return–Purchase Item	1:*n*	A return may be composed of several purchase items.
Supplier–Part	*m:n*	A supplier can usually provide many different parts. The same parts could be supplied by more than one supplier.
Part–Purchase Item	1:*n*	Any one item may appear as a purchase item on several different orders whereas a single line item on an order relates to only one part.

At this stage the reader may be wondering why we chose this particular model of a purchase system. It is not difficult to think of other entity types that might have been included, e.g. a supplier's quotation for a part. Some of the data could have been modelled in different ways; for example, instead of a relationship type connecting the entity types SUPPLIER and ORDER we could have included the supplier number, SUPPLIER #, as another attribute of ORDER, or both representations of the connection between an order and a supplier could have been included in the model. One of the objectives of a database is to eliminate unnecessary redundancy. This applies to the logical as well as the physical description of the data. However, redundancy in a logical definition does not necessarily imply redundancy in the physical representation.

It is also important to appreciate that a database models only part of the real world; it cannot include absolutely every entity and relationship type that might be required. If the model is well constructed then it can evolve and be modified to meet the changing requirements of the users. In our simple model we have included only a small part of any real purchasing system.

Once the identification and definition of appropriate entity types and relationship types, and analysis of how these concepts fit together is completed it is useful to portray the structure of the object system in an Entity – Relationship (E–R) diagram. An oval box is used to indicate an entity type to distinguish it from the rectangular box normally used to represent a record at the storage level. Relationship types are indicated by lines connecting pairs of boxes and the degree of a relationship type is indicated by arrows on the connections. Different forms of relationship types are illustrated in Figure 6.9. The E–R diagram corresponding to all the entities and relations identified in our purchasing system is shown in Figure 6.10.

Although we have already identified and recorded some of the attribute types associated with each entity type, these are not included in the E–R diagram; they add nothing to our appreciation of the overall structure of the purchase system, and the additional detail would obscure the E–R diagram. The full details of definitions of entity, attribute and relationship types are recorded in the documentation of the system usually maintained by the DP department together with information about the origin of the data, volumes of data, frequency of use, useful life of the data, who has right of access to the data and so on.

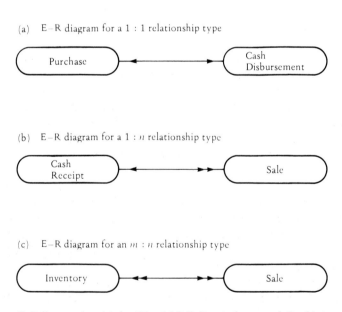

(a)   E–R diagram for a 1 : 1 relationship type

Purchase   Cash Disbursement

(b)   E–R diagram for a 1 : *n* relationship type

Cash Receipt   Sale

(c)   E–R diagram for an *m* : *n* relationship type

Inventory   Sale

Figure 6.9   *E–R diagrams for related entities: (a) E–R diagram for a 1:1 relationship type, (b) E–R diagram for a 1:n relationship type, (c) E–R diagram for an m:n relationship type*

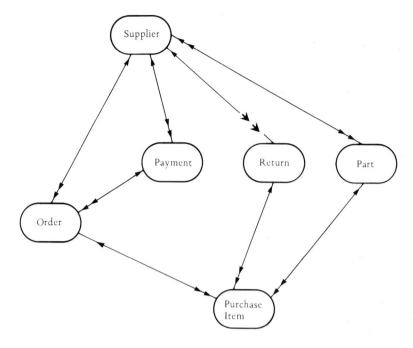

Figure 6.10   *E–R diagram for simple purchasing system*

Functional analysis

In performing data analysis we can draw a distinction between the process of identifying and defining the entities, attributes and relationship
types in the system and the consideration of ways in which the entities
and relationships are used. The functional analysis is more application-
dependent than the entity analysis and should therefore play a secondary
role in the construction of a conceptual model of a system. The objective
of the functional analysis is to identify which entities and relationships
are used and in what order. It includes consideration of the kind of access
required and for what purpose, e.g. to retrieve, update, delete or create
data. This process can throw new light on the meaning of the entities
identified in the entity analysis and can provide useful cross checks on the
validity, completeness and redundancy of the conceptual model. Any
discrepancies between the results of entity analysis and functional analysis should be investigated and reconciled.

The results of functional analysis are fully documented as for entity
analysis and for each function is constructed a model showing the data
structure and the order of use of entities and relationships. These functional models appear as subsets of the entity model.

Data dictionaries

The process of data analysis generates a considerable body of information about the data in an organization. This information must be organized, updated and made available when required. This definition and documentation is often achieved through the *data dictionary*. There are a number of commercially available data dictionary systems which provide some degree of automated data supervision. The information one might expect in a data dictionary includes:

List of entity, attribute and relationship types with their properties;
List and definitions of functions and events;
For each entity type, a list of all the functions which use it;
For each function, a list of all access paths and entity types required;
Keyword indexes;
Synonyms and homonyms;
Directories specific to particular departments.

One of the objectives is to ensure that no data-item can exist in more than one form. All users of that data must agree and understand precisely what it means and thereafter it cannot be changed without the data administrator's approval. Agreement on the data dictionary can be a long and difficult task. Once established, the dictionary can itself be automated, being a file which is referred to by the user's Data Description Language so ensuring that users conform to the agreed standards.

Network and hierarchical databases

The process of identifying entity and attribute types and the relationships between them leads to a conceptual model of the data in the system. Whether this model is expressed in terms of hierarchical (tree) structures or plex (network) structures depends upon the data-management software to be used.

A summary of the main categories of schema that may be permitted is given in Figure 6.11. This summary may be useful in making comparisons of supplier's database software.

Database management systems and languages differ in which of these structures they can handle. Some can handle tree structures but not plex structures. Others can handle simple plex structures but not complex plex structures. Systems differ in the number of levels they can handle. Few, if any, can handle loops.

A plex without cycles can always be restructured and expressed as a tree structure, or as a set of trees, with redundant elements. For some plex structures the amount of redundancy introduced is acceptable, for others it may be excessive. To illustrate alternative representations of the same

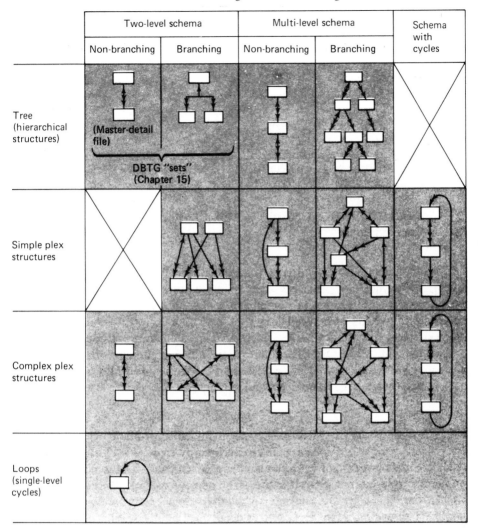

	Two-level schema		Multi-level schema		Schema with cycles
	Non-branching	Branching	Non-branching	Branching	
Tree (hierarchical structures)	(Master-detail file)				
Simple plex structures					
Complex plex structures					
Loops (single-level cycles)					

Figure 6.11   Source: *Martin*, Principles of Database Management, *1976, Prentice-Hall, p. 94*

logical model of data we consider again the simple purchasing system described earlier in this chapter. Figure 6.12 shows a model of a purchase system expressed as a plex or network. This is essentially based on the E–R diagram in Figure 6.10. A tree representation of a similar system is given in Figure 6.13. Note the duplication necessary in the tree representation.

Relational databases

Most database softwares use tree or plex structures, so these structures

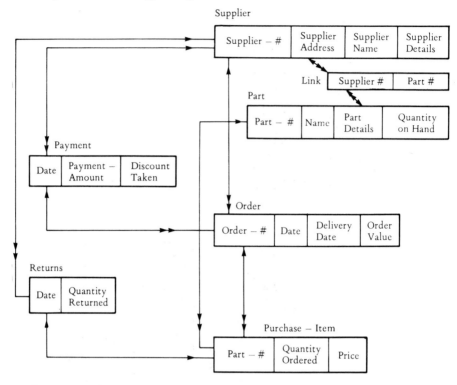

Figure 6.12   *Plex structure model of purchase system* Source: *After Martin, 1976, p. 188*

are particularly important. However, it is not essential to use tree or plex structures to represent complex structures in the logical definition of data. The most storage-independent approach currently available is the relational approach. Nearly all recently developed database systems use the relational model, probably the most important conceptual advance in database theory. The essential feature of a relational database is that all the data are seen by the user as residing in tables or relations. Taking the definition of C. J. Date (1986, p.96), we can state that 'a relational database is a database that is perceived by its users as a collection of tables (and nothing but tables).' For example, the entity type ORDER in our purchase system is viewed as a relation or table in which each row represents an instance of an order and the columns correspond to the attributes associated with the entity type ORDER. This and other typical relations for a purchasing system are shown in Figure 6.14.

Whereas plex and hierarchical systems go to great lengths to represent all types of connections within a set of information, the relational systems use only one method. Each relation itself represents an association between certain data items. For example, in the relation PAYMENT (Figure

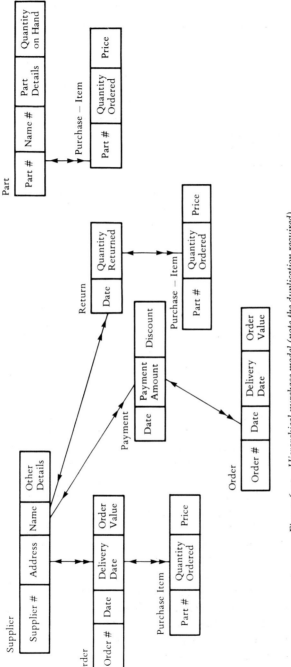

Figure 6.13 *Hierarchical purchase model (note the duplication required)*

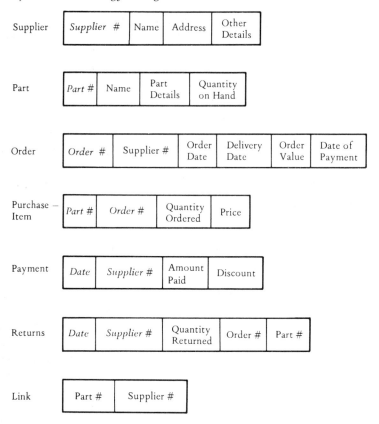

Figure 6.14   *Relational model of purchase system*

6.14) there is an association between the date of the payment, the number of the supplier to whom payment is made, the amount paid and the discount. Outside a relation, the only way of establishing an association is when two rows have related values for some common attributes. Thus, we can deduce that certain payments are associated with certain orders when the date of payment and the supplier number attributes of rows of these relations are identical.

Just as a plex representation can be reduced to a tree representation of data, with some redundancy, so also, any representation can be reduced to a set of tables or relations. The tables must be set up in such a way that no information about the associations between data items is lost. There is a step-by-step process for replacing associations between data, such as those represented in tree and plex structures, with associations in a two dimensional tabular form. This process is called *normalization*.

To illustrate the relational model we refer again to our model of a simple purchasing system. In that system we identified entity types

PURCHASE ORDER (*ORDER#*, ORDER DATE, DELIVERY DATE,
ORDER VALUE, DATE OF PAYMENT)
PURCHASE ITEM (*PART#*, QUANTITY ORDERED, PRICE)

(The key attributes are italicized).

Each instance of a purchase order is composed of a number of purchase items, i.e. there is a relationship type, of degree 1:n between entity types PURCHASE ORDER and PURCHASE ITEM. This connection can be represented by including the order number ORDER# as an additional attribute of PURCHASE ITEM giving the relation PURCHASE ITEM (PART#, ORDER#, QUANTITY ORDERED, PRICE). Similarly, the relationship between SUPPLIER and PURCHASE ORDER is represented by an additional attribute, SUPPLIER#, associated with each instance of a PURCHASE ORDER, and an attribute SUPPLIER# associated with the entity PAYMENT represents the relationship between the entity type SUPPLIER and PAYMENT. Proceeding in this way we can represent all of the relationships in the data structure by suitably chosen attributes as shown in Figure 6.14. In other words, if we think of each entity type as being represented by a two dimensional table or relation in which the columns correspond to attributes associated with the entity type, **then** relationships between entity types may be represented by further columns (key attributes) which identify instances of the related entity type.

Relationships of any degree can be represented in relations. For a relationship of degree 1:n we simply include the key attributes of the parent in the child relation. For m:n relationships we introduce a new relation composed of the key fields of each of the connected relations. Thus, the m:n relationship between a PART and a SUPPLIER can be represented by a relation LINK with attributes

(SUPPLIER#, PART#)

We have glossed over a number of important details of the normalization procedure. The reader who is interested in these details is referred to the relevant literature cited in the bibliography at the end of this part of the book. It is perhaps worth stating here that every row of a relation must have a key with which it can be identified. The row may be identifiable by means of one attribute, for example ORDER# in Figure 6.14 uniquely identifies an instance of a PURCHASE ORDER. To identify an instance of a PURCHASE ITEM we need more than one attribute; the key in this case consists of two attributes ORDER# and PART#. The key must have two properties:

1 *Unique identification:* in each row of a relation, the value of the key must uniquely identify that row.
2 *Non-redundancy:* no attribute in the key can be discarded without destroying the property of unique identification.

In normalizing a structure, extra data items may be added to a relation for two reasons. First, key data items may be added in order to identify each row uniquely. Second, attribute data items may be added to represent the connections that we draw with lines and arrows in E–R diagrams.

We introduced this section on relational databases with the claim that they provide the highest level, most storage-independent approach currently available. This implies that there exist not only convenient means of describing the logical data structure but also high-level languages for the interrogation of the database.

The terminal user or application programmers will usually employ different relations to those in the schema, that is the user's view of data is not the same as the conceptual scheme. It is therefore necessary to derive the user's relations from those in the schema. An important feature of a relational database is the ease with which relations can be manipulated to derive other relations representing a subset of the information. Three operations are particularly useful.

SELECT   Choose all rows in a relation for which some predicate is satisfied, e.g.
SELECT ORDER WHERE VALUE > 500.

PROJECT   This operator enables a user to select what columns he wants from an existing relation, and to specify what order he wants them in. No duplicate rows exist in a relation so there may be fewer rows in the derived relation as duplicates resulting from the contraction are deleted, e.g.
PROJECT PART OVER PART#, QUANTITY ON HAND.

JOIN   When two relations have a common attribute they may be joined. Thus if R_1 (A,B,C,) and R_2 (B,D,E,) are two relations with the common attribute B, then R_1 and R_2 may be joined to form a third relation R_3 (A,B,C,D,E) which contains rows formed from rows of R_1 and rows of R_2 having identical values of B.

A user may wish to join projections of two relations; he may join a relation R_1 containing only one attribute with another relation R_2 and so obtain a selection of the rows of R_2.

Many different operations and combinations of operations are possible including the standard set operations of *Union, Difference* and *Intersection*, but our brief description of SELECT, PROJECT and JOIN is sufficient to indicate ways in which data described in a user's (external) scheme may be derived from that described in the conceptual schema.

By making explicit use of the relational operators, the user can express how his required relational result is to be constructed. This is the relational algebra approach. However, most relational systems provide a higher-level user interface enabling the user to *define* his required relations in the form of a predicate. To illustrate these two levels of inquiry we consider the following problem.

Construct a table of part numbers and quantities received over a given period of time, from a given named supplier, and not subsequently returned.

All of the required information exists in the relational model of our purchasing system (Figure 6.14). The problem is how to construct the required relation from the existing relations in the conceptual schema. The supplier number corresponding to the given supplier name is readily available from the relation SUPPLIER. This supplier number can then be used to select rows from the relation ORDER having the specified supplier number. This result can be further reduced by selecting the order numbers from those rows with a delivery date in the specified period. These order numbers are then used to construct a table of purchase items associated with the specified orders and a table of returns associated with these orders. A projection of the difference between these two tables is the required result. This is the basic method. The order in which the reductions are performed is not unique and can affect the efficiency of the search for the required information. At this stage we are more concerned with the nature of the operations involved than with the efficiency with which they can be performed. First, we shall express them making explicit use of relational operators and then we shall give an equivalent definition in a high-level language. The instructions used are not based on any particular query language although there is some resemblance to SEQUEL in which instructions have the general form

SELECT attribute list
FROM   relation
WHERE conditions.

Solution using relational algebra

S_1 : = SELECT SUPPLIER WHERE SUPPLIER NAME = given name
S_2 : = PROJECT S_1 OVER SUPPLIER#
S_3 : = JOIN S_2 AND ORDER
S_4 : = SELECT S_3 WHERE DELIVERY DATE $\geq$ start AND DELIVERY DATE $\leq$ finish
S_5 : = PROJECT S_4 OVER ORDER#
S_6 : = JOIN S_5 AND PURCHASE ITEM
S_7 : = PROJECT S_6 OVER ORDER#, PART#, QUANTITY

S8 : = JOIN S5 AND RETURN
S9 : = PROJECT S8 OVER ORDER#, PART#, QUANTITY

RESULT : = S8 MINUS S9

Solution using high-level language

ASSIGN TO R1 (ORDER#)

    SELECT ORDER#
    FROM ORDER
    WHERE DELIVERY DATE ≥ start
        AND DELIVERY DATE ≤ finish
        AND SUPPLIER# = SELECT SUPPLIER#
                        FROM SUPPLIER
                WHERE SUPPLIER NAME = given

ASSIGN TO RESULT (ORDER#, PART#, QUANTITY)

    SELECT ORDER#, PART#, QUANTITY
    FROM PURCHASE ITEM
    WHERE ORDER# IS IN R1
    MINUS
    SELECT ORDER#, PART#, QUANTITY
    FROM RETURNS
    WHERE ORDER# IS IN R1

Developments in relational databases

The relational database market is now well served, particularly the micro-based environment where numerous products are available. The first PC relational database to be developed was dBase II. This has now progressed to a fourth version which offers the user mobility between PCs, 'workgroup environments', and mainframe SQL databases. Among the features available on dBase IV are a code compiler, a structured query language and a view database.

Structured Query Language (SQL) is now a common feature of many database environments and is rapidly becoming an industry-standard means of managing database servers and client/server database architectures. SQL is both a database program which can be used with most relational database management systems (e.g. Ingres, Informix SQL and DB2) and an interactive or retrieval query language. It comprises a data definition language (DDL) and a data manipulation language (DML). DDL provides a description of database objects, while DML supports the manipulation and processing of these objects.

SQL provides the user with a standard means of accessing data from any database, and obtaining it in an easily processable format. When combined with OS/2 and networking facilities (see Chapter 7), it is expected to provide real distributed PC databases, in which database queries are dispatched on to the local network and the reply comes from a local PC, a local file server, or even a mainframe located on the other side of the world.

Normalization

An issue of concern to database designers is what data items should be grouped together in one record or one row of a relation. There are many different ways of grouping data items and some are better than others. With data in the wrong form, problems of semantic integrity can arise in the use of project and join operators to create new relations. Some of the objectives in designing a database are to eliminate unnecessary redundancy, to reduce the need for restructuring relations if new types of data arise and to separate logically distinct aspects of the data so that modifications which concern only one area can be made without affecting other areas. To achieve these objectives, Codd [1970] defined a step-by-step process of normalization in which a set of relations is refined into new sets having progressively simpler and more regular structure. Starting with an unnormalized set of relations we derive what is formally described as *first normal form* (1NF), then *second normal form* (2NF), and finally *third normal form* (3NF). If relations are in third normal form, problems of semantic integrity arising from project and join operations can be avoided. The steps are summarized as follows:

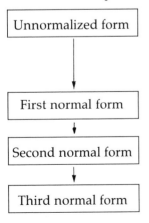

1 Decompose all data structures that are not two-dimensional into two-dimensional relations. In other words, create separate relations for any repeating groups in a relation.

2 Create a separate relation for any attributes which depend on only a subset of the key of their relation.

3 Create a separate relation for any attributes which depend on some other non-key attribute(s) within their relation.

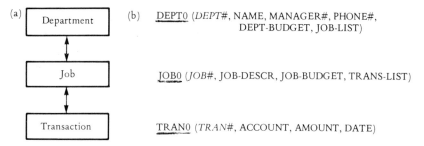

Figure 6.15   *(a) E–R diagram of managerial model, (b) Information for each entity, key fields are underlined*

The concept of third normal form might be summarized as follows:

> All data items in a record are functionally dependent on the key of that record, the whole key, and nothing but the key.

An example (taken from Everest and Weber (1977)) will illustrate the process of normalization. Figure 6.15 shows a managerial accounting model in which costs are accumulated for a job, jobs are carried out within particular departments and there are a number of departments within the firm. The costs may be overheads, materials or labour. We assume that a transaction relates to only one job and a job relates to only one department.

Each department is described by a unique department number (the key field), the department name, the personnel number of the manager, the manager's telephone number, a departmental budget and the list of jobs associated with the department. For each job is stored a unique job number, a job description, a job budget and a list of transactions for the job. For each transaction is stored a transaction number, the account to be debited or credited, the amount (negative for a credit) and the date of the transaction.

Note first that these descriptions are not two-dimensional relations since the attributes JOB-LIST and TRANS-LIST are repeating groups. The first step in the normalization process is to transform the unnormalized set to 1NF by removing the repeating groups:

DEPT 1 (DEPT#, NAME, MANAGER#, PHONE#, DEPT-BUDGET)
JOB 1 (DEPT#, JOB#, JOB-DESCR, JOB-BUDGET)
TRAN 1 (DEPT#, JOB#, TRAN#, ACCOUNT, AMOUNT, DATE)

To reduce these relations to 2NF we must remove any attributes which depend on only a subset of the primary key. Dept 1 is already in 2NF. To have the DEPT# in the key of JOB1 is unnecessary since JOB-DESCR and JOB-BUDGET are dependent only on JOB#. Likewise in TRAN1, DEPT#

and JOB# need not be in the key since the non-key attributes are dependent only on TRAN#. We note also that DEPT# could be deleted altogether from TRAN1 since the department number could be determined from the join of JOB1 and TRAN1 on the JOB#. The relations in 2NF are as follows:

DEPT2 (*DEPT#*, NAME, MANAGER#, PHONE#, DEPT-BUDGET)
JOB2 (*JOB#*, DEPT#, JOB-DESCR, JOB-BUDGET)
TRAN2 (JOB#, *TRAN#*, ACCOUNT, AMOUNT, DATE)

Finally, the 2NF relations are reduced to 3NF by creating a separate relation for any non-key attributes that depend on some other (non-key) attribute within this relation. This is the case for PHONE# on the non-key attribute MANAGER. We remove this dependency by projecting DEPT2 first over DEPT#, NAME, MANAGER# and BUDGET, and then over MANAGER# and PHONE#. The 3NF relations are as follows:

DEPT3 (*DEPT#*, NAME, MANAGER#, DEPT-BUDGET)
PHONE (*MANAGER#*, PHONE#)
JOB3 (*JOB#*, DEPT#, JOB-DESCR, JOB-BUDGET)
TRAN3 (*TRAN#*, JOB#, ACCOUNT, AMOUNT, DATE)

Almost all of our discussion so far has been concerned with the logical description of data. We have looked very briefly at some of the data structures (trees and plexes) commonly used in a database. We have not studied their physical representations in detail; such details are of interest only to the systems specialist and are fully covered in the relevant literature. It is worth emphasizing once again the important distinction between the user's view of data and the system implementor's view, i.e. the logical description and the physical representation, and to point out that redundancy in a logical description does not necessarily imply redundancy and inefficiency in the physical representation. The efficiency of the physical representation is a matter for the system specialist.

We have confined our discussion to database systems in general and made no reference to particular database systems currently available. A few of the commonly used systems are listed in Table 6.1.

There are other aspects of database systems of particular interest to the user, namely the managerial and administrative aspects, and, of course, the question of security of data.

Table 6.1 Some commonly used database systems

Package	Vendor	Remarks
ADABAS	Software AG	A unique system with many special features. Based on the inverted file approach. Has a good query language.
DMA-1100	Univac	Available free to users of UNIVAC equipment. Not compatible with other vendors' equipment.
IDMS	Cullinane Corporation	A widely used system which ranks high in user satisfaction.
IDS	Honeywell	One of the first systems developed and implemented
IMS	IBM	A relatively complex system, but widely used. DL/1 is the query language.
RAPPORT	Logica	A relational system which can fit many computer systems as it is written in FORTRAN.
SYSTEM 2000	MRI Systems Corporation	Easy-to-use system based on the inverted file approach. Has an excellent query language.
SYSTEM 38	IBM	A relational database that is the standard method of file organization.
TOTAL	Cincom Systems, Inc.	A relatively simple system. Is the most widely used of all DBMS packages.

Data administration

Because the database concept is concerned with data relationships which cross functional and departmental boundaries and data is a resource of the organization as a whole, key administrative issues are raised. Corporate objectives must outweigh factional interests, some conflicts will arise and must be resolved as early as possible. The concept of a database independently updated, but available to widespread applications, demands control at a high managerial level. Two distinct roles can be identified. The first is that of the *data administrator*. The duties of this post might include:

Data analysis;
Design and maintenance of the corporate data model;
Design and maintenance of a data dictionary;
Establishment and maintenance of coding systems, standards and documentation;
Data security and access control;
Rules for data ownership, rights of access;
Resolution of conflicts of interest.

The data administrator has a delicate role to play. He must have the authority to control departmental use of data and the status and qualities necessary to guide senior management. His duties do not include responsibility for the details of database implementation and management. These are normally associated with a second level appointment – that of *database administrator*, whose responsibilities might include:

Design of the logical model (as distinct from the corporate data model);
Integration of new applications;
Database consistency and validity;
Database integrity and recovery procedures;
Performance monitoring;
Re-organization of data representations for greater efficiency;
Database documentation and procedures.

Frequently, the functions of the data administrator and the database administrator are performed by a group or team but it is convenient to separate the roles of database administration and overall responsibility for data occurring in an organization. It is also important that the senior data administrator has the authority to take decisions and the tact to win support for them; he has an important and demanding task providing an interface between the different views of data in the organization.

Data protection

Very considerable efforts are devoted in database implementations to ensuring the highest possible level of data protection.

The concern for integrity and security of data is understandable and proper. Integrity means that the data are accurate, consistent and free from accidental corruption. Security means the prevention of unauthorized access, modification or destruction. Possible forms of control to ensure security of data are:

Control of terminal access (unlocked by card or key);
User identification (password checked by the operating system);
Restrictions on subschema contents;
Restrictions on access to certain entities, relations;
Restrictions on use of functions or programs.

Users may be classified into categories and different types of access allowed for each category. For example the system might recognize the following categories:

The database administrator;
The owner of the data;
Individual named users;
Groups of users having a common identity code or range of passwords;
All other users.

Some of these categories might be allowed both read and write access to certain files whilst others could be allowed read only access, and some no access at all. The overheads of exercising control over access to files will certainly be significant in terms of system performance but flexible and powerful controls must become an important feature of any database management system.

Data reliability, accuracy and consistency are encouraged by having one common database updated by one subsystem only. Nevertheless, some constraints are necessary to protect the integrity of the data. These constraints can arise in various ways. There are constraints which must be maintained because of the semantics of the data, such as salaries of certain categories of employees being in certain ranges. These constraints can be specified in the data dictionary. There are constraints imposed on the operation of a database to guard against a conflict of transactions. For example, if two users require simultaneous access to data which is currently in the process of being updated by one of them, then the other must be locked out until the update is completed. Simultaneous access may be allowed so long as the data is not being modified.

Despite increased attention to reliability and security, computer systems will fail through hardware, software, user or operator error. There must be procedures to alleviate failure in some parts of the system. Images of data items immediately before or after each transaction are recorded in transaction logs. The state of current processes and their data can be recorded at various check points. In the event of a system failure it is then possible to revert to a checkpoint at which the database was known to be consistent. Occasionally, a more extensive dump of the whole system may be taken as an additional precaution but this is an expensive and disruptive process.

Conclusion

We conclude this chapter with a brief summary of the implications of databases. First we review the advantages and then some problems.

Information has been described as a resource and data as raw material. The database concept encourages the management of data as a resource. It encourages a thorough analysis of data and how it is used in different applications. Waste is reduced. Redundancy through duplication can be controlled to achieve a balance between efficiency of file storage and speed of access.

The organization of data in a logically related database with connections between data items rather than files encourages integration of information and makes more data more widely available.

Data independence leads to greater flexibility and facilitates extensions such as the addition of new entity, attribute and relationship types. It also allows the existing data to be used in new applications. New and unforeseen information needs tend to be more dependent on programming than on data. Unanticipated needs can be met without the cost and upheaval experienced hitherto. Any restriction of data needed to increase processing efficiency can be achieved without impairing existing applications programs.

The programmer's task is easier. He has less responsibility for file design; he need not concern himself with physical representations and file organization, and can concentrate on his logical view of data. The details of physical organization are looked after by the database management software. Problems of data security and recovery are increasingly handled by database software.

Initial database development costs are high but once the database is established the maintenance costs are potentially less than for a traditional DP system. The development and running costs of new applications based on the same data are significantly lower in a database system.

Common data in a database can imply centralized storage, but this may conflict with the company's needs. Database access can be distributed to satellite computers and remote terminals. The database itself can also be distributed but the costs of data communications are high and must be carefully assessed; consistency is complicated by the unreliability of communication lines.

There are real problems of privacy and security. Much can be done to protect the security and reliability of data but users and managers should question the assumptions built into the database. Administrative procedures are required to supplement the software controls.

Since the data is held only once and its use is widespread, the problem of recovery in the event of system failure is one of the most crucial. Database management software is constantly being improved in terms of recovery capability.

7 On-line systems and networks

In Chapter 2 we introduced the concepts of real-time and on-line processing in relation to situations where the user has a direct link to a computer. In this chapter we consider interconnected computing facilities in more detail, together with the related concept of data communications. The importance of on-line computing is the ability to receive input and produce output quickly and effectively, thereby allowing a business or process to react more rapidly to changing conditions. The time interval to process and respond to input data has to be so small that the response itself is useful in controlling an activity or process. The length of response time that will be acceptable is actually dependent on the nature of the activity being controlled. If the activity is the launching of a space satellite then a response time measured in fractions of a second may be required. In an airline seat reservation system a much longer response time is adequate, although some form of response in five seconds or so is psychologically desirable.

The need for quick-response business systems originated in critical inventory applications such as airline and hotel reservations systems. Other examples of such processing include systems for immediate updating of customers' records in savings banks, e.g. building society share accounts, and systems for process control. An essential component of many of these systems is master files which are updated immediately after a transaction occurs and in which the data accurately represents the status of the system at any point in time. When an airline customer reserves a seat, the agent immediately keys in the transaction and the inventory of non-reserved seats on that flight is updated. An agent might have access to information for several different airlines. Airlines are international organizations with reservations being made and operations taking place simultaneously all over the world. Customers frequently book or cancel seats at short notice. Each unsold seat represents the loss of a significant contribution to the fixed costs of a flight. On the other hand overbooking will result in disgruntled and unhappy customers. Direct on-line access to update master files and fast response to queries via elaborate international telecommunications networks are important features of an airline reservation system. Obviously, a batch system would be totally inadequate. Immediate processing is required because of the perishability of the service sold and the need to provide the best possible service for the customer.

Not all applications require immediate access to information. For example, information for management decisions at the tactical and strategic levels, such as profit and loss statements, can be just as useful if it is a day old, a week old or even a month old.

A computer configuration to support a real-time system must allow on-line, direct access. The files must be organized to allow direct access, since immediate updating and rapid response to users' enquiries are required. However, not all on-line systems involve immediate updating of master files. As the cost of storage and processing has declined, on-line capture of data has become more feasible, even though the data may not be required for immediate use. One example is on-line capture of data at points of sale which at a later stage may be used for sales analysis. When the time limits are not so severe, on-line data entry with periodic updating of master files will frequently replace traditional batch-processing methods.

The basic building blocks for a quick-response business computer system are:

A fast central processor with large amounts of random access memory;
A large direct-access file store;
Terminals and other on-line, data-capture devices;
A sophisticated multi-programming operating system capable of looking after many devices and users linked to the system simultaneously;
Recovery facilities including a log of all transactions for back-up purposes;
Data communication facilities to connect and service remote terminals and other input/output stations.

Not all these facilities will be required by all users at all times but it is important that the full capacity of the system is available when required for any particular processing activity. Increasingly, a network of computing facilities, any of which can be accessed by any authorized user, is seen as the most effective way of sharing the available resources.

In the following sections we consider networks and distributed com-

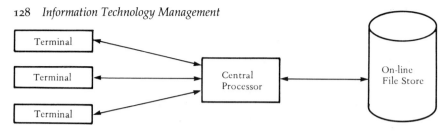

Figure 7.1   *Simple multi-user system*

puting systems, the facilities necessary to support data transmission and some example applications of networked facilities.

Hardware configurations for multi-user systems

The simplest hardware configuration offering processing capabilities for a number of users at the lowest possible cost is a single processor with on-line, direct-access file storage and with a number of on-line input/output terminals. Such a system is illustrated in Figure 7.1. The chief disadvantage of any single processor system is that it cannot be available for the kind of uninterrupted use so often required because of the need for periodic preventive maintenance and because of the inevitability of occasional machine failures. The software system required to support such a system has a minimum of complexity.

A slightly more complex system using a *front-end processor* between the terminals and the host computer is illustrated in Figure 7.2. The job of the front-end processor is to handle the data communications, that is to organize all incoming messages from terminals and to despatch all outgoing messages. The precise nature of this task depends upon the particular configuration of on-line terminals and other input/output stations.

There may be a variety of different terminals arranged and connected in different patterns. The front-end processor has to convert all messages in accordance with a standard 'protocol' (set of conventions) so that, as far as

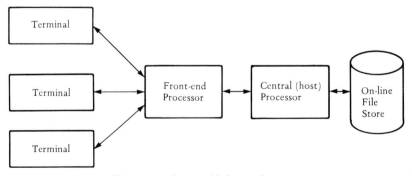

Figure 7.2   *System with front-end processor*

the host computer is concerned it is dealing in effect with a simple homogeneous star network, in which each terminal is independently connected to the computer.

For increased availability and reliability more than one main processor may be used. Figure 7.3 shows an arrangement based on two central processors. The advantage of this system is the availability of one processor for on-line access while the other processor is undergoing routine preventive maintenance or is unavailable because of a failure. When not needed for real-time processing the second processor is available for ordinary batch processing and other less urgent work. The operating system to run a multi-processor system is complicated by the software needed to switch on-line users from one processor to the other.

Connections between terminals and a central computer are in two basic patterns: the point-to-point or *star* formation (Figure 7.4(*a*)), in which each terminal is independently connected to the processor, and the *multidrop* formation (Figure 7.4(*b*)) in which a number of terminals share a single line to the processor. The star pattern has the disadvantage that line utilization may be low but it is simple and the failure of a line affects only one terminal. The multidrop pattern reduces the total length of lines and increases line utilization, but any savings in cost are offset by the need for more sophisticated hardware. Messages to and from the computers are each preceded by a code which identifies the message with a particular terminal. The front-end processor to which the multidrop line is connected must sort out which message comes from which terminal by means of the identification code.

When several terminals are connected to a computer there is the possibility that more than one of them will wish to transmit messages simul-

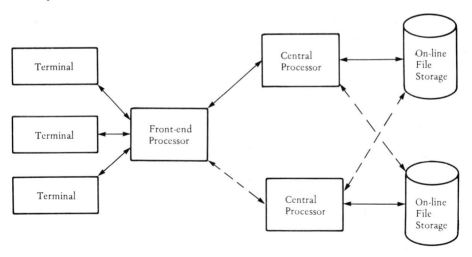

Figure 7.3 *Two-processor system*

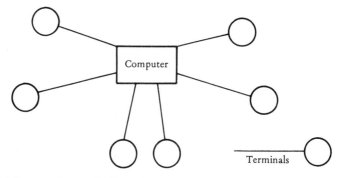

(a) Star or point-to-point formation

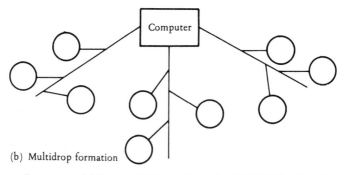

(b) Multidrop formation

Figure 7.4   (a) *Star or point-to-point formation, (b) Multidrop formation*

taneously. This can be catered for by the computer 'polling' each terminal in turn to ask if it has anything in its buffer to be transmitted. If so, the transmission goes ahead, otherwise the next terminal in sequence is polled.

In all but the simplest systems some form of *concentrator* is used to receive input from many low-speed devices. This input is compressed to form a compact, smooth stream of data to be sent down a high-speed line to the central processor. Similarly, messages received from the central computer are despatched to appropriate terminals. This message processing may be carried out by a special, 'hard-wired' unit such as a multiplexor, or by software in a front-end processor. The use of a programmable processor offers more flexibility with the potential for a certain amount of message checking and processing.

Most communications processors have storage facilities for messages so that several messages can be packaged and held until a suitable line is available. There is a variety of data communications hardware available as well as combinations of concentrators and front-ends, different devices having overlapping functions.

Networks

So far we have considered relatively unsophisticated configurations in which typically one or two host processors support a number of terminals connected via a front-end processor. This model of one or two computers serving all of the organization's computational needs is rapidly being replaced by a model in which a large number of separate but interconnected computers do the job. These systems are called *computer networks*. The term is used to mean an *interconnected* collection of *autonomous* computers. The connections need not be via cables; lasers, microwaves and earth satellites can also be used. In a network there is no master/slave relationship between the connected computers. No one computer controls the others; each is truly autonomous. With this definition, a large mainframe with many terminals is not a network. Each user, or group of users, may have his own computer, usually a micro computer, to perform particular functions independently of the other computers in the network. From time to time the user may need to access data held on other components in the network, to extract and correlate information pertaining to other sectors of the organization, or to the entire company. The network facility makes this possible.

The main driving force behind computer networking is the much superior price/performance ratio of small computers over large computers. Mainframe computers may operate roughly ten times faster than the currently available single chip microprocessors, but they cost up to a thousand times more. An interconnected collection of microcomputers is therefore potentially much more powerful than a more expensive mainframe computer.

Advantages of networks

An organization's existing computers can be connected together to increase the total computing resource available to each user. Authorized users are able to extract and correlate information about the entire organization. It is possible to make all programs, data and other resources available to anyone on the network without regard to the physical location of the user or of the resource.

By having alternative sources of computing processing power, higher reliability is achieved. If a particular processor is unavailable due to failure another processor on the network may be able to take over the job, so achieving graceful degradation rather than total loss of service.

With a computer network a company can take advantage of the relatively low cost of computer processing power compared with the higher cost of communications. In a single mainframe processor system, data captured at remote locations (e.g. points of sale) must all be transmitted to the central mainframe for processing. With a network, the data can be processed by a small computer located at the point of capture, occasional summaries being sent to the user over the network rather than all data being sent for processing at the user's location.

Incremental growth of the system is facilitated. Processing power can be enhanced by the connection of an additional processor to the network rather than by the replacement of an existing single mainframe by a more powerful mainframe.

An important side effect of a computer network is that it can provide a powerful communication medium among widely separated people. Electronic mail may be received at its destination as soon as the addressee is ready to receive it. Joint authors of company reports may have access to and comment on the contributions of co-authors immediately each draft is created and regardless of the distance separating them. It is no longer necessary to suffer the frustrations caused by communications delayed in the mail. We shall discuss electronic mail in more detail in Chapter 16 in the context of office automation.

Distributed computing systems

Distributed computing systems are sometimes confused with computer networks. One view of a distributed computing system requires it to have a system-wide operating system which services requests by name and not by location. The user of a distributed system should be unaware that the system has multi-processors. It should look like a virtual uni-processor system. Allocation of jobs to processors, job scheduling, allocation of files to disks, movement of files from where they are stored to where they are needed and all other system functions should be automatic, and the user should be unaware of such activities.

Another, more general view of a distributed system is one in which the computing functions are dispersed among several physical computing elements. This description includes some systems which are not covered by the previous more restricted view of distributed systems.

A distributed system is a special case of a network, one which exhibits a high degree of cohesiveness and transparency. A network on the other hand may or may not be a distributed system depending on how it is used. The lack of any generally accepted nomenclature allows us to use the term *computer network* generally to cover both networks as defined above and distributed systems in a broad sense.

Network structures

Autonomous computers in a computer network are called *hosts*. A host may be a simple single-user microcomputer system or a more sophisticated computer system capable of supporting many users as depicted in Figures 7.1 and 7.2. The host computers are connected by a *communications subnet*, sometimes referred to simply as a *subnet* or, alternatively, as a *transport system*, or a *transmission system*. The subnet comprises a number of *nodes* or *switching elements* and *transmission lines*.

A switching element is itself a computer, an interface message processor (IMP), having a special function. Its job is to receive messages on their way through the network, to store them temporarily if necessary, depending on the volume of traffic through the network, and to send them on through the network towards their destination, i.e. towards some specified host machine. IMPs are variously described as communication computers, packet switches and data switching exchanges.

Each host in the network is connected to an IMP. All messages to and from the host go via its IMP. Figure 7.5 shows the relation between hosts and the communications subnet. The separation of the special function of the communication aspects (on the IMPs) of the network from the general applications (of the hosts) greatly simplifies the overall design of the network.

Transmission lines may be either point to point channels or broadcast channels.

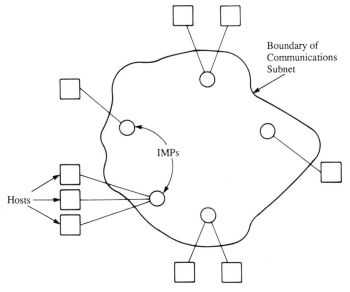

Figure 7.5 *Relationship between hosts and IMPs in the subnet* Source: *Tanenbaum, Figure 1.2, modified*

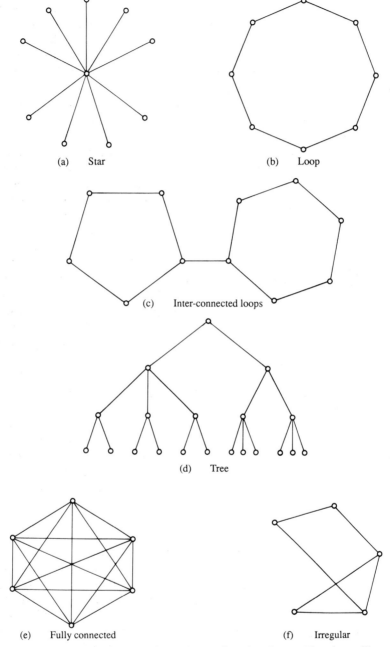

(a)   Star

(b)   Loop

(c)   Inter-connected loops

(d)   Tree

(e)   Fully connected

(f)   Irregular

Figure 7.6   *Some possible topologies for a point-to-point subnet* Source: *Tanenbaum, Figure 1.3,*
modified

A subnet using point to point channels has numerous cables or leased telephone lines, each line being a connection between a pair of IMPs in the subnet. If there is no direct link between a particular pair of IMPs which need to communicate then the message is sent via an indirect route through other IMPs. Each IMP on the route from the source host to the destination host receives the whole message and stores it until an appropriate output channel is free, then the message is forwarded to the next IMP on its route. A subnet using point-to-point channels is sometimes called a *store-and-forward* subnet.

There is a wide range of possible topologies for point-to-point subnets, some of which are shown in Figure 7.6. Generally, a local network, designed as such, i.e. one confined to a single building or to a number of neighbouring buildings, exhibits a symmetric topology, whereas irregular topologies are normally the result of connecting widely separated existing computers through the public telephone network.

A subnet using broadcast channels has a single communication channel shared by all IMPs. A message sent by one IMP is received by all IMPs on the channel. A message must contain a code which identifies its destination. An IMP receiving a message which is not intended for it simply ignores the message. Figure 7.7 illustrates some possibilities for broadcast subnets. In a bus or cable subnet only one IMP is permitted to transmit at any one time. Some mechanism is needed for deciding which IMP may transmit next.

In a satellite system, each IMP can transmit messages to the satellite, and receives *all* output from the satellite, but ignores those messages intended for other IMPs.

In a ring system each bit propagates around the ring on its own without waiting for the remainder of the message. This is in contrast to the point-to-point loop channel in which each IMP in turn receives and stores the whole message before sending it on to the next IMP in the loop. As in other broadcast systems, some mechanism is needed for arbitrating simultaneous attempts to access the ring.

Both point-to-point channels and broadcast channels can be implemented by means of common storage shared by all the host processors. For a network with n processors $n \times (n-1)$ storage locations (communication words) are needed to represent all possible source-destination pairs. If processor i wishes to send a message to processor j it simply stores the address of the message in the communication word (i, j) in the common store. The presence of the address in (i, j) is detected by processor j which will then receive the message when free to do so. Such a system does not need IMPs at nodal points of the subnet.

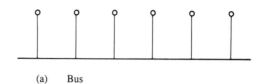

(a)   Bus

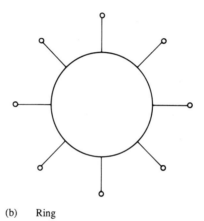

(b)   Ring

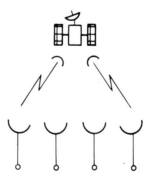

(c)   Earth satellite

Figure 7.7   *Some communication subnets using broadcasting* Source: *Tanenbaum, Figure 1.4, modified*

Network architectures: layers, protocols, interfaces

Most modern computer networks are designed in a highly structured way. Complexity is reduced by organizing the network as a number of layers, each layer being built upon its predecessor. Associated with each layer is one major function, or possibly several related functions, but complexity is reduced by separating essentially different functions into different layers. The number of layers depends upon the particular network architecture; the standard proposed by the International Standards Organization happens to have seven layers which we list later in this section. Figure 7.8 shows a conceptual reference model with seven layers. For each level or layer there are conventions and rules called *protocols* for communication between the two computers at that level. In reality no data are directly transferred from one host to another at any level except level 1. The communication links at the higher levels are virtual links. When a message is to be transmitted, the message passes from one layer to the layer below. There it is transformed as necessary and has infor-

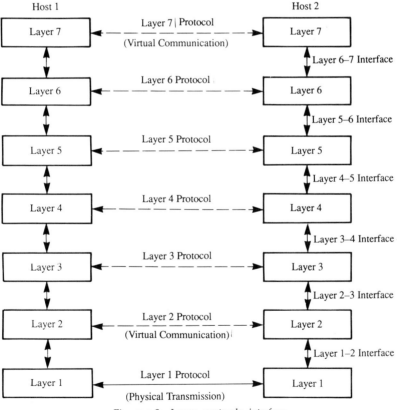

Figure 7.8   *Layers, protocols, interfaces*

mation added to it to implement that layer's protocol before being passed down to the next layer. The lowest layer implements the physical transmission of electrical impulses, electro magnetic radiation or optical signals, representing bits, to convey the data from one geographical location to another. When the message is received, the data relevant only to a particular layer is removed by that layer as the message is passed up from each layer to the one above and finally to the recipient at the application layer.

Design issues

There are a number of fundamental design issues for layers. For each layer there must be a mechanism for establishing a connection with another host. A mechanism is also needed for terminating a connection. Rules are needed for the data transfer: e.g. in one direction only (called *simplex*), or in either direction but only one direction at a time (*half duplex*), or in both directions simultaneously (*full duplex*). How is a fast sender to be prevented from swamping a slow receiver? Feedback from receiver to sender is needed to control this. What is to be the length of a message? Mechanisms are needed for breaking a long message into parts of appropriate length, transmitting each part and reassembling the constituent parts on receipt. Another design issue is the means for determining the route by which a message is to be transmitted. These are just a few of the functions to be performed by the various layers.

Clearly the number of layers should be sufficiently large that distinct functions need not be thrown together unnaturally in the same layer and sufficiently small that the architecture does not become too unwieldy.

Layer boundaries should be chosen so as to minimize the information flow across the interfaces.

Each layer should perform a well-defined function and the function of the layer should be chosen with a view to conforming to internationally standardized layer protocols.

The ISO reference model

In the ISO reference model, the layers have been created where different layers of abstraction were considered to be needed. This has led to the seven layers shown in Table 7.1

The management accountant need not be concerned with the detailed technical function of each layer. It is sufficient to know that the first four layers (numbered 1 to 4) provide a transport service shielding the higher

Table 7.1 The seven layers of the ISO reference model

1 The physical layer	Concerned with the physical transmission of raw bits over communication lines.
2 The data link layer	Maintains an error free link between two nodes.
3 The network layer	Controls the operation of the subnet and routing of messages.
4 The transport layer	Deals with such functions as multiplexing of messages, disassembling messages for transmission and reassembling them at their destination.
5 The session layer	This is the user's main interface with the network. Through this layer connections are made and terminated.
6 The presentation layer	Performs functions, such as text compression, encryption, character code conversions
7 The application layer	The content of this layer depends on the particular application. For example, industry specific protocols for banking and reservation systems

layers from technical details of how the communication is achieved. The three highest layers (5 to 7) provide an application service for the user, transforming data to and from the forms required by the lower layers in accordance with transport service protocols.

For a detailed description of the function of each layer you are referred to one of the standard texts: *Computer Networks* by Andrew Tanenbaum.

Some well-known computer networks

It is not possible in this text to give even a brief account of all the major network systems in common use but there are some which deserve a mention. None of these is a full implementation of the ISO model; some actually pre-date that model but influenced the design considerations leading to the establishment of the model. As examples of computer network systems we have chosen: ARPANET, a wide area network of interest because it is a global network connecting computers across the world; IBM's Systems Network Architecture (SNA) intended to allow IBM customers to construct their own private networks; DECNET, a set of programs and protocols produced by Digital Equipment Corporation for use on its computer systems; Apple Talk designed for communications among Apple microcomputers; and *public network* systems offered by the government or private companies as a communications service for customers' hosts and terminals. We shall also refer to two application-specific networks: the SWIFT banking network and TRADANET used by retailers and suppliers.

ARPANET

Development of ARPANET commenced in the late 1960s and resulted in the first working version going live in December 1969. ARPANET was the creation of ARPA, now DARPA, the Defense Advanced Research Projects Agency of the US Department of Defense. It has been operating ever since, and now spans the globe from Hawaii to Norway, connecting hundreds of host computer systems. There is only one ARPANET. Although it is not of direct relevance to the needs of most management accountants we include this brief reference because much of our present knowledge about networking stems from the ARPANET project.

SNA

IBM customers may construct their own private networks using Systems Network Architecture (SNA). A bank, for example, might have several central IBM computers in its data processing department and numerous IBM microcomputers and terminals located in branch offices. Using SNA these isolated components could be transformed into a coherent computer networked system.

The original version of SNA introduced in 1974 was designed for a single host supporting many terminals and was therefore not a computer network system in the true sense. The topology of the connections was a tree structure (similar to a multidrop formation). Later (1976) versions of SNA were extended to cope with multiple hosts each having its own tree structure of connections but with inter-tree connection possible only between the root nodes of trees. This restriction was removed in 1979 allowing more general interconnection.

Because of its history, in particular the need for compatibility with the many earlier non-standard network systems supported by IBM, SNA is more complicated than it need be. An SNA network has nodes of several types: terminals, controllers that supervise the behaviour of terminals and other peripherals, front-end processors to relieve the hosts of the task of handling communications, and the host computers themselves. The controllers are usually microprocessors which have some of the capabilities of host computers.

DECNET

The intention of DECNET is to allow any of DEC's customers to create a private network based on DEC's set of network programs and protocols. An interesting feature of DECNET is that unlike SNA and ARPANET, there is no distinction between the hosts and the IMPs. A DECNET is just a collection of machines of which some may run users' applications programs, others may do message switching and some may do both. DECNET has only five layers, the first four of which correspond very roughly to layers 1 to 4 of the ISO model. There is no session layer and the applications layer performs a combination of the functions of the two highest layers of the ISO model.

AppleTalk

The AppleTalk Personal Computer Network is a simple serial bus network (see Figure 7.7(*a*)) to which up to 32 devices such as Macintosh computers, printers and file servers can be connected. The network hardware comprises a series of connection boxes linked in a daisychain by cables and cable extenders. Each device on the network is connected to a connection box by a connection cable which plugs into the printer port of the device. Installation and extension of an AppleTalk network is extremely straightforward. A new device is connected to a connection box by an AppleTalk plug to its printer port and the connection box is linked into the daisychain where required.

Each device to be connected to the network must have the appropriate software such as programs for electronic mail and software to allow access to shared disks, printers, or other devices on the network.

When a network device is switched on, it is automatically assigned a unique network identification number by the AppleTalk Manager without any special action by the user. This number then serves as a device address when sending or receiving messages.

When one device wants to communicate with another device, it sends a message, addressed to the destination device, out of the printer port to its connection box. This message, which includes the address of both the destination and the source, is 'broadcast' from the connection box on the network to all devices connected to the network. Devices respond only when they receive a message addressed to them.

No more than 32 devices can be connected to an AppleTalk network and Apple recommend that the total length of cable from one end of the network to the other should not exceed 300 metres. However, this does not represent a serious constraint for it is possible to connect two separate AppleTalk networks by means of an intelligent hardware device called a *bridge*. A 'local bridge' connects two networks located in close proximity, for example, on two different floors of the same building. A 'remote bridge' connects two networks in different geographical areas by modem or satellite link. AppleTalk networks can also be connected via gateways to other networks using different protocols.

The AppleTalk system architecture consists of five main protocols arranged in layers. In the usual way, each protocol in a specific layer provides services to higher layers by building on the services provided by lower-level layers.

At the lowest level is the *AppleTalk Link Access Protocol (ALAP)* whose main function is to control access to the network among competing devices. It ensures that each device is assigned a unique identification number when it is switched on. It also provides device-to-device delivery of variable length packets (data frames) of up to 600 bytes within a single AppleTalk network. A sending device can ask ALAP for a *broadcast service*: to send a frame to all devices on the network.

The protocol in the next level up is the *Datagram Delivery Protocol (DDL)* which manages the delivery of packets of data (datagrams) over Apple-Talk internets. A datagram is sent from its source through a series of AppleTalk networks, being passed on from bridge to bridge, until the destination network is reached. The ALAP in the destination network then delivers the datagram to the destination device in that network.

Bridges on AppleTalk internets use a *Routing Table Maintenance Protocol* to maintain routing tables for controlling the passage of datagrams through the internet.

The highest level protocol is the *Name-binding Protocol (NBP)* which maintains a name table in each node (device) containing the name and internet address of each entity in that node.

The ALAP and DDP provide simple delivery services with no recovery mechanism when packets are lost or discarded following corruption. For many purposes this is sufficient, but AppleTalk can also provide an error-free transport service by means of its *AppleTalk Transaction Protocol (ATP)*. This uses *transactions* consisting of a *transaction request* and a *transaction response* for safe delivery of data. A transaction request is retransmitted at specified intervals until a complete response is received, so allowing for recovery from packet-loss situations.

The AppleTalk network facility is highly popular among Apple Macintosh users.

Public networks and X25

In many countries public network services are now provided by governments and private companies. In the UK, British Telecom is the major provider but with some competition from Mercury.

The major problem with a public network is the great variety of computers and terminals that users may wish to connect to the network. Many terminals do not conform to the standard protocols.

There are internationally agreed protocols for public network access. These are of benefit to vendors who can market their products worldwide and to customers because users may connect terminals and hosts from different suppliers so long as the standard protocols are used. The three lowest-layer protocols have been standardized for public networks and are collectively known as X25. The physical (level 1) layer protocol requires digital rather than analogue signalling and can therefore be fully implemented on the public network only when conversion to digital exchanges is complete. As an interim measure, an analogue interface, similar to the RS232C standard, has been defined. For those devices which do not speak X25, another set of standards exists and a *black box* is installed through which the device can connect. The black box is called an X25 Packet Assembler Disassembler (PAD). A standard protocol exists between the PAD and the public network.

Tradanet

Tradanet is a wide area network developed by ICL and now operated by International Network Services. It provides facilities for electronic trading, transmitting messages such as orders and invoices between companies' computers in such a way that these messages can be immediately acted upon. The service is available 24 hours a day, seven days a week, and is therefore accessible at all times to suit the user. The network is being extensively used by the retailing sector. Tradanet offers a complete trading environment to its users but it is a closed system; the services are available only to subscribers.

The Article Numbering Association has created a set of standards for the exchange of trading documents, such as invoices, orders, credit notes, etc., known as *Tradacoms*. This standard, together with a variety of data transfer protocols, allows any member of the company to communicate with any other member via a central bureau. Users from anywhere in the country are able to send their trading data in Tradacom format quickly, securely and economically to their trading partners as and when it suits them.

Tradanet overcomes the problem of document format compatibility by requiring all users to convert their data to the standard Tradacom format prior to transmission. Similarly, on receipt, messages are converted from Tradacoms back to the local format. This ensures that any message travelling around the network conforms to a single unified format. Users again benefit from the fact that the format is manufacturer and machine independent and provides an industry-wide standard. The Tradacoms data format is specific to Tradanet.

Tradanet works like a postal service. Each subscriber or user is allocated a postbox and a mailbox located at a local, computer-controlled, network node. These local nodes are connected by high-speed telecommunications links to the central bureau, which acts as a clearing house for all messages and which manages the whole system. The network is illustrated in Figure 7.9.

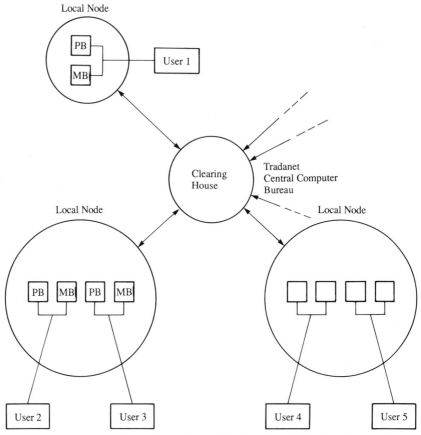

Figure 7.9   *The Tradanet network: PB, postbox (outgoing): MB, mailbox (incoming)*

A user's outgoing messages are posted via a local, often low-speed, telecommunications channel to the local postbox and the central bureau collects the messages from the postbox. The messages are sorted by reference to addresses and are then posted to the appropriate recipients' mailboxes. A user's incoming messages are collected from the mailbox by the user. The service is a passive one, in which initiatives come from the system user; it is at the user's discretion when messages are posted or when mail is received.

The system is concerned with security and, by use of passwords, ensures that messages are made available only to the intended recipient. The use of new passwords, or the changing of old passwords is entirely under the control of the user. To guard against accidental loss of messages through errors, back copies of messages in mailboxes are made, which allows recovery from data corruption. Reports are available to allow the progress of a message through the system to be indicated. These, together with system error messages and warnings, allow an audit trail to be constructed in the event of any problems.

If a malfunction occurs within the network, such that a particular channel becomes unavailable, the system is capable of rerouting the message to its destination without the user being aware of the malfunction. The user is concerned only with mail arriving in the mailbox free from error, not with the route by which it arrives.

Tradanet offers one solution to problems of inter-company communications, but as yet it does not offer links to other wide area networks. This could be resolved by special gateways between networks, but the current level of demand does not justify the cost of standard solutions for data transfer protocols and data format conversion between networks. Future large-scale developments are likely to be based on new international standards for electronic data interchange. Meanwhile gateways to other networks require ad-hoc solutions.

Data transmission via PSTNs

We have referred to communication lines between a central processor and remote terminals and to communication lines connecting one processor to other processors in a network. The transmission of data is usually accomplished through the facilities of the telecommunications companies: British Telecom and Mercury in the UK, the Bell System, Western Union and numerous other companies offering data transmission facilities in the USA. Any organization operating a computer system in which some of the components are geographically dispersed must use the services provided by the communications companies.

In a computer system, binary-coded data may be transmitted in the form of a signal having a rectangular waveform, corresponding to the stage levels, representing os and 1s (see Figure 7.10(a)). Such waveforms are suitable for transmission over short distances only as the pulses become distorted and indistinguishable if the line is long. Also, most public switched telephone networks (PSTNs) are designed for voice communication in analogue form. The digital information must be transformed into voice frequency signals before it can be transmitted over significant distances through the PSTN. This is done by MOdulators and DEModulators (commonly called MODEMS) at either end of the telephone line. The modulator codes the digital signal for transmission as an analogue signal and the demodulator decodes it on arrival.

In the last few years the demand on the PSTN to pass more and more digital data has increased dramatically as we have entered the so-called digital age. The PSTN cannot be improved overnight and until we have a nationwide digital network designed to carry data the demand for modems will continue to grow. (In 1984 there were about 30 million telephones in the UK but only about 70,000 modems.) Faster and faster modems are required. The development of microprocessors, used for both the transmit and receive circuits, has increased the speed, reliability and flexibility of modems and at the same time reduced the size, power consumption and cost.

The process of modulation makes use of the fact that there are certain waveforms and frequencies that can travel over telephone lines without much distortion, e.g. a sine wave (of say, 1500 cycles per second) may be used as a carrier on which the data can be superimposed. Figure 7.10 demonstrates a variety of waveforms. In practice, it is common to use *frequency modulation* for low-speed transmission and *phase modulation* for high-speed lines.

It is also usual to interleave signals from several lines into one channel. This technique is known as *multiplexing* and the device which combines or distributes channel signals is a *multiplexor*. Several methods of combination are possible. For example, frequency multiplexing divides the bandwidth of the channel into a number of narrower bandwidths, so that several carrier waves, widely separated in frequency, can be transmitted simultaneously.

In networks, communication is required not only between terminals and a central processor but also between two processors. Since processors are not limited by human operation, much greater volumes of data may be generated for transmission. Interprocessor communication may require the use of a *broadband* channel designed to carry data at speeds of up to one million bits per second. This might be achieved by using a group of voice grade lines, or, depending on the distance, by a series of microwave circuits, possibly needing repeater stations to allow for the earth's curvature; alternatively, transmission may be via a satellite.

Data transmission can be either *synchronous* or *asynchronous*. In asynchronous mode, transmission commences with a start signal and terminates with a stop signal. Between the start and stop signals are a number of bits representing a character. Bits are detected by an oscillator sampling the pulses along the line at regular intervals, but the process begins only on receipt of the start signal and terminates on receipt of the stop signal.

Synchronous transmission is more efficient in that start and stop signals are not required. Transmission between two machines takes place at a constant rate with the bits of one character followed immediately by those of the next. The receiving and transmitting devices have oscillators in synchronization; hence there is no need for start and stop signals between successive characters.

Synchronous transmission is less susceptible to errors and can tolerate a higher degree of distortion in the signal. It can also provide faster transmissions than asynchronous mode, though it requires more expensive equipment. Asynchronous communication channels are used for slower-speed devices without a buffer, on which characters are sent down the line at more or less random intervals – in this situation it is useful to have a start signal since there is an indeterminate interval between the characters.

As mentioned earlier in this chapter, three common conventions are used for data transmission:

1 A *simplex* line allows data to flow in only one direction (i.e. servicing a *send only* or *receive only* device);
2 A *half-duplex* line can either receive data from or send data to a computing device, but not both at once;
3 A *full-duplex* line allows the simultaneous transmission of data in both directions.

The most common types of transmission line are capable of full-duplex operation. Speeds of transmission, however, vary enormously. Standard

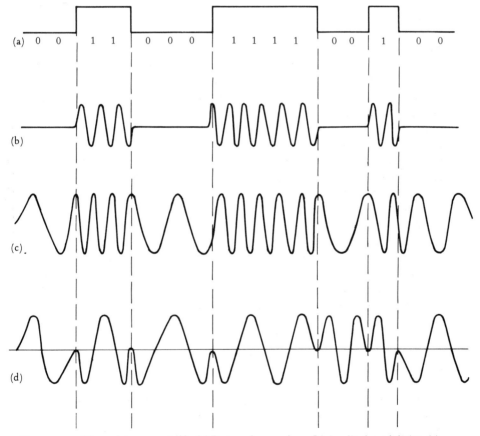

Figure 7.10 *Binary data represented by (a) Rectangular-waveform, (b) Amplitude modulation, (c) Frequency modulation, (d) Phase modulation*

voice-grade telephone lines are capable of speeds up to 2,400 bits per second (i.e. 300 bytes or characters per second), although telephone companies will normally only guarantee 600 bits per second. Lines that operate at 9,600 or even 48,000 bits per second are available from British Telecom but they tend to be special-purpose lines. The speed of transmission is usually described in *bauds*, with one baud normally being one bit of data per second. Assuming that each signal event or discrete condition corresponds to exactly one bit, 2,400 baud is 2,400 bits per second.

Standard voice-grade telephone lines can be hired in one of two ways. If data volume is small, then a standard 'dial-up' facility may be used to obtain a line through the normal public telephone switching network. The risk is that this may turn out to be a bad line with an unacceptable amount of 'noise', 'fading' and 'cross-talk' which interferes with the accurate transmission of data. The cost of a dial-up line is proportional to the time used. Alternatively, a *private* line may be leased at an annual charge (related to the length of the line). This is permanently connected irrespective of use and free from the interference caused by other users.

In the U.S.A., specialized common carriers (as opposed to telephone companies) are often used. Telenet is an example of a 'value-added packet switching service'. Data is received by a network of computers via telephone lines and temporarily organized into convenient parcels of 128 characters in length. These parcels, under the control of computers, are routed to a Telenet office near their final destinations by a series of high-speed dedicated A.T.&T. telephone lines. At the appropriate Telenet office, the data in the parcels is reassembled into complete messages for transmission via ordinary telephone lines.

Software for fast response systems

The requirement for fast responses to input in real-time systems, and in general to all on-line terminal users, constrains the design of both the software for handling communications and the operational programs. The operational programs accomplish the actual processing of transactions, updating of data files and production of responses to input. The response time is defined as the time between the last action taken by the operator on input and the printing or display of the first character of the output response. Some systems on the market have a response time of 3 seconds or less for 90 per cent of the messages. In such systems, the average response time will normally be less than 2 seconds which is little more than the response time in human conversations.

In order to achieve a level of performance which is psychologically acceptable (i.e. response times ≤ 2 seconds) it is sometimes necessary to sacrifice certain desirable features of software such as portability and to make full use of any special features of the hardware on which the system is to be run. Careful attention must be paid to the organization of data files possibly minimizing search times at the expense of storage space. The number of seeks required to locate a desired record on a disk must be kept to a minimum; there is no hope of fast access if embedded pointer chains must be followed from record to record with seeks between records. Every fraction of a second spent in accessing and processing files is time which is not then available for handling data communications.

In general, methods for speeding up access to and processing of data include combinations of the following:

Storage of frequently accessed data on fast devices;
Organizing data so that lengthy seeks are avoided if possible, e.g. clustering frequently accessed data near the middle cylinders of disk packs to minimize disk head movements;
Selection of addressing and search schemes which require few (preferably only one) seeks per retrieval;
The use of multiple operations in parallel.

It is not essential to design a real-time system so that all operations can be performed in a uniformly fast time. For example, in an airline reservation system, response times of less than 2 seconds are desirable during the dialogue between the operator and the system while investigating the availability of seats, but once the customer has made his reservation the end of transaction process (often called the *closure* process) of updating the master file need not be performed quite as quickly, 4 or 5 seconds might be acceptable.

On some systems, whilst enquiries may be dealt with in real-time, it may be possible to defer the insertion of new records into files until some more convenient time. Similarly, old records need not be deleted in real-time, but simply flagged to indicate that they are not available. In highly volatile files it is usually better to remove the deleted records in a planned periodic operation which releases the space for new records rather than remove them in real-time as each deletion occurs.

The operating system software to control on-line, real-time systems is much more complex than that required for a conventional batch-processing system. This is simply because there are many more functions to be performed.

We can summarize the functions of any operating system under six main headings:

Control and allocation of resources;
Scheduling resources;

Communication with operators;
Emergency procedures;
Dealing with errors;
Housekeeping routines.

The operating system's control functions are concerned with the scheduling of the operations of the input and output units and checking for their correct functioning. In an on-line system it will also be concerned with the control of communications lines, the terminals and messages passed to and from user terminals. It will have to build and maintain queues of enquiries and commands awaiting processing. It will also have to decide whether applications programs required to deal with users enquiries and commands are already in primary store or must be read in from disk. If programs are to be read in then the operating system must decide which programs in the store can be overwritten by new incoming programs.

The operating system assigns primary storage to the various programs or routines as it is required. In a real-time system small areas of store may be allocated dynamically to incoming messages or to programs as they are needed. It is necessary to keep track of the use of each piece of store, the purpose for which it is used and when it becomes free again. Such dynamic allocation of storage is essential to the flexibility of a real-time system.

The operating system must decide which message is to be handled next as well as scheduling the machine functions. It handles communications with on-line terminal operators, including validation of input, notification of errors and exception reporting. A system of priorities for processing has to be administered together with different levels of interrupts.

Emergency procedures need to be handled carefully, for the operating system must respond to malfunctions in any part of the system and must be able to handle a 'graceful degradation' in the mode of operation when a component of the system fails. It also has to take some action when there is a danger of the system becoming overloaded.

The housekeeping routines involve the editing and validation of input messages before handing them over to applications programs for processing. Random access to data files must be controlled and the performance of the system as a whole monitored. In a multiprocessor network, the system must interface with other computers in the network.

The increased variety and complexity of the hardware and the need for rapid responses to a multiplicity of on-line users in a real-time system introduces a higher level of complexity into the operating system.

The accountant should be interested in software from several points of view. First, he is interested in the cost of development of the increasingly complex software needed to supervise and control a real-time system.

This may affect the feasibility of the system. Secondly, he is particularly concerned with file design and the operational programs for maintenance of files. Thirdly, he is concerned with the problems of data reliability, security, and provision for an audit trail. In order to meet the requirement to provide fast responses some pressure will be put on the accountant to keep his requirements to a minimum.

With the processing of transactions individually instead of in batches a more elaborate system of checking is required at the point of entry. The accountant will need to be involved in the design of software for input validation and tests of reasonableness. The software must request re-entry of any data which does not satisfy these tests. One advantage of on-line data entry is that data is keyed in by the person originating the source data who is in the best position to verify its accuracy.

A major problem in an on-line system with remote terminals is the question of unauthorized access. We shall return to the question of security in Chapter 8. Most of the methods discussed in Chapter 6 for controlling access to databases apply equally to any on-line application.

The spectrum of on-line computer systems

We have described a real-time system as one which can react to input from the environment with which the system is interacting on a time scale which allows the environment to take a decision based on the response from the computer and for this decision to be effective in influencing and controlling the activities of the environment. Failure to react quickly could lead to an inadmissible situation in the environment. In highly competitive business situations, when customers can easily go to other suppliers for perishable goods or services, sellers can use a real-time computer system to provide an up-to-the-minute record of the availability of a product. A potential airline passenger who makes an enquiry can be given an immediate answer and his booking confirmed on the spot. In some situations, quick price or delivery quotations may help to clinch a sale. Real-time computer systems have been installed in stock markets to help stockbrokers in the buying and selling of stocks and shares for their clients.

Other examples, outside the business environment, include the control of a chemical process, in which failure to react immediately to rises in temperature or pressure beyond critical limits could be dangerous; real-time monitoring of hospital patients can give early warning of any deterioration in a patient's condition.

So far, we have not given a precise definition of what we mean by on-line operation. Strictly speaking, if one unit of a computer system can be controlled by another without human intervention then the first unit is said to be on-line to and under the direct control of the second unit. This strict definition has become extended by common usage to include tele-processing, i.e. the transmission and receipt of data over long distances via a telecommunications link. We have used the term on-line to include remote terminals connected to a processing unit via telephone lines and modems.

The factor which distinguishes a real-time system from other on-line systems is the response time between a user sending a message to the computer system and getting the answer back. James Martin (1967) sum-marizes the choice:

> 'Ideally one would like the response time of all data processing to be very short. However, this is too costly and one has to compromise, evaluating where a fast response is needed and where it is not. Systems worth calling real-time may respond in seconds or minutes; other on-line systems may take an hour or so before a transaction is processed. Systems with off-line data-transmission links may possibly take several hours. When a periodic batch-processing job cycle is used, the work may have to wait its turn for several days, and when the mail is used for sending transactions to the computer, the response will also take days.'

When examining the various available system configurations it is possible to work out the *cost* of having different response times. If this is done, the *value* of different response times should also be considered. This is more difficult because often so many intangibles are involved, such as the value of improved customer service, the value of giving management up-to-the-minute information whenever they want it, and the improvements that result from shortening an organization's reaction time. The various functions carried out by any one system need different response times, and it is part of the job of a systems analyst to determine what these differences are. Some systems may need immediate processing of urgent transactions and enquiries, processing in an hour or so of other trans-actions and background processing of transactions with no urgency. Broadly speaking, response times can be divided into a number of categories:

1   Immediate response (microseconds), required by systems controlling a technical process.
2   Conventional response with users at terminals – a response time of not more than 5 seconds is usually considered necessary.
3   Conversational response to terminals after 'closure', for example when a user has told the computer to close a procedure or start something new. In the normal input of transactions, a response time of up to 15 seconds is acceptable after a closure.
4   Response as soon as it is convenient. This type of response is geared to the situation where computing responses are required quickly (e.g.

seconds/minutes) but are not geared to the speed of a human conversation.

There is a spectrum of on-line and real-time systems, but it is useful to categorize three broad types.

Batch input and processing with on-line enquiries

Transactions are batched, sorted and input and the master files are periodically updated by batch processing. However, to allow fast responses to enquiries, the files will be organized as indexed sequential files to facilitate fast access to information. This organization is not suitable for immediate updating and no update of the file is allowed at this point. Typical applications include the on-line enquiry about a customer's account in a computerized sales ledger: if statement details sent to a customer do not accord with the customer's own record, then a telephone enquiry can sort out the problem whereas reminder or delinquent letters may be sent in error.

On-line input, with batch processing and on-line enquiry

In this system the primary means of input is via terminals, often enabling the data to be captured 'at source', and output sent to the point where it is needed. Usually, the system provides for a fair amount of on-line data checking and validation and sometimes this will require information from a master file. Once again these files are usually organized in indexed sequential form. The resulting input will normally be stored on a temporary file and the updating of the master file will take place periodically – at the end of the day, week or month. Nearly all systems in this category also permit the on-line interrogation of files.

On-line input and real-time update

Information is keyed in via terminals as in the previous system. The information keyed-in is not, however, written to temporary files, but after validation is used immediately to create or update various records on the master files. These real-time updating systems provide up-to-date information at all times. Various banks and building societies are moving towards real-time systems with the immediate updating of customer records. Although it would be wrong to assume that real-time processing should be applied to all data-processing applications, businesses generally are finding that timeliness is becoming more important. Some situations which are not strictly time-critical but where it is nevertheless valuable to have up-to-the-minute information are customer orders, finished goods stock control, production scheduling, new material stock control, pricing and description of products and so on. Even within the routine accounting system, the savings achieved from prompt credit control of overdue customers has led some firms to implement a real-time sales ledger.

Time-sharing systems

Real-time systems often employ the technique of time-sharing which permits a number of programs to use various computer resources one at a time in rapid succession. Time-sharing in computer systems is adopted as a means of allowing the use of the system by a number of distinct and independent users. From the user's point of view they appear to be using the system concurrently, whereas in fact each user is attended to in turn and has only intermittent use of the system. The illusion of continuous use is a consequence of the rapidity of switching between one on-line user and the next. The user is in real-time contact with the computer but the system operates in time-sharing mode, since each user shares the system with all other users. Such a multi-access arrangement is perfectly satisfactory for many users operating in conversational mode. An on-line terminal will have commands obeyed immediately although the processing initiated by a command may take some time.

All on-line, real-time, multi-access and distributed processing systems imply some time-sharing of computer resources. Such sharing can result in higher CPU utilization.

The availability of a large number-crunching computer in a network, larger file stores and extensive libraries of applications programs brings more facilities to all users connected to the network. The availability of multiple processors permits peak-load sharing and provides back-up in the event of equipment failure. A wider body of knowledge becomes available when DP and systems personnel co-operate in the development of software. The enhanced facilities may enable managers to react more quickly to new developments. The chief disadvantage of larger complex systems is the increased complexity and cost of the software necessary to supervise the system and to handle communications between the various processors and users in the network. The reliability, speed and cost of data transmission is often disappointing.

In time-critical, real-time processing systems, reliability is even more vital than in conventional systems. A customer who wants to make a reservation when the system is not available and is told to come back next day may simply go elsewhere. Obviously, the seriousness of a system interruption is related to the response time requirements. Hardware failures can be planned for in three ways:

1 *Duplication of equipment*. This is expensive and cannot give 100 per cent reliability since the second piece of equipment may also fail. Further duplication is possible but the cost can only be justified in exceptional circumstances.
2 *Fallback procedures*. When a fault develops in one component of a system, a fallback procedure may be invoked whereby the system modifies its mode of operation so as to circumvent the problem. The modified mode of operation will probably provide a degraded form of service. A popular term is 'fail soft' or 'graceful degradation'. This means that rather than fail completely the system attempts to find an alternative means of processing through a hierarchy of fallback procedures dealing with different eventualities.
3 *Bypass procedures*. Once a system has failed and terminals are no longer operative, the users have one of two choices: (1) not to process any more transactions, which usually entails a loss of business or (2) to have some alternative procedures for processing transactions or dealing with enquiries.

Bypass procedures often involve writing down certain information for subsequent input to the computer. Sometimes reference is made to 'old' (but nevertheless quite up-to-date) printouts. Sometimes terminals may have a limited storage capacity of their own where data can be held for a short time until the system can be re-established. For more serious breakdowns, a company may arrange standby rights on another similar computer system, so that essential work such as the payroll can be transferred in an emergency.

Different functions in a system often have different reliability requirements. Some functions are so vital that their failure, or the use of a bypass procedure would mean the loss of so much revenue that it would be worthwhile providing a completely reliable system regardless of cost. Unfortunately, no computer system is absolutely reliable, but it is certainly possible to devise configurations which improve reliability. One way of doing this is to have duplicate facilities on a network.

The man/machine interface

One of the major arguments in favour of on-line systems is that they enable the user to get 'closer' to the computer – in other words it is easier for the user to react to and control the way in which his work is processed. However, it is important to remember that, in moving data capture away from a specialist data preparation department and bringing the task to users, terminals will frequently be operated by people who are not experienced programmers and have no wish to spend the time necessary to acquire programming skills.

If the benefits of on-line access are not to be lost, this means that the use of terminals must be made as straightforward as possible, with simple instructions to guide the user about the options open to him at each step. This list of options is often called a 'menu'. By typing in the appropriate number identifying an item on a menu, the user can select one of the various facilities available. In some cases this will result in the user being presented with a further list, or sub-menu. For example, one of the items on the main menu might be a sales ledger routine, but this could itself have a number of submodules such as sales transaction, cash payment, sales enquiry, and so on.

In the event of a mistake, or if the user changes his mind, then by typing a special control or hybrid character such as .R he can return to the main menu.

Once a particular module has been selected, there are two basic approaches:

1 *Form filling.* The user simply fills in a form displayed on the screen of the VDU. For this method to be effective the VDU must be equipped with page-mode, cursor addressing, and protected fields. Cursor addressing takes the user to the relevant field of the form, and protected fields permit the user to input only a certain number of characters of an appropriate type.
2 *Computer-initiated dialogue.* No special VDU requirements are necessary for this form of man-machine dialogue which consists of questions posed by the computer with appropriate answers supplied by the user. Sometimes a mini-menu is necessary. The computer may, for example, wish to know which transaction type is required and provide a number of alternatives from which the operator must make his or her selection. Sometimes the question will simply ask for data (e.g. ADDRESS OR CUSTOMER?). Whatever the question, good systems normally provide some procedure whereby the operator can, if necessary, escape from the strait-jacket of questions imposed by the computer. For example, .R may take the user back to the main menu and disregard all data input in this particular session, .E may have the same effect but might store the data, and .S may terminate a sub-procedure (for example end of address, where the number of address lines is variable).

An alternative to the menu systems, but one which retains a form-filling or computer-initiated dialogue, is the provision of a number of discrete procedures. The user in this case must know all the procedures and would type on the terminal a command such as

RUN SALESLEDGER

in order to gain access to the set of facilities embodied in the 'Sales Ledger'.

Some systems, particularly complex reservation or enquiry systems, have a dialogue using mnemonics. This essentially condenses some form of limited natural language input into a set of mnemonics. Other systems allow a more verbose but still limited English-like input. As opposed to the menu system, the computer will simply issue a prompt e.g.

COMMAND?

and the user must lead the computer to answer his or her questions by means of a number of single word or phrase instructions. For sophisticated financial modelling or statistical procedures (see Chapter 14) the user may have to become involved with statements which are program-like in nature.

This raises a question about the level of intelligence and training which is expected of the user. In general, a casual and unskilled operator will always respond better to computer-initiated dialogue. But for simplicity, economy, or security reasons it may be desirable to have *special terminal hardware* such as that used as cash-dispensing terminals for banks. In this case, only a very limited range of terminal commands will be available to the user.

Benefits of on-line systems

The benefits of on-line systems which we have commented on in the preceding sections can be summarized as follows:

Data can be entered into the computer system directly at its point of origin.
This makes it easier to observe and correct errors at source and may also reduce the occurrence of errors.
Files can be centralized or, where appropriate, logically dispersed.
This avoids duplication and improves the consistency of the data.
Files can be updated more quickly.
Many queries can be answered immediately.

Output can be made available directly at the point where it is needed. A range of terminal prompts and commands makes it possible for both experienced and casual users to obtain efficient access to files.

These advantages can also be viewed from a business standpoint; the commercial benefits which they can be expected to yield include:

Management decisions based on up-to-date information;
Easier standardization of operational procedures;
An improved level of service to customers, including enquiry facilities;
Better availability of goods, and faster confirmation of orders;
Tighter stock control;
A reduction in data preparation cost and often in operating costs generally, at the expense of some increase in capital costs;
Fast response to competitive market situations.

We shall conclude this chapter by looking at some business applications in which network systems are used to provide a better service for the customer and to assist management in the control of the business.

Reservation systems

Among the earliest examples of reservation systems were those of the airlines. The main objectives of such systems apply to all reservation systems:

1   To improve the service to customers and potential customers;
2   To save staff (or prevent increases in staff to meet an anticipated growth in business);
3   To improve the utilization of resources such as planes, hotels, holidays etc. but without the risk of conflicts such as overbooking.

In many systems reservation handling is simply a subset of a larger system. For example, the operation of an airline will include functions such as:

Crew scheduling;
Aircraft scheduling;
Passenger check-in;
Baggage check-in;
Aircraft load and trim calculations (for take-off);
Aircraft maintenance schedules;
Cargo handling;

Flight information.

All these are in addition to the handling of seat bookings, which itself is a complicated task involving:

Enquiries for seat availability;
Provisional bookings (e.g. from passengers who wish to switch to a more convenient flight if possible);
Firm bookings;
Reconfirmation;
Cancellations.

Some of the areas above, such as aircraft maintenance, may be handled by separate systems, but many of them are clearly intimately connected with reservations and must be performed as part of an integrated system.

The particular problems of airline reservation systems are:

The large standing costs incurred and the *high unit cost of the product* being sold (i.e. seats), which make it essential to aim for a high percentage of seat occupancy, but without overbooking;
The volatility of customers, who frequently book or cancel seats at short notice. If an airline is prepared to allow some overbooking, gambling on cancellations to correct this, the booking pattern may look like Figure 7.11;
On multi-stop flights the demand may not be uniform throughout. Clearly, the airline will try to give preference to passengers who wish to fly the longest or most profitable legs of the flight;

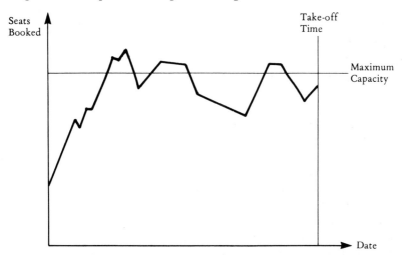

Figure 7.11   *Typical booking variations (note spare capacity at take-off)*

Airlines are international organizations with *reservations being made and operations taking place simultaneously in widely separated areas*; *Unpredictable circumstances* such as bad weather can lead to rescheduling at short notice.

In this section we do not aim to do more than point out the many difficulties to be overcome, but clearly the solutions will involve *inter alia*, very fast response times to avoid inconsistency and conflict (such as double bookings), elaborate international telecommunication networks, and substantial duplication of components to provide adequate reliability and back-up.

A supermarket network

Figure 7.12 shows an example of a local area network suitable for use in a supermarket. The network consists of a ring operating at 10 megabits per second.* The physical transmission line is a coaxial cable. The computers and terminals connected to the ring are all intelligent devices capable of sending and receiving messages, checking for errors in messages received and asking for retransmission. The minicomputer monitors the operation of the ring, detects and reports any malfunction of devices connected to the ring and deals with any problems associated with messages passing round the ring. The minicomputer also provides a means of access to other remote local networks via a wide area network (Tradanet).

In a ring system such as that shown, information is sent round the ring in *packets*. Each packet of information has digits giving the address not only of the destination device but also of the source. This facilitates certain checking; a packet which is not accepted, perhaps because the receiving device is too busy, or has been made deaf to the transmitting device, or for any other reason, will arrive back at the source after making a complete circuit of the ring. No packet is permitted to pass the minicomputer more than once. Thus a message whose destination address has become corrupted can be prevented from continuing round the ring indefinitely.

Each device is connected to the ring by an access box, called a transceiver, which in the case of a computer can be relatively simple since much of the processing required can be performed by the computer itself. For a terminal, or more usually a group of terminals, a more sophisticated interface to the ring is required to perform some of the functions of a small processor.

The importance of a ring system is its simplicity. Its traffic-carrying capacity is high. It provides a convenient, more economical alternative to a star network. It is not suitable for connecting geographically remote

*10 million binary digits per second.

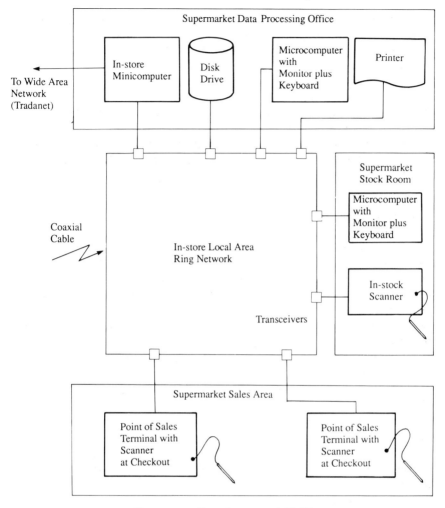

Figure 7.12 *Example supermarket LAN*

devices but, of course, all the devices on the ring can be connected to remote devices through the minicomputer which provides a gateway to Tradanet.

The network is used in the following ways.

Each product has a unique identifying number represented by a standard barcode symbol. Barcodes are read at point-of-sale (POS) terminals equipped with light pens or low-powered laser scanners. The barcode is decoded by the terminal and used as a key providing access to a full description, in the in-store database, of the product being sold. Details such as the product description and price are transmitted back over the ring to the terminal, displayed at the checkout and simultaneously printed on the till receipt. The benefits to the customer are fast, accurate processing at the checkout and production of a till receipt with both prices and names of items purchased. Details of the total payment can be printed on the customer's own cheque at the checkout and before long full electronic payment from the customer's bank account may replace the use of cheques entirely.

Sales information from all POS terminals is transmitted to the in-store minicomputer where it forms the basis of the supermarket's management information system, involving stock control, ordering, financial records, special offers and promotions.

In the stockroom, details of goods coming in can also be entered into the system by scanning barcodes on boxes and cartons, or by keying in at the stockroom microcomputer.

To facilitate electronic exchange of information between the supermarket and its suppliers, a set of standards, called Tradacoms, has been developed by the Article Numbering Association. Electronic information exchange dispenses with the need for paper transfers of information. Using the Tradacoms standards, the supermarket can access other retailers, wholesalers and manufacturers via the Tradanet wide area network.

An advantage of using the ring network in the supermarket environment is that access to the transmission medium is guaranteed even when the system is very busy. Its capacity is shared among all users, resulting in a highly efficient operation with no undue delays for any single user. Error rates are usually very small. Devices which do produce errors are quickly identified by the minicomputer as it monitors the ring. A faulty terminal can be detached from its transceiver without disturbing the operation of the ring.

The connection of additional devices to the ring requires the ring to be broken, so such additions must be carried out outside normal supermarket opening hours.

A bank network

Next we describe a star network in the context of a typical high street branch bank (see Figure 7.13). The star topology is typical of many in use in that it is based upon experience with a centralized data processing system. The hub of the system is a minicomputer which controls the operation of all devices connected to it in a star configuration. The intelligence necessary to monitor and control the network is located at the hub. This configuration, in which each peripheral device is polled in turn on a regular basis to see if it requires service, also accommodates the different transmission media and transmission rates found in the very wide range of equipment available for the banking operations.

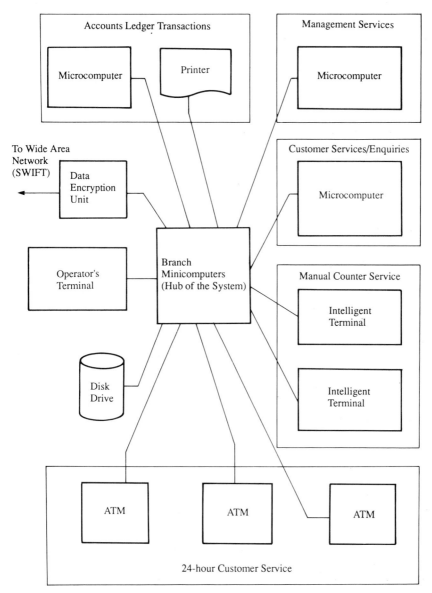

Figure 7.13 *Example bank network*

Automatic Teller Machines (ATMs) located outside the bank facilitate a 24-hour customer service; customers can withdraw cash, request statements, order cheque books, deposit cash and enter payment instructions at any time of day or night. Access to the system requires the use of a personalized plastic card with a code recorded in a magnetic strip on the back. Before a transaction is allowed to proceed the computer matches a Personal Identification Number (PIN) against the code on the plastic card. Alternatively, because of the possibility of fraud, some banking systems use a central data file to record all the PIN numbers. The number entered by the user is checked against the file record for the card being used. This is more secure because, even if the card were stolen and the PIN number known, access could be denied by altering the central file and locking out the user. Transactions entered at the ATMs are sent via the local network to the microcomputer at the hub where they are processed, and instructions transmitted back to the ATM to complete the transaction.

The hub computer is connected to remote local area networks via a wide area network (SWIFT – banking network of the Society for World-wide Interbank Financial Telecommunications) in order to confirm any details necessary before or after completing a transaction. A customer can therefore make use of any ATM regardless of its geographical location in relation to the branch where their account is held.

Counter service machines are used by cashiers for obtaining details of customers' accounts, lists of missing cheque cards or indications of other problem areas and for entering details of cheques being paid in. Customer account number, branch sorting code and cheque number are read by a magnetic ink character reader connected to the teller's machine and then communicated to the hub microcomputer via the network.

Accounting and management information is provided for the bank by terminals dedicated to this task. Permanent copies of information are available from a printer attached to the network.

From the bank's point of view, the star network represents the application of a technology that is well established and proven. Data security can be maintained at a high level with all accesses being checked and controlled by one central computer at the hub.

A savings bank system

This description relates to the savings or trustee banks; it also has some relevance to building societies. We will assume that each customer has a passbook in which all transactions (i.e. withdrawals, receipts and interest) and an updated balance are entered. Some systems use a dedicated terminal: the terminal is so designed that the passbook fits into it, and a printing mechanism writes in the appropriate place. Other systems rely on manual maintenance of the passbook with the teller using an on-line terminal to check the passbook, find out the interest due and then in some cases to update the customer's record. (Some building societies still prefer the updating function to be done in batch mode with batch control totals.) However, the fact that the interest payment has been entered into the passbook must be recorded in real-time to prevent the same interest being paid out later that day.

Whether or not a special-purpose terminal is used, the functions of the system are essentially the same. A customer hands the passbook to a teller together with the transaction details (which may be written down on a standard form to provide a source document). The teller will input to the computer the customer's account number, the transaction details (if this is to be input on-line) and the old balance (for checking purposes). The computer will then display the customer's name and address, any discrepancy between the balance held in the computer and on the passbook (with the exception of accrued interest), the amount of accrued interest, and so on. The system may ask the teller whether or not the interest is to be reset to zero (i.e. implying that the teller will enter the interest details in a manual system). In a dedicated terminal system, the passbook will be entered into a document-reading part of the terminal (with automatic read-in of the input information, though the teller would have to key-in the transaction details). The dedicated terminal could then print the interest details, the transaction details and the new balance. On a dedicated terminal there may be some special purpose keys to indicate transaction type and other special messages to the computer. Other transactions not yet recorded in the book (e.g. transactions made at a cash-point till or transactions made when the computer was off-line) can also be entered.

On these terminals it would be usual for some hard copy of all transactions to be kept and for messages from the computer to be retained. The computer system may also keep individual cash and transaction details and totals for each teller. Such a terminal will usually have a lock and each teller may have a unique key which can be identified by the computer. Alternatively, each teller can have a unique identification code (with an associated password). In this way, the teller's job of balancing the cash at the end of a day can be facilitated as well as an audit trail being provided.

With any banking system or system dealing with cash transactions, control is very important. The computer can aid control by rapidly producing balancing and listing runs. A record of all transactions indexed by teller and customer will be kept at branch level. This, together with appropriate totals, will be used for cross-checking and balancing. Cash or other discrepancies can be identified and either rectified that day or filed for subsequent investigation and analysis.

Such a system will also produce a number of reports and perform other functions. A savings journal may be maintained, an account activity report may be listed, customers' statements can be produced, details can be printed for tax authorities, managerial reports can be produced and an audit trail maintained possibly in a special form for use by external auditors.

Obviously, any computer system in such an organization would also handle the purchase and nominal ledger as well as payroll and cost accounting applications, which would be organized on a branch as well as a function level. In a building society, mortgage payments would be handled by the system. In a banking system, loan repayments, account enquiries and the status of a loan may be handled on-line. The computer may also be able to inform tellers of exception or hold conditions when an account is overdrawn, a loan repayment is in arrears, when there are other unpaid penalties, or when the bank manager would like to talk to a client.

Current developments in connected systems

The scientific and technological revolution now under way is creating new business methods and new opportunities. Connected systems of the type discussed in this chapter and new uses of data communication techniques are having a radical effect upon the business environment. Some developments are mentioned below.

Electronic invoicing

A computer-produced invoice is prepared in the usual way, but instead of being printed and mailed it is transmitted via a network directly to the computer system of the customer. Unique identifying numbers for the transmitting and receiving organizations are essential, as well as the normal invoice number, and a standard protocol must be used. When the invoice is received and understood, the receiving computer system can send a message back to the transmitting computer saying 'invoice received and understood' (but not necessarily authorized for payment; this occurs at a later stage). If a breakdown occurs in either computer system or in the data transmission system then the sending computer can continue to send the invoice at suitable intervals until it is correctly received. If the invoice is received but does not make sense, then the receiving computer can ask for clarification or ask for the whole invoice to be retransmitted.

Electronic ordering

If electronic invoicing is taken back one stage, then it is natural for ordering also to be carried out electronically. The same types of pro- cedures are undertaken in a manual or electronic ordering system as in the invoicing system, with one exception. If an order cannot be completed or can only be part-fulfilled, then a much more sophisticated reply system is necessary.

Electronic payment

Payroll tapes are passed to banks and security firms for crediting employees' bank accounts and making up payroll packets. It will not be long before electronic cancelling of mutual debt through contra-payments will be routinely undertaken automatically, e.g. when Firm A owes £100 to Firm B and Firm B owed £75 to Firm A, a contra payment by Firm B to Firm A of £75 would leave Firm A owing only £25 to Firm B. However, this step will be overshadowed by the following major development in electronic payment.

Electronic funds transfer system (EFTS)

Electronic Funds Transfer Systems (EFTS) will permit the widespread use of electronic money between individuals and organizations, rendering the current system of cheques, pay-in books and credit cards redundant.

An EFTS would involve EFTS stations or *automated teller machines* that could be situated in banks and connected to point-of-sale equipment at shops. All stations would be capable of debiting and crediting bank accounts. Some stations would also be able to receive and dispense cash. The updating of bank accounts would involve an EFTS card, similar to current credit cards but probably with a magnetically encoded strip of material (to supply the computer with the account number) and would let the card holder choose which account to credit.

Thus, automated teller machines in an EFTS placed in a bank could be used to:

1   Make a deposit to one's own account;
2   Withdraw cash;
3   Transfer cash electronically from one's own account to the account of a creditor; or
4   Inquire about the balance in one's own account.

A combined point-of-sale/EFTS terminal in a retail store would provide further functions. Figure 7.14 shows how the retail store's accounting, sales analysis and stock control updating, together with the banking transactions, can all be performed by means of one scan of the bar code on the goods, together with the insertion of a customer's EFTS card. Such a system would require common standard protocols between trading organizations and banks. There are still a number of issues of security and control to be resolved before payment for goods by automatic transfer from customers' bank accounts becomes widely accepted.

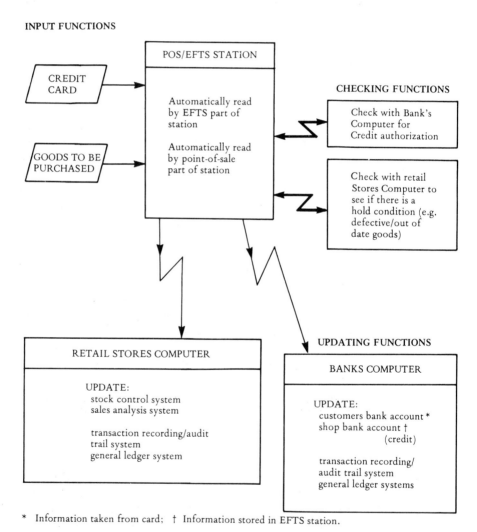

* Information taken from card; † Information stored in EFTS station.

Figure 7.14   *A cash sale using a point-of-sale and an electronic funds transfer system*

Electronic mail

The use of electronic invoices, ordering, and payment systems will reduce the burden on the postal service. With new and improved data communications services, the transmission of other information will also be faster and cheaper than the current postal service. The transmission of letters and facsimile images (i.e. signatures, diagrams and photographs) takes only a few seconds. Routine letters can simply be typed by the receiver's computer. Letters requiring signatures can either be typed with a password (known to the receiver) or sent through facsimile image printers.

The electronic office

Word-processing facilities which are already used in many offices will become just one of many computer and data communication functions. All paper files can be stored in a company-wide electronic document, mail and message system that can provide immediate delivery of words and pictures, together with the interrogation of the firm's data processing files. Furthermore, input to the computer system may be possible in the future either by a keyboard, or by scanning a printed document, or by spoken voice input. There need be no distinction between mail and a phone call. Such an electronic mail and message system may provide the following functions:

1   A message distribution service with messages delivered to specified individuals or identified groups;
2   A message reception service which can automatically receive or hold messages, redirect them if necessary, and possibly operate a priority algorithm to select the most important messages to be transmitted onwards;
3   A computerized conference facility; since all conference material may be stored (dialogue as well as papers), a person may sit down at a terminal at any convenient time, call up unseen conversations or papers, make additional comments and respond to questions.

We shall return to the subject of automated office systems in a later chapter.

Although it is difficult to be sure of the timescale, there is little doubt that most of these developments could be implemented within the next few years – particularly the electronic funds transfer system. Of course, the changes will not appear overnight, nor will every business take part; there are many problems of security and control still to be overcome, as well as a need to train existing personnel, but the developments which have been described show the potential which interconnected computing systems have to offer.

8 Computer systems – control and security

Introduction

The general concept of control is often misleading. Management theory has sometimes divided control systems into three distinctive types: feedback control systems, feedforward control systems and preventive control systems. These systems are defined from the standpoint of management theory. Budgeting and standard costing systems are examples of feedback control systems – they operate by measuring some aspect of the firm being controlled and adjusting the process when the measure indicates that the firm is deviating from the budget. Such a system is basically a detection system which highlights out-of-control situations for management, who then take the appropriate corrective action.

A feedforward control system attempts to predict potential deviations from the firm's plans so that corrective action can be taken to avert problems before they occur. Examples of feedforward control systems are cash planning and inventory control. The latter case includes prediction of desired stock levels in order not to carry excess stocks and to reduce the risk of a stock-out situation.

We shall return to feedback and feedforward control systems in Chapter 9 and again in Part 4 (applications). In this chapter, we are concerned with preventive control systems that operate from within the system, by placing restrictions on and requiring documentation of employee actions in such a way that the occurrence of errors (whether deliberate or accidental) and deviations from standards are obviated. Since preventive controls operate within the firm they are sometimes classified as internal controls.

The functions of an internal control system are to safeguard assets and provide an internal check usually through batch or control totals. Sound organizational practices imply the separation of three functions:

1   Functions involving custody of assets (such as writing cheques, receiving cheques in mail, handling cash, handling inventories);
2   Recording functions (such as preparing source documents, maintaining journals, ledgers or other files, preparing reconciliations, preparing performance reports);
3   Performance of line-operating functions (such as performance of the production, marketing and finance functions and the authorization and execution of transactions).

The effective segregation of duties makes it impossible for a single employee to commit embezzlement. For this to happen collusion between two or more persons is necessary.

It is assumed that the basic tenets of internal control are appreciated and understood by the reader. Such basics include the competence of employees, segregation of duties, proper supervision, job rotation and forced vacations, written manuals and documentation, proper clerical procedures with adequate approval and authorization of certain documents and/or transactions.

Control and security in computer-based systems

A computer should be accurate, reliable and consistent. Yet the lack of adequate security and control over computer systems has threatened the existence of some organizations. Problems that have arisen include the following:

1   Fire, flood, riots, war, accidents and sabotage have destroyed irreplaceable computer files;
2   Acts of deliberate fraud have led to the manipulation of computer programs and resulted in stolen assets – e.g. goods being delivered and not paid for, accounts being understated, the payment of wages or salaries to fictitious employees, and so on;
3   Mistakes do happen and a mistake on a computer system can be costly – an employee mistakenly underpaid will usually complain whilst the same employee if over-paid will probably 'keep quiet' hoping that the mistake is not discovered;
4   Other privacy and confidentiality issues arise, trade secrets (e.g. a list of customers has been copied and sold to competitors) or the security controls of a system have been broken and access gained to sensitive information (e.g. the tender price on a large order).

Control problems arising from the use of a computer

Page and Hooper (1979) describe the major internal control problems which are specific to computer-based systems as opposed to basic manual problems. These are summarized in Table 8.1 where the problem, the typical result of the problem, and the general solution are given. It is perhaps worthwhile to look at some of these problems very briefly.

In a manual system one can usually rely on the people doing the work not to do something ridiculous such as issuing a cheque for £5 million instead of £500, issuing a final demand for a negative or zero amount or paying an employee for 200 hours of overtime worked in one week. The computer has no judgement and, unless programmed to detect and report exceptional or unreasonable events, will process all input data without discretion. The programs should constantly check that data and results are reasonable and within established limits.

Outside checks on a system's accuracy are important; for example, it is quite usual to rely on customers to check the accuracy of statements of account. However, it is not uncommon for people to assume that what has been processed by the computer is correct simply because it has been

Table 8.1 Internal control problems specific to computer systems
Source: **Page and Hooper (1979)**

Control problem	Typical result	General solution
The machine lacks judgment	Spectacular errors	Build in judgment with reasonableness tests
The user is in awe of the computer	User does not check computer output	Use control totals; check results of the computer
Duties are concentrated within the computer	Person in charge of computer can circumvent controls	Segregate duties within data processing
Records and the audit trail are invisible	Audit trail hard to use, if it is there	Use the computer to analyse records and audit trail
Information can be changed without physical traces	Change account balances without a trace	Use physical controls and cross-checks
Sophisticated tampering can cause unauthorized actions	Add name to pension rolls when fired	Ensure proper authorization
Great speed extends one person's capabilities	Accumulate round-off error in one account	Review programs, limit access to programs
Vast capabilities can create a different reality	Equity funding creates fictitious policyholders	Independent checks with 'real world'
Concentrated information is easier to steal	Social Security gets over 1 million records stolen	Physical controls and proper authorization
Electronic information is easy to lose	Fund raising loses millions in pledges	Proper backup
There are new sources and potentials for error	Incorrect use of the system	Complete debugging and proper system design
Source documents are eliminated	Loss of audit trail	Physical control on access to terminals

done by the computer. This is a serious problem and cannot be completely solved. One general solution, which should foil the potential computer thief, is to perform manual checks on random samples of computer output. Checks by user departments are aided by the provision of control totals and other information.

We have already recognized the need for segregation of duties as one means of internal control in a system. However, in a computer system, all the duties are performed by the computer and unless proper control is exercised the standard separation of duties will not be effective. Any person gaining unauthorized access to or control over the computer can abuse the system. One instance was the programmer who modified a bank program which produced lists of overdrawn accounts. He had the program simply omit his account so that he could overdraw without being detected. Another programmer instructed the computer to pay him several times. Such cases eventually come to light when the computer breaks down and lists are prepared manually or the programmer is away and pay cheques pile up on his desk. Segregation of duties in the computer department is critical. Six separate functions can be identified: (1) supervision or management, (2) systems analysis, (3) programming, (4) operating, (5) data entry, and (6) correction and investigation of errors.

Checking accuracy, cross-checking and the analysis of support for figures on financial statements are made more difficult when all records and the audit trail are invisible and exist only in machine-readable form. Nevertheless, the information does exist, although not in a form suitable for manual checking, and the computer itself must be used to analyse records and the audit trail. The system must be designed to include the data necessary for such analysis.

In a manual system, records are in ink, any changes are difficult if not impossible to conceal; even replacement of a whole page can be detected by analysis of the tint of the page or the age of the ink on the page. Similar changes on a magnetic storage medium can be made without physical trace, indeed one of the great advantages of magnetic tapes and disks is that they can be used many times over. Unauthorized changes to data are not the only potential problem; the programs can be changed by a sophisticated embezzler and used regularly on a production basis. Protection against changes without trace is difficult but there must be physical controls to reduce access to the computer by unauthorized personnel, and cross-checks to ensure that all data file changes are backed up by properly authorized transactions.

There is a tendency to believe that data adequately checked before entry to the computer will be correct, and that all computer stored transactions are authorized. Thus, if the input controls can be bypassed the potential thief can get his transactions 'authorized'. If a proper audit trail exists and unauthorized transactions are checked at various stages during processing then any tampering will be detected.

In a manual system there is a limit to what any one person can achieve by alteration of records and transactions. The great speed of a computer extends this capability. Insignificant changes such as a rounding error when applied to tens of thousands of accounts can yield a significant total sum. It is difficult to detect such errors as each account is only accurate to a specified number of decimal places, the proceeds of the fraud are credited to one account and the accounts all appear to balance. The only protection is proper supervision of all modifications to programs, regular review of programs by a supervisor and possibly occasional replacement of production versions by copies of protected master copies of programs.

Manual records are so bulky that their theft presents serious logistic problems. The thief cannot easily walk off with several filing cabinets full of information, nor copy the contents. However, concentrated information is relatively easy to steal. A magnetic tape or disk file can be copied quickly and the stolen file taken away in a briefcase. Again, the only adequate protection is rigorous control over access to files and to the computer.

So far we have emphasized the dangers of loss through deliberate manipulation of the system. We should not overlook the problems of accidental loss of information through malfunctioning of the computer. For example, the contents of disk files may be rendered unreadable by a disk head crash damaging the surface of the disk. This could be caused by an accumulation of dust on the disks or on the disk read/write heads. Regular cleaning and preventive maintenance will reduce the risk but will not eliminate it altogether. When a disk becomes unreadable, a well-designed recovery procedure is necessary; if the damage results from a fault on the disk drive then use of the only back-up copy on the same disk drive could turn a relatively minor problem into a total disaster. If master files are lost they can only be reconstructed by processing all the transactions again.

The numerous potential problems of manual systems, such as errors in calculations and mispostings, are well known. A computer system overcomes most of these problems but introduces new sources and potentials for error. Least serious perhaps is the risk of breakdown through hardware faults or vendor-supplied software. Such problems quickly become apparent and can be corrected before serious damage is done. There is a wide range of hardware controls and it is safe to assume that the hardware performs its function accurately. Faults in operating system software once corrected will not recur. When the computer does something wrong, the fault can usually be found in a user program, or is the result of misusing standard software such as incorrect input of data, data values supplied in the wrong order and so on. The only solution is thorough testing of all user-produced software. This is easier said than done and some errors do not become apparent until weeks, months or even years after a program is accepted for production runs. Another source of error is poor design of either programs or the system. Some people actually enjoy breaking the system and getting the computer to make mistakes. Some mistakes may be deliberate but most are inadvertent or the result of inexperience. The solution is, of course, good design in the first place of a robust system which can handle unusual situations and circumstances.

In a computer system, source documents are often eliminated or reduced. For example, in an on-line data entry situation the terminal operator may enter the data directly into the computer without creating a source document. Orders or reservations may be received over the telephone and entered directly without any written record. The problem is that without source documents there is no indication of proper authorization and the audit trail is lost. The solution is first to control access to the terminal so that only authorized personnel enter data, second the system should log all transactions, keeping a record of the operator, the terminal and the time of initiation of each transaction. This assigns responsibility and provides a check on the authorization of transactions.

The risks described above do not give the reader a real feeling for the full extent of the problems involved. The average annual computer embezzlement loss in the U.S.A. according to Sanders [1979] was between half and one million dollars, which was 5 to 10 times higher than the average manual system loss. Let us investigate a few more typical types of computer frauds.

A teller at a savings bank in New York was charged with stealing about $1.5 million from the bank. The teller did not have direct access to the computer. It was however alleged that hundreds of legitimate accounts were manipulated and money was transferred to fraudulent accounts and then withdrawn. False information was fed into the bank's computer so that when period checks were made, or when quarterly interest was due, all the legitimate accounts remained intact and in order.

A second type of fraud concerns the salami principle. There are many instances of this type of fraud. In general, this involves the deduction of a few pence in excess service charges, interest, taxes or dividends from thousands of accounts and writing the defrauder a cheque for the total amount of the excess. One was in a very large organization with many thousands of employees. All the half-pennies were accumulated to a bogus account and collected by the fraudulent programmer. No-one noticed a half-penny error (cheques cannot be made out for a half-penny anyway) and the total wages bill balanced exactly with the control total. Another variation again involved cheating from fellow employees. The programmer changed the tax module so that his tax withholdings were over-stated and the tax withholdings of all other employees were understated. The total tax amount was correct since the over- and under-stating of tax balanced out. To prevent other employees becoming suspicious, the programmer only under-stated each of his colleagues pay by a small amount (i.e. 50p).

In the former case the fraud was discovered when the employee left (and no-one collected the bogus pay-cheques). In the latter case, the fraud was discovered several years after it was put into operation when the deductions reported on an employee's weekly pay-cheque stubs did not match the annual PAYE tax return by around 50p.

The Equity Funding insurance fraud is another example in which the alleged conspirators included both senior management and computer personnel. Fictitious insurance policies and other assets were created in the computer files along with equally fictitious transactions. Such a fraud must inevitably collapse if the reported results are significantly at variance with the underlying reality. Here, the reality was insurance policies of bogus individuals. But eventually the company created a bubble which meant that to survive it had to keep on growing, which in turn meant the creation of more and more fictitious insurance policies until the whole fabric of the company was undermined.

Another type of fraud involves reporting inventory items as broken or lost and then transferring the items to accomplices. A more ambitious form is to initiate a bogus order to a valid customer and have it delivered to a fraudulent address and hope the legitimate customer pays up without fuss. Even if the mistake is discovered the embezzlers may have disappeared. Alternatively, release of goods and the incorrect charging (e.g. under-statement of prices) is another effective method.

Payroll frauds can occur in many separate ways. There is always the ubiquitous 'ghost' – a fictitious employee inserted into the payroll file. Over-statement of hours worked and the problem of the ghost are no more serious in a computer system than in a manual system. Automated badge readers acting as clocking-in devices may lead to a more reliable input. Over-statement of the rate of pay or salary scale is another type of fraud which must be carefully controlled.

As well as the problems of fraudulent use of computer programs by authorized users, there are various security risks which arise from using a computer system. The system is vulnerable to attack and penetration from people both inside and outside the organization and for motives as diverse as personal financial reward and the challenge of breaking into, *hacking*, a supposedly secure system. Let us examine some of the risks.

The first problem for the would-be criminal is to gain physical access to the computer system. An isolated computer system is relatively secure from the outsider who wishes to gain access to it. However, systems which use telecommunications networks are at risk of outside interference from *hackers*. A hacker is someone who tries illegally to break into a computer network. Although hackers may not damage systems to which they gain access, the potential to do damage clearly exists. With the increasing availability of personal computers and modems the problem of individuals trying to gain illegal access to systems just for the challenge is likely to increase. For the more determined criminal an alternative approach is *piggybacking* where a *bootleg* terminal is attached to a tapped communication line. Even the simple recording of data (e.g. prices to customers or from suppliers) may be of great value. Because of the speed at which the computer operates and the size of storage media it is easy to duplicate data files.

Physical access to a system is not a problem for the normal user. How can they overcome the security measures? Security of some larger systems usually involves levels of access. The systems manager, for example, will be in a position to know and modify all users' passwords, while ordinary users may have access only to their own files. Security would be breached if a user with a low level of access gained access to a higher level. There are a number of ways in which this can occur. The first is carelessness on the part of higher level users, for example, they are not vigilant when putting in their passwords, they use passwords which are easy to guess, or they have them written down. All these possibilities mean that passwords can get into the wrong hands, perhaps accidentally. Another way in which passwords can be stolen is by *spoofing*. Here a small program which mimics the normal logging-on procedure makes the user think they are logging on. The program records the password and then makes the user think that there is a fault by giving a standard error message. He/she then logs-in again, this time successfully, not knowing that the password has been written to a file. A rather more sophisticated approach to stealing passwords and data is a *Trojan horse*. This is a piece of code usually added to a common utility program, such as an editor. When the utility is run the Trojan horse code also operates. Unlike spoofing, everything appears perfectly normal to the user. Because a Trojan horse is part of another program the user can be encouraged inadvertently to load it on to the computer system. For example, system updates are usually sent through the post. If these are intercepted and a Trojan horse added, then the user will load an offending program.

Stealing passwords allows the security to be overcome through the front door. However, while developing a system a programmer can include code in such a way that it provides a *trap-door* for future penetration. This code may be benign and legitimate, in that it may have been used for *debugging* the program during systems testing, or may be used in some way for maintenance of the system. However, the code could also be included deliberately for fraudulent purposes. This unauthorized code is unlikely to be documented and may bypass some of the security measures of the system, for example, the system may not register that it has been accessed. In the wrong hands knowledge of such code would represent a serious risk to the integrity of the system and the data it contained.

Access to the system to steal data is not the only crime that can be perpetrated on a computer system. There is the potential for malicious damage and possibly bribery. In the same way that systems programmers can include trap-doors in their programs they can also leave *logic bombs*. A logic bomb is a section of code that goes off as a result of some criteria being met, thereby disrupting the system in some way. For example, if a specific date is entered into the system all the files on the system are deleted.

One further control issue which has been highlighted in recent years is the growth of computer *viruses*. A computer virus is a program that can attach itself to other programs and modify or destroy them. As the name suggests, viruses have the ability to 'infect' a whole computer system. Every program that becomes infected may then act as a carrier for the computer virus, with the result that the infection process can have a rapidly spiralling effect. There are three main types of virus, depending on the part of the computer they infect: the boot record, the operating system or the applications program.

Boot record viruses attach themselves to the boot record, which is used by the computer when it is first started up. The virus remains in control of the computer at all times. When a new floppy is inserted into one of the drives it will infect the boot record of the floppy. The virus cannot infect another machine except by being loaded from a floppy disk.

System viruses attach themselves to the operating system and will remain in control at all times, infecting any floppies used in the system. The Lehigh Virus modifies the main system command file, infects four times and then destroys all systems data.

Applications viruses attach themselves to specific programs and operate only when these programs are run. For example, the Israeli Virus, which makes the system unusable on any Friday 13th, infects all executable files. Applications viruses can infect by the user loading programs via modems.

Given the mobility between computerized systems and the sharing of resources and data, the threat posed by a viral attack is considerable. Although much research has been carried out to prevent the unauthorized access and dissemination of information, and many security measures are now available, very little has been done to safeguard against the entry into a system of potentially damaging information. Figure 8.1 shows how a computer virus can spread.

There are many possible entry paths for a virus, some open and authorized, others covert and unauthorized. Most commonly, viruses are introduced inadvertently by the computer user. Worldwide, computer

ORIGIN

A programmer writes a small piece of
computer code which can attach itself to
other programs and modify or destroy them.
The virus can also reproduce by copying
itself to other programs stored in the same
computer.

DISTRIBUTION

Usually the virus attaches itself to a piece of
software which will act as a Trojan horse in
the transformation process. As the owner of
the Trojan horse exchanges software with
other computer users (e.g. swapping disks
and through electronic bulletin boards), the
virus spreads.

INFECTION

As the host program is swapped, the virus
duplicates itself undetected and soon
becomes widespread.

ATTACK

At a predefined time (usually determined by
the computer clock/calendar), the virus
manifests itself and takes control of the
computer, causing the loss or modification of
data.

Figure 8.1 *The origin and spread of a computer virus*

enthusiasts use electronic bulletin boards on communication networks to
'chat' by computer. Often programs are swapped, and any one of them
may contain a virus.

With such global networking capabilities there have been some remark-
able viral outbreaks. A good example would be the so-called Pakistani
Brain, a virus which originated in the Punjab province and spread, with
pernicious results, to Europe, the Middle East and America. Clearly, a
viral attack can inflict very great damage upon governments, businesses
and other institutions. What, then, are the possible countermeasures?

The only total guarantee against a viral attack is complete isolationism.
To be perfectly secure, a system must protect against an incoming flow of
information, while at the same time ensuring against the leakage of
information. However, this is not really a practical solution since there
will always be a need for the interchange of computerized data. At

present the only real safeguard against viral attacks is an awareness of how the problem originates. At its most basic this involves vetting software and avoiding any that may be of questionable origin. It may also be possible to institute some limited forms of isolationism to arrest the spread of a viral infection, though the need for sharing will always render this problematic. Although a number of specifically designed 'vaccine' programs are now available, an effective answer to viral attack remains to be found.

The problems of deliberate fraud should not be overstated. Accidental mistakes and lack of care or insufficient concentration are still the major concern of an internal control system and, by a very large order of magnitude, are the most frequent type of control problem encountered.

Planning

Security planning includes a systematic approach to the identification of all the possible threats and hazards to the computer system. Remember that the hazards to a computer system include not only the problems identified in Table 8.1. Equipment may be damaged due to fire, floods or riots. Basically, all other types of problem arise from both accidental as well as deliberate acts.

A good control system should not only recognize all the possible threats, but should also minimize the likelihood of each hazard, reduce any consequential loss or problem in the event of adversity and provide for recovery from damage. In other words, it should:

Prevent the problem if possible;
Reduce the consequences if it does happen; and
Have a recovery plan.

Such a plan includes the entire spectrum of internal control policies and security procedures. We analyse these policies and procedures under the following major headings:

Management and organization controls;
Procedural controls;
Access controls and security;
Application controls.

First, we examine types of control described as management and organizational controls. The second area is concerned with procedures for prevention of errors, minimizing the damage and recovery procedures. The third concerns the physical and actual access to a system. Application

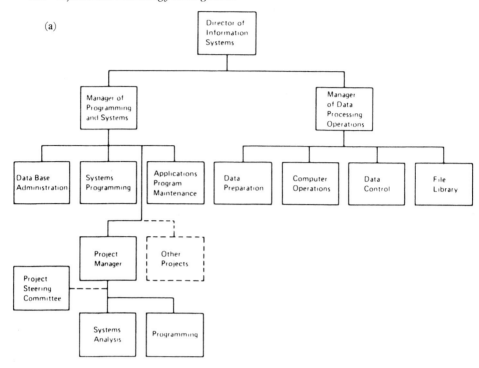

Figure 8.2 (a) *Organization of the information systems function* Source: *Cushing (1982), p. 416,*
(b) *Alternative organization of a large computer department* Source: *Hicks and Leininger (1981), p.*
288

controls concern controls built into the application program whilst in
production (i.e. routine data processing).

Management and organizational controls

Management control of the computer department includes the planning
and implementation of the overall information processing strategy for a
firm, the segregation of functions, the documentation of procedures, the
usual budgetary control of all expenses (and revenue, if any), and the
selection and training of personnel.

In looking at the managerial function, one important aspect is the
structure and organization of the computer department. Cushing (1982)
describes (1) the *operations* activity which is concerned with the day-to-
day activity of processing data and (2) the *systems* activity involving the
development and maintenance of software (including applications programs, utilities, data management systems and operating systems). This
split emphasizes the cardinal principle of good internal control – the
segregation of functions, those responsible for operations and custody of

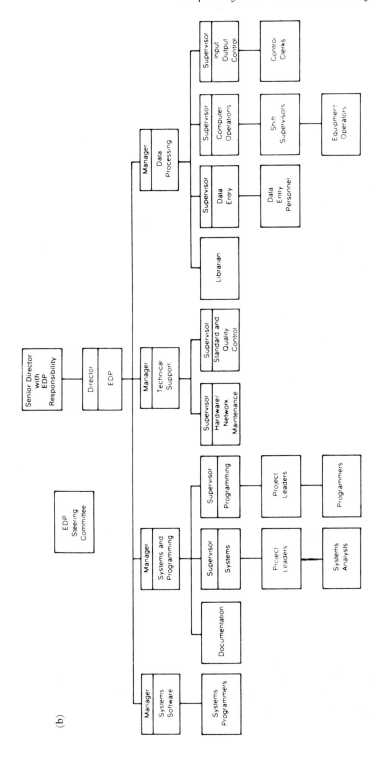

(b)

assets should be separate from those who record transactions relating to those assets. The reason why the principle is so important in computer departments is the ease with which data or programs can be changed and the changes concealed.

In Figure 8.2 (a) one example of an organizational chart for a computer department is given. This structure emphasizes the distinction between operations and systems. Regardless of the status of the top computer executive, this person must perform the role of manager of information systems which includes the development of profitable new applications and the efficient processing of existing applications. In this particular organizational structure there are a variety of different functions.

On the programming and systems side, tasks such as design, program-ming and documentation are performed. The database administration function has already been referred to. The systems-programming group is responsible for the efficient running and maintenance of all the systems software. This includes the operating system and utilities, database management systems, telecommunications and other software. In this example, a distinction is made between new applications and mainten-ance of applications software. This latter concept involves all aspects of maintenance including the design, development, programming, and testing of modifications and extensions to existing programs. The design and implementation of new applications systems are the responsibility of project managers who direct a group of analysts and programmers.

The data-processing operations in this organization (Figure 8.2 (a)) are divided into four distinct areas:

1   Data preparation, which involves the preparation and verification of source data;
2   Computer operations, which runs the computer and operates the input, output, storage devices (including changing disk packs and magnetic tapes);
3   Data control, which is responsible for checking the accuracy of input and output against control totals, for following up detected errors by computer editing and validation, and for ensuring that established control procedures are adhered to;
4   File custodianship/library function which maintains an inventory of all files and program copies irrespective of the storage media used.

The following areas are not clearly defined: the monitoring of work-in-progress, the flow of work through the systems and the distribution of output for completion of processing. This work may be a combination of 'data control' and 'operations'; the exact split depending on the actual firm or business set-up.

Figure 8.2 (b) shows an entirely different organization chart with four functional boundaries drawn around the following areas:

1   A data-processing department which is broadly similar to the previous organizational chart (for data control, input, output control);
2   A systems software group which in this chart warrants a department; this probably indicates an IBM mainframe where there are several layers of system software;
3   A systems and programming section which has three sub-sections; documentation, systems design and analysis, and programming;
4   The technical support services would supervise the standard of support and supervise any communication of network maintenance.

Modern hardware and software trends indicate that the effort devoted to systems software maintenance should be reduced. Conventional operating support with fixed disks should become increasingly automatic, except for archiving.

A typical large mainframe environment employing 150–300 people probably has personnel allocated to various functions in the following approximate percentages:

Data entry,	20
Operators and telecommunications,	20
System analysis and applications programming,	40
Systems software,	10
Management and other support functions,	10

Note that data entry will probably decrease whilst the role of systems analysis and applications programmers will increase, although some of this effort may be performed by accounting personnel acting in both an *ad-hoc* and full-time capacity.

It is conventional to separate the computer department from the users. The computer department usually has control over the data, files and systems and it should only correct those errors which have originated in the computer department. The above organizational structures aim to segregate functions and this can only be achieved to the extent shown in Figure 8.2 in large departments.

In smaller departments some segregation is possible as follows:

Operators should be segregated from programming and data entry activities;

Data entry personnel should not have the opportunity to operate or to program; and

Systems analysts and programmers should not be allowed to operate or enter data.

This minimal segregation is quote logical. If a potential fraudulent programmer can modify a program, as long as he or she does not enter the data or operate the machine, the modified program may neither be run nor have the appropriate data entered which would trigger the fraud. Obviously, the testing of the programs is vital and the close control of subsequent changes or amendments to programs is of extreme importance.

Data entry input-output and data control are increasingly being devolved or 'distributed' to user departments. Programmers/analysts and operators should not have access to data controls since fraudulent changes could be concealed by the modification of an application's control totals. By making a user department responsible, there is some segregation, although the data entry and data control are in the same (user) department. In some organizations, a control group within the computer department is established which maintains controls in addition to those in user departments. This provides a more secure system but at a considerable extra cost.

Other management controls

Other management controls include functions such as the selection and training of personnel. Obviously, the skills of the personnel implementing an internal control system play a vital part in its success. At the same time the computer department does have people in positions which are difficult to control and may therefore lend themselves to fraud.

Another useful control is the encouragement of an appreciation of the cost of computing and an efficient use of information. Often users treat the computer as a free and limitless resource. To ensure an efficient use of the resources, users should be charged for services. Such a user-charging system may lead to a sub-optimal situation for an organization, with managers being afraid of or not using the computer sufficiently. There must obviously be a trade-off and some discretion must be used.

The computer department should be a cost (even if not a profit) centre and should form an integral part of the organization's budgetary control processes. New equipment should undergo investment appraisals. This is also true of software except that software development staff may be a 'fixed' cost and it may be difficult to quantify the benefits of additional or better information. Nevertheless some form of cost/benefit appraisal should be undertaken, though mechanization and automation may be preferable because of (a) reliability, (b) ability to cope with increased work-loads and (c) no personnel or wage/salary problems.

Procedural controls

Although documentation was only briefly mentioned in the previous section, good documentation is important for the efficient running and control of a computer system. However, there are a number of other procedural controls which are vital to security and control in a computer department.

Hardware controls

Whenever data are copied or transcribed from one unit or storage location to another in the computer it is necessary to check the accuracy of the transfer. One safeguard is the parity check: each byte (or word) of binary data has one bit which is set to 'on' or not so that the number of on bits in the byte (or word) is even (or odd, depending on the machine). Whenever data are transferred in the machine, the parity of the result is checked.

Another type of hardware control involves redundancy checks, where two hardware units perform an identical task. The accuracy of a write operation (to a magnetic device) can be checked by an immediate read and comparison; this is a form of redundancy check.

One type of file protection control is the write ring on a magnetic tape (a similar device may be set on a disk drive). When a plastic write ring is removed from a tape reel, the computer is physically prevented from writing to the tape.

Preventive maintenance checks involve the regular testing of all the system components and the replacement of those thought likely to cause trouble in the near future. An uninterruptable power system smooths the flow of power to a system by having an auxiliary power supply which can act as a buffer. This prevents the loss of data and/or processing power during temporary fluctuations in electricity. In the event of a complete power failure, the system should either keep the machine functioning by the generation of its own supply (e.g. auxiliary power back-up system linked to a diesel generator) or should have sufficient reserves to allow the system to close down in an orderly fashion and preserve all the data in a tidy state.

In the event of a hardware failure the system should attempt to provide a partial or slow response system enabling a graceful degradation until the hardware (or software) fault has been rectified. Duplexed systems or partially duplexed systems are sometimes used in critical real-time applications. As businesses increasingly depend upon on-line and quick response systems some computer manufacturers are providing fully duplexed systems. One example of a mini computer manufacturer doing this is TANDEM computers.

System development controls

In Part 3 of this book the system development cycle is discussed and part of the systems development controls will be related to the control of the system development cycle. One aspect of systems development – documentation – is very important as it is the primary means of communication between systems analysts, programmers, management and auditors. Again the subject of documentation is discussed in the next section.

Documentation

Briefly, documentation is one important safeguard against someone threatening to leave or trying to hold the organization to ransom on account of the person's indispensability to the firm since he or she is the only one who can run the system. Since pressure is usually exerted to meet deadlines for software, documentation is often left as a non-essential, low-priority task or, at best, a necessary evil. Management must, for their own safety, ensure that there is adequate documentation and continually stress its importance.

Other advantages of good documentation include communication and independence of different people developing systems which can then be integrated (or coupled to existing systems) with the minimum of fuss. But the major safeguard must be to cover the possibility of a programmer leaving an organization in the middle of a major project. The need for documentation can thus be argued on both an efficiency or productivity (long-run) basis as well as for security.

Documentation can be divided into different categories. First, there is *operating* documentation which includes all the information, procedures and responses necessary to run a program or suite of programs. This should include such items as the hardware configuration, the various program parameters, the various options on the computer's control terminal (commonly called the console), conditions leading to errors and program malfunction, any corrective actions, and so on.

Second, there is the *user* documentation describing the necessary actions and terminal responses and variations of a response for a user to run a program and reply to any computer-initiated dialogue. Third, there is *administrative* documentation dealing with a description of overall standards and procedures for data processing in general. Finally, there is *systems* documentation which should include a complete description of all aspects of each application including narrative, flow-charts or decision tables, program listings.

Program changes

One control which is important is that over program changes. One authority likens the uncontrolled ability to make changes in production (as opposed to developing) applications programs as equivalent to having direct uncontrolled access to a firm's cash. Changes to all applications programs should follow a carefully specified set of procedures.

First, a change should be approved by the user and the appropriate level of management. A programmer/analyst should analyse what the changes mean in terms of program code modifications. A programmer should then obtain a copy of the production source program from the librarian and all the documentation for the program. The changes should be made and the program tested. The modified program and the up-to-date documentation should then be handed over to an independent person who should list the new program and approve and review the new program and its modifications. The new program is then released to the librarian as the production version. Close monitoring and scrutiny of the revised program should take place until the production program has been demonstrated to be reliable.

Internal audit review

One of the control devices which spans the analysis, design, coding, implementation, periodic review and routine production activities of computer departments is the internal auditing function (if one exists). Such a function should be part of the complete life-cycle of the development, testing and operation of a system.

Security of files

Files may be destroyed either deliberately, or accidentally due to equipment malfunction or electrical power failure. Occasionally, a terminal operator accidentally deletes all his files by typing, for example,

DELETE *.*

instead of

DELETE *.OLD

where OLD is a file name extension specifying that the file is an OLD or superseded security copy. This incorrect command, instead of deleting just the files with extension 'OLD' would delete all files from the user's file store directory. The damage can only be repaired if back-up copies exist elsewhere.

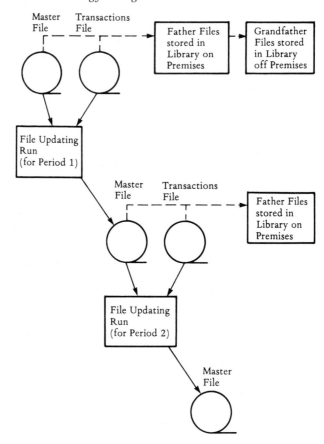

Figure 8.3   *Flows of files in grandfather-father-son back-up: vertical dimension illustrates the flow of grandfather-father-son master files in processing, and horizontal dimension illustrates the flow of these files for back-up storage*

To safeguard against the loss of files by whatever means, it is necessary to adopt a strict procedure for security copying. One back-up mechanism in common use is the grandfather-father-son technique which we describe in Chapter 5. Such a procedure is part of the normal flow of activities. At any stage, if the current master file becomes corrupted or is destroyed then it should be possible to recreate it by running again the program which created it using saved copies of the old master file and the transactions file for that period. The procedure is shown in Figure 8.3 where the vertical dimension depicts successive generations of files (grandfather, father and son) through successive processing periods, and the horizontal dimension shows the flow of files for back-up storage.

At each stage, the files used as input to the file updating run are the old master file, called the *father* file, and the transactions file for the period. The new (updated) master file created by the updating run is called the *son* file. On the next updating run, the son created on the previous run becomes the new father, i.e. the old master file, and a new son is created. The old father, from the previous period, is then the *grandfather* file. Thus, at any one time three generations of master files (grandfather, father and son) and the corresponding transactions files are retained. The current master file (the son) and the father file from which it was created might be stored in a library on the premises, whereas the grandfather files might be stored more remotely in a library off the premises. This sort of technique was originally devised for magnetic tape-based, batch-processing systems. It is sufficient to cover all events which are likely to occur. A similar technique can be applied to removable disk packs.

However, for on-line and real-time or fixed disk systems a slightly different approach must be adopted. If the master file is updated on-line by overwriting selected individual records then no old master (father) file is created. The grandfather-father-son effect can be achieved by period-ically copying the master file (i.e. dumping the entire contents) onto another (removable) disk pack or magnetic tape. For large files this can be very time-consuming and if file record activity is low, to dump the whole file is wasteful of time. Selective dumping of records that have changed as a result of updating may be more efficient. It is also necessary to create a file of transactions input during each period, i.e. between successive dumps. The periodic dumps together with transaction logs give us the equivalent of grandfather, father and son files from which the master file can be reconstructed in the event of corruption or loss.

In Figure 8.4, transactions received via communications equipment come from both central and remote locations and are input to the system. These transactions are logged onto tape drives or a disk drive. If the transactions come in bursts which are too rapid to be written directly onto the tape in real-time then an intermediate disk may be used as a buffer. Two tape drives are normally used in large applications so that when one tape is full the second tape can immediately take over.

Sometimes as a further security, between file back-up dumps, in addition to all transactions being logged, all changes to a file are also recorded on a file amendment log. Such logging can occur on tapes as portrayed in Figure 8.4 but, alternatively, the logs may be written to:

1 Any spare fixed disk (as shown in Figure 8.5) which are rotated in a grandfather-father-son procedure;
2 Removable disk packs used in a similar manner to tapes; or
3 In smaller systems, a number of floppy disks.

The use of fixed disks is beginning to change the way back-up pro-cedures work. In Figure 8.5 we assume a small system with four separate disk drives on two controllers and two channels (alternatively this may be

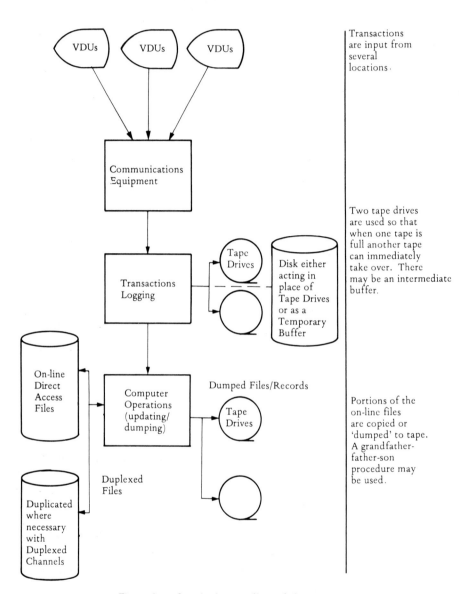

Figure 8.4   *Security in an on-line real-time system*

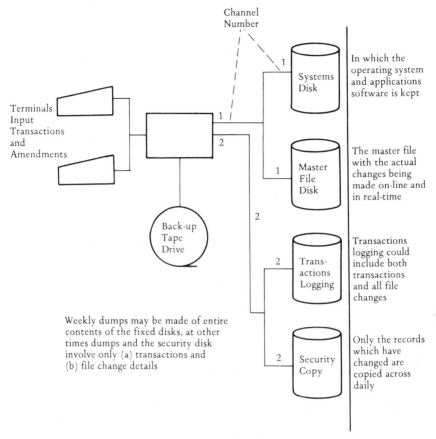

Channel Number

Systems Disk — In which the operating system and applications software is kept

Terminals Input Transactions and Amendments

Master File Disk — The master file with the actual changes being made on-line and in real-time

Back-up Tape Drive

Transactions Logging — Transactions logging could include both transactions and all file changes

Weekly dumps may be made of entire contents of the fixed disks, at other times dumps and the security disk involve only (a) transactions and (b) file change details

Security Copy — Only the records which have changed are copied across daily

Figure 8.5 *Security of files with fixed disks*

three drives on three controllers and channels, or some such variation). The basic concept is to spread the master files, back-up copies, and transaction logs across as many drives and channels as possible. Critical portions of the systems disk and the day's transactions disk may be copied to tape. The master file may take too long to copy – except weekly. Therefore, security requirements may dictate simply taking a security copy of the master file (i.e. the son). Even this process may be simplified and only those records which have been changed actually copied both to tape and to the security disk.

If a high proportion of all records on the master file are updated each day then it may be sensible to dump the entire master file every day, but if file activity is low then the dumping of the whole file cannot be justified and is a waste of time. It is normal practice for the daily tape dump to record only incoming transactions and to record only changes to master files. The transactions and the master file changes may be dumped to two separate files. Thus, at any time, we have the old security file (the weekly dump of the entire master file) and for each day since the last weekly dump, records of all input transactions and amendments to the master file. Application of the grandfather, father, son procedure to these dumped files is adequate insurance against all likely problems.

Hierarchical archiving

Some systems (particularly IBM) have a system of hierarchical archiving. What this does is to copy files onto successively slower access devices unless there is some kind of lock on so doing. Files or individual records (in, for example, a transactions file of all sales) would be copied from:

1 Fast-access fixed disks to
2 Slower-access fixed disks to
3 Either a mass storage system (e.g. disk cartridge) or a removable disk pack and then stored in a library of disk packs and thence to
4 Tape which is then stored in a tape library.

Since (4) always involves operator action, it is the last resort. The criteria for moving information can either be frequency of use – i.e. keep the most frequently used data on the fastest-access storage device – or some other criteria.

Librarian functions

With all the above systems and especially with older tape-based systems, librarian functions are vitally important. Manual libraries consist of a separate room, extremely physically secure, in which tapes, disk packs and any other removable storage media are kept. Access to such a library should be restricted to authorized library personnel. Usually, each tape or disk pack has an external label (i.e. a gummed paper label) on which is written the file identification, date of last processing and other information.

As well as a manual library the system also sets up and maintains its internal library of files through its systems software. These library files have internal labels used by the systems software for identification and control of access.

Software file controls

The internal librarianship function and other controls necessary to manage and control the resources of the computer are provided by the systems software. Usually, in all but the smallest systems, the systems software provides a number of built-in control features. One of these is password access to the system, this is discussed later. Another is the library function of a set of files – often called a directory – and the cataloguing system associated with the file library on the on-line secondary store. Most files have a *header* and a *trailer* label signifying the start and end of the file. Physically, this was literally true of a tape file but may be only logically true of a non-contiguous disk file (i.e. a disk file whose records may be scattered over several physical areas on disk). The header record usually contains certain details about the file organization (and indices) of the file. It will include the file name, creation data, logical record length, blockage, date of last access and so on. Sometimes, this information is not stored in the header record but is stored in a separate file directory.

Sometimes the trailer record, as well as acting as a label signifying end of file, also contains control totals for checking against the totals accumulated (or carried forward) during processing.

Access controls and security

The investment in hardware and software may be very considerable. The control of access to hardware, software, documentation and data is therefore important. A computer centre destroyed, or a set of master files lost can lead to the collapse of a business. For example, in Iran, one computer centre was located above a garage which, being associated with 'western' products, was set alight and the computer centre, located on a higher storey, was completely destroyed. Similarly, a bank with special input/output and cash dispensing terminals located in each branch throughout the country and linked to a real-time computer system came to a standstill when most of the terminals were confiscated or destroyed in the process of revolutionary fervour. Nearer home the case of a multinational company having its master files and security copies of the sales ledger stolen and ransomed nearly led to a new form of hi-jacking. This attempt was foiled at the hand-over of the ransom but it could have been a disaster for the firm.

Access to program documentation

Access to all documentation should only be made available on a need-to-know basis. Certain documentation such as passwords, directory listings and privacy locks for example should be kept in a safe. Documentation should take one of several forms: (a) what is needed for routine operations and (b) what a programmer or systems analyst, or accountant may need to now about the detailed specification, file layouts and program code.

Program documentation of type (a) may allow an unauthorized person to operate a fraudulent transaction but the person would also need to know the password to a user account with the appropriate access privileges in order to run the program and update the various data files. Documentation of type (b) may allow a programmer to make changes to the code to his or her advantage. Access should therefore be restricted to that documentation necessary for the programmer to perform his or her duties.

Back-up systems and procedures

For complete security the following precautions should be taken.

1 Copies of programs, grandfather or monthly data files and associated transaction logs, documentation and so on should be held in a separate physical location.
2 Fire-proof safes should be used to store current security copies and transaction logs, system disks, etc.
3 A set-up procedure is necessary with documentation outlining the steps to be taken in the event of a disruption, according to its severity.
   This disaster recovery plan will prepare an organization to recover its data-processing capacity as efficiently as possible.
4 There should be access to back-up hardware. This could include support from a computer bureau or the computer manufacturer but, more commonly, it is from another company with similar equipment which has agreed to provide back-up on a reciprocal basis.

Physical security

Physical security begins with the consideration of such threats as floods, fire, riots and so on. Companies proud to have computers used to show them off to visitors or passers-by by locating them on the ground floor behind large windows. This is a weakness. A more practical approach dictates that the PR advantages of having a computer on display are outweighed by the ease of physical access. Hence, the computer should be located in a physically fire- and riot-proof place with the maxim 'keep people out'. Other physical aspects include protection against power surges, uninterruptible power sources, closed circuit television monitoring access to and from the computer room, and the appropriate environmental control equipment to regulate temperature, humidity and to extract dust particles from the air.

Other controls should ensure that, if the worst possible happens, then back-up files exist, alternative computers are available and that back-up manual procedures exist. An insurance policy covering partial or full loss is an essential part of the security cover with the usual risks of fire, flooding, exceptional weather, riots, sabotage and some cover to guard against risk of loss from embezzlement.

Physical controls should ensure that a computer system is physically lockable and secure. Security copies of files (on disk packs or tapes) should be kept in a fire-proof safe. File libraries should be physically secure and lockable. Terminals should be kept in secure positions, although there is some security value in placing terminals where access and the actual use of the machine is in clear view of many people.

System software controls

More advanced computer systems have programs and data files stored on-line and access to both is by means of terminals, or batch programs (initiated to run at a certain time or placed in a batch queue which is run sequentially and at a lower priority than on-line terminals or real-time computing requests). Access to files and programs is controlled using directories (i.e. an index of files kept in a certain area). Password schemes, device authorization tables and the encoding of data are related to this access control.

To gain access to the system the user enters a unique ID username or account number. The system will then ask the user for a password and on correctly submitting this* the user will be allowed entry to the system.

Each user account can have a range of privileges and access facilities which may be kept in a user number authorization table. Users may be granted read, write, create or delete access to certain files. Sometimes to access a particular file, the file name or dataset name must be entered. In order to read or write to a file, password systems may also be used – individuals may have a read-access password but not a write-access password. However, a more common form of control is to allow different classes of users different types of access. For example, program X run from user number Y at terminal Z may be allowed read-access. User A may be allowed write-status from any terminal and to any program which also has write-status built in. Usually, such authorization tables are either maintained with each file or with each user account.

In some systems not only do files require certain privileges (right of access is a privilege) but certain fields or records within a file may have 'privacy locks' requiring a special password for access. A managing director's salary is an example of a record which might have a privacy lock. On a sales system, the gross profit made on each customer may be a field for which a privacy lock is maintained.

The encoding of data can be used for particularly sensitive data since, if unauthorized access occurs, the data is then unintelligible unless the code

---

*On good systems, the password will either not appear on a screen (this requires a duplexed line, i.e. send and receive) or, on a printing terminal, the password could be printed over a mask.

is known. Access to data must be through an encoding and decoding function which can only be performed by certain software modules.

Application controls

Application controls can be classified in many different ways but their basic function is to ensure that (1) input data are accurately and completely input, (2) the input data are processed accurately and completely against correctly maintained files, (3) the output of the system is distributed on a timely basis to those authorized to receive it. In general, application controls rely on a wider set of controls than input, processing and output. They involve the data inputs, the maintenance of files and programs, as well as the outputs from a computer application. However, they do not refer to the computer system in general.

Input

Most transaction inputs are based on a source document which should be properly authorized. The various functions which have to be controlled are:

(a) Input authorizations and the process of collecting source documents and passing them on for
(b) Data conversion which often takes two steps (i) transcribing the data to a special source document, or form, and then (ii) keying the data onto a machine-readable input medium,
(c) The validation and editing of the input data to ensure that only accurate data is processed by the computer system.

It is in these stages of manual preparation of data for input to the computer that errors are most likely to arise. The more times data are transcribed the higher the incidence of errors; source documents become misplaced; transaction records may be lost. In this respect, the advantages of direct and on-line data entry, from points of sale for example, cannot be over-emphasized. However, on-line data input has its own problems of security and control to which we have already referred. There are a number of precautions which can be taken to avoid or detect errors in batch-processing systems.

Batch totals

In a computerized batch-processing application, batch totals are accumulated manually from source documents prior to input preparation. The original totals are then compared with machine-generated totals at each subsequent processing step. A discrepancy indicates an error in one of the two systems (manual or computer), or a loss of a record, or an error in data transcription. Batch totals are sometimes called control totals and can be any of the following:

(a) Record counts – a total of the number of input documents or records processed in a run;
(b) A financial total of a money field such as total cash receipts;
(c) A hash total which may be generated from totalling a field that would not otherwise be added, e.g. total of all customer account numbers on sales transactions.

For efficient use of batching, the originating department should submit batch source documents in limited numbers (these may form natural logical groupings such as a day's transactions). If numbers are kept small then errors will be isolated to within a relatively small number of transactions and this makes it easier to find the specific record or records which are in error. Each batch usually has an identification number which is keyed in as part of the input record. If batches are based on logical groupings such as departments or days, then the department number or date can serve as an additional identification.

Use of pre-numbered forms

An effective control is to use serially numbered forms so that documents may be accounted for. A missing number or two identical numbers in a sequence signifies an error. (However, a missing number may simply represent a voided transaction.)

Use of transcription methods

Data input may be controlled by the visual check of experienced clerks who conduct a pre-audit of source documents prior to recording the transactions in a machine-readable form.

Use of redundancy (i.e. duplication)

If input is by means of punched cards (now very rare), a card verifier can be used. This technique involves a second person re-inputting the source data and any discrepancies noted. Note that this duplication of input can be performed on any system. However, no information is necessarily available as to which is correct. A badly written document is open to misinterpretation.

Use of programmed checks on input

Programs can be written to edit and check the data on input. Input validation and editing routines utilize the computer to check the validity and accuracy of the input data. Generally, this is performed by a separate program prior to the main processing.

1   A *sequence check* checks whether the data is in proper order. If forms are not pre-numbered the check may take the form of a date order or departmental number check.
2   *Check digit verification* involves the use of an additional digit or character for the purpose of producing a 'self-checking' number. Each check digit is derived arithmetically from the other digits and bears a unique mathematical relationship to them. Thus, with a check digit the internal consistency of the number can be verified.

For example, the check digit calculation for a part number 57382 may be performed as follows:

(a)   Multiply each digit of the part number by a selected weight and form a sum of products:

Part number	5	7	3	8	2	
Weights	5	4	3	2	1	
Sum of products	25 +	28 +	9 +	16 +	2 =	80.

(b)   Subtract the sum of products from the next highest multiple of some selected modulus, 11, say, to obtain a check digit (moduli in common use are 7, 10, 11, 13):

$$88 - 80 = 8.$$

The part number complete with its check digit is

$$573828.$$

The check digit thus becomes an integral part of the number. On input the number is subjected to check digit verification by the data validation routine as follows:

Form sum of products:

Part number	5	7	3	8	2	8
Weights	5	4	3	2	1	1
Sum of products	25 +	28 +	9	+ 16 +	2	+ 8 = 88.

Divide by the modulus (11) and note the remainder:

$$88/11 \rightarrow \text{remainder } 0.$$

Since the remainder is zero the number passes the check digit verification.

If a transcription error or a transposition of digits occurs then the number will not usually check digit verify. For example, suppose the number is input as

(a) 578328 (a transposition)
or (b) 513828 (the 7 being mistaken for a 1)
then check digit verification yields the following results:

(a) 5   7   8   3   2   8
     5   4   3   2   1   1
    25 + 28 + 24 + 6 + 2 + 8 = 93.

93/11 => non-zero remainder.

(b) 5   1   3   8   2   8
     5   4   3   2   1   1
    25 + 4 + 9 + 16 + 2 + 8 = 64.

64/11 => non-zero remainder.

In each case the error is detected by check digit verification. Check digits can be very useful for account numbers, part numbers or employee numbers.

The most common forms of error include transcription (the miscopying of a digit such as 543682 for 548682), transposition (the interchanging of two digits such as 471352 for 473152). Transcription errors are particularly common forming over 80% of the total field errors. Many errors are caused not by an arbitrary miscopy but by confusion between similar digits, e.g. 1 and 7, 3 and 8 or 4 and 9. It is also easy to confuse certain digits and letters (e.g. 2 and Z, 1 and I, zero and O) but these may be caught by a numeric and alphabetic check.

3 *Range checks* involve comparing the input values with certain known bounds or characteristics. Some typical examples are;

   Hours worked per week $\leq$ 168 and $\geq$ o
   Sex code = M or F.

   Another form of this check is *limit, feasibility* or *reasonableness* check. A form of reasonablness check may be that
      Hours paid $\leq$ 84 and $\geq$ o.
4 *Field checks*. This type of check includes the anticipation, numeric and alphabetic checks. An *anticipation* check is based on the fact that certain fields in an input record should be blank and some should be non-blank (e.g. hours worked should always be non-blank even if the input is zero). *Numeric* and *alphabetic* checks ascertain that certain parts

of the input are numeric (e.g. hours worked) whilst alphabetic fields contain only alphabetic characters (e.g. a name). A U.K. national insurance number must have the form

where A stands for a letter, b is a blank and 9 for a numeric digit. In some systems the blank spaces may be automatically created so that a form is effectively displayed as

but even here the various positions can be checked for correctness of character type. A *sign* check may also be incorporated within a field check to ensure that the data in a field are of the appropriate arithmetic sign.

5   *Arithmetic proof checks* can be used to verify the results of other computations. One example is that the total of debits should equal the total of credits for general journal inputs. Batch-control total checks are a further example of this form of check.

6   *Invalid code checks* may be able to verify codes contained in input records. For example sales territory codes may be limited to the range 21–99. Alternatively, they may be checked against a table of valid codes. Sometimes certain codes always start with the same digit. A sales ledger payment record may always start with a certain digit.

7   *Redundant data checks* require that two identifiers (e.g. account number and name) be included for each input record that is to be updated in order to confirm that the correct record is retrieved by cross-referring both identifiers. In a payroll file an example would be the employee number and the name of the individual (it may just be the first few letters of the employee's name). The computer can check whether the name (or the first few letters) also match those on the file after obtaining the employee name.

Computer systems and input

Having described a variety of input checks, it is useful to categorize the most common input forms:

1   *Punched card- or paper taped-based systems* are batched systems with a second process of verification. The input transactions are then subject

to data validation and editing routines. Batch-control totals are keyed into a separate control record for each batch. Usually, the balancing and edit program verifies that each input batch balances with its control totals prior to further processing. Alternatively, a report can be produced if the totals do not balance and this report can be used to track down the errors in the input.

2 *On-line input* is usually also arranged in batches before files are updated, though the data validation and editing can be performed in real-time. In these circumstances, closed loop verification can occur with the aid of the terminal user. On prompting for an account number, the system may retrieve the account name and address, display it on the terminal and wait for confirmation from the user that the name and address corresponds to the account number originally entered. However, once the input transactions are recorded on a separate file and the batch control information has been input the system is faced with one of several options:
   (a) Reject the whole batch;
   (b) Wait until the error has been found and corrected;
   (c) Put through a correction error record which balances the batch but which must be subsequently corrected; or
   (d) Deduct all transactions with errors (e.g. check-digit verification or reasonableness errors) recalculate the batch and the sum of the transaction totals and proceed.

   Especially important in either of the above batch systems are the procedures for investigation and correction of errors identified by edit programs, batch-total checks and other source data controls.

3 *Key-to-disk or magnetic tape encoders* are two other input systems which fall somewhere in between the two above systems depending on the intelligence and power of the local system.

4 *Turnaround documents* can also be used to input information. Part of an invoice or request for payment is detached and sent with a customer's cheque, the detachable part will have, in machine-readable form, the account number, amount and transaction number. Thus, the input for most cases can be automatically read. (Queries or instances where the customer sends in an amount of money different to that demanded will have to be dealt with by a separate clerical and input procedure.)

Error handling

Sometimes, a special data control department exists to carry out the investigation and correction of errors. The main features of error handling include:

   (a) Well-defined procedures for correction and re-entry of erroneous input and adequate supervision to ensure that these procedures are being carried out (in some firms, errors have just been ignored and hence piled-up);

(b)   Re-submission of corrected input to the full validation procedure (often the error rate on error corrections is high).

Obviously, to ensure a self-correcting system, the user department responsible should be notified of its incorrect input. One technique which is widely used is the maintenance of an error log. This contains errors detected in the current processing run and all the previous errors detected in previous runs that have not been corrected. Each error in the log would include the date and time of error, type of record, the transaction identification number, the information on the whole record, the specific field or fields in error and the type of error. Note that the error log may be maintained either manually or by the computer. The error log would be maintained by senior personnel and reports listing all outstanding errors and the number of errors should be regularly provided to management who will wish to monitor the level of input errors as well as the status and number of uncorrected errors.

On-line input

Since most modern systems are accessed from terminals located at a distance from the computer, it is necessary to re-iterate the controls on on-line input. A number of unique problems arise; some of the solutions are similar to a batch input system, others are very different.

One of the most important concepts is that system access controls must also apply to terminals. However, restrictions on the physical access to a terminal are not always effective. A number of controls exist:

1   Each authorized user is assigned a unique user number and password that must be keyed into the system to allow access;
2   Each terminal may have an electronic identification number and certain applications and commands are accepted only from authorized terminals.

With a user number/password plus a terminal identifier, the system may apply a compatibility test to transactions or enquiries demanded by the user. A sales ledger clerk would not be allowed to view the managing director's salary. Similarly, a dispatch clerk would only be allowed to enter dispatches and returns – but not deliveries.

In this way the system attempts to prevent both unintentional mistakes and deliberate manipulation of the system. The system may maintain, in access control, a table consisting of:

1   A list of user numbers, the names of the individuals authorized to use each number and the corresponding password;
2   A list of all files and programs maintained on the system; and
3   A record of the type of access allowed for different users or groups of users.

Type of access can mean read only, read and copy, modify or update, addition of record, or deletion of record. However, more sophisticated systems would allow access to summarized information or the reading of certain fields within a record. In order to obtain access to certain fields an authorized user may have to supply the key (i.e. a password) to a privacy lock on certain sensitive fields (e.g. the profit made on a particular sale – information that you may not wish customers to find out).

Batch controls can be used in on-line and even real-time systems. If the system is only on-line data entry then the batch control totals as well as the individual transactions are input. With real-time data input batch processing can still be used, since input is normally based on some hardcopy document (orders received over the telephone or counter should give rise to some hardcopy documentation). Ex-post batch controls can be constructed periodically and can be based on natural input groupings such as departments. These totals can be balanced to totals produced by the computer system.

User numbers and passwords are effective only if they are kept secret. However, people tend to write down the numbers or ask a colleague to finish a set procedure. Some security measures can be taken, for example, the computer should never print a password and users should be constantly reminded of the need for security. All passwords should be periodically changed as this reduces the likelihood that a password will become known to an unauthorized user. Some systems, where system security is important, record all attempts to access the system from an unauthorized terminal or using an unauthorized password. A record of such attempts would then be scrutinized by a security officer.

Some of the more advanced computer systems create new problems for the auditor. The expansion of on-line data entry systems has caused particular concern since some conventional controls, such as batching, control totals and balancing, may no longer be appropriate. In these cases great care and attention must be given to the checks on accuracy which are made when data is input. These checks, summarized in Table 8.2, use whatever information is available in the system to analyse the consistency and reliability of the input data (see also Martin, 1973).

There are important implications for analysts, designers and administrators. An on-line system must be designed to catch as many errors as possible immediately on input; any errors so caught must be immediately corrected; self-checking operations should be built into the terminal dia-

Table 8.2   On-line and real-time accuracy checks

Single transaction checks	*Group transaction checks*
Descriptive read back	Periodic item balances
Character and field checks	Running totals
Links to earlier transactions	Checkpoints at which the
Check for a valid sequence of transactions	operator must inspect the
Use of machine-readable documents	input or status of the entry
Check for internal contradictions	and verify that it is correct
Check that all facts have been entered	

logue with the user and the linkage of this dialogue to file inspection routines.

Furthermore, control is improved when the real-time error detection process is backed up by off-line file inspection and balancing routines. Consequently, systems analysts must play an active part in the design of controls in computer systems, even if some of these may fall in users' areas, and computer administrators must give close attention to the quality of the manual and administrative controls which surround and protect the on-line computer controls.

Other on-line data entry controls

Most on-line systems have special input controls over and above those found on purely batch-processing systems. Techniques such as *prompting* are used where the system displays a request to the user for each item of input data and waits for a valid response before requesting the next required item. Another procedure is to display a *pre-formatted* scheme. This puts up the equivalent of a form – this document is displayed on the screen with blanks or a format (highlighted by a different colour or a series of lines) for the data items which the user must fill in. The input routines supporting such methods can obviously perform data editing and vetting checks (e.g. reasonableness, existence and so on). Another check which an on-line data entry system can perform is a *completeness* test on each input record to check whether all of the data items required for a transaction have been entered. A null response or a blank may not be allowed. If a mistake has been made the operator may have to fill up with blanks and then reject the whole transaction.

One of the advantages of on-line input and real-time validation is that error messages can be displayed at the terminal immediately one of the conditions has been violated. These error messages should be as clear as possible. There are three objectives of the error message: (1) to indicate which data item is in error, (2) to state what the error is, and (3) to suggest what should be done to correct it. For example, if the error is the date of the transaction, the error message should clearly state that it is the date that is incorrect and the correct format or the factor that is wrong in the date (e.g. the operator may have input 31.06.84 and the mistake of there being only 30 days in June may not be immediately obvious to the operator).

Processing controls

Processing controls are necessary to ensure that data are not lost or not omitted from processing. Processing controls are also necessary to check the arithmetic and processing accuracy of the update technique.

Essentially, processing controls are similar to input controls. The output of one stage of a system often forms the input to another stage. Prior to each stage, or program run, in the system various checks may be performed:

1 Run-to-run control totals on such fields as value, quantity and record counts. This verification is essential and should be followed throughout all processing operations;
2 Reasonableness checks to isolate any errors that escaped the various input checking routines or to highlight unauthorized changes that occurred after input.
3 External and internal file-labelling systems should ensure that the correct file is being used and that it is the correct version of that file.

Many of the other controls discussed previously can be used. The essential aim of processing controls is a further chance to capture undetected input errors, prevent accidental or deliberate operator errors and to detect intentional or accidental errors made after input.

Output controls

Output controls ensure the accuracy of the computer operations and control the distribution of the output. Hicks and Leininger (1981) identify the following six controls:

1 Output control totals should be reconciled with input and processing totals before the reports are released;
2 The computer console log or the job execution stream on the computer output should be reviewed to determine whether any unusual interrupts or patterns of processing occurred that would affect the validity of the output;
3 Job Control Language listings should be checked to ensure that no unauthorized programs have been executed during processing;
4 The output reports should be visually scanned to make sure that they

look correct. Critical input transactions should be compared individually with output reports to ensure that the changes were made correctly. Other techniques, such as statistical sampling, are sometimes used to review output;

5   Copies of output reports should be delivered only to the authorized recipients. An integral part of a system's documentation is a list of all system output and the recipient of each copy;

6   The use of accountable documents (for example, blank cheques) should be verified by comparing computer-generated counts to actual usage recorded from pre-printed sequence numbers on the documents.

Legal controls

Having described the various managerial, organizational and application controls placed on a system, we must now go on to discuss another important safeguard: legal controls.

The 1984 Data Protection Act came into force in Britain in November 1987. This important piece of legislation, which requires all data users to be registered, was long overdue given the nature of the computer revolution and its potential for abuse. Under the terms of the act the need for privacy is recognized by the requirement that all data should be held for clearly designated purposes. Accuracy or integrity must be maintained and data must be open to inspection. Only legitimate parties can access data, and information must be secured against alteration, accidental loss or deliberate damage. Furthermore, the act states that data must be obtained fairly, to precise specifications, and must not be kept for longer than required.

One omission, however, which has occasioned some criticism is the fact that data held to prevent or detect crime are exempt from these provisions. Additionally, while going some way to protect the rights of individuals and offer legal redress, the act can only deter and not prevent the activities of hackers who gain illegal access to privileged information.

Although much needed legislation and other control measures are now emerging to protect privacy and maintain data security, the pace of technological change has been so dramatic that the full social and economic implications of the computer revolution are yet to be felt.

Part Two: Further reading

Anderson, R. G. *Data Processing and Management Information Systems* (McDonald and Evans, 1978)

Clifton, H. D. *Business Data Systems* (Prentice-Hall International, 1978)

Codd, E. F. 'A Relational Model of Data for Large Shared Data Banks', *Communications of the ACM*, June 1970

Cushing, B. E. *Accounting Information Systems and Business Organizations* (Addison-Wesley, 1982)

Date, C. J. *An Introduction to Database Systems* vol 1 (Addison-Wesley, 1986)

Everest, G. C. 'The Objectives of Database Management' in Tou, J. T. (ed.) *Information Systems: COINS IV* (Plenus, 1974)

Everest, G. C. and Weber, R. 'A Relational Approach to Accounting Models', *The Accounting Review*, April 1977, 340–59

Fitzgerald, J. *Designing Controls into Computerized Systems* (Jerry Fitzgerald and Associates, 1981)

Gregory, R. H. and Van Horn, R. L. *Automatic Data-Processing Systems: Principles and Procedures* (Chatto and Windus, 2nd edn. 1963)

Hicks, J. O. and Leininger, W. E. *Accounting Information Systems* (West Publishing, 1981)

Hunt, R. and Shelley, J. *Computers and Common Sense* (Prentice-Hall, 3rd edn. 1983)

Kroenke, D. *Database Processing: Fundamentals, Modeling, Applications* (Science Research Associates, 1977)

Martin, J. *Design of Real-time Computer Systems* (Prentice-Hall, 1967)

Martin, J. *Systems Analysis for Data Transmission* (Prentice-Hall, 1972)

Martin, J. *Security, Accuracy and Privacy in Computer Systems* (Prentice-Hall, 1973)

Martin, J. *Computer Database Organisation* (Prentice-Hall International, 1975)

Martin, J. *Principles of Database Management* (Prentice-Hall, 1976)

Murdick, R. G., Fuller, T. C., Ross, J E. and Winnermark, J. E. *Accounting Information Systems* (Prentice-Hall, 1978)

NCC *Introducing Systems Analysis and Design* vol. 1 (National Computing Centre, 1979)

NCC *Introducing Data Processing* (National Computing Centre, 1981)

Page, J. and Hooper, P. *Accounting and Information Systems* (Prentice-Hall International, 1979)

Sanders, D. H. *Computers in Business: An Introduction* (McGraw-Hill Kogakusha, 1979)

Shave, M. *Data Structures* (McGraw-Hill, 1975)

Shave, M. J. R. and Bhaskar, K. N. *Computer Science applied to Business Systems* (Addison-Wesley, 1982)

Skok, W. *Systems and Programming Exercises in Data Processing* (D. P. Publications, 1982)

Thierauf, R. J. *Systems Analysis and Design of Real-Time Management Information Systems* (Prentice-Hall, 1975)

Thierauf, R. J. *Distributed Processing Systems* (Prentice-Hall, 1978)

Yourdon, E. *Design of On-Line Computer Systems* (Prentice-Hall, 1972)

Some useful texts on programming languages

Alcock, D. *Illustrating BASIC: A Simple Programming Language* (Cambridge University Press, 1977)

Atherton, R. *Structured Programming in BBC BASIC* (Ellis Horwood, 1982)

Balfour, A. and Marwick, D. H. *Programming in Standard Fortran 77* (Heinemann, 1979)

Ellis, T. M. R. *A Structured Approach to Fortran 77 Programming* (Addison-Wesley, 1982)

Findlay, W. and Watt, D. A. *Pascal: An Introduction to Methodical Programming* (Pitman, 1978)

Gear, C. W. *Programming and Languages* (Science Research Associates, 1978)

Parker, A. J. and Silbey, V. *BASIC for Business for the PDP11* (Prentice-Hall, 1980)

Parkin, A. *COBOL for Students* (Edward Arnold, 2nd edn. 1982)

Poole, L., Borchers, M. and Donahue, C. *Some Common BASIC Programs: PET/CBM Edition* (Osborne/McGraw-Hill, 1980)

Sawatzky, J. J. and Chen, S.-J. *Programming in BASIC-PLUS* (John Wiley & Sons, 1981)

Part Three

Systems Analysis and the Business Environment

9 Systems theory and control systems

Introduction

In Chapter 1 we gave a very brief introduction to business activities and indicated ways in which computer systems could be used to improve the availability, accuracy, timeliness and value of information. Part Two of the book dealt with computer systems in more detail. In this part, we turn our attention to business organizations and how a business works, accounting information systems and systems control.

A business is primarily an organization of people with resources at their disposal and certain objectives to be attained. For the organization to function properly it requires information systems to support managerial decision-making functions and properly designed procedures for performing activities. The business as a whole consists of a number of subsystems with complex inter-relationships. We shall consider the variety of organizational structures and the information flow in a business but, first, it is worthwhile to consider the theoretical aspects of systems in general and of business systems in particular. Then, in the next chapter, we shall consider the problems and techniques of systems analysis and design. The final chapter in this section will describe business organizations and activities, and accounting information systems.

What is a system?

The term 'system' is used extensively, and sometimes rather loosely, in connection with many different facets of life. We talk of business systems, computer systems, information systems, biological systems, educational systems, social systems and so on. Why can we refer to each of these very different examples as a system? What do they have in common? There are a number of common elements that can be found in the systems mentioned so far. They all interact with the world around them; each system receives inputs from its environment and produces outputs for the environment. They all have a purpose and are composed of a number of parts that interact to achieve a goal or a result. For example, a business system may have as its purpose a corporate goal, such as making a profit. Another important characteristic of a system is that it tends to maintain itself in a steady state. In this sense it is said to be self-regulating. Self-regulation is internal; it is accomplished through the dynamic interaction of component parts or subsystems. Interaction with the environment can result in conditions which upset the normal self-regulation of a system and corrective action may be necessary. Systems are often self-correcting or self-adjusting. The self-correcting capability of a system is partly explained through the concept of 'feedback'. When the system produces an output, it samples that output and information about the effects of that output, and compares it to expected or required output. This information is called feedback as it is fed back into the system as input. It is on the basis of feedback that any required corrective action is taken.

The self-regulating and self-correcting characteristics of systems remind us that most systems are loop-like and not just a linear progression of activities.

We have introduced the concept of a system as a set of inter-related elements that perform some activity, function or operation. The basic elements of a system include:

One or more *inputs* from the environment;
One or more *processes* which are carried out by the system; and
One or more *outputs* from the system.

We have also recognized the loop-like nature of a system indicated by its self-regulating and self-correcting characteristics. Figure 9.1(a) shows a simple system with feedback. A more complex model of a system is illustrated in Figure 9.1(b). This model has n inputs, m outputs, four subsystems and four interfaces between the subsystems. All the inputs and outputs are 'handled' through subsystem 1; the outputs are sampled and the system is informed of any necessary corrective action by feedback.

Every system has a boundary within which it lies and outside of which is its environment. The environment of a business system includes any human, business or political activity that infringes on the business operation. The environment of a management information system includes

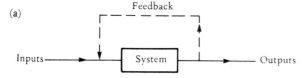

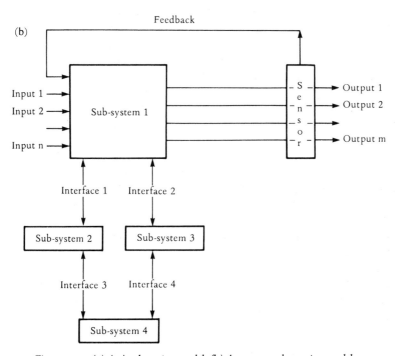

Figure 9.1 (a) *A simple system model,* (b) *A more complex system model*

any source of data for input to the system and anything that responds to or is affected by output from the system. The details of a boundary are sometimes difficult to define and will depend upon the scope of the project or study under consideration. To some extent, the scope may be defined subjectively. For example, when we speak of 'the payroll system' we mean those components and processes of the payroll that we choose to consider relevant and important.

For the management accountant the definition of the boundary of a system is especially important. What might be thought to be externally induced and hence uncontrollable disturbances may in fact originate within the organization. Control might be exerted by extending the boundaries of the system beyond the normal organizational boundaries. A classic case illustrating this is one in which competition depends on *delivery time* rather than price or product reliability:

Firm A, a component manufacturer, sold its products to another manufacturer, Firm B, who incorporated them in their own product. The management of Firm B were faced with the problem of a highly unstable order book, a fluctuation which they passed on to Firm A. The time and rate at which these orders were placed was partly dependent also on Firm A's lead time, changes in which in turn affected Firm B's rate of ordering. This interdependence created a feedback loop which had not been taken account of in Firm A's control system, and by stabilizing their own lead time, unnecessary fluctuations in order rate were eliminated. Firm B's ordering decisions had to be incorporated into Firm A's control system boundaries in order to bring this about.

In this example, what were thought to be externally induced (hence uncontrollable) disturbances were, in fact, shown to have originated within the firm, but were controllable only by extending the boundaries of the system beyond the normal organizational boundaries of the firm.

Levels of systems

Every system consists of other (sub)systems that interface with each other, and this hierarchy often extends through several levels. For example, an order-processing system is a part of the total business system. It is also made up of a number of other subsystems including systems for the order department function, inventory management, credit management, the accounts receivable function, the shipping and receiving function. Some of the subsystems of a system interface with the system's environment and take the form of input or output sensors, e.g. the salesmen of a business system, the input/output peripherals of a computer system, the canvassers of a political system.

Classification of systems

A system whose processes and subsystems are not defined, because for example the objectives of the study do not require it, is called a *black box* system (so called because we need not concern ourselves with what is inside it). For most systems, it is necessary to identify and define carefully the processes that occur and the significant features at each level. Each system is considered in relation to its *level of predictability*, whether it is *open* or *closed*, and its *level of complexity*.

Deterministic and probabilistic systems

A *deterministic* system operates according to a predetermined set of rules. Its future behaviour can be predicted exactly if its current state and operating characteristics are known. A good example of a deterministic system is a computer program. Mechanical systems are also normally deterministic as they are designed to perform in a pre-defined manner receiving certain defined inputs. Business and economic systems are not deterministic because there are many indeterminates such as customer behaviour, supplier reliability, and the national economic situation.

A *probabilistic* system is controlled by chance events and its future behaviour is a matter of probability rather than certainty. Such systems are sometimes called *stochastic* systems. Business and economic systems are probabilistic in nature. For example, stocks of raw materials, parts and finished products are influenced by changes in demand and variations in supply. Stock control systems are implemented to detect such variations and to minimize their effect. Similarly, production activities are subject to variations in respect of availability of manpower and materials, equipment breakdowns, industrial disputes. In such systems, it is not certain what outputs will be obtained from specific inputs and not possible to know precisely what events will occur during processing.

Adaptive (self-organizing) systems

Adaptive and self-organizing systems are dynamic systems which respond to changing circumstances by adjusting their behaviour to achieve and maintain desired levels of performance. This is done by monitoring performance and using feedback to modify system parameters and so achieve self-regulation. Computerized stock control systems are often adaptive. Changes in demand may be sensed and changes implemented to avoid overstocking and stock-out situations. The parameters which may be changed include order point, safety stock level, order quantity, maximum stock level and the frequency of placing an order. Most of the computerized stock control systems currently implemented are not self-adjusting in the sense that changes to parameters must be input manually, but recent advances in self-organizing database management systems, for example, show that fully automatic self-adjusting adaptive systems are feasible.

Open and closed systems

A *closed* system is one that is self-contained and has no interaction with its environment. The concept has more relevance to scientific situations such as a chemical reaction in a sealed container. Such a system, which receives no input from its environment, will eventually run down and become disorganized. The term *entropy* is used as a measure of disorganization. Thus, the entropy of a closed system tends to increase and the system reaches an inert equilibrium state in which its entropy is at a maximum.

Open systems have many interfaces with their environments and are capable of exchanging material energy and information with the environment. An open system will tend to increase its entropy unless it receives 'negative entropy' from its environment and adapts to changes in its environment so that it can continue to exist and to attain its purpose. A business system must be capable of re-organization to cope with its changing environment: products become obsolete, customer preferences change, markets wax and wane. Unless the system feeds on negative entropy it will run down and become disorganized. When functioning properly, an open system reaches a state of dynamic equilibrium. This is a steady state in which the system readily adapts to external influences by re-organizing itself according to the internal forces of its subsystems. With a manufacturing company, for instance, the steady state is buying raw materials, manufacturing and selling products. An environmental factor is an increase in the cost of raw materials. The internal force of its subsystem is increased manufacturing costs, and the consequent re-organization is an increase in the selling prices of the finished products.

For a management information system, the equipment elements, such as the computer, are relatively closed and deterministic; the human element provides an interface with the environment and transforms the system to an open, probabilistic one. The combination of man and the machine can, at one extreme, emphasize the machine with the human simply monitoring the machine's operations whilst, at the other extreme, the human aspects are predominant and the machine has a supporting role (e.g. computation power or the ability to search through large files of data).

Closed systems obey the second law of thermodynamics: they go from less probable to more probable states and eventually reach a stable equilibrium in which entropy is at a maximum. This increase in entropy is an irreversible process. Open systems are fundamentally different; they too are subject to increases in entropy but are able to react with their environment, feed on negative entropy and arrest or reverse the increase in entropy. We call this *entropy transfer*. A system capable of entropy transfer is a net importer from its environment.

The steady state for a closed system is one of maximum entropy (or rundownness). For the completely open system, a steady state is a dynamic equilibrium in which the various subsystems are operating to achieve the system's global objective by recognizing, responding to and adapting to environmental forces and in the process re-organizing itself to adjust its internal working.

A commercial organization is usually a complex, probabilistic, open system which is self-organizing and will change in response to new conditions in the environment. Management decisions affect many of the subsystems of the global system; decisions thus made enable a global system, such as a corporation, to respond to changes in the environment.

Survival and success in a business organization depend upon the ability to monitor the system outputs, to recognize changes in the outside world and to adapt to or react to new opportunities. Like the chemical reaction in a sealed container (a closed system), a firm which is not sensitive to customer demands and other external forces will eventually collapse in the same way as the chemical reaction runs down.

Subsystems

Most systems consist of a number of inter-related subsystems each of which may be further divided, or factored, into smaller subsystems until a level is reached at which the subsystems are of a manageable size. This process is important as an aid to simplifying what might otherwise be a very complex situation. The process of repeated divisions into sub-systems can introduce another problem: communication between the various subsystems. A system with four subsystems has six interfaces as illustrated in Figure 9.2; for 20 subsystems there can be up to 190 inter-faces and in general for n subsystems there are either $n/2$ $(n-1)$ or $n(n-1)/2$ interfaces. Of course, not all subsystems interconnect with all others, nevertheless the problem of communication between subsystems can be a serious one and two techniques are commonly used to simplify the interfaces and communication among subsystems. The first is to establish clusters of subsystems and define a single communication chan-nel between one cluster and another (see Figure 9.3). A second method is to reduce the co-ordination required between two subsystems. A system which is tightly coupled requires close co-ordination and timing between subsystems.

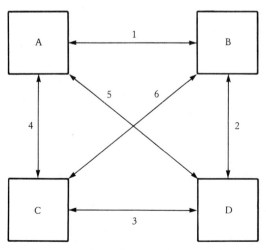

Figure 9.2   *Four subsystems with six interfaces*

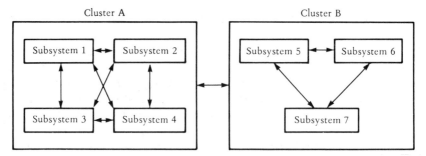

Figure 9.3   *Single communication between two clusters*

The above system is connected within a cluster, and the two clusters are interconnected via a single interface. If all the subsystems were linked, then the total number of interfaces would be 21; in the above it has been reduced to 10.

Methods of decoupling fall into three categories:

1   *Inventories, buffers or waiting lines;*
2   *Slack and flexible resources* allowing subsystems to be somewhat independent and yet responsive when the output of one subsystem is the input to another system;
3   *Standards* (e.g. specifications or standard costs) allow a subsystem to plan and operate with reduced need to communicate with other subsystems.

The process of decoupling confers benefits in allowing subsystems a degree of independence in managing their affairs, but at a cost of the decoupling mechanism itself (e.g. inventories, additional capacity or a standard costing system). Davies (1974)* has this to say about the choice:

> 'The issue of alternating structures can be seen in questions of centralized (tightly coupled) versus decentralized (loosely coupled) organizations. As one proceeds from the loosely coupled system to a more tightly coupled one, there are benefits from system-wide optimization, but there are also costs of co-ordination and communication. The changing level of independent responsibility assigned to each subsystem (generally less in a tightly coupled system) may affect productivity by the human components. Thus, each system structure has advantages and disadvantages. There is no single, general answer. However, the experience of system designers in man-dominated and in man/machine systems suggests the need for at least some decoupling. These types of systems have so many random and probabilistic elements that individual subsystems must have some independence.'

*Pages 94–95.

Communication in business systems

For a system to function effectively it must be controlled. This involves an element of communication. Information must be conveyed between one subsystem and another; information must be provided for management as a basis for decisions to control the state of a system. The information provided must be timely, sufficiently detailed, and accurate. Distorted, inaccurate, or out-of-date information may result in the state of the system being misinterpreted and incorrect action to remedy the situation may be applied.

There is an extensive mathematical theory of communications developed mainly in relation to telecommunications, but the concepts are relevant to data communications in digital computer systems including computerized business systems and, to a lesser extent, to other business systems. The theory also provides insight into the nature of information.

A simple model of the communication system is shown in Figure 9.4.

A message is transmitted from its source by sending coded symbols through a channel to a receiver which decodes the symbols and passes the message to its destination. The channel is subject to noise and distortion: noise is random or unpredictable interference, distortion is caused by a known operation (correctable by an inverse operation). In more general terms, noise alters the content of a message received from that which is meant to be conveyed. In a business system this can arise simply by misinterpretation of the context of a message, the use of jargon not understood by the recipient, interference on a telephone line during a conversation, too much padding in a report which hides essential facts, and inadequately worded communications.

A management accountant may also communicate in the way portrayed in Figure 9.4. An accountant may be the originator or source of a message that material costs are out of control. This message will probably be transmitted through the 'code' of a variance analysis and report. A manager – the recipient of the message – will receive the coded message by means of the internal mail (the communication channel) and will decode it so that the appropriate action can be taken to reduce material costs.

Redundancy

Some redundancy is often incorporated into communications to overcome the problem of noise. Redundancy implies that additional bits or characters are included in the transmitted message so that in the event of loss or distortion of some elements the original message can be reconstructed at its destination. For example, a message written in English can

Source → **Transmitter** → **Channel** → **Receiver** → Destination
Encoder   **Decoder**

↑

Noise and
Distortion

Figure 9.4   *Representation of a communications system*

suffer a number of changes in the spelling or in the characters transmitted. The message 'How are you?' could still be understood if the characters received were

	H*W	ARE	Y*U?
or even	HOW	AER	YUO?
or possibly even	H	R	U	?

However, the transposition of the first word to give

WHO ARE YOU?

would result in misinterpretation of the original message.

The concept of redundancy means that the receiver need not decode every element of the message in order to deduce its meaning. The greater the degree of redundancy, the more noise and distortion that can be tolerated without destroying the information content to the recipient. In data transmission, the incorporation of suitable additional bits of information enables errors in the message to be automatically detected and corrected.

Accountants often store the same information twice to prevent mistakes or fraud; an example of which is the control account. Other examples of redundancy are:

The spelling out of a value in addition to presenting it in the normal way, e.g. £35 (thirty five pounds);
The inclusion of a parity bit in binary-coded information in computer systems;
The use of check digits to ensure the accuracy of stock numbers, etc. in data-processing applications.

These and other examples of techniques for control and security were discussed in Chapter 8.

Redundancy and management reports

Redundancy incorporated in management reports tends to obscure the essential facts. There is a limit to the amount of information that humans can digest; reports should therefore be restricted to important details and highlight the most significant facts. For example, a complete listing of cost-centre budgeted expenditure and actual expenditure, although conveying all the facts, does not convey a clear picture of the situation directly. The manager concerned would have to go through the whole list item by item and establish the significance of each fact for himself. If the reporting is restricted to items with significant variations of actual expenditure from budgeted expenditure, then a much greater impact is made and the manager can quickly respond to the situation disclosed.

Data reduction

Since humans have limited data-processing capacity, constraints must be applied to information systems in order to limit the volume of data presented to humans. Figure 9.5 illustrates some of the concepts applied in the reduction of data volume.

Classification and compression

Data may be classified or summarized under various heads or codes (e.g. product groupings) rather than transmitting all the individual data items.

Organizational summarizing and filtering

Messages are summarized and filtered in various ways as they are reported up a hierarchical organization structure (i.e. only important messages are subsequently passed on to the next higher level).

Information, as distinct from data, is defined in terms of its usefulness to the recipient. As such, information usually refers to the result of some processing of raw data. Hence the process of data reduction can yield useful information from raw data. Another way of generating information from raw data is to draw *inferences* from the body of data and to communicate the inferences instead of the data itself to the decision makers.

Data reduction techniques simplify the problems of communication among subsystems of a system by reducing the volumes of data communicated. However, they do imply a certain risk of noise or distortion; the wrong information may be excluded, or the information may be distorted to achieve the objectives of one particular subsystem rather than of the organization as a whole. For example, customer complaints of salesmen's tactics in a sales district may be blocked by the district sales manager who does not wish the criticism to reflect on him since he initiated these tactics in the first place.

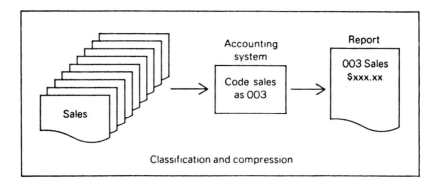

Classification and compression

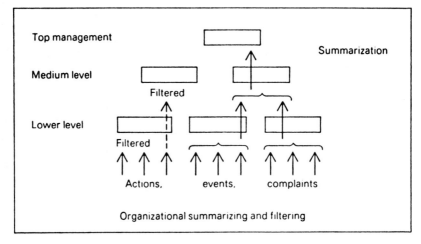

Organizational summarizing and filtering

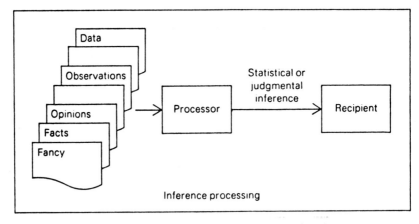

Inference processing

Figure 9.5   *Data reduction methods* Source: *Davies (1974), p. 43*

Controlling systems

A prior concept to control within an organization is the recognition that systems are goal-seeking and that planning provides the criteria managers must meet in order to achieve prescribed goals. Planning is vital for an organization and is the foundation of good management. Without plans it would be impossible to determine whether a system was under control, since there would be nothing with which to compare its actual progress. The basic systems model (see Figure 9.1) includes a feedback loop for regulation and control of the system. Figure 9.6 shows the model in more detail. Outputs from the system are compared with the designed output and any difference causes an input signal to be sent to the process to adjust operations so that the output will be close to the plan. This corrective signal is the result of *negative feedback* because the feedback seeks to dampen or reduce the fluctuation from the standard. Positive feedback would cause a system to repeat or amplify its deviation.

An example of negative feedback in an accounting system is the examination of debts due from customers. These are compared with predetermined standards (credit limits) and those outside the standards give rise to an input control signal that restricts the customer's future trading with the company. Without this negative feedback the customer's debts would tend to increase, more bad debts would be incurred and the system would become disorganized.

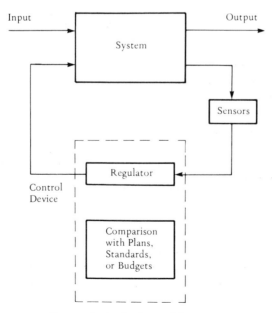

Figure 9.6   *Feedback control for a system*

Controlling is a process which involves a number of stages:

Establishment of desired goals of the system;

Production of detailed plans or budgets to meet the desired performance;

Design and implementation of a measuring device (i.e. sensor) which gathers data related to the output of the system;

Communication of the information from the previous stage to management;

Evaluation by management of the actual performance against that planned, this stage can be likened to a control unit which compares the actual measurement with a standard;

Generation of a corrective input signal to the system; this process is the consequent managerial action necessary to keep an organization in control (i.e. according to the plan plus or minus some range).

A large deviation from a plan may be caused by a number of factors which include the following:

1   Unforeseen change in the environment (e.g. dramatic change in the price of raw material);
2   Incorrect plans (e.g. failure to correctly forecast demand for a new product);
3   Inefficiency within the system;
4   Lack of motivation by workforce and/or management.

A deviation from the target may be due to a combination of several reasons. In some cases, the difference between unforeseen changes in the environment and incorrect plans is a marginal one – good planning should allow for many of the 'unforeseen changes' identified in a less accurate planning framework. For example, a good planning system should be able to forecast changes in the prices of raw materials. Sudden switches in policy by a government are a better example of what may be classified as unforeseen changes.

Once a deviation or variance from a plan has been detected, management has the difficult job of determining whether to follow up the variance with an investigation of what went wrong. Without correctly identifying the reason for the variance it is unlikely that any action by management will permanently correct the problem. On the other hand, management resources are limited and one of the costs of such an investigation is the increased benefit that might accrue to the system by management spending its time elsewhere. (This is the opportunity cost concept.) In general, management might obey the following decision rule*: choose that course of action which minimizes total costs.

*This is set within a cost framework but, with the inclusion of revenue, could be set within a total profit framework.

If investigation occurs, then

> total cost = cost of investigation plus total planned costs for all future periods – this assumes permanent correction of the problem;

else, if there is no investigation, then

> total cost = total actual costs which may be permanently out of control.

Note that the above assumes a two-state process: once a system has gone out of control, it is deemed to remain out of control. In practice, in a probabilistic system, there are always some random disturbances, and management may wish to be convinced that a variable is out of control (and not merely subject to a random disturbance) before taking action. The likely probabilities of whether a process is in or out of control and whether an investigation should ensue is a matter for the judgement of management.

Techniques for aiding control

There are two other techniques for aiding control, one, that of filtering, we have already come across. Filters should be used to reduce unneeded or irrelevant data being passed on to another subsystem. Filtering can occur either by reducing the number of inputs to another system or reducing the quantity of information transmitted to another subsystem.

A second aid to obtaining control concerns the *law of requisite variety*: there must be as many variations of controls to be applied as there are ways for the system to get out of control. If an element in a system gets out of control, for example the inventory of a particular piece of raw material, then there must be a mechanism to respond to that particular control-state independently and without detrimentally affecting any other elements within the subsystem or any other subsystem. In this example, a person or machine must be able to reduce the inventory of that raw material without affecting the other inventories; this can be achieved by designing the system in such a way that it is possible to take decisions about that specific raw material and, moreover, someone has the responsibility to ensure that decisions are made routinely to achieve this end.

Another principle which is useful in controlling a system is the *principle of equifinality*: a relatively open system can reach a given objective from a number of different initial conditions – there is often no single best way of achieving the system's global objectives. Management, in controlling an organization, may require new o⁻ different information, necessitated by changing events in the environment. One objective in designing a system should be, subject to cost considerations, to design systems which promote the maximum flexibility towards information.

Feedback control systems

The justification for a feedback control system is that it should create a dynamic, self-regulating system. Because the system has a built-in ability to restore the process to equilibrium, the system can operate for long periods of time, correcting itself when necessary without external intervention. In the science of *Cybernetics*, which involves the study of such feedback control systems, the process of restoring a system to the desired state when it is subjected to changing environmental conditions is called *homeostasis*. We may interpret homeostasis as the process of holding steady the parameters essential to system effectiveness despite disturbances and buffeting. In a stock control system, unusual variations in demand and supply may be interpreted as disturbances to normal behaviour. Safety stocks are designed to cope with this situation to some extent but, in the case of extreme variations, the stock control parameters may require modification to allow for the changing trends. Cushing (1978) lists four essential properties for the successful application of feedback control systems in a business organization.

1 A control system should have a benefit value at least as great as the cost of advertising it.
2 The measurement part of the control system should report deviations from standards on a timely basis. (The longer the information lag, the less successful will be the control system.)
3 Feedback reports should be simple and easy to understand. Important relationships should be highlighted and factors requiring attention should be directed to the manager responsible.
4 A feedback control system should be integrated with the organizational structure of which they are part.

The classic example of a feedback control system is a central heating system. The components of the system include a boiler linked to radiators (the process), a thermostat (the measurement system), heat (the characteristic of the process which is the subject of control), the desired temperature (the standard or criteria against which the measured state of the process is evaluated) and a switch linked to the desired temperature and the thermostat (the regulator). The system, on detecting that the temperature of the room has fallen below that desired, will take action by switching on the boiler and thereby heating the room. Once the room has reached its desired temperature the regulator will switch the boiler off until a comparison with the desired temperature once again signals action.

Although a business cannot operate as precisely and automatically as a thermostat, the analogy is useful. Some examples of control systems commonly found in businesses are shown in Table 9.1; these are credit control, standard costing systems, internal auditing, and responsibility accounting systems.

Feedforward control systems

Feedback control systems suffer the disadvantage that they do not signal a deviation until after it has become significant; costly deviation from plans may worsen before corrective action can be taken or become effective. The elements of a feedforward control system include:

A measurement and a prediction system which assesses the system and predicts the output of the system at some future date;
A regulator which compares predictions of the system's output to a set of standards and takes corrective action when this comparison indicates a possible future deviation (see Figure 9.7.)

The distinguishing feature of a feedforward control system is that it also

Table 9.1   Examples of feedback systems After Cushing (1982) pp. 81–82

Responsibility accounting systems.   The assignment of responsibilities within an organization to organizational units is called responsibility accounting.

Standard cost systems.   A standard cost refers to the cost that should be incurred in producing a unit of product under efficient operating conditions; the total standard cost per unit of product may be broken down into costs of material components, labour and overhead elements, and by departments or other cost centres. Actual costs are compiled on a per unit basis and compared with standards to obtain two or more general types of standard cost variances such as a price variance which indicates that portion of a total variance which is attributable to a deviation from a standard rate or price (e.g. a labour rate or a material price) and an efficiency or usage variance which indicates that portion of a total variance which is attributable to a deviation from some standard amount of usage, say labour hours, or material quantities.

Credit control.   The characteristic of the credit system which is the subject of control is the loss from bad debts. The information system can provide information about the aging of debtors' balances and information relating to bad debts written off as uncollectable during a given period.

Internal audit.   There are two aspects of internal audit function which provide feedback for management control. First, the independent appraisal of the performance of various levels of management provides information on the effectiveness of subordinate managers. Second reviewing and assessing the system of preventive controls within an organization provides information on the effectiveness of that system.

Production control.   The production control process is concerned with efficiency in the production process. The characteristic being controlled is often time or material usage.

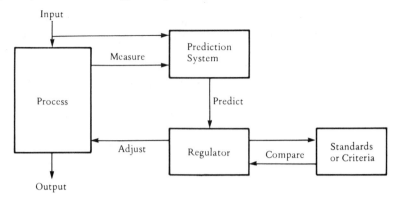

Figure 9.7   *A feedforward control system* Source: *Cushing (1982), p. 83*

involves monitoring of inputs to the system. Examples of feedforward control systems are shown in Table 9.2.

Preventive control systems

Preventive control systems can be distinguished from the feedback and feedforward control systems in that they are an internal part of the process encompassing policies and procedures which form part of the system – i.e. they exercise a measure of *internal control*. Very often, such internal controls are viewed as an integral part of the accounting system.

One important example of a preventive control system is the separation of assigned duties (sometimes known as organizational independence). For example, it is common to segregate those functions involving the custody of assets (e.g. writing cheques or handling cash) from those functions involving the recording of transactions. Another important example of a preventive control system is the physical protection of assets. For example, access to cash should be limited to responsible employees following written-down policies and procedures.

Preventive control systems are usually especially relevant where there is the possibility of fraud; examples include: payment of a wage to a non-existent employee ('the ghost'), payment for goods (which have not

Table 9.2   Examples of feedforward control systems

Cash planning.   Cash planning systems help to maintain the organization's cash balance at some desired level.

Inventory control.   An inventory control system controls the operation of ordering, storing, and making available when needed within the organization, various items of raw materials, parts and supplies, and finished goods inventories.

New product development.   A new-product development program will attempt to introduce a successful new product while making efficient use of time, cost, and other resources.

been received) to a hypothetical company, sale of a commodity to a person which has not been recorded, and so on. Any operation which involves the payment of money must be closely monitored and checked. But the organization's raw materials, work-in-progress (partly finished goods) and finished goods must also be closely controlled – their loss is just as important as the loss of cash.

The design of documents, especially those which capture the transaction information (often called *source documents*), is also important; documents should be designed to facilitate the collection of all necessary information about the transaction or event. A sound business practice is the sequential pre-numbering of all documents; this ensures that every document is accounted for.

One important facility in preventive control systems is concerned with the ability to trace individual transactions through the system; this facilitates correction of errors and the verification of output information in a system. The term *audit trail* is given to the path which a transaction takes through a system starting from a source document and ending up as an aggregate figure in a summary report.

Conclusion

The management accountant and systems analyst are interested in breaking down a complex organization into a system which itself can be divided into a number of subsystems, each of which has a boundary and interfaces to other subsystems. Each subsystem, however, must be integrated into the whole and operate in accordance with the global objectives of the system. A systems analyst is also concerned with the behaviour of business organizations which are complex, human, probabilistic, open systems. One of the principal objectives is to allow a system to adapt to its environment; this can be achieved by means of feedback and feedforward systems. However, preventive control systems form an integral part of the basic system. The key problem areas that confront the systems analyst include*:

Identifying the whole system boundaries;
Identifying subsystems and their boundaries;
Dealing with problems of interface;
Maintaining a system's dynamic interaction with its environment;
Building control into systems;
Building flexibility into systems;
Resolving conflicting objectives in a system.

From the point of view of the management accountant, one of the major

*Based on NCC (1978) p. 20.

lessons to be learnt from systems theory is that systems must be designed to increase the firm's ability to learn and adapt rapidly. The firm's information system must enable the management accountant, and through him (or her) management in general, to identify problems and their inter-relationships both quickly and effectively. The information system should also allow management to plan and make decisions and implement and control those decisions and plans once made. If the system is to adapt and learn effectively, it must not be too mechanistic or inflexible. Amey (1980) emphasizes this point:

> 'It should enable the firm to learn from its own mistakes, be self-correcting, and become better at doing this over time. It should also increase the firm's ability to cope with variety in its environment – in short, to learn more about its changing environment, and to stimulate curiosity, experimentation, innovation, and creativity.
>
> Probably most existing management information systems do not come close to meeting these needs by encouraging organisational flexibility rather than rigidity, ensuring that relevant information is communicated where it should be (between interdependent functions or activities), and not communicated where it should not be (unrelated functions) and providing sufficient information on the environment so that the system can seek to match its orientation to the environment, if that is its objective, or at least keeping it fully informed about its relevant environment if its objective is to change parts of that environment to its own design. In a rapidly changing environment, rigidly prescribed information search and collection routines and screening rules, and standard operating procedures, can exert strong inertial or even destabilising effects, inhibiting adaptation and learning.'

10 Systems analysis and design

Introduction

The objective of systems analysis is to study in depth the aims and problems of existing business activities and to design new systems that will correct or overcome problems, make more effective use of available resources and enable the organization to attain its goals as efficiently as possible. What makes the task particularly challenging is that the system goals are not static. The requirements of a system are continually evolving as the business objectives of the organization are modified in response to the environment. The design of a system should be 'open ended' so that further applications and enhancements to existing applications can be introduced without duplication of work or records.

The systems analyst has a very delicate role to play. He needs a thorough understanding not only of the business structure and organization, of system development methodologies and of the latest technology, but also of human relations. The systems analyst is highly reliant upon other people to answer questions about particular job functions: What is being done? Why is it being done? Who is doing it? How is it being done? What are the major problems involved in doing it? What is not being done that should be done? The systems analyst requires basic communications skills; effective communication is necessary to ensure that the right systems and procedures are developed to attain the company's objectives and in ways that meet the needs of management, operators, users, and all who are affected either directly or indirectly by the system.

In this chapter we consider the problems of system development, then we discuss the role of the systems analyst in the various systems activities, and the tools and techniques available to assist the analyst in these activities.

Problems associated with systems analysis and design

Problems of communication between the user and the systems analyst give rise to major difficulties in understanding the user's environment and in the subsequent specification of the user's requirements. These difficulties are compounded by continuous change in the user's environment and in the detailed requirements for the new system.

It is very hard for a systems analyst to learn enough about the user's environment to observe the existing system from the user's point of view. Similarly, the user does not have the appropriate knowledge to formulate a clear, consistent and complete specification of requirements. The analysis task therefore requires close cooperation between the user and the analyst in a partnership which the analyst is usually expected to manage.

Much of the investigation and analysis phase in any project is spent acquiring detailed information about the existing system. The volume of such information can be overwhelming and if the analyst is not to become overloaded with facts and paper some scheme or structure is necessary to organize the details. The detail is needed and must be readily available when required, so the analyst must have tools and techniques to control it.

The document which specifies the detail of the new system is effectively a contract between the user and the designer. It must be possible for the user to understand and at the same time must be sufficiently formal to serve as a specification for the design. If the document is vague, inconsistent or incomplete, then it is not a satisfactory basis for the design. On the other hand, if it is too formal for the user to understand then the user may not feel bound by it, no contract will exist, and the user will feel free to change the requirements at any time. Changing the requirements at a late stage is a major reason for late delivery and overspend.

A particular problem at the design stage is the difficulty of separating detailed technical design, i.e. *how* the design can be implemented, from *what* is to be implemented. Ideally, logical design of processes and data structures should be determined and documented before technical details of the physical implementation are added to the documentation.

Another problem with systems development is the absence of any agreed notation common to all stages of development. Changes from one notation to another as the development project progresses from one stage to the next can introduce errors of interpretation. The notation used must be intelligible both to the customer and to the designer of the new system. This is particularly true of the notation used to describe the existing

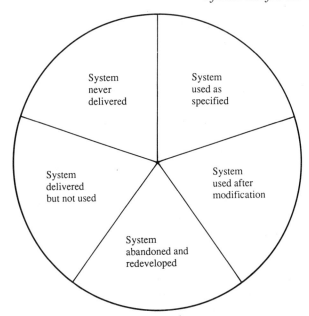

Figure 10.1   *Typical results of developing a system*

system and to specify the requirements of the new system. Misunderstandings at this level are a major cause of systems not meeting the user's requirements. Figure 10.1 shows typical proportions of the results of developing a system.

If a specification is written in 'natural' language only, it is impossible to ensure that the system design meets the specification of requirements. Natural language is vague and a complex specification in natural language is likely to be incomplete and contradictory.

The development of computer systems is a complex, problem-solving activity. The major problems associated with it can be deduced from the symptoms evident in many development projects. These appear in the form of:

Development costs which are over budget;
Development timescales in excess of planned timescales;
Production systems which do not meet the user's requirements, are unreliable and which are difficult to modify and maintain.

The root cause of the problem is the scale and complexity of many system development projects. Computers make some things more efficient and have opened up areas of application that were once impossible to contemplate. We need a framework within which the complexity of such applications can be managed.

A methodology for the development of the specification of requirements and for the design specification is required to overcome these problems. A methodology is a way of structuring one's thinking about an area of study. It facilitates the decomposition of a large complex task into smaller subtasks each of which can be considered in appropriate detail, at the appropriate time without loss of information and without risk of distraction by other subtasks which, for the time being, are irrelevant. A systems analysis and design methodology should provide a framework which leads towards the achievement of specific objectives. However, use of such a structured methodology does not guarantee success; the achievement of objectives depends upon a number of criteria. A number of tools and techniques have been developed to help cope with complexity. Later in this chapter we shall describe a structured systems analysis and design methodology but first we present an overview of the system life-cycle and the principal phases of the system development process.

The system life-cycle

A new system project may be triggered off by any one of a number of events, such as those listed below.

(a) A difficulty encountered in operating an existing system: changing patterns in workloads may result in unacceptable delays in issuing invoices, perhaps not enough staff can be recruited to do the processing, a lot of mistakes are being reported, there may be an increasing number of customer complaints;

(b) A manager may hear of a successful system in another organization and see a similar application in his own;

(c) There may be dissatisfaction with the level of indirect expenses such as administrative costs;

(d) A sales representative from a computer manufacturer, service bureau, or software house may encourage a manager to take an interest in a particular applications package or system;

(e) There may be a review of the business objectives of an organization in response to changing external factors.

Prior to initiation of the project, little formal analysis of the existing or possible alternative systems may have been carried out, although the possibility of a change may have been in the minds of management for some time. Figure 10.2 shows a simplified view of the life-cycle of a system. First, we have a project selection phase during which the current system is investigated, the problem is identified and defined, terms of reference and objectives are determined and a new project is selected according to certain criteria, possibly from among a number of alternative projects. There follows a series of development phases: analysis,

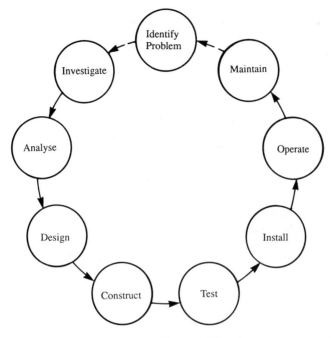

Figure 10.2   *The system life-cycle*

design, construction, testing and installation of the new system, all of which take place while the existing system is in operation. There is usually a period of parallel operation during which account is taken of users' reactions while the old system is still in use. When the new system has been thoroughly checked out, the old system is dropped and the new system becomes fully operational. During the development phases, a *conversion system* may have to be developed and brought into operation prior to the introduction of the new system. For example, if an existing manual system is to be replaced by a new computer-based system, it may be necessary to produce a conversion system which establishes and maintains files of data on disks prior to implementation of the new system when these files will be used and maintained by the new system.

Even when the new system is fully operational there will be maintenance tasks to be performed which will involve the systems analyst; errors will arise, performance may need to be enhanced, and applications extended or modified to meet the changing needs of the organization.

The systems development process

The systems process commences with the definition of the problem. The systems analyst is rarely asked to find out if a problem exists. Usually, management becomes aware of a problem and asks the analyst to assess the existing system and propose ways of improving it. It is not always easy for the analyst to discover the precise nature of a problem. Much fact-finding is necessary and many answers need to be obtained before a clear systems definition of the problem can be determined. This can be a time-consuming and expensive stage in the systems process, but it is important to do it thoroughly, for after this stage the analyst has to formulate clear objectives for the remainder of the project. Errors or misunderstandings at this stage can be very expensive to correct if not discovered until late in the design or implementation phases. It is not necessary to discover all possible facts and information before beginning to define the requirements of any proposed system, indeed it is doubtful whether it is possible to discover all the facts as that would be a never-ending task. Nevertheless, the volume of information could be overwhelming unless it is well structured. The experienced analyst will be able to organize the information so that he or she can access what is relevant at any particular time. This fact-finding involves personal consultations not only with top management but with managers of affected departments, the data processing department (particularly those members involved in operating the system), internal users of the system and possibly some external users such as customers who will be affected by any proposed changes.

In the first report to management the analyst will present a clear systems definition of the problem, together with outlines of some alternative proposals for its solution with a qualitative assessment of their relative advantages and disadvantages. It is not for the analyst to decide which system should be adopted for further detailed investigation, although, of course, recommendations can be made and the way in which the report is presented can influence management in their decision. It is important for the analyst to present relevant facts and information on which a decision can be based but preferably not to become too involved in the actual selection of the system. The analyst should be, and should be seen to be, impartial.

Figure 10.3 presents a simple overview of the activities described so far. Whilst we may isolate the activities in an attempt to obtain a clear understanding of them, they are highly inter-related. We start with a statement of the problem from management, collect some relevant data, analyse and assess it. This may enable us to refine the definition of the problem, or the need for more data may become apparent before further progress can be made. Eventually, a tentative specification of requirements may be formulated and outline designs of alternative systems considered, but these too will need to be tested, evaluated and modified, and will possibly show the need for more fact-finding. This is a complex iterative process with the problem definition becoming more precise as more relevant facts

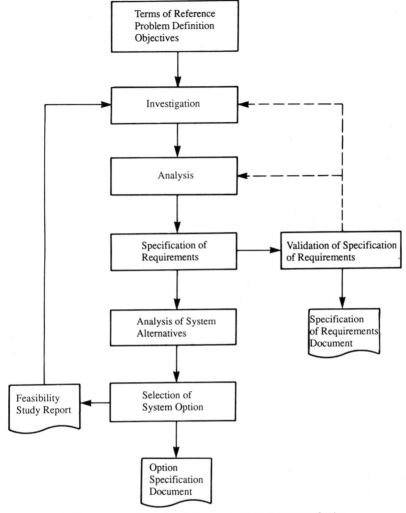

Figure 10.3   *Overview of system process up to system selection*

are found. Requirements become more firm and eventually one or more alternative systems will be outlined from which one will be selected for detailed investigation and development.

The first major activity after system selection is the detailed feasibility study. This includes determination of a number of fine measures of the effectiveness of the selected system and the application of these measures. The results may lead to further modifications to the specifications of requirements but very rarely to rejection of the selected system in favour of one of the alternatives. The system has already been subjected to a number of coarse measures of effectiveness in the evaluation prior to selection.

The feasibility study will include an analysis of estimated costs and benefits of the system. The cost of the system has a significant bearing on its feasibility. However, until some programs have actually been designed, developed and tested it is difficult to obtain reliable estimates of costs. Software development costs seem always to be grossly under-estimated! Feasibility is something which has to be reviewed throughout the development process.

Development of the systems proposal

If the selected system is to be developed and implemented successfully the systems analyst will need the confidence and full support of everyone affected by the proposed system. All concerned must understand what is being proposed and appreciate how it will solve existing problems. The 'systems proposal' is a formal written document containing a detailed specification of requirements and setting out the nature and scope of the proposed solution. It is studied by each party concerned, modified as required and eventually formally agreed to. Thereafter, it serves as a contractual basis for the remainder of the project. Any further modification must be agreed to in writing by the parties affected. This degree of formality is desirable since the agreed proposal is an agreement between the parties, and mutual understanding is essential from the beginning.

Pilot systems and prototyping

If a proposed solution is so novel or the techniques so unfamiliar that people are not easily convinced that it will work, it may be necessary first to develop only a part of the system or to produce a quick and 'dirty' prototype version at limited cost. This enables the organization to test the proposed ideas without committing the full resources needed to develop the system as a whole. A substantial number of projects fail to realize the full benefits originally anticipated. There may well be high risks in the project which are not fully understood at the time of the feasibility study. The proposed system may meet resistance from the company's work force or from customers. A proposal to change established patterns of work of a large number of employees should be reviewed carefully by representatives from each affected section. A limited pilot scheme may be a convenient means of demonstrating some of the advantages of the system. For example, when a new software tool is acquired, users will want to know how it compares with existing systems. A prototype would give the user the 'look' and 'feel' of the new system without all the features being available.

The advantages of producing a prototype are:

(a) The prototype can form a clear reference point for the user and systems developer to discuss the features of the system. The prototype can be modified so that different options and facilities can be experimented with. In some cases the whole system may be developed by modification and enlargement. This is known as iterative prototyping.

(b) The user gets to experience the user interface at an early stage in design process and any major design faults – from the user's point of view – can be eliminated at this stage. The last thing the systems designer wants to be told at the end of the project is that the system is not what the user envisaged.

(c) Normally systems requirements would be clearly defined, but where this proves difficult a prototype can be used as a basis for the progressive refinement of system requirements.

Systems design and program development

Once agreement has been reached on the specification of requirements, the design phase can proceed (see Figure 10.4). This involves logical design of processes and data including details of inputs and outputs, file structures and database design. This overall systems design is followed by physical design: translation of logical data design into more detailed file or database specifications and process outlines into structured operations which can be refined step by step until they are at a level suitable for implementation and testing. Successive levels of design are inspected and validated for consistency with the formally agreed specification of requirements. An important part of the design process is the design of a test strategy in parallel with the process design. It is inevitable that errors will be introduced in the complex process of software development. A structured methodology is required to facilitate the earliest possible detection of errors in design and to ensure that all necessary testing of relevant components is repeated when any change is made to the system.

Ideally the systems analyst has no involvement in the detailed design and testing of programs. The job of the analyst is to provide clear specifications of system requirements, to be available to provide additional information and clarify requirements if requested by programmers, to establish a basis for testing the reliability and accuracy of programs as they are developed, and to maintain close contact with programming management to ensure that programs are developed to specification and on time.

As more firm information becomes available throughout the design and development stages of the project, estimated costs are updated and the

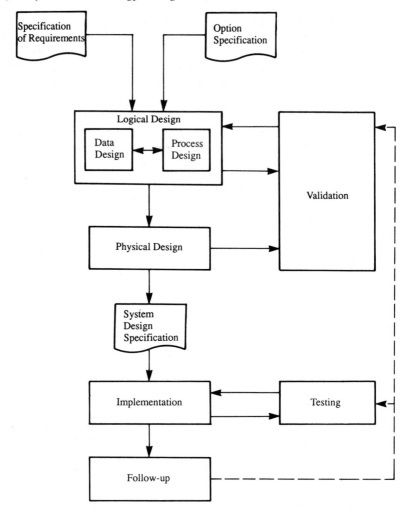

Figure 10.4   *Overview of system process from design to completion*

assessment and evaluation of the project is reviewed. Detailed requirements and objectives may need to be revised subject to the agreement of all parties affected by them. The results of testing and evaluation can affect the design and construction activities and provide further data needed for the feasibility study.

Final testing of the system as a whole can be carried out during a period of parallel running: that is, all the procedures of the new system are carried out whilst the old system is still in operation, giving a final opportunity to check user reaction to the new system before the old one is superseded. This is the point at which the new system can be said to be fully implemented. The costs of running the two systems in parallel may be high but the safety factor involved may well be worth the additional cost. Even after full implementation, some problems may arise: errors will be found in some of the programs, operators and users may have difficulty in adjusting to new procedures for doing the work. For a short period after implementation the systems analyst should be available to offer advice and to supervise any modifications that may be necessary to ensure the smooth operation of the system. This follow-up activity must be of limited duration; there must be some point at which the systems analyst's involvement in the project comes to an end.

In the preceding paragraphs we have given a brief overview of the main activities involved in the system development process. These include:

Problem definition and statement of objectives;
Investigation;
Specification of requirements;
Analysis of systems alternatives;
Selection of system option;
Feasibility study;
Logical design of data and processes;
Detailed physical design;
Implementation;
Follow-up.

Throughout the process the analyst is responsible for testing and evaluating data, and measuring and reviewing the effectiveness of the proposed system as more concrete information becomes available. Reliable estimates of costs are not available until the project is well advanced. The value of some benefits cannot be estimated until after implementation; even then it is difficult to evaluate intangible benefits of the system. Documentation must be produced at each stage of the process; this will include: reports for the initiators of the project and for those who authorize continuation to the next stage; detailed specifications for those who will construct the programs; and finally, separate documentation for users of the system and for those who will maintain the system. Table 10.1 sets out some of the deliverables at various stages of the process.

The structured systems analysis and design methodology

We have referred to the need for a structured methodology to organize the enormous amount of information relating to a project and to cope with the complexity of projects. Many computer applications are so large that no one individual can comprehend the full detail of the entire system. We need to decompose a system into a number of smaller subsystems or

Table 10.1   Documentation deliverable at the end of each phase of the project

Phase	End of phase deliverables
Project selection	Terms of reference, statement of objectives
Feasibility study	Feasibility report to the sponsor including estimated costs and likely benefits
Analysis	Formal specification of requirements Revised project plan Analysis of costs and benefits

Design	System design specification including:
	    hardware specifications where relevant
	    logical data design and logical process design
	    physical design of detailed files and data base
	    detailed program design
	    test strategy
	Revised project plan
	Revised analysis of costs and benefits
	Training manuals

Construction	Documented programs Test data and results The working system Consumables requirements
Follow-up	Post-implementation evaluation report to the sponsor Analysis of costs and benefits

functions. Further decomposition and thus a greater level of detail and understanding can be obtained by zooming in and decomposing each of the subsystems until a level is reached at which each subsystem can be described accurately, precisely and unambiguously. There are a number of well-established tools and techniques to assist the analyst and software developer with such an approach. The *Structured Systems Analysis and Design Methodology (SSADM)* is a structuring of well-known techniques into a comprehensive methodology.

SSADM commences with the organization of investigation notes and concludes with the production of a detailed design specification for implementors. It does not include stages for fact-finding or implementation. The investigation phase relies on techniques such as interviewing which are common to many business situations. We shall return to these in a later section. Implementation commences with programming and testing, for which structured techniques are already well established. SSADM fills the gap between investigation and implementation. It does not concentrate on any one technique but is a collection of techniques, each being chosen for its appropriateness to a particular task. In the following sections we give brief descriptions of some of the most important tools and techniques. These include:

(a) Data flow diagrams which show the boundary of a system and its relationship to the environment. They also show the functions, data stores, input and output for the system;

(b) Entity/function matrices showing the entities affected by each function;

(c) Entity models which show the data structures and data relationships for the system;

(d) Entity life histories which provide a dynamic view of the system showing how each entity is affected by system functions and the sequence in which the functions are carried out;

(e) Process outlines which specify the operations necessary to process a transaction in the system and lead towards the production of program specifications.

A basic technique used in logical data design is normalization. This is a process for transforming complex data structures into simple list structures. It is used to identify entities and to create an entity model which can be checked against the entity model constructed in the analysis stage; any differences can then be resolved. Normalization was discussed in Chapter 6 and is not considered further here.

SSADM includes an integrated set of documents which support the methodology. User reviews of the documents are a formal part of SSADM. These take the form of inspections and walk-throughs for quality control purposes; they also serve as a useful way of monitoring project progress.

Data flow diagrams

A key goal of structured analysis is to partition the system that is to be specified; then we can produce an integrated set of mini-specs. A data flow diagram is a network representation of a system. It portrays the component pieces with all the interfaces among the components and between the system and the external environment. Figure 10.5(a) and (b) show an example – a simple graphical representation of data flow, data storage and functions, in a form which users can readily understand. This really is a situation where a picture is worth more than a thousand words, so we shall pass over the details of the system itself and focus on basic elements which make up a data flow diagram. These are:

1 Data flows, represented by named vectors connecting nodes in the network;

2 Processes or functions which transform the data, represented by rectangular nodes. It is helpful to label these nodes for reference

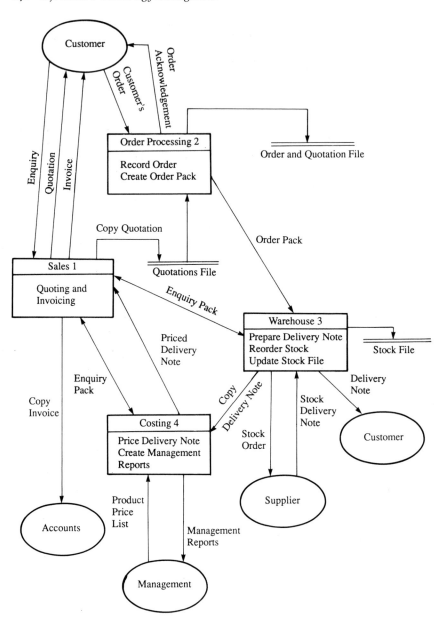

Figure 10.5   (a) *A data flow diagram: top level,* (b) *Second level data flow diagram showing details of order processing function*

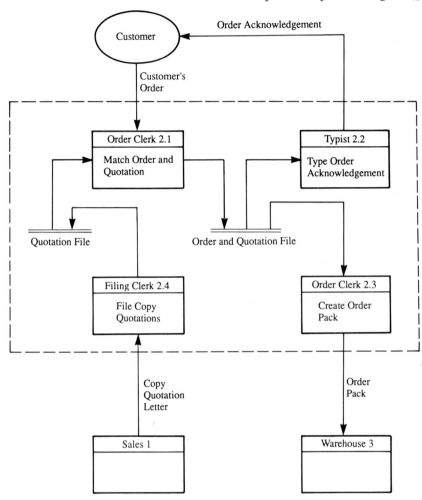

purposes. Note that the boxes numbered 2.1 to 2.4 in Figure 10.5(b) are the result of presenting the function of Box 2 in Figure 10.5(a) in more detail. If further refinement of Box 2.4, say, were necessary then the more detailed boxes would be numbered 2.4.1, 2.4.2, and so on;

3   Data stores, represented by double horizontal lines;
4   Data sources and sinks, outside the (sub)system boundary, represented by ellipses.

How much detail to show at each level is a matter of judgement. Too much detail adds to the complexity. Trivial error flows should be omitted. In our example the inclusion of the quotation file and the matched order and quotation file in the top-level diagram rather than as files internal to the order processing function as in Figure 10.5(b) is perhaps questionable; it depends what other functions need access to these files.

Data flow diagrams are a good means of communication between the systems analyst and the user. Following the interview with users, the analyst might draw data flow diagrams as in Figures 10.5(a), and (b), showing understanding of the system. There is then a validation process in the form of a walk-through with the appropriate users, to check the data flows into and out of each process. The user will see immediately if there have been any misunderstandings; for example, if preparation of delivery notes in Figure 10.5 is not a part of the warehouse function but the responsibility of some other area, the user will spot the error.

The main characteristics of data flow diagrams are readily apparent:

They are graphic and clearly descriptive;
They are partitioned and so aid control of complexity;
They emphasize flow of data;
They de-emphasize flow of control, the order of events is a matter for the detailed process design phase.

Entity models

Entity models are complementary to data flow diagrams in that they provide a logical view of data structures and data relationships which is missing from the data flow diagram. In Chapter 6 (Figure 6.10) we presented an entity relationship diagram for a simple purchasing system. We saw that relationships can be one-to-one, one-to-many, or many-to-many.

Some examples of entities in the system described in Figure 10.5 are *customers, orders, invoices* and *suppliers*. Relationships are expressed as:

Customer	*places many*	orders	(one-to-many)
Invoice	*is for one*	delivery	(one-to-one)
Product	*is supplied by many*	suppliers ⎫	(many-to-many)
Supplier	*supplies many*	products ⎭	

These and some of the other entities and relationships for this system are shown in Figure 10.6.

The entity model produced during the analysis phase can be checked at a later stage against the entities derived from the normalization process. How then does the analyst produce this first entity model from the results of his or her investigations? A list of candidate entities can be compiled from investigation notes by scanning the notes and listing nouns or noun phrases. This inevitably produces more candidate entities than will be required for the model but it is better at this stage to have too many than to overlook some entity. Similarly an analysis of the notes for verbs provides candidate relationships between entities.

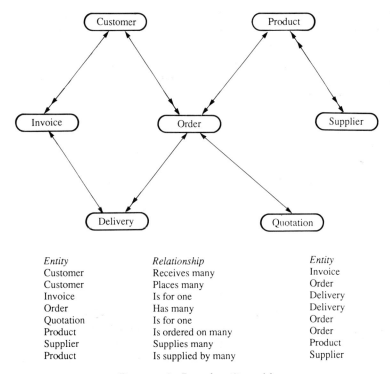

Entity	Relationship	Entity
Customer	Receives many	Invoice
Customer	Places many	Order
Invoice	Is for one	Delivery
Order	Has many	Delivery
Quotation	Is for one	Order
Product	Is ordered on many	Order
Supplier	Supplies many	Product
Product	Is supplied by many	Supplier

Figure 10.6   *Example entity model*

Cross references

The technique of cross-referencing one set of data objects to another is used during the analysis and specification of requirement phases of a project to provide tests of completeness and accuracy.

The data stores represented on a data flow diagram comprise one or more entities or parts of entities. These data stores can be cross-referenced with the entity model. If any data store cannot be associated with one or more entities then either the data store is not needed in the system or the entity model is incomplete.

Entity–function matrix

A technique which leads to the construction of entity life histories is the construction of an entity function matrix. This involves construction of a matrix in which the entities form the rows, and the functions – from the data flow diagram – form the columns. The matrix entries comprise single letters or combinations of the letters I, R, M and D, or are left blank, where:

I   indicates that an entity occurrence is inserted by the function, e.g. an *order* is inserted by the *order entry* function;

R   indicates that an entity occurrence is read by the function, e.g. the *order acknowledgement* process refers to a *customer* entity occurrence;

M   indicates that the function modifies an entity occurrence; the process of acknowledging an order might modify the *order* entity occurrence to show the date on which it was acknowledged; the *order* entity occurrence would also be modified by the *record delivery* function to show that the order, or part of it, has been satisfied;

D   indicates that the entity occurrence is deleted by the function; one of the actions of the *produce invoice* function might be to delete the corresponding *order* entity occurrence.

A blank entry indicates that the function is not relevant to the entity.

A partially constructed entity–function matrix derived from the data flow diagram of Figure 10.5 and the entity model of Figure 10.6 is shown in Figure 10.7. Clearly we cannot construct the complete matrix without first completing the details of the data flow diagram and the entity model.

Each row of the entity–function matrix shows how an entity is affected by functions. It provides a means of checking that every entity occurrence is inserted by some function, that it undergoes any necessary modifications and is finally deleted from the system. However, it does not show the order in which these events take place. For this we need to construct a life history for each entity showing the sequence of functions and when it is acceptable to apply a function to an occurrence of the entity.

Entity Name \ Function Name	2.1 Order Entry	2.2 Acknowledge Order	2.3 Create Order Pack	2.4 File Quotation Copy	1.1 Prepare Quote	1.2 Produce Invoice	3.1 Record Delivery		4.1 Price Delivery Note	
Customer	R	R								
Order	I	M	M			D				
Product					R		M			
Quotation	R			M	I	R, D				
Delivery						D	I		M	
Invoice						I				

Figure 10.7   *Partially constructed entity–function matrix*

Process outlines

A process outline collects together all the operations necessary for a process to execute. The entities affected by the processing can be determined from the entity–function matrix. The sequence in which functions may be carried out on an entity is established from the entity life history. Each function sets the state of an entity to indicate what further processing is then acceptable. Before any function is carried out the previous state of the entity must be checked to ensure that the function is acceptable. For example it is clearly not acceptable to process transactions against an account before the account is set up, nor can an account be closed before it has been set up. A process outline therefore lists not only the entities affected by the processing but also the preconditions that

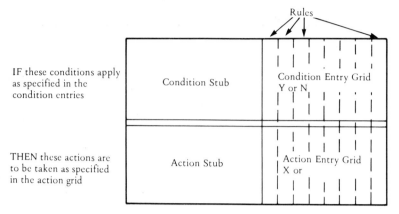

Figure 10.8   *Decision table quadrants*

must be satisfied for the processing to be acceptable. The process outline is then expanded to include a description of the processing for each operation required to complete the process. This information provides a basis for the specification of logical process designs which can be developed into detailed physical designs.

Decision tables

Most of the tools and techniques described so far are graphic and are therefore especially useful when an extensive system or process is being discussed with users, with non-technical staff, or in presentations to management. One alternative which is often used to specify a process at the design stage is the decision table. This tool is most useful when the alternative actions which can be taken depend upon complicated preconditions. The decision alternatives are represented in a table divided into quadrants as shown in Figure 10.8.

Each line in the condition stub is a statement representing a single condition which might affect the decision outcome. These lines, which can be expressed as IF statements, may be written in any order. However, some conditions pre-empt others, that is, depending on the result of testing one condition, a number of other conditions may be irrelevant and need not then be tested. The best order to test the conditions is to deal with the most pre-emptive first.

Each line in the action stub specifies some action which might possibly be required. These lines are equivalent to THEN statements.

The condition entry grid in the right half of the table is used to record various combinations of conditions that may be relevant. Generally, we use Y to denote that a condition is true and N for false. A dash indicates that a condition is irrelevant as a consequence of previous tests. Thus, if

Credit Determination Table

Cash with order?	Y	N	N	N	N
Customer has record card?	--	N	Y	Y	Y
Outstanding balance older than 3 months?	—	—	N	Y	N
Outstanding balance exceeds £10,000?	—	—	N	N	Y
Allow credit	.	.	X	.	.
Refuse credit	.	X	.	X	X
Advise customer to apply for record card	.	X	.	.	.

Figure 10.9   *A limited-entry decision table*

we apply three condition tests in sequence we might obtain the result (Y,N,Y), or if the third condition is irrelevant as a result of the first two we might have (Y,N,−). For three conditions, at most $2^3 = 8$ different relevant combinations of Ys and Ns exist. Each of these combinations is recorded as a column in the condition entry grid. For n conditions we need at most 2^n columns.

For each relevant combination in the columns of the condition entry grid there is a corresponding set of required actions. These are recorded in the columns of the action entry grid where an X denotes that an action is required and a blank, or a period, that it is not required.

Consider the following problem:

Customers with an approved account hold a record card. Customers without a record card are not allowed credit. Credit is allowed to a record card holder unless there is an outstanding balance older than three months or a short-term balance exceeding £10,000. None of this applies if payment is tendered with the order.

Figure 10.9 is a completed decision table for this problem. Although four separate conditions have been identified, suggesting a possible $2^4 = 16$ rules, some conditions are pre-empted by others and, in this case, only five distinct rules are needed to describe the solution. This table is called a *limited entry* table because the result of each test can be represented by one of only two states, Y or N.

If we now extend the problem by the further conditions that card holders with a balance not exceeding £5,000 may be allowed credit, if the age of the balance does not exceed 6 months, then significantly more rules are introduced. However, we can reduce the size of the table if we extend the conditions so that more than two states are needed to represent the results of tests. The decision table is then called an *extended entry table*, or if some condition entries involve only two states and others more than two,

Credit Determination Table

Cash with order?	Y	N	N	N	N	N	N
Customer has record card?	–	N	Y	Y	Y	Y	Y
Age of outstanding balance (months)	–	–	≤3	≤3	>3,≤6	>3,≤6	>6
Amount of outstanding balance (£1,000)	–	–	≤10	>10	≤5	>5	–
Allow credit	.	.	X	.	X	.	.
Refuse credit	.	X	.	X	.	X	X
Advise customer to apply for record card	.	X	.	.	.	.	.

Figure 10.10   *A mixed-entry decision table*

then the table is a *mixed entry table*. Figure 10.10 shows a mixed entry decision table for our extended problem.

Multiple decision tables

At times, decisions may be sufficiently complex to be expressed as a set of related decision tables as opposed to a single decision table. Action statements are included which permit interaction between the various tables. Figure 10.11 shows how the decisions expressed in the table of Figure 10.10 may be represented by two related tables.

Credit Determination

Cash with order?	Y	N	N
Customer has record card?	–	N	Y
Refuse credit	.	X	.
Advise customer to apply for record card	.	X	.
PERFORM Credit Detail	.	.	X

Credit Detail

Age of outstanding balance (months)	≤3	≤3	>3,≤6	>3,≤6	>6
Amount of outstanding balance (£1,000)	≤10	>10	≤5	>5	–
Allow credit	X	.	X	.	.
Refuse credit	.	X	.	X	X

Figure 10.11   *A simple example of a multiple decision table*

Decision table applications

Decision tables are a concise, easily understood, non-procedural method of documenting information. The alternative rules are side by side and it is easy to determine the preconditions that lead to a sequence of actions. They work best in instances which are both specific and detailed. They can be used with a minimum of instruction.

The systems analyst can provide programmers with decision tables from which coded routines can be developed. Decision tables can also be used as a basis for automatic generation of computer programs. The details of this are beyond the scope of this book but all that is necessary is to automate the selection of a rule which matches a given set of condition states, and hence to determine the actions to be taken. For a brief description of automatic program generation from decision tables the reader is referred to *Computer Science Applied to Business Systems* (Shave and Bhaskar, 1982, pp. 100–105) where two such methods are described: *The rule mask method* (King, 1966) and the *index method* (Smithe and Shave, 1975).

Investigation techniques

Two important activities in the systems process – probably the two requiring the most skill and experience and for which few formal tools are available – are:

1   Data collection (for fact-finding the analyst requires exceptional communication skills);
2   The feasibility study, which is normally carried out by a small, carefully selected team of top-calibre personnel.

In the following sections we consider these activities in more detail.

Fact-finding

The systems analyst is concerned with collecting data for two principal purposes. First, it is necessary to observe, understand and evaluate all aspects of the job under investigation. This is primarily for the analyst's own benefit, for without a clear understanding of the nature of the existing system it is not possible to decide what to look for in order to determine the exact nature of the problem. These facts are probably already well known to the management and certainly to those directly involved in operating the existing system. It is essential that the analyst has a good personal model of the processes of the business, or at least of that part of it under investigation, in terms that are meaningful; that is, in terms of real objects, physical locations, movements and events. This model is for the analyst's own education; it need not be fully documented.

There are also facts which are public and must be shared with or communicated to others. These facts need to be fully documented in a form which can be understood by all concerned.

The assessment objective

As a part of the assessment of the existing system the analyst must obtain answers to the following questions:

What is being done?
Why is it being done?
Who is doing it?
How is it being done?
What are the major problems involved in doing it?

The analyst will need full and clear answers to the first four questions in order to assess the significance of the data collected in answers to the fifth.

The assistance objective

A second objective is to discover and propose operational alternatives to the existing system. The analyst must offer specific suggestions for improving the effectiveness in getting a job done, and must seek answers to the two questions:

What other ways exist for dealing with the problem?
What benefits and liabilities are associated with these alternative approaches?

The processes of assessment and assistance are on-going and inter-related activities in the systems process. Better assistance can be offered as the analyst gains a better assessment of the problem. Also, a knowledge of the operational alternatives available gives a broader perspective for true assessment.

Participants in the process

To be effective in meeting both the assessment and the assistance objectives the analyst must establish good communications with all participants in the systems process. These include:

Top management, who are responsible for most of the decision-taking and are probably the initiators of the project;

Managers of the affected departments, who may be allowed or required to take many decisions without referring to higher authority;
The data-processing department: data-processing manager, programming manager, programmers and operators (systems analysts are usually employed in this department);
Staff whose work may be affected.

The analyst may also wish to consult people outside the departments most affected: people in other departments, external auditors, customers and suppliers. He largely depends upon others for both information and co-operation. Communication skills are therefore essential in performing effective systems analysis.

Interviews

How does the analyst set about collecting relevant data? The data required for an assessment of the existing system are most effectively obtained by means of planned discussions or interviews. It is through personal contact during private discussions that the participant gets a real sense of involvement in the system process. Users can be powerful as regards the success or otherwise of that part of the system with which they are concerned. It is important that they contribute any relevant information, are involved in and have the opportunity to influence the design of the system, and *feel* that they are involved. Other forms of communication such as staff meetings, presentations, newsletters and questionnaires rarely engender the same feeling of involvement as the private discussion.

The best order for a series of discussions and interviews is probably from top management down. It is helpful if, at each stage, the analyst is introduced to the participant by that participant's immediate superior. In this way, the importance of the investigation is endorsed from above. Several meetings with each participant may be necessary: the first for a general preparatory discussion, then more detailed discussions on various aspects of the job and, finally, a session in which the analyst confirms with the interviewee the matters agreed and facts recorded during the discussions. Errors and wrong impressions can be reduced if after the interview the analyst sends the interviewee a resume of these facts. This is also an opportunity to clarify responsibility for any further action required.

We shall not go into the details of interviewing techniques, precisely what information should be sought, and how, but it is perhaps useful to give a sample of standardized guidelines that might be used by a systems analyst to structure interviews during data collection (see Semprevivo (1976) p. 54).

Interview each member of the user department and focus on gaining information about each of the following:

1   *Office organization.* How does the management organize its personnel? How does this organization relate to the major functions which the office performs?
   (a)   Construct a general description of the major functions performed by the office.
   (b)   Construct a chart which depicts lines of authority and responsibility and/or other kinds of formal and informal organizational interaction.
2   *Functional flow.* For each important function determine the steps required and describe their significance.
   (a)   Construct a procedure and/or flow chart which illustrates in detail the work that is performed.
   (b)   Explain which personnel are involved in or affect the problems, decisions, and materials used at each step in the process.
3   *Resource requirements.* Determine what resources are applied by the organization in getting the job done.
   (a)   What personnel requirements such as specialized training and experience are required in doing the job?
   (b)   What equipment and materials are required to support the work efforts of personnel?
   (c)   How do the resource requirements utilized translate into a cost of doing business?
4   *Time relationships.* How does the work performed relate to specific times of the year or other business cycles?
   (a)   Are there workload peaks and valleys?
   (b)   What are the actual work volumes by time?
5   *Forms, procedures, and reports.* What forms, written procedures, and reports are utilized in the course of performing work?
   (a)   Include examples for each form, procedure, and report used.
   (b)   Note whether the material is originated by the office, modified by the office, and/or transmitted to another office.
   (c)   Make comparisons which determine usefulness, duplication and incompleteness.
6   *Non-existent desirable functions.* Record the opinions of people as they relate to job improvement.

To answer all the questions raised in these guidelines the analyst will need to talk to many 'users' at various levels. They may each be asked many of the same questions and different and sometimes conflicting answers may call for further investigation. The way in which questions are posed is important. The analyst should avoid questions which suggest obvious answers or which can be answered yes or no. Neutrality must be preserved and the analyst is more likely to ask the right questions and in the right way, and is less apt to overlook important areas of concern if the interview is well structured. However, the interviewee must also be given the opportunity to offer information which might not have been anticipated. After the interview the analyst has to consider the information obtained and decide whether to accept the picture given by the interviewee or to seek confirmation from another source.

Fact-finding from documents

Documents are an important source of information about data and terminology used in a system. The analyst should aim to collect a completed specimen (or a photocopy) of each relevant document, together with its copies, discover and record who completes the document, what happens to each copy of it, where copies are filed, and for how long and for what purpose filed copies are retained. The analyst will find it useful to draw a data flow diagram showing the input of data, documents and copies recording the data, the flow of copies through departments and between departments, and the documents output from the system. In this way any gaps in his understanding of the purpose of each document in the system will be revealed. Figure 12.2 is an example of such a diagram showing the flow of information in an order processing system.

Sometimes, the analyst needs to quantify answers to questions such as:

What is the mean time between receipt of order and despatch of goods?
What proportion of customers accounts have more than eight transactions per month?
What proportion of orders qualify for discount?

The answers to such questions can normally be obtained by sampling from filed documents.

It is also useful to browse through filed documents observing any points of special interest. In this way, the analyst may discover exceptional cases of which he might otherwise not become aware because his questions during data collection might not lead to these items of information and the interviewee might not think to mention them. The analyst should also see for himself the actual working conditions under which jobs are done, physical layout, pace of movement, noise levels, clutter and so on. All of these have some bearing on the efficiency and accuracy with which work is done.

External search for equivalent systems

Most of what we have described so far is concerned with the analyst's assessment objective. In order to achieve the assistance objective and discover specific operational alternatives to the existing system, it may be necessary to search outside the present system. During planned discussions with users, possible alternatives may be volunteered by users who are educated in computing and systems design. Whatever the nature of the problem it is highly likely that another organization somewhere has experienced a similar problem and implemented a new system to solve it. Time spent finding and studying the details of a close parallel system is likely to repay itself many fold. It can provide prompts for the analyst's fact-finding questions, suggest alternatives and avoid pitfalls. Good starting points for an external search are as follows:

> *Computer suppliers' representative.* Most large computer companies employ specialists who can offer advice or direct the analyst to an example application similar to his own;
> *Computer users' groups.* These are self-help consumer associations of purchasers of computers. Exchange of information between members is encouraged;
> *Packages.* Even if a program package is not entirely suitable for the particular application under investigation it can be a good source of ideas. Information about packages is published annually in the Computer Users Year Book Directory of Software;
> *Literature.* Published books, journals and reports are a useful source of information but are not always readily available to the analyst and, unless he has some help such as a computer-search service which given appropriate keywords will list relevant references, this course can be very time-consuming.

Questionnaires

The questionnaire is probably the most frequently misused of the tools available to the systems analyst for collecting, recording and organizing information. Constructing, issuing and evaluating questionnaires is a highly skilled job and unless the analyst really understands the basic principles of questionnaire design he would be most unwise to use this method for collecting facts and opinions for business systems design. Parkin (1980) offers the following advice for questionnaire designers:

1   Read Berdie and Anderson, *Questionnaires: Design and Use* (1974);
2   State your precise objectives in sending the questionnaire – What

decisions will the questionnaire influence? What different decisions will be taken for different hypothetical questionnaire results?

3   Estimate the time and cost of conducting the study.

If still interested,

4   Plan a questionnaire with a personal tone, with a purpose, which will be clear to the recipients and plan how you are going to process the responses;
5   Ask short questions which call for short, objective answers;
6   Test the questions by showing them to your peers;
7   Test the revised questions by asking a small sample of the target population to complete the questionnaire blind (i.e. with no more explanation or personal contact than is planned for the other recipients). Repeat the questions in interview to elicit difficulties, ambiguities, unreliability.

There is no doubt that people are prejudiced against questionnaires and as a result they are often careless about the way they answer them. One major advantage is that answers to a well-designed, fixed-format questionnaire are easily prepared for automatic processing and tabulation by computer. The systems analyst can therefore obtain summaries of answers in tabular form with useful statistics, or as computer-produced graphs or bar charts.

The only satisfactory way to issue a questionnaire is in person. A higher degree of confidence can be placed in the accuracy and reliability of answers given in the presence of the investigator or representative. This suggests that the questions should be included in the analyst's guidelines for structured interviews and discussions.

Written procedures

In addition to the pictorial and tabular methods of recording and summarizing information, the analyst makes frequent use of written procedures to describe a process. Sometimes, written procedures are already available for the guidance of operators carrying out the tasks involved. In such cases the analyst has to follow jobs through each procedural step noting any exceptions and problems as they occur. When they are not available he can construct a set of written procedures as each step of the job is being reviewed. The written procedure is not just a check list of job steps; it should define the nature and purpose of the process, the resources used, the role of each employee involved and how the process relates to other processes which precede it and follow it, or are in any way dependent on it.

Documentation

There is little point in collecting information about existing systems and user requirements unless the findings are adequately documented. The documentation serves as a record of the investigation which can be agreed with all participants in the systems process and as a basis for subsequent analysis and design work. The documentation is most useful if it is based on some widely accepted standard providing facilities for recording relatively unstructured data such as reports of meetings and more structured descriptions of processes, document flows, data relationships and computer programs. Some of the tools available to the analyst to assist him in organizing and recording his findings have been described in the preceding sections. Good documentation greatly aids the analyst in his communication and in the analysis and design activities.

Systems feasibility

The purpose of a feasibility study is to assess the effectiveness of the complete systems plan in terms of its ability to meet users' needs, its use of resources, impact on the organization, and general workability. Determination of feasibility is in many ways a continuous feature of the systems process but once a particular proposal has passed through a coarse sieve of tests and been accepted in preference to possible alternatives, it must then be tested and evaluated in more detail and on a scale which might not be possible for several systems. The cost of failing to carry out a rigorous feasibility study is all too evident.

The feasibility study is usually the responsibility of a small team of top-calibre personnel carefully selected by a project steering committee or by management to maximize know-how and minimize any risks to the organization in adopting the proposed system. In addition to each having a good understanding of long- and medium-term planning for DP, conduct of feasibility studies and the principles and practice of systems analysis and design, collectively members of the team should be competent to:

Make up measures of effectiveness (MOE);
Design and document systems;
Predict effects of the system;
Plan DP projects;
Make reports to management.

If there are special risks associated with the project such as unfamiliar technology (e.g. distributed database, new or untried software, first-time users), or the system directly affects the organization's dealings with customers, or the system needs to fit the requirements of human operators, then the chances or cost of failure can be reduced by including in the study team one or more members with experience in the particular high-risk area. The study team would normally include representatives of the DP department, user departments, and, if necessary, external consultants.

Measures of effectiveness

It is the responsibility of the study team to propose suitable MOEs for the project. Some common MOEs, listed by Parkin (1980), are:

Money cost of system operation (measured by project accounting system);

Money cost of system operation (measured by cost of accounting system);

Ease of use (e.g. number of times *ad hoc* enquiry service used, number of official complaints from users);

Speed per transaction, or response time (measured by a specially-kept log; both the average and the distribution are of interest);

Accuracy (error correction entries per 1,000 transactions);

Timespan to develop system (project event log);

Money return on investment (e.g. measured money return on measured money investment);

Congruence with DP policies (lack of revision to this system to permit the development of subsequent systems).

Of these, 'number of complaints' is a lumpy measure of an existing system since some complaints are more serious than others. Measures of the kind listed are called *close MOEs*, since external events have relatively little influence upon them. More *distant MOEs* such as:

Customer satisfaction (proportion of customers closing accounts);

Job satisfaction (labour turnover); and

Productivity;

may be affected by the DP system but external influences are likely to be more significant.

Objective

Following project selection, the study team:

Proposes the close MOEs;

Develops the design of the system to the point where, with acceptable reliability,

a forecast can be made of the effect on the MOEs, thereby defining targets, and

an assurance can be given that the project is free from unacceptable risks and side effects;

Lays the foundations for subsequent planning and control of the project, should continuation be authorized, by preparing an outline plan for the whole project and a more detailed plan of activities to the end of the analysis phase;

Documents the objectives, design and plan in a way that allows analysis, design and post-implementation evaluation team to benefit from the feasibility study;

Presents the findings in a form suitable for the management to decide whether or not to authorize continuation.

Terms of reference

Clear terms of reference are essential for the study team. Often these will be proposed by the team leader for approval by management. It is helpful if the terms refer to desired outputs or achievements of the team and indicate how much licence management are prepared to give the team, or how much initiative is expected. Any constraints caused by company policy should be mentioned. Bounds of the study may be included to avoid the risk of misapplied effort, or to ensure referral to management for further guidance or authorization if necessary. The resources available to the team should be made clear. Method guidance may be needed, for example the team may be required to study a known similar system. When high-risk factors are present the team may be required to prepare contingency plans which could be called upon should the selected system prove unfeasible after implementation (one such plan might be to return to or to continue with the existing system until the problems are overcome). The team should also be told the expected duration of the study. An example of fairly specific terms of reference is given below:

From: Steering Committee   To: Order Entry Study Team
                                   (G. Hall, Systems
                                   J. Steel, Orders
                                   B. Goodhand, Warehouse)

Terms of reference

1   Propose objective measures of effectiveness of the sales order entry system. Of particular concern are the speed of getting orders to the

warehouse, the speed of raising invoices and the proportion of invoices which need retyping or which are sent out containing errors.

2 List the advantages and disadvantages of two alternative possibilities (or more at the team's discretion), including:
(a) On-line order entry using minicomputer with terminals in sales department and warehouse;
(b) Off-line order entry, input from sales department by optical mark read documents.

3 For the system recommended by the team, provide firm forecasts of the effect on each of the proposed measures of effectiveness and of the cost of development and operation. Define in detail the inputs and outputs of the system, with draft order forms/displays, picking lists and invoices. Document the manual processes foreseen in the sales department and warehouse.

4 J. Steel is particularly to appraise the effect of the proposed system on customer service, order staff job satisfaction and other side-effects. B. Goodhand is particularly to appraise the effect of the proposed system on picking speed, and the productivity and job satisfaction of picking staff.

Messrs. Steel and Goodhand are also to ensure that each person in their departments is kept fully informed of plans and possibilities and that interested staff and shop stewards are invited to participate in the team's activities. It is company policy that no redundancies take place as a result of computerization and that established work-groups will not be broken up if this can be avoided.

The authority of the study team does not extend to negotiating wage rates nor to other matters connected with sharing any productivity benefits which might result.

5 Make the proposed system extensible so that stock control and sales ledger systems can be added at a later date. Investigation of these systems is authorized only to the extent necessary to establish extensibility.

6 Furnish plans for standby operation in the event of prolonged cessation of computer facilities or electricity supply.

7 The expected duration of the study is five weeks. The team is to submit forthwith a detailed plan of their activities, stating their planned achievements at approximately weekly intervals.

8 The feasibility report is to be drawn up as outlined in the company standards manual. The report is to be copied to Steering Committee members, order/warehouse personnel at supervisor level and above, and warehouse shop stewards. A management presentation should be made approximately three days after submitting the report.

Terms of reference	As modified.
Justifications	Statement of system objectives and scope:
	What messages will be supplied by system;
	What processes will be controlled;
	What decisions will be supported.
	Summary of major operational alternatives considered and preferred solution:
	Premises, assumptions and unknowns influencing choice should be emphasized.
	Fit with organization's long- and medium-term plans.
	Cost and benefit summary.
	Project targets.
	Limitations of preferred solution.
	Other implications of interest to management.
Present system	Background information if necessary.
	Summary of procedures, staffing, equipment.
	List of inputs, outputs and files.
	Control and security features.
Proposed system	Summary of procedures, staffing, equipment.
	Outline design of the inputs, outputs and business procedures.
	Data dictionary or summary of the database content:
	Entities, relationships and their attributes which are to be recorded by the system.
	Control, integrity and security features.
	Other implications.
Conversion	Conversion requirements and conversion plan.
Future plan	Overall project plan.
	Detailed plan for the analysis phase.
	Recommendations for participation in the next phase.
Appendices	References to documents read or mentioned in report.
	Supporting detail of present system, proposed system, conversion plans, volumes, estimates, costs, benefits, hardware, software, data transmission, terminal network, etc., being mainly copies of or extracts from the standard system documentation files.

Figure 10.12 *Feasibility study report content*

Results of feasibility study

The deliverable product at the end of the study is the feasibility report. Depending on the scale and duration of the study one or more interim reports may be produced. These might serve as a basis for further input to the study from the management. There is no question but that the formal requirements for a feasibility report (and afterwards for a full systems proposal) are time-consuming. To approach the matter informally is risky. The formal agreement to a systems proposal following acceptance of the feasibility report serves as a basis for resolving differences and misunderstandings which can arise between the time of the commitment and the completion of the project. A possible content of the feasibility report is outlined in Figure 10.12.

All other documentation collected or produced by the study team should be filed for use in the later phases of the project. The feasibility report is not just for acceptance or rejection. It is for management to study and make any modifications to remedy specific weaknesses or take advantage of strengths not previously recognized, and to weigh up their confidence in the feasibility effort. Other interested parties (e.g. user departments) may be invited to review and critically assess the report. Further investigations may be requested by management.

Throughout this review the analyst should attempt to:

Remain flexible with respect to possible modification;
Fully evaluate the consequence of any proposed modifications;
Remain firm when it can be demonstrated that proposed modifications would severely limit or undermine the advantages of the proposal.

Eventually, unless the proposal is shelved, the amended feasibility report will form the basis of the detailed systems plan which then serves as a reference for detailed design and construction. Figure 10.13 gives an overview of feasibility study conduct.

System cost determination

To communicate effectively with management the analyst will have to express the money costs and benefits of a system in accordance with the organization's Chart of Accounts, that is, the classifications under which transactions may be recorded. The conventions may vary from one organization to another according to the nature of the business and its traditions.

There are several different types of systems costs and benefits which the analyst is concerned with:

Tangible and intangible;
Direct and indirect;
Recurring and non-recurring.

If a cost can be identified as actual or provable and its amount estimated, then it is tangible. An intangible cost is one which is assumed to

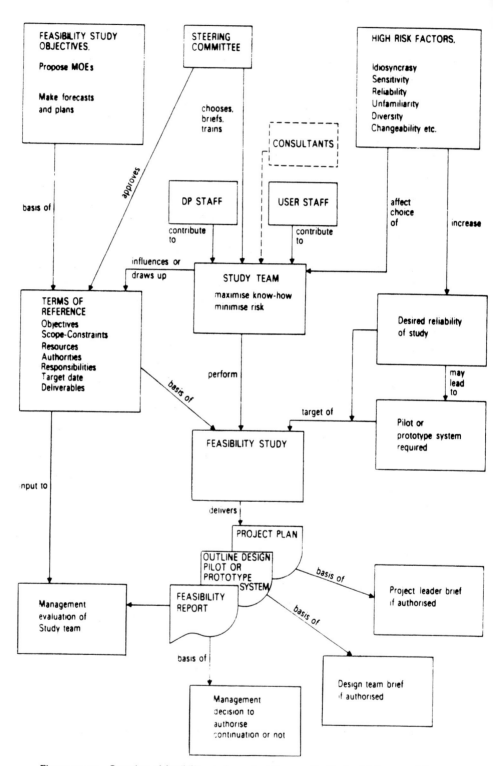

Figure 10.13 *Overview of feasibility study conduct* Source: *Parkin (1980)* Systems Management, *p. 25*

exist; the amount is estimated but cannot be proven. Many important systems benefits are intangibles:

Will the customer order more goods because of better service?
Will other customers learn of the improved service and bring their business to the company?
Will the improved system result in higher staff morale and productivity?

It is necessary to try and estimate the extent to which these intangibles occur. However, if there are more tangible benefits then more emphasis will be placed on these.

Most business systems are really subsystems within the organization as a whole. They therefore affect and are affected by other subsystems with which they interact. Direct system costs are those directly related to the expense of developing and operating the subsystem in question. Indirect costs are those associated with other subsystems, such as central adminis-tration, supporting the one in question.

The cost of developing a new system is a one-time, non-recurring cost. Maintaining and operating a new system will be a continuous or recurring cost. The analyst's task is to identify all the various kinds of cost associ-ated with a proposed system. He must estimate the changed cash flows associated with each money MOE associated with the system. The main money MOEs with which he is concerned will be cost of development and changed cost of operation (relative to the existing system). We assume that if a source of cash flow can be identified then the amount of cash flow can be estimated. This is a big assumption and the analyst's task is complicated by the fact that, in some situations, basic cost data may not be readily available.

Cost categories

The main tactic is to partition the money MOE orthogonally, i.e. so that all significant costs or revenues are included and no significant double count-ing occurs. A useful starting point is to partition the money according to the following five classifications (the five Ms):

Men, Machines, Materials, Money, Miscellaneous.

Men

The cost of personnel has two parts: the salary of personnel, and ad-ditional costs (employee benefits) such as holiday pay, employers pension and national insurance contributions, sick leave. The cost of these benefits usually amount to 20–25 per cent of salary costs and should be added to the salary costs. The analyst should estimate the proportion of each employee's time spent in developing or operating the system to determine that component of non-recurring and recurring personnel costs. Other fixed personnel costs, such as training, supervision and workspace may be more significant than employee benefits but are usually regarded as overheads and may be classified as miscellaneous costs.

Machine

The cost of equipment includes the costs incurred in purchase, rental or leasing, maintenance and repair costs. When only a part of a machine's hours are attributed to the MOE, the general rule is to count the cost as a proportion of attributable hours to total hours used.

An hour of computer time is frequently costed to include all of the people and supplies which enable the computer to operate. The determination of this cost may be further complicated if some computer time is sold to external users.

Materials

Just as people and equipment are required to develop and operate a new system, so a wide range of consumable supplies are required to support these efforts. These costs are included in the materials category.

Money

The cost of increased or reduced indebtedness attributable to the system should be estimated. An improved invoicing system may result in more frequent payments by customers resulting in a reduction in the average amount of credit they take. Interest earnable as a result of improved cash flow should be counted. An improved stock control system could lead to a similar improvement if working capital tied up in stock can be reduced.

Miscellaneous

This category includes anything that is not accounted for in the other four categories. It may include such overheads as management, secretarial and administrative support, furniture, heat, light. Such cost can usually be added in some form to items in the other four categories and there may be little or nothing left to enter under miscellaneous items.

Strictly, it is the opportunity cost that should be counted, although the costs measured by the usual conventions of accounting are normally taken as a sufficient approximation.

We must remember that we are interested in changes in costs and revenues relative to the existing system, and relative to alternative systems under consideration. Two quantitative methods of cost comparison frequently employed by the analyst are break-even analysis and payback-period analysis. The accountant will be familiar with these techniques so we shall not discuss them here.

11 Business activities and organization

The concept of MIS

As we have seen in Chapter 1, a modern organization requires information systems to support its managerial and decision-making functions. These systems are often called management information systems (MIS) or information processing systems.

One role of the MIS in an organization is to establish a link between the market for a product and the organization's internal control systems. The economics of each organization imposes constraints on what can be done. With these constraints in mind, a firm must make full and efficient use of all the resources it has available. The success of a product depends on its acceptability to the market: this means that not only the price and quality must be acceptable but the product must be tailored to meet the needs of its customers. Thus, the product, production technology and management style together must meet the economic constraints of the external environment (including demand for the product, competitor actions, customers' ability to pay, and so on). The two relevant control aspects are quality control systems and the cost control system. Both need market information for the formulation of their objectives. Such information should be readily available through the organization's MIS. Companies operating in a large number of countries with varied economic and social conditions have found it necessary to vary their information systems from country to country.

In designing a MIS the functions and style of management must be borne in mind. It is important to:

Develop an hierarchical view of the organization;
Understand the functional, line and staff relationships;

Realize the different managerial tasks and management style of each position.

Each manager will manage in a different way to his predecessor. The MIS must be able to adapt to the managerial style and information needs of the current managerial team.

The broad view of MIS encompasses four distinct types of information, supporting different types of users:

1   Information regarding the routine processing of transactions;
2   Information necessary for day-to-day operations, planning and decision making (i.e. operational control);
3   Information to aid tactical planning and decision making;
4   Information for the support of strategic planning and decision making.

This is illustrated in Figure 11.1 where each management level relates to a different type of activity. These levels may be regarded as a pyramid with the bottom level providing information for the higher levels; the fourth level (strategic planning) represents the pinnacle for which all information is filtered and summarized. Allied to each information layer or level is the associated concept of information as the means of enabling the organization to control its activities or to ensure that the organization does not deviate from its plans.

Strategic planning can best be exemplified by the product/market mix. Should we move into new markets, new products or both? Should we take over another company or expand internally? Other aspects of strate-

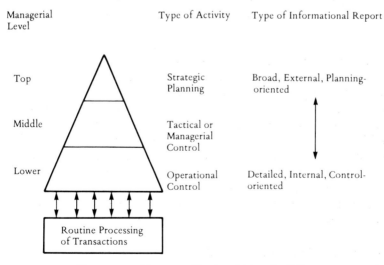

Figure 11.1   *Management levels and types of activity*

gic planning are such issues as the competitiveness of the business and the overall assignment of resources (long-term capital, manpower, management, etc.). The ability of top management, and company strengths and weaknesses, are also identified.

Tactical planning is concerned with short-run planning: recruitment, redeployment or redundancy of personnel, the budgeting process for 1 to 5 year periods and so on. Operational planning is concerned with day-to-day decisions such as: What do we produce today? Which order do we satisfy first?

The origin of the MIS concept predates computers, essentially MIS evolved as an extension of management accounting, using ideas and techniques in the area of management service, decision theory and behavioural theories of management. However, the capabilities of computers have undoubtedly added to the development of the MIS concept, as new hardware and software have offered new dimensions to be considered in providing information for all levels of planning, decision making and control within an organization.

Computer applications

Figure 11.2 demonstrates how the various computer applications may be viewed by an accountant.

The inner-most core is defined as the AIS (Accounting Information Systems). This includes:

1　The conventional subsidiary and general ledgers associated with routine book-keeping and financial accounting; and
2　The cost collection, cost allocation and budgeting tasks associated with management accounts.

Of equal interest to the management accountant is the wider concept of an MIS. This would include such applications as: order entry, order processing, sales analysis, finished-goods stock control, production monitoring, raw-material stock control, cost estimation and more specific applications such as personnel information systems. Most of these systems are designed to deal with historical data.

The new type of information system designed to help management in the area of predictive or futuristic systems is in the Decision Support Systems (DSS) area. Consideration is given to this area in later chapters.

Better information leads to better decisions not just through a direct or indirect relationship, but by means of a feedback relationship which enables the decision-maker to learn about the organization and how it interacts with the environment, and the consequences of a range of actions and decisions.

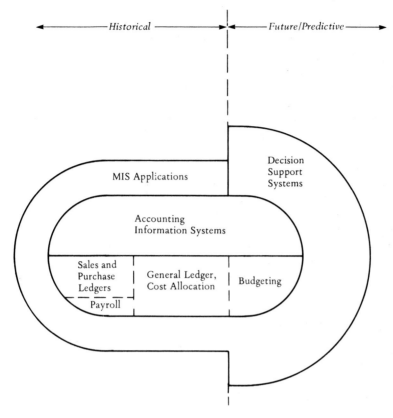

Figure 11.2 *Computer applications*

Functional areas of a business

At the highest level of management people tend to be all-rounders. Below this level, managers usually specialize in one of the following functional areas:

Marketing;
Production or manufacturing;
Purchasing;
Finance and accounting (this may include the data-processing or infor-
mation function);
Personnel and industrial relations;
Research and development.

The marketing or sales function generally includes all activities relating to the promotion, selling and distribution of the products or services produced by the firm. This may also include the finished-goods inventory. The production or manufacturing function includes all responsibility for product engineering, production facilities (planning, scheduling and operation), employment of the production labour force and quality control and inspection. The manufacturing function may include responsibility for the finished-goods stock. The purchasing function encompasses such activities as purchasing, receiving, inventory and distribution to manufacturing. The personnel function includes recruitment, training, record-keeping, wage or salary negotiations and dismissal of personnel. The finance function is responsible for ensuring sufficient financing for the organization at the lowest cost possible and it sometimes includes an appraisal of the alternative investment opportunities. Accounting covers the classification of financial transactions and their summary in standard financial reports; these include the Balance Sheet (which is a snapshot of the financial structure of a business), the Profit and Loss Account (which measures the performance of a company over a designated period), the Sources and Application of Funds Statement (which shows where the money came from and where it went over a designated period) and other reports (e.g. Current Cost Statement, Value-Added Statement). The research and development function carries out all research into the product and techniques of production. Its function may also include data processing and management services.

This list is neither exhaustive nor representative; many of the functions may be split over a number of heads, e.g. marketing and sales may be segregated. Table 11.1 illustrates how a matrix of organizational functions and management activities may be formed.

Functional areas are also determined by the nature of the organization's business, which can be categorized into one or more of the following groups:

Manufacturing and selling a product which has been produced from raw materials with some input from labour and machines;
Manufacturing and selling a product by the further processing of products purchased from other organizations;
Purchasing, storing (not essential) and distributing finished products either by wholesaling (selling to other firms) or by retailing (selling to the public);
Selling of a service such as banking, insurance, cleaning and so on.

Types of organization

Although the range of business organizations is vast, some major types can be identified. The owner of a small one-man shop is called a sole

Table 11.1 Matrix of functional areas and management activities

Activity	Marketing	Production	Purchasing	Personnel	Accounting and finance
Transaction	Sales orders, Promotion orders	Production orders, Assembly orders, Time-keeping tickets	Purchase requisitions, Manufacturing orders, Receiving orders, Bills of lading	Clock cards, Paycheques, Benefits	All source documents involving value
Operational	Day-to-day scheduling of sales force, Promotional efforts, Status of customer deliveries	Order scheduling, Machine scheduling, Overtime allocations	Out-of-stock items, Over-stocked items, Inventory turnover reports	Changing pay rates, Training schemes, Negotiation with trades unions	Comparison of actual versus budgeted costs
Tactical (including all planned versus actual deviations)	Hiring and training of sales force, Data on customers, competitors, lost orders, advertising budget	Planned actual production, Efficiency variances, Down-time analyses	Analysis of stockouts, Cost of purchases, Performance of suppliers	Labour turnover rates, Distribution of skills, Competitiveness of wage rates	Arranging short-run finance, Taxation policies
Strategic	New customers, New products, New markets, Customer surveys	Alternative plant layouts, New machinery, Automation	New materials, New suppliers, New storage techniques	Alternative recruiting, Salary and training strategies	Long-run finance

trader. Firms of solicitors or accountants include several partners (equal owners, but not always quite so equal in practice!) and are termed partnerships. Private companies can be either 'close' (owned by a small number of people or a family), or of a more dispersed ownership. Public companies have shares which can be bought and sold on a stock exchange. All companies and some partnerships have limited liability – this usually means that owners' liability is limited to the amount they paid for their share of the concern.

Organizations can also be classified into private-enterprise firms and state-owned businesses; in the U.K. in the 1980s the latter included steel, coal, oil, mining, electricity, gas, the Post Office, British Rail and British Leyland (which was 98 per cent state-owned). Most of the private-enterprise firms and some of the state-owned businesses (e.g. British Leyland) operated within a competitive economy. In such organizations, the profit motive is generally considered to be the primary goal towards which the system strives. However, profit is sometimes traded against business risk, perhaps accepting a lower profit in exchange for a lower risk. Such a course of action would be classified as 'risk-averse'. New capital investment is financed either by long-term loans or by new equity finance (additional money from the shareholders). In this context, it is vitally important to keep the shareholders informed so that they will be encouraged to contribute more money at a later date. If a company is unable to raise money for new product developments or new production techniques then ultimately that firm will decline (like the decaying chemical reaction in a container).

The state-owned businesses are characterized by state capital investment, a virtual monopoly of the home market, and state intervention. Nevertheless these organizations are controlled in a similar manner to private enterprise, with performance being measured by the accounting system and summarized in a profit-and-loss report. Another control measure may be the ability of the organization to compete in international markets and to attract staff and capital resources.

Business organizations can also be characterized by the number of competitors in a particular market. A monopoly is a market structure in which there is only one firm. Duopoly consists of two firms and an oligopoly of many. With the duopoly and oligopolistic forms, the quantity of a product sold depends on price, advertising strategy and the behaviour of a competitor (e.g. if you reduce your price, will that lead to a price war?). Another market structure is perfect competition. In this structure, it is assumed that there are so many producers that no single product can affect the market price – price is essentially given (e.g. as in farming) and no advertising is undertaken.

Organizational structure

An organizational structure defines the distribution of authority and responsibility within an organization. The structure of an information system must closely parallel the organizational structure of the entity it serves – information over which a manager has no control may be interesting but is not particularly helpful. Different organizations develop different organizational structures, so the information provided here must again be noted as representative rather than typical.

An organizational structure can be described by the number of levels of supervision and by the span of control. Figure 11.3 shows a hierarchical structure in which there are four levels of supervision, i.e. there are four distinct ranks. Span of control describes the number of subordinates reporting to a superior.

In this case the median, mode and average span of control is around two. A wide and a narrow span of control are shown in Figure 11.4. How a span of control is actually determined depends on the organization itself. Some common methods of departmentalization are by function, product, territory, customer, process and project. Figure 11.5 shows a hierarchical structure with alternative ways to departmentalize.

A line organization is the simplistic structure where the lines of communication flow directly through a hierarchical structure from top to bottom. Each manager has a responsibility to the person immediately

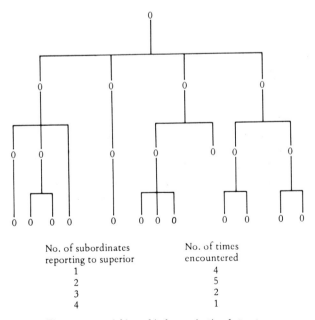

No. of subordinates reporting to superior	No. of times encountered
1	4
2	5
3	2
4	1

Figure 11.3 *A hierarchical organizational structure*

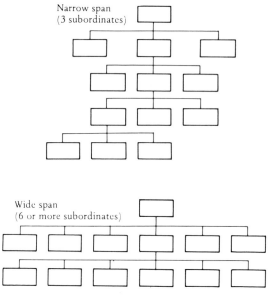

Figure 11.4   *Two approaches to span-of-control*

above and controls those immediately below. A functional or staff organization is more concerned with support activities such as analysis or consultation. Staff organizations have no direct responsibility over those in lower levels, but they do have a degree of authority over certain people in the level below them. For example in a company which is split into a number of divisions according to product, a group personnel director has a functional responsibility for divisional personnel managers who formally report (in a line role) to a divisional managing director. Figure 11.6 illustrates the two concepts.

Classification of organizations

Some organizations can be classified on the basis of their adaptation to their environment: mechanistic systems and organismic systems can be distinguished. Mechanistic organizations are often found in traditional industries where innovation is slow and where management control and information are based on elaborate rules and procedure (e.g. the steel industry). Organismic organizations have a rapid rate of innovation with a less structured and a more consultative style of management. For example, the computing industry (apart from the large mainframe manufacturers) is facing constant threats of innovation which force it to develop a managerial style conducive to the rapidly changing nature of the business (see McCosh, Rahman and Earl (1981), Chapter 1). The MIS system

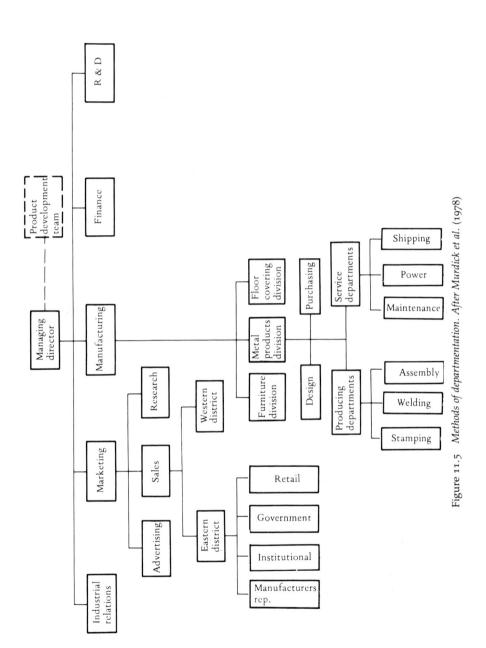

Figure 11.5 *Methods of departmentation. After Murdick et al.* (1978)

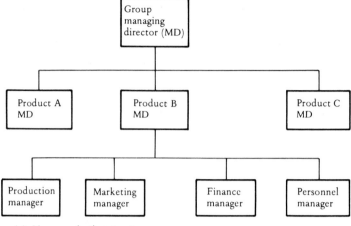

(a) Line organization structure

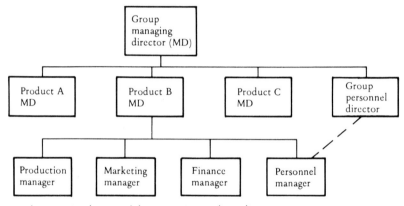

(b) Functional responsibilities superimposed on a line organization

Figure 11.6   *Alternative organizational structures*

in this environment must provide management control and information relevant to a relatively uncertain and unstructured situation.

The organization must also take into account the type of technology available: managerial style and the MIS will depend upon the type of technology as this will influence the line of command, span of control, and managerial style. Table 11.2 shows the differing requirements of unit production, mass production and process production.

There are other ways of approaching the question of the type of MIS an organization requires which depend more on the nature of decision making. For example, different decision-making levels demand different characteristics of information. Two examples are shown in Tables 11.3(a)

Table 11.2 Technology, organization and the MIS After McCosh, Rahman and Earl (1981) p. 24

	Unit production	*Mass production*	*Process production*
Number of levels of management	Small	Medium	Large
Span of control of top and middle management	Small	Medium	Large
Span of control of first-line supervisors	Small	Large	Small
Relationship between personnel	Intimate and personal	Impersonal	Personal
Flexibility of organization	Fewer rules	More rules (more clear-cut definition of authority and responsibility)	Fewer rules
Adaptation to environment	More organismic	More mechanistic	More organismic
Paperwork	Small	Large	Small
Predominant means of communication	Verbal	Written	Verbal
Power of functional areas	Engineering and development	Production	Marketing

and 11.3(b). Table 11.3(a) shows the characteristics of information as it relates to different levels of decision making. Table 11.3(b) shows how the classification of information changes between different categories of decision making.

Problems associated with organizational structure

Four of the most prominent problems of modern organizations are:

1 *Rigidity*   Organizations tend to resist change.
2 *Information failures*   Failures in communication may occur between organizational subunits due to their physical separation and specialization of functions.
3 *Suboptimization*   This refers to the problem whereby an organizational subunit, by attempting to optimize its assigned subgoal, makes it more difficult for the organization as a whole to achieve its global goal.
4 *Individual motivation*   There is an area of conflict between individual goals and organizational goals.

Table 11.3(a)   Characteristics of information which meet the requirements for different kinds of decision-making (b) Classification of information as related to the three categories of decision-making *Source*: Thierauf (1982)

(a)

Types of information	Essential characteristics
Strategic	1 External information
	(a) Competitive actions
	(b) Customer actions
	(c) Availability of resources
	(d) Demographic studies
	(e) Government actions
	2 Predictive information concerning long-term trends
	3 Simulated 'what if' information of a long-term nature
Tactical	1 Descriptive-historical information
	2 Current performance information
	3 Short-term future information
	4 Simulated 'what if' information of a short-term nature
Operational	1 Descriptive-historical information
	2 Current performance information
	3 Accent on exception reporting

(b)

Characteristic of information	Categories of decision-making		
	Strategic	*Tactical*	*Operational*
Dependence on external information	Very high	Moderate	Very low
Dependence on internal information	Moderate	High	Very high
Information on-line	High	High	Very high
Information reported periodically	Moderate	High	Very high
Information that is descriptive-historical in nature	Low	High	Very high
Current performance information	Moderate	High	Very high
Predictive information concerning long-term trends	Very high	High	Low
Predictive information concerning short-term trends	High	Very high	Moderate
Information that is simulated 'what if' in nature	Very high	High	Low

The problem of encouraging the flow of consistent, accurate and relevant information to the top of the hierarchy is difficult. For example, reports which are summarized from a number of departments in the hierarchy may be based on different timescales, different assumptions, different interpretations of rules and so on. Such problems have led the NCC (the U.K. National Computing Centre) to state

'Hierarchical structures tend to encourage formal, highly structural information flows in which information is inconsistent, incomplete and filtered (possibly in the wrong way).'

This view is supported by the problem of empire-building which leads to a duplication of effort and information. For instance, a lack of trust or an inappropriate organizational structure may cause both the sales department and the production department to maintain records of customers' orders. As a result the production of reports across the departmental boundaries would often be frustrated.

Responsibility accounting

As management accountants will know, responsibility accounting is a term describing the reporting of financial results in accordance with the assignment of managerial responsibilities within a business organization. It is characterized by three functions. First, the assignment of managerial responsibilities is based on an organizational chart; then a formal statement of these responsibilities is prepared with the given objectives and plans being translated into financial terms – i.e. the budget; thirdly, the actual performance as compared to the budget is reported. In order to achieve this, an organization sometimes has to be split into a number of cost or profit centres – where costs (and revenues where relevant) are collected. Sometimes, these cost centres will be split in such a way that profitability can be reported via product groupings as well as by a summary of costs-by-function.

Reports on a cost centre focus on the variances from planned costs which are controllable by the manager of that centre. This is demonstrated in Figure 11.7 where successively more detailed reports are provided as one proceeds down the organizational chart to lower cost centres.

Management decision making is sometimes defined as being made up of planning, controlling and operating. Planning is concerned with deciding in advance what has to be done, when it has to be done and who has to do it. The control system measures the performance and provides information for control. The operating system is the part of the system which causes the business organization to work; it includes orders, instructions, and specifications. The operating system basically converts the plans into the actual results – the performance can then be measured against plans. Information, however, must be rigidly confined to an organization structure; the information system must have access to all levels in the organization and the operating system. Figure 11.8 shows how information may be obtained from a number of different functional areas within an operating system.

Information levels and flows

Within a business there are a number of distinct types of information. First, there are information types corresponding to strategic, tactical and

ABC MANUFACTURING COMPANY
DEPARTMENTAL COST SUMMARY

MANAGING DIRECTOR AND GENERAL MANAGER	AMOUNT		(OVER) OR UNDER BUDGET	
CONTROLLABLE EXPENSES	THIS MONTH	YEAR TO DATE	THIS MONTH	YEAR TO DATE
	£	£	£	£
M.D.'s Office	3,120	18,410	(30)	(155)
Production Manager	42,635	254,705	(1,020)	(3,655)
Controller	7,520	44,830	135	780
Personnel Manager	2,540	15,135	(40)	90
Marketing Manager	25,860	151,380	(345)	(670)
Treasurer	9,230	55,460	(85)	125
TOTALS	90,905	539,920	(1,385)	(3,485)

	STANDARD		VARIANCE	
	THIS MONTH	YEAR TO DATE	THIS MONTH	YEAR TO DATE
PRODUCTIVE LABOUR	27,120	161,970	3,020	5,130

£254,705

ABC MANUFACTURING COMPANY
PRODUCTION DEPARTMENT : COST SUMMARY

PRODUCTION SUPERVISOR	AMOUNT		(OVER) OR UNDER BUDGET	
CONTROLLABLE EXPENSES	THIS MONTH	YEAR TO DATE	THIS MONTH	YEAR TO DATE
	£	£	£	£
Production Supervisor's Office	960	6,300	(115)	(675)
Drill Press	1,465	8,160	35	(95)
Automatic Screw Machine	5,960	35,530	25	(60)
Punch Press	5,740	33,335	(65)	(1,240)
Heat Treatment	5,060	27,810	35	860
Assembly	5,340	35,845	(625)	(1,380)
TOTALS	24,525	147,280	(210)	(2,590)

	STANDARD		VARIANCE	
PRODUCTIVE LABOUR	THIS MONTH	YEAR TO DATE	THIS MONTH	YEAR TO DATE
Drill Press	2,550	14,250	250	400
Automatic Screw Machine	6,550	39,650	650	2,300
Punch Press	3,720	23,850	215	940
Heat Treatment	3,040	15,880	335	1,800
Assembly	11,260	68,340	1,570	(310)
TOTALS	27,120	161,970	3,020	5,130

£8,160

ABC MANUFACTURING COMPANY
FACTORY COST SUMMARY

PRODUCTION MANAGER	AMOUNT		(OVER) OR UNDER BUDGET	
CONTROLLABLE EXPENSES	THIS MONTH	YEAR TO DATE	THIS MONTH	YEAR TO DATE
	£	£	£	£
P.M.'s Office	2,110	12,030	(115)	35
Production Supervisor's Departments	24,525	147,280	(210)	(2,590)
Production Planning	1,235	7,570	(125)	(210)
Purchasing	1,180	7,045		
Engineering	9,955	57,815	95	75
Receiving, Shipping, Stores	3,630	22,965	(95)	(235)
TOTALS	42,635	254,705	(1,020)	(3,655)

	STANDARD		VARIANCE	
PRODUCTIVE LABOUR	THIS MONTH	YEAR TO DATE	THIS MONTH	YEAR TO DATE
	27,120	161,970	3,020	5,130

£147,280

ABC MANUFACTURING COMPANY
DRILL PRESS COSTS

FOREMAN	AMOUNT		(OVER) OR UNDER BUDGET	
CONTROLLABLE EXPENSES	THIS MONTH	YEAR TO DATE	THIS MONTH	YEAR TO DATE
	£	£	£	£
Supervision	350	2,100		
Setup	175	910		
Repair and Rework	240	1,215		
Overtime Premium	215	1,145	20	40
Supplies	95	545	(25)	35
Small Tools	115	625	(10)	(215)
Other	285			
TOTALS	1,465	4,160		

	STANDARD		VARIANCE	
PRODUCTIVE LABOUR	THIS MONTH	YEAR TO DATE	THIS MONTH	YEAR TO DATE
Amount	2,550	14,250	250	
Hours	850	9,500		
Per Hour	3.00	3.00		

Level	Report
1st level	Managing Director
2nd level	Production Manager
3rd level	Production Supervisor
4th level	Drill Press Foreman

Figure 11.7   *The hierarchy of performance reports*

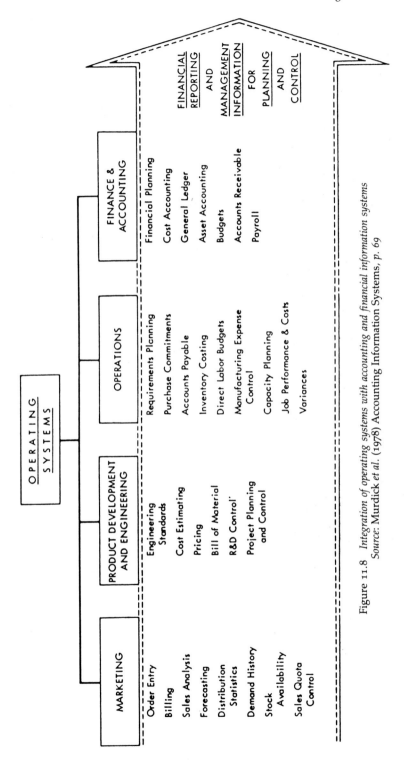

Figure 11.8 *Integration of operating systems with accounting and financial information systems*
Source: Murdick et al. (1978) Accounting Information Systems, p. 69

operational decisions. Assuming that we have now focused on the operating and transaction-processing system, what information flows could
there be?

1   Information relating to a transaction such as a customer purchase
    order, or an acknowledgement of an order.
2   Information relating to the monitoring of the physical movement or
    use of goods, labour or raw materials.
3   Information relating to the payment of cash.

These flows relating to the transactions, the physical movement of goods
and the receipt of cash are all markedly different. Perhaps it is worthwhile
to follow these flows for a particular sale.

A customer purchase order is received. An acknowledgement of the
order may or may not be given. Several possibilities immediately arise
and must be acted upon.

Is this customer a credit customer and is he in the information system?
If yes, is he over his credit limit? Do we have the product he is asking for
in stock?

Obviously, for each question a procedure for dealing with all alternatives
must be specified. If the item is not in stock, for example, the next
question is can we make it? To answer this question we would have to
know the loading on the machines, the raw material situation and the
availability of labour. Let us suppose the item asked for is available from a
finished goods inventory. An instruction has to be issued to take the item
to a loading bay. Another instruction has to be issued to obtain a lorry or
van to come to the loading bay and take the goods to the customer,
accompanied by a delivery note. A consignment note may be sent to the
customer in parallel with the delivery note which may be signed on
delivery and brought back to the company as evidence of delivery. An
invoice must be raised which is essentially the delivery note with pricing
information added and totalled together with VAT (Value-Added Tax).
The amount of the invoice must be added to the amount that particular
customer owes. At the end of the month, a statement must be produced
and sent to the customer, detailing the various invoices and showing the
total amount owed. Finally, a cheque will be received; this will be paid
into the company's bank account and the customer's financial debt will be
decreased by the amount of the cheque.

All the above assumes that nothing goes wrong. What happens if the
goods get lost or damaged in transit? What happens if the customer does
not send a cheque? What happens if the bank does not allow clearance of
the cheque because the customer is overdrawn? What happens if the

wrong item is shipped to the customer? These and many other eventualities must be recorded and monitored by the information system with
relevant reports being fed to the correct person in the organizational
structure.

Distinguishing flows and tasks

In terms of the internal functions associated with a sale, there are three
paramount functions:

Receiving, recording and monitoring the customer order;
Invoicing, generation of a statement of account (containing the current
level of indebtedness of the customer) and receipt of cheque;
Production scheduling/picking the commodity from a warehouse,
packing and despatching the goods to the customer.

However let us broaden our outlook from the sales side of a business to
more general matters.

A distinction must be made between a number of different tasks.
Information flows can either be formal or informal. Formal information
flows usually comprise the transmission of some type of document or an
entry in a file stored on a computer. A diagram of the document flows
within an organization (a document flowchart) is concerned only with the
flow of documents; it leaves out what is done with each of the forms at
each department. Sometimes it is obvious what must occur at each stage
in the system but this is not always the case. In general, a document
flowchart provides a good overview of the information processing, un-
cluttered by detail. Examples of a document flowchart are provided in
Chapter 12.

Systems flowcharts usually specify not only the dcouments in a system
but also the procedures involved (e.g. files to be accessed/updated, customer details and other information to be looked up or recorded) and the
processing steps to be carried out (e.g. prepare invoice, arrange batch of
invoices in alphabetical order). A systems flowchart will also show all
flows of information and other items (e.g. physical movement, cash
movement, electronic transmission of documents and/or information).
The tasks which do not involve document flows are in general, caught by
a systems flowchart.

There are some tasks which are not caught by a systems flowchart.
These tasks include forecasting possible trends in the market, prod-
uct/market appraisals, constant monitoring as to the competitiveness of
the firm and so on. Sales forecasting for example affects the rate of
production which, in turn, will affect purchasing. Forecasting may be

included in a very formal way by surveys or by the use of econometric forecasting, or economic models, or it may be a much more intuitive process based on some or all of the information in a particular department. We will now attempt to provide a simplified example of all information and other flows.

An example

Each firm in each industry is an open probabilistic system and therefore its organizational structure and information flows respond dynamically to environmental forces. No two firms will be subjected to exactly the same forces. Not surprisingly, therefore, each firm develops its own unique structure and, similarly, its own unique document and information flows. This preamble to providing an example of the information flows in a firm is a cautionary warning that every firm or organization is different and that there is no necessary presumption of a better or right way of doing things. On the other hand, evidence of poor performance or organizational objectives in the real world is evidence that not everything is always as efficient and smooth as it could be; because a system is different does not necessarily mean it is inefficient in terms of that particular organization. Very often the job of a systems analyst is to analyse how a firm works and to recommend improvements; his job is not to change for the sake of change – that may very well be worse than no change at all. So with these caveats in mind, an example is now given that is neither claimed to be representative nor typical of a 'good' system. It is simply an example of one approach.

Our example has four functional areas:

Sales and marketing;
Accounting and finance;
Production;
Stores and purchasing.

Each function involves a number of specific jobs.

The sales and marketing department must make sales forecasts, receive orders, deal with quality complaints, develop new products and undertake enquiries as to prices of products, which may involve 'costing', i.e. estimating the cost of special orders.

The main function of the sales department is to achieve certain sales volumes, to advise on product/market developments and instigate continuing product improvement programmes. In order to achieve these aims, the sales department may have to launch advertising campaigns, devise selling strategies, set up distribution networks and so on. It is therefore quite logical that the sales and marketing function should look after all information and document flows associated with customers, and information relating to product availability and markets.

The production department has specific responsibility for producing the goods; this will include production scheduling, job despatching, shipping, shop floor control, and quality control. The actual organization of labour, components and raw materials will be the responsibility of this department. An appraisal of current capacity, efficiency of production and productivity, and new production techniques are the province of this particular department.

The accounting and finance department maintains all records concerned with how much customers owe the organization (the sales ledger*), how much is owed to suppliers (the purchase or bought ledger†) and a list of all other expenditure and other value items (the nominal ledger or general ledger). In addition, this department deals with the payroll. All budgeting operations are performed here, and to help achieve this aim, all costing details are maintained by this department. Cash flow forecasting and longer-term forecasting/financial planning are also undertaken here.

The final function in our example is that of stores and purchasing. This function includes maintenance of the inventory of raw materials and bought-in-components, deciding material requirements and orders appropriately, and, as well as purchasing, receiving the goods when they arrive. Let us consider the most simple information flows within our commercial organization.

Figure 11.9 shows some of the flows of information and tasks required in our simplified example. We assume that there are two inventories: the raw materials and bought-in-components stock, shown as the supply storage, and the finished goods stocks. The order-processing task is handled as a part of the sales and marketing function. Orders are received and invoices sent to customers. Goods are picked from the finished goods inventory or an instruction passed to production to manufacture some more if there is insufficient stock – at this point a continuing dialogue may be entered into with the customer, e.g. can he wait? Once picked from the warehouse or store, the goods are then packed and despatched to the customer. The production department receives a list of orders, knows what is in its finished goods stock and decides on an appropriate production schedule. Product specifications and other information can be passed back to the sales department. Production in turn will pass on its material and parts requirements to purchasing and stores, who will periodically purchase items after examining the raw material inventory. The department responsible for the accounting and finance function must keep track of all the information flows as well as deal with cash receipts from

*Accounts receivable in U.S. jargon.
†Accounts payable in U.S. jargon.

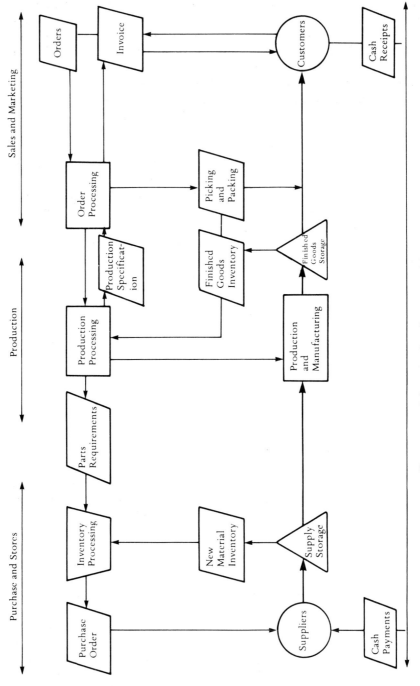

Figure 11.9 *Information flows in a commercial organization*

customers and cash payments to suppliers. Tasks such as pricing will involve the accounting and finance department who should know various current costs; the sales department, who would know what their competitors charge as well as what the market may bear; the production department which will furnish material and parts usage details as well as product specifications, and the purchasing and stores department who provide information on the latest price of raw materials and parts.

The information flows contained in the diagram are not sufficient to run a business. Management would need to continuously monitor orders received, unfilled orders and cancellations. Sales (both in volume and value terms) would also require continual monitoring. For strategic and managerial decisions sales should be regularly analysed by area, customer, salesmen, product group and so on. If possible, the profitability of sales for each analysis head should also be analysed. Complex questions such as the profitability of product groups by area (and even by customer) might provide some interesting insights. Many managements receive a rude shock when profitability by product line information shows that a cherished product is actually unprofitable whilst the real profits are generated from other bread and butter lines.

Similarly, suppliers can be analysed by assessing their price competitiveness, delivery record, quality of product, volume of business, shortfall record, and degree to which alternative suppliers can be found (i.e. multi-sourcing which reduces a firm's dependence on a single supplying firm).

Transactions between the firm and its environment

Having roughly sketched some of the information flows in broad outline, we will now be much more specific. Figure 11.10 shows the transactions and information flows between the firm and its environment. Ignoring the various government agencies, information flows are shown between labour and shareholders as well as customers and suppliers.

Frequency

Different tasks and operations have varying degrees of frequency of operation. Orders are usually recorded as soon as they arrive, whereas pay cheques are usually paid weekly or monthly; VAT returns are made quarterly and so on. In the printing of reports for use by management, use should be made of facilities whereby only that information is printed which in some way deserves special managerial attention. Table 11.4 shows the frequency of operation of some typical procedures.

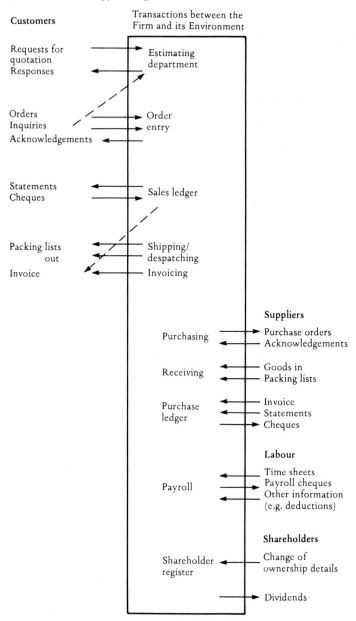

Figure 11.10

Table 11.4 Frequency of operation

Continuous	Order entry
	Inquiries (if by telephone)
Daily	Order costing
	Inventory control
	Invoicing
	Sales ledger
	Production scheduling
	Job despatching
	Shop floor control
	Shipping
	Purchasing
	Receiving
	Material requirements
	Estimating
	Quality control
	Purchase ledger
Weekly	Labour costing
	Payroll
Monthly	Budgeting
	Cost accounting
	Nominal ledger
Periodic	Shareholder register and dividend payments
	Special order processing
	Short-order production planning
	Development of new product specifications

Basic types of operation within a MIS

In terms of the overall functional tasks that must be performed, certain broad categories of procedures may be identifed. These include:

1 Basic information;
2 Management science;
3 Detailed planning;
4 Data processing.

The basic information includes maintaining data on certain key functions and operations. The management science function, in contrast, deals with planning, forecasting, scheduling and operations research. These two areas together allow management to make a decision which is transformed into detailed plans and then implemented. The data-processing function involves updating the basic information in (1) and a comparison of actual results against the detailed plans from (3).

Information characteristics*

Returning to the three sets of managerial control activities: operational, managerial and strategic, the information requirements at the various levels may be characterized as in Figure 11.11. The range of management activities is large and their information requirements diverse. Gorry and Scott-Morton (1971) identified systems developed for senior management which had little impact on managerial activities: a direct result of the failure to understand the different information needs of the different activities. Some problems can be defined as *structured* in which well-defined, rigid and routine decisions can be made. Other problems are *unstructured*, these problems have ambiguous solution procedures and incomplete data (on which to base a decision). Figure 11.12 shows activities with classifications ranging from structured to unstructured. *Decision support systems* are systems designed to help with unstructured problems: such a system must be able to provide models of the decision-making environment which allow the decision-maker maximum insight into the problem, despite the inability to structure it, and in a way that makes this aid effective within the organizational structure. A further distinction can be made between institutional and non-institutional decision support systems. *Institutional* decision support systems are concerned with decision-making problems that are recurrent in their nature and deal with known information needs. Often these systems are characterized by the need for constant revision and modification during their development in order to achieve the fine-tuning and efficiency required by a system that may be frequently used and be expected to have a long life-time. *Ad hoc* decision support systems deal with non-recurrent types of decisions. In these one-off situations managements' information requirements tend to

Characteristics of Information	Operational Control	Management Control	Strategic Planning
Source	Largely internal	———————▶	External
Scope	Well-defined, narrow	———————▶	Very wide
Level of aggregation	Detailed	———————▶	Aggregate
Time horizon	Historical	———————▶	Future
Currency	Highly current	———————▶	Quite old
Required accuracy	High	———————▶	Low
Frequency of use	Very frequent	———————▶	Infrequent

Figure 11.11   *Information requirements by decision category*

*This section is based on Short (1979).

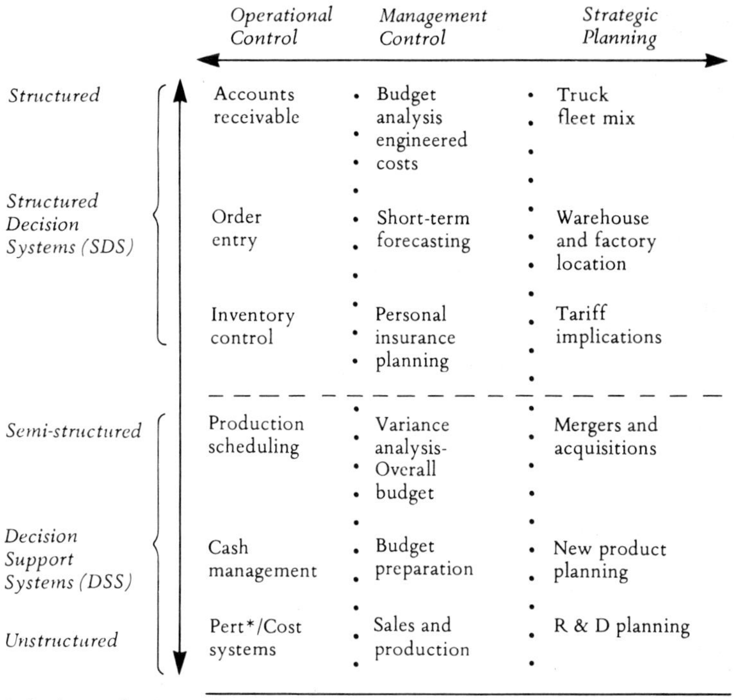

	Operational Control	Management Control	Strategic Planning
Structured	Accounts receivable	• Budget analysis • engineered • costs	• Truck • fleet mix •
Structured Decision Systems (SDS)	Order entry	• Short-term • forecasting	• Warehouse • and factory • location
	Inventory control	• Personal • insurance • planning	• Tariff implications

Semi-structured	Production scheduling	• Variance
		  analysis-
		• Overall
		• budget
			• Mergers and
			  acquisitions
			•

Decision Support Systems (DSS)	Cash management	• Budget • preparation	• New product • planning
Unstructured	Pert*/Cost systems	• Sales and production	• R & D planning

* Project evaluation and review systems

Figure 11.12   *The Gorry and Scott-Morton framework*

be wider, appear suddenly, and often require a rapid solution. With the *ad hoc* decision-support system, managerial needs are not known in advance, and the system must be flexible enough to change or to incorporate new models and data, either as the decision-maker becomes more knowledgeable about the problem on hand, or as the decision situation itself changes. In these systems, the emphasis is on rapidly constituting a flexible system, with operational efficiency being of less importance.

Conclusion

In this section we have discussed the fundamentals of systems in general, and business and management information systems in particular. We have studied the problems and techniques of systems analysis and design and the more mundane realities of commercial organizations and how a business works. It is now time to turn our attention to actual computer applications in business. In Chapter 12, we shall consider the nature and meaning of the heart of a business data-processing system, the accounting system. Although some computerized business systems include subsystems such as stock control, for example, the vast majority of systems include the routine data-processing of the accounting subsystem. We shall then focus on the sales subsystem of the total firm in order to illustrate some of the aspects of computerized systems discussed so far.

Part Three: Further reading

Amey, L. R. *Budget Planning and Control Systems* (Pitman Publishing, 1979)

Berdie, D. R. and Anderson, J. F. *Questionnaires: Design and Use* (Scarecrow Press, 1974)

Clifton, H. D. *Systems Analysis for Business Data Processing* (Business Books, 2nd edn. 1972)

Clifton, H. D. *Business Data Systems* (Prentice-Hall International, 1978)

Cushing, B. E. *Accounting Information Systems and Business Organisations* (Addison-Wesley, 1978)

Cutts, G. *Structured Systems Analysis and Design Methodology* (Paradigm, 1987)

Davis, G. B. *Management Information Systems: Conceptual Foundations, Structures and Development* (McGraw-Hill, 1974)

Davis, J. R. and Cushing, B. E. *Accounting Information Systems: A Book of Readings with Cases* (Addison-Wesley, 1980)

Gallagher, J. D. *Management Information Systems and the Computer* (American Management Association, 1961)

Gorry, G. A. and Scott-Morton, M. S. 'A Framework for Management Information Systems', *Sloan Management Review*, 1971, 13, No. 1, 55–70.

King, P. J. H. 'Conversion of Decision Tables to Computer Programs by Rule Mask Techniques', *Communications of the ACM*, 1966, 9, 11, 796–801.

Lucas, H. C., Jr. *Information Systems Concepts for Management* (McGraw-Hill, 1978)

de Marco, T. *Structured Analysis and Systems specification* (Prentice-Hall, 1978)

Murdick, R. G. *MIS: Concepts and Design* (Prentice-Hall, 1980)

NCC *Introducing Systems Analysis and Design* vol. 1 (National Computing Centre, 1978)

NCC *Introducing Systems Analysis and Design* vol. 2 (National Computing Centre, 1979)

Oliver, E. C. and Chapman, R. J. *Data processing: An Instructional Manual for Business and Accountancy Students* (D. P. Publications, 4th edn. 1979)

Parkin, A. *Systems Analysis* (Edward Arnold, 1980)

Parkin, A. *Systems Management* (Edward Arnold, 1980)

Semprevivo, P. C. *Systems Analysis: Definition, Process and Design* (Science Research Associates, 1976)

Shave, M. J. R. and Bhaskar, K. N. *Computer Science applied to Business Systems* (Addison-Wesley, 1982)

Smillie, K. W. and Shave, M. J. E. 'Converting Decision Tables to Computer Programs', *The Computer Journal*, 1975, 18, 2, 108–111

Thierauf, R. J. and Reynolds, G. W. *Systems Analysis and Design: A Case-Study Approach* (Charles E. Merrill, 1980)

Thierauf, R. J. and Reynolds, G. W. *Effective Information Systems Management* (Charles E. Merrill, 1982)

Part Four

Applications

12 Basic accounting systems

The purpose of this part is to introduce the reader to management accounting and MIS applications. In Part 2, we described technical details of hardware and software, and the techniques for organizing files of information stored in a computer system. Part 3 was concerned with business information systems in general and the role of the systems analyst in the design, implementation and analysis of systems. A knowledge of such details is of vital importance to the management accountant, but he is likely to be more interested in applying these features and techniques to his own particular area. The applications described in the following chapters have been selected to illustrate and bring together the concepts and techniques introduced previously. It is in this section that the relevance of many of the techniques will become apparent.

In this chapter we deal with the conventional data-processing applications of computers to financial accounting. The more exciting and new computer concepts are not fully explored until later chapters. First we shall consider the more mundane applications associated with the purchase ledger, sales ledger, payroll and general ledger application areas. Any cost must be collected and recorded and then allocated to at least one of the following: (1) a job or process, (2) a cost or profit centre, (3) a product, and (4) a cost classification. Similarly, the management accountant will monitor costs against budgets for each of the above categories. As will be seen, what may seem a difficult or tedious manual task can be performed quickly and efficiently by a computer. For the moment the costing and budgeting systems will be ignored, allowing us to focus on the conventional data-processing area which the management accountant will deal with directly and may be responsible for. Our objective is simply to show the reader how the conventional accounting functions are performed with the aid of a computer.

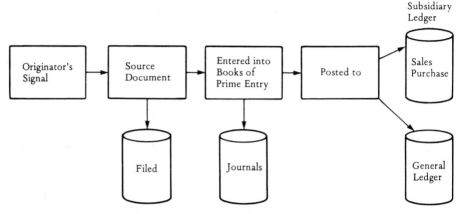

Figure 12.1   *The basic accounting system*

Although the major area of interest to a management accountant will be that of decision support, budgeting and the control process, and planning, most management accountants will still have to keep (or understand the keeping of) the basic books of accounts. The equivalent manual system would involve:

(a)   The books of prime entry such as the sales journal, purchase journal, cash book and general journal;
(b)   The subsidiary ledgers including the sales and purchase ledgers;
(c)   The payroll system; and
(d)   The general or nominal ledger.

Figure 12.1 shows how the basic accounting system operates. Some sort of originating signal occurs: this could be a telephone call or receipt of an order or some other initiating document. From this signal an internal source document is raised. Copies of this document will be filed away. At some later point, these source documents will be entered into the books of prime entry (which is essentially a file) and then subsequently posted to the subsidiary and general ledgers.

Since the general ledger area is or can be more closely associated with the specialist work of the management accountant, we will defer all consideration of the general ledger until the next chapter. The sales ledger, purchase ledger and payroll are essentially all similar; they deal with customers, suppliers and personnel. It is summaries of transactions affecting these detailed records which are posted to the general ledger. In order to provide a more comprehensive treatment this chapter will primarily focus on a sales system. However, a purchase or payroll system is similar and the lessons learnt from a computerized sales system can be carried over, with some differences, to these areas. The differences will be discussed at the end of the chapter.

Reason for mechanization

A computerized book-keeping or basic accounting system performs the same functions as a manual system. Why should you computerize? One answer is speed. Another reason, which is also essentially an argument that depends on speed, is that a business may find that an existing manual system cannot adequately cope with the volume of work. Speed is not the only argument; the computerized system should be capable of doing more. Traditionally, there are two reasons for advocating the use of the computer in basic accounting systems:

1 *Cost:* By computerizing certain basic clerical operations, it is hoped that staff costs may be reduced for a given volume of transactions;
2 *Improved information:* Computers allow for better (i.e. more timely/relevant/accurate) information.

Historically, computers always produced better information or more information than that available on a manual system. However, cost savings were not always achieved; the savings made on low-grade clerical personnel were outweighed by more expensive specialist computer staff. With the advent of cheaper micro- and minicomputers the need for specialist staff is less, but the maintenance and running costs of the computer (usually significant and sometimes equal to the purchase price of the hardware) must be taken into account.

Duplication of information: a manual example

One advantage of computers which can give rise to cost savings as well as better/additional information is the centralization of data with the possibility of many different users and departments being able to access the data. Not only is centralized access a significant advantage (as will be demonstrated below) but modern data-management systems (e.g. multiple keys in indexed sequential files) allow some data to be accessed in different ways by different people. Invoices could be accessed, for example, by date (i.e. all invoices on a particular day), by invoice number, by customer, by item ordered and so on. An example will illustrate this.

In order to illustrate the difference between a computerized and manual system, we will describe a manual sales system and then discuss how a computerized system would differ from this. The sales system given below is a simple system and deals with:

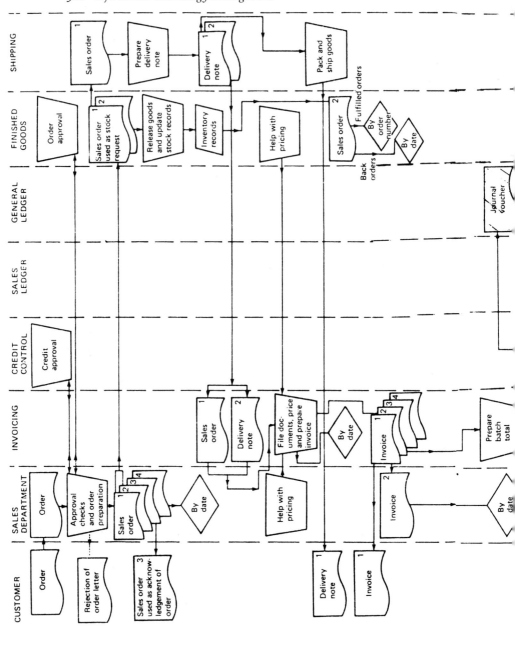

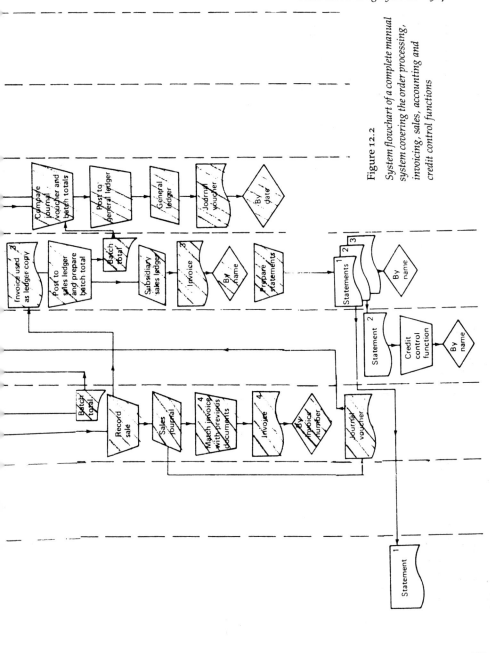

Figure 12.2

System flowchart of a complete manual system covering the order processing, invoicing, sales, accounting and credit control functions

Order processing;
Invoicing;
Sales recording;
Credit control.

This system does not deal with sales return or cost receipts. (Similar systems were more fully developed in Part 3.)

Figure 12.2 begins with a customer order, which is either sent to the sales department or obtained over the phone by the sales department. Before the order can be accepted, a number of checks must be made. First, approval for this particular order must be obtained from credit control. Sometimes, this check can take the simple form of verifying that the value of this order combined with the customers current balance does not exceed his credit limit. Second, the sales department must check whether there is sufficient stock to cover this order or, failing this, whether the production department can fulfil this order within a reasonable period of time. Once through these checks, the order is then transcribed onto a four-part internal order document – the sales order. Copy 4 of the sales order is filed by date in the sales department. (An extra degree of control could be placed on unfulfilled orders by temporarily splitting these from the main file and routinely checking up on their progress.) Copy 3 is sent to the customer as an acknowledgement of order. Copies 1 and 2 are sent to the finished goods department. Copy 2 is used to release the goods and update the inventory records. Orders which have been fulfilled are then filed by order number. Orders for which a back-order has been issued are temporarily filed separately where a measure of control on these orders can be exerted. Copy 1 is used by the shipping department to prepare a two-part delivery note. Delivery note 1 accompanies the goods which are sent to the customer. Delivery note 2, together with sales order 1 are sent to the invoicing department and matched. An invoice is prepared with full pricing details appended – help being forthcoming from the sales and finished goods departments. (An acknowledgement of the delivery may be received separately or the person delivering the goods may return a third copy of the delivery note duly signed – i.e. goods as specified in the delivery note were received by the customer.)

A four-part invoice is then raised with copy 1 being sent to the customer. Copy 2, sent to the sales department, is filed by date and can provide a check on the sales order (i.e. what was requested) and the invoice (what was actually sold). Copy 3 of the invoice is used as a sales ledger copy; this means that a batch total is prepared by printing the calculator listings prior to being sent to the general ledger. Copy 4 is matched by the invoicing department with the sales order (3) and the delivery note (2). The general ledger is updated by using the batch control totals derived in the invoicing and sales ledger departments. Finally, statements are prepared and sent to the customer, and the credit-control function attempts to minimize the amount and length of credit extended to customers. In this system, the delivery note accompanies the goods and shows what the shipment should contain.

The sales department receives the orders, deals with order-approval checks, raises a four-part order, helps with pricing and stores a copy of the sales order (no. 4) and invoice (no. 2) in date order. A degree of control on unfilled orders can be exerted by periodically scanning this file. The invoicing department matches the sales order (no. 1) and delivery note (no. 2), files these documents by date order, prepares a four-part invoice, prices the invoice, prepares a batch total, enters the sales journal, raises a journal voucher, matches the previous documents with the invoice and stores by invoice number. The credit-control function approves credit, receives statements and constantly monitors customers' accounts; any customer whose account is overdue must be followed up and pressure brought to bear on that customer to pay up as soon as possible.

The sales ledger department is responsible for maintaining the subsidiary ledgers. Individual customers' enquiries could be quickly answered as all invoices will be stored by customer name (and then by date order). Statements are also generated by the sales ledger department. The general ledger department is solely responsible for the debtors' control account. The finished goods department is responsible for the maintenance of stock records, release of goods and control over back orders and unfulfilled orders. The shipping department prepares a delivery note and packs and ships the goods.

The control of the system is exercised through separation of functions and the duplication of effort. Handling of the goods, record-keeping, and authorization are segregated. Note that batch totals are prepared twice in the invoicing department, once as a pre-list of invoices and once as a total from the sales journal. A third total is prepared in the postings to a subsidiary ledger and all three are compared prior to acceptance by the general ledger function. Tight control is necessary, since a missing invoice (either accidental or deliberate) means a free gift to a customer. If free gifts through missing invoices continue unchecked, then this could lead to the bankruptcy of the business. Any batch totals which have been raised are documented and either kept separately with detailed notes, or are appended to the journal entry or posting. In both cases, sufficient notes and details must be provided to explain to a third party exactly what was done, when and to which documents.

In some systems, the sales order, delivery note and invoice are combined into one multi-purpose six-part invoice. The purpose of each invoice is as follows:*

---

*See, for example, Page and Hooper (1979) pages 113–118.

Copy
1   Goes to the customer as his invoice;
2   Is filed by invoice number in the sales department: this maintains control over the invoices;
3   Goes to the sales ledger where it is filed by customer name;
4   Goes to the customer as a delivery note;
5   Is filed by date in the invoicing department to back up the batch control total sent to the general ledger department;
6   Goes to the customer as acknowledgement of his order.

Duplication of information within the sales system

Notice that in the order processing/invoicing sales recording/sales accounting part of the system, much of the same information is retained in different ways by the firm. The reason for this is that the firm must access the same information in different ways and for differing purposes. Consider the following uses:

1   A copy of the sales order (no. 4) is retained in the sales department. A copy of the invoice (no. 2) is also retained in the sales department. Together they provide a measure of control over the progress of all sales.
2   The invoicing department maintains a record of all invoices (no. 4) by invoice number together with a sales order (no. 1) and a delivery note (no. 2). This provides a physical control over all invoices (gaps in a consecutive numbering system can be spotted easily) as well as providing quick access to an invoice by identifying number.
3   The sales ledger department stores a copy of the invoice (no. 3) and statement (no. 3); this is partly to provide a convenient enquiry service to customers as all relevant documents are grouped together by customer name to provide a quick access.
4   Statements (no. 2) are also stored by name in the credit control department.
5   Sales order (no. 2) is also stored by date in the finished goods department.

Some of this duplication is to provide a proper audit trail; for example, the keeping of sales orders and invoices by date, in the sales department; the filing of invoices, sales orders and delivery notes by invoice number in the invoicing department; and the filing of all relevant documents by customer name in the sales ledger department. Other documents are stored either to provide useful information at some future date (i.e. what price did we charge customer X for product Y last time?) or as a means for providing a control over the proper processing of that sale (i.e. have we dealt with all outstanding orders?). Obviously, one impact of a computer is to minimize this duplication. Information can be stored fewer times and by using the file-access capabilities of the computer the same information can be accessed in different ways. For control and auditing reasons, some duplication is inevitable and cannot be eradicated; some redundancy must also be maintained for security purposes.

A computerized debtors sales system

Having looked at a manual sales accounting system, we now turn our attention to a particular example of a simple computer-based accounting system. The system described is based on a simplified version of the accounting package implemented by *Systime*. To some extent the title of this section is a misnomer since we shall only cover those points of the package dealing with credit control, sales ledger and general ledger.

Although the package deals with invoicing and finished goods, we shall assume that these operations are not covered by the computerized system. The package does not cover the shipping, receiving, order-entry or order-processing functions. These operations either have to be, or are assumed to be, performed manually. However, a substantial part of the accounting system is computerized; this corresponds to the shaded part of the systems flowchart in Figure 12.2. Manual files may still be maintained of the various copies of the invoices. How the manual system and the computer system dovetail is something that the management accountant can influence.

The system has four types of files. There is the customer or debtors file with details of each customer plus some totals and other information (e.g. name, address, credit limit, total debt outstanding). There is a transaction file in which details of all 'current' transactions are stored. What 'current' means is very much up to the user. There is a temporary transaction file to which all transactions are first input. Finally, there is a file to which all transactions are input and which records only the summary details of each transaction. The system described is interactive with on-line input and some real-time updating of master files.

Figures 12.3 and 12.4 show a run diagram of the file-processing cycle. In Run 1 in Figure 12.3(a) data is entered and stored on a temporary file. Figure 12.3(b) shows the display on a VDU screen after invoice details have just been input.

One of the advantages of a computerized system is that not all the information has to be keyed in for each invoice. For example, on entering the account – 000066 in Figure 12.3(b) – the screen will fill in the name and address automatically. The invoice number and the date may be auto-

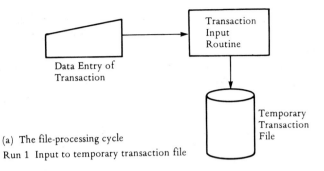

(a) The file-processing cycle

Run 1 Input to temporary transaction file

FIRE QUEEN LIMITED 195 CHAPEL STREET SALFORD M3 5EQ		ACCT.NO: 000066 BRANCH: 01 REP: NO: NA				INVOICE NO: 001254 DATE: 03/07/84 ORDER NO: 123654	
	PRODUCT CODE	DESCRIPTION		QTY	UNIT PRICE	GOODS AMOUNT	VAT%
01	FIR002	400 FT. ASBESTOS	HOST 2"	12	70.00	840.00	0.00
02	KET001	SWAN AUTOMATIC	KETTLE	5	16.50	82.50	15.00
03	KET003	HOTPOINT CHROME	KETTLE	4	10.60	42.40	15.00
04	DRESS002	BLUE GINGHAM DRESS	SIZE 10	2	18.50	37.00	15.00
05							
06							
07							
08							
09							
10							
				GOODS TOTAL		1001.90	
				VAT TOTAL		24.29	
				INVOICE		1026.19	

OK TO LOAD INVOICE (Y/N)?

(b) On-line Invoice Production on a VDU

Figure 12.3   (a) *The file-processing cycle, (b) On-line invoice production on a VDU*

matically generated. If the computer system also has a product file, then all that is needed for each line of the invoice is:

Product code;
Quantity.

The description and price can be looked up by the computer and arithmetic (including VAT and total price) performed automatically. Hence, computerizing the invoice can save time and effort as well as guaranteeing the accuracy of calculations. (A flexible system would allow the input of a special price but, from the auditing viewpoint, this has certain risks unless adequately controlled – both in authorization and the recording of this event.)

In Run 2, probably carried out at the end of a day, the data stored in the temporary transactions file are transferred to the permanent transaction file. This is shown in Figure 12.4. As well as the permanent transactions file being updated, the customer/debtors file and the sales analysis file are also updated. Normally, two types of reports may be printed, a list of all transactions and a summary of the data contained in the files. At the same time as updating the customer file, the daily processing cycle will also post a batch total to the general ledger.

Another advantage of the computerized system is the complete documentation of the inputs and what has been updated. A good system, in this respect, is bliss to audit and easy to keep track of. A bad system can be disastrous.

Sales analysis

A minimal sales/debtors system would not have a sales analysis section. A sales analysis section usually summarizes sales, or orders the transactions in a variety of ways, for example an analysis of all sales made:

By product;
By salesman/rep code;
By area code;
By branch or division;
By company type.

The system described also generates the invoice. Not every transaction in-put would give rise to an output document such as an invoice. Hence Figure 12.4 shows three output reports.

Table 12.1 shows an analysis of sales by customer within certain area codes. In this particular system, targets (or budgets) are set for each area. This ability to capture data which occur in a random fashion and re-arrange or sort them under various codes and then provide sub-totals is a classic example of converting 'raw data' into useful 'information'. It imposes a structure on the data which can become far more meaningful to management. Again, this is an advantage of a computer system. To do the scan manually would be both tedious and time consuming. Although it is possible to perform a sales analysis function manually, most firms with manual systems would not 'waste' their time doing so – even if they realized important information was being lost.

Table 12.1   Sample sales analysis report

No.	Description	Quantity				Value			
		This year		Last year		This year		Last year	
		Current	To date	Current	To date	Current	To date	Current	To date
1	*Area*								
0101	Advertising Bureau	0	0	0	0	1523.67	3899.44	0.00	0.00
0706	Car Care Plan	0	0	0	0	7739.63	11677.40	0.00	0.00
2402	General Transport Co. Ltd.	0	0	0	0	2577.87	2914.75	0.00	0.00
2506	Hepworths Industrial Plastics	0	0	0	0	428.93	678.77	0.00	0.00
	Total	0	0	0	0	12270.12	19170.36	0.00	0.00
	Targets					10500.00	19800.00		
	Difference					1770.10	629.64—		
2	*Area 2*								
0101	E. J. Arnold Ltd.	0	0	0	0	0.00	753.44	0.00	0.00
2702	Nalfloc Ltd.	0	0	0	0	0.00	4028.45	0.00	0.00
3220	Oxbridge Garages Ltd	0	0	0	0	0.00	22.67	0.00	0.00
3445	St Peters Sporting Goods	0	0	0	0	6758.69	3433.34	0.00	0.00
3705	Read Medway Sacks	0	0	0	0	1548.97	3164.52	0.00	0.00
	Total	0	0	0	0	8307.66	16402.42	0.00	0.00
	Targets					14500.00	26100.00		
	Difference					6192.34—	9697.58—		

3	*Area 3*									
0323	Jack L. Barnett	o	o	o	o	2137.91	5851.63	0.00	0.00	
0720	Charlie Brown's Mot. Supermkts Ltd.	o	o	o	o	15904.18	28063.47	0.00	0.00	
1515	Courier Printing & Publishing Ltd	o	o	o	o	1566.89	3169.00	0.00	0.00	
3728	Roevin Ltd.	o	o	o	o	632.44	956.70	0.00	0.00	
	Total					20241.42	38040.80			
	Targets					25000.00	48600.00			
	Difference					4758.58—	10559.20—			
4	*Area 4*									
0357	Buchan Meat Producers	o	o	o	o	1136.69	1497.84	0.00	0.00	
2707	George Morrell & Sons Ltd	o	o	o	o	2449.86	4955.93	0.00	0.00	
2927	University of Newcastle-upon-Tyne	o	o	o	o	812.20	2268.29	0.00	0.00	
	Total					4398.75	8722.06			
	Targets					6500.00	11600.00			
	Difference					2105.25—	2877.94—			
6	*Area 6*									
2002	Discount for Beauty	o	o	o	o	1415.70	3848.99	0.00	0.00	
2711	Motaproducts Automotive Ltd.	o	o	o	o	25.30	196.88	0.00	0.00	
4101	Yorkshire General Life Insurance	o	o	o	o	1181.98	1903.86	0.00	0.00	
	Total					2622.98	5949.73			
	Targets					4000.00	6800.00			
	Difference					1377.02—	850.27—			

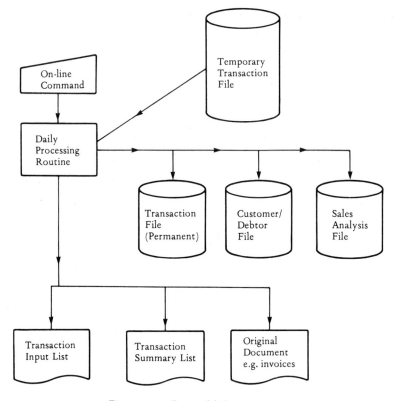

Figure 12.4   *Run 2 of daily processing cycle*

Transaction processing

Having outlined the system in global terms, it is useful to take a closer look at it. First, we will examine the transaction-processing facilities. There will be a number of separate data entry routines dealing with:

Invoices;
Credit notes;
Cash;
Journal entry;
Contras;
Discount.

Each type of distinct transaction involves a slightly different conversation with the user. Hence, each routine is separately distinguished.

There are two reports which are prepared in the course of the daily

Table 12.2 Listing of all current or unpaid transactions for a customer

Advertising Bureau
Newton Road
Chapeltown Leeds LS7

0101						14-Dec-79		1		0101				14-Dec-79	
06 Nov 79	80219 103	INV	4.40	201.84			P		06 Nov 79	4.40	80219 103	INV		201.84	P
12 Oct 79	82001	INV	6.21	284.74			P		12 Oct 79	6.21	82001	INV		284.74	P
04 Oct 79	78766 103	INV	1.81	83.20			P		04 Oct 79	1.81	78766 103	INV		83.20	P
06 Sep 79	74758 130	INV	0.00	183.56			P		06 Sep 79	0.00	74758 130	INV		183.56	P
10 Sep 79	76019 130	INV	0.00	165.14			P		10 Sep 79	0.00	76019 130	INV		165.14	P
14 Dec 79	12512	CSH	0.00		686.31		P		14 Dec 79	0.00	12512	CSH		636.31-	P
14 Dec 79	12513	CSH	0.00		348.70		P		14 Dec 79	0.00	12513	CSH		348.70-	P
14 Dec 79	12514	CSH	0.00		434.09		P		14 Dec 79	0.00	12514	CSH		434.09-	P
14 Dec 79	78886	SET	0.00		8.42		P		14 Dec 79	0.00	78836	SET		8.42-	P
14 Dec 79	82001	SET	0.00		6.21		P		14 Dec 79	0.00	82001	SET		6.21-	P
14 Dec 79	82506	SET	0.00		0.66		P		14 Dec 79	0.00	82506	SET		0.66-	P
14 Dec 79	2	TFP	0.00	348.70			P		14 Dec 79	0.00	2	TFP		348.70	P
14 Dec 79	3	TFP	0.00	434.09			P		14 Dec 79	0.00	3	TFP		434.09	P
14 Dec 79	78766 103	SET	0.00		1.81		P		14 Dec 79	0.00	78766 103	SET		1.81-	P
14 Dec 79	30219 103	SET	0.00		4.40		P		14 Dec 79	0.00	80219 103	SET		4.40-	P
14 Dec 79	80220 103	SET	0.00		3.46		P		14 Dec 79	0.00	80220 103	SET		3.46-	P
14 Dec 79	3	103 TFP	0.00		434.09		P		14 Dec 79	0.00	3	103 TFP		434.09-	P
14 Dec 79	2	130 TFP	0.00		348.70		P		14 Dec 79	0.00	2	130 TFP		348.70-	P
04 Oct 79	78886	INV	8.42	386.35			P		04 Oct 79	8.42	78886	INV		386.35	P
10 Oct 79	82506	INV	0.66	30.51			P		14 Oct 79	0.66	82506	INV		30.51	P
06 Nov 79	80220 103	INV	3.46	158.72			P		06 Nov 79	3.46	80220 103	INV		153.72	P
23 Nov 79		BAL	0.00	1.41					14 Dec 79	0.00		BAL		1.41	
16 Oct 79	10364	CRD	0.00			50.61			30 Dec 79	0.00	10364	CRD		50.61-	
14 Dec 79	78885	PDB	0.00	354.30					30 Dec 79	0.00	78885	PDB		354.30	
			0.00	305.10										305.10	
			0.00	303.69		0.00		1.41							

processing cycle. These include a *batch list* and a *sales day book* or *sales journal*. In addition, there is a routine which allows entries on the temporary transactions file to be deleted or amended.

Another type of operation which may be required is the interactive inquiry concerning the status of a customer's debit – this may be used to help credit control. Figure 12.5 shows the run diagram and the VDU display of the account details.

The display of the customer's details as in Figure 12.5(b) to various parts of the organization (e.g. sales, credit control, marketing and so on) is important. A full list of transactions is shown on another page. Table 12.2 is a listing of all the current or unpaid transactions for a particular customer.

Details kept on the file

At this stage the reader may wish to find out what details are stored on the files. The temporary transaction file and the transaction file are broadly similar. The customer file has two types of information:

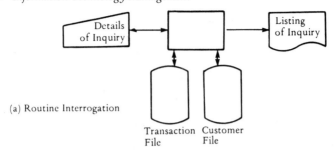

(a) Routine Interrogation

Transaction   Customer
File   File

DRF020   *DEBTORS ACCOUNT ENQUIRY*

ACCOUNT	0000581
NAME	NU-SWIFT INTERNATIONAL
	LIMITED
ADDRESS	SALISBURY MILLS
	NUTTALL STREET
	BLACKBURN
TELEPHONE	56518

REP CODE	NA
BRANCH CODE	01
AREA CODE	P
ALPHA SORT	NUSWIFT
ACCOUNT TYPE	F
TERMS	30
CREDIT LIMIT	2000
YTD DEBITS	1230.00
YTD CREDITS	0.00

BALANCE B/F	1900.00
ACCOUNT BALANCE	3130.00
CURRENT	1630.00
30 DAYS	500.00
60 DAYS	600.00
90 DAYS	400.00
120 DAYS	0.00
CURR MONTH DR	1230.00
CURR MONTH CR	0.00

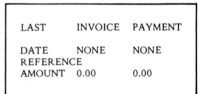

LAST	INVOICE	PAYMENT
DATE	NONE	NONE
REFERENCE		
AMOUNT	0.00	0.00

NO OF TRANS THIS MONTH 1

(b) VDU display of inquiry

DO YOU WISH TO VIEW THIS ACCOUNTS TRANSACTION? (Y/N):

Figure 12.5   (a) *Routine interrogation*, (b) *VDU display of inquiry*

1   Permanent or static (standing) information such as the account number, customer name, etc. Even some items, such as address, may change from time to time.
2   Changing or volatile information such as the current balance.

Although the account details are shown in Figure 12.5, Table 12.3 shows the information which may be contained in the customer file. There is an above average degree of flexibility in terms of discount and settlement procedures. Table 12.3 also shows the sort of information that may be contained in a transaction file. The sales ledger system automatically defines a unique document reference number for each entry in the

Table 12.3 Details of the type of information stored on the sales ledger

Customer file	Transaction file
Account number	Account number
Customer name	Document date
Address	Document reference.
	Date to which the transaction is to be
	allocated.
Current balance	Total amount
Turnover Year to date*	Goods amount
Turnover previous Year to date*	VAT amount(s)‡
Credit limit	Sundries amount (e.g. insurance, packing)
Balance forward or open item	Sundry charge type
Account type†	Quantity
Account term	Product analysis code
Settlement discount terms	Customer analysis code
Settlement discount	
Trade discount	
Analysis codes	

*Calendar and financial.
†Head office, branch or sub-branch.
‡There may be several for differing rates.
N.B. A sales budget for each customer may also be appropriate but is not supplied in this particular system.

file. One problem that has to be faced is the analysis code. It may be that the whole invoice can be analysed under one code, for example, product analysis code. On the other hand, certain lines on the invoice may be analysed under one product code, whilst other lines are allocated to other codes. The system must be capable of analysing a total amount into a number of different analysis heads.

There is a simple routine to create and amend the static details relating to a customer account and to perform enquiries into the current status of the account. Typical operations used to maintain customers/debtors amounts include:

Insert a new account;
Amend an account (but not the balance);
Print account details;
Delete account details (but only a zero balance account).

Figure 12.6(a) shows the run diagram for file maintenance. Each customer account has a number of static details which are invariant with the number of transactions. The user runs the program by typing the appropriate number on a file maintenance menu; the VDU layout as shown in Figure 12.6(b) is displayed. The square brackets on the right show the maximum allowable size of each field. Obviously, not all the fields are displayed since we should not wish certain items (e.g. account balance) to

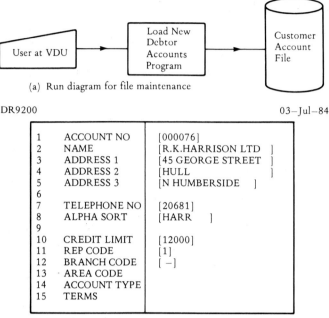

(a) Run diagram for file maintenance

DR9200   03–Jul–84

1	ACCOUNT NO	[000076]
2	NAME	[R.K.HARRISON LTD]
3	ADDRESS 1	[45 GEORGE STREET]
4	ADDRESS 2	[HULL]
5	ADDRESS 3	[N HUMBERSIDE]
6		
7	TELEPHONE NO	[20681]
8	ALPHA SORT	[HARR]
9		
10	CREDIT LIMIT	[12000]
11	REP CODE	[1]
12	BRANCH CODE	[–]
13	AREA CODE	
14	ACCOUNT TYPE	
15	TERMS	

(b) VDU layout for inserting a new customer account

Figure 12.6 (a) *Run diagram for file maintenance,* (b) *VDU layout for inserting a new customer account*

be altered without a proper input of authorized transactions or adjustments.

Ledger maintenance

The permanent transactions file and the customer file together make up the sales ledger. Neither the balance on the customer file nor the individual transactions on the transaction file can be modified (but it is possible to delete certain transactions e.g. invoices after they have been paid). If there is a mistake on the sales ledger (transactions file plus customer file) then the only way to correct the mistake is to input appropriate entries through the daily processing routine and on the temporary (or daily) transaction file.

The way in which the information on the temporary file eventually gets incorporated into the sales ledger is by means of a ledger updating routine (sometimes called a day-end routine to match the notion of a daily transaction file). This routine will insert the new transactions into the transactions file, update the balances on the customer file, add any invoices or credit notes to the sales analysis transactions file (see below) and prepare a report on the various operations undertaken in this run.

Accounting functions

Various accounting functions such as the generation of statements, prints of the debtors schedule and label printing (for envelopes) may be required. Up to now we have assumed an open-item ledger system (rather than a balance-brought-forward). If we were running a balance-brought-forward system (opening balance plus any transactions that have occurred subsequently), then a procedure would be required to bring forward the opening balance. With an open-item system, two additional routines are required: firstly, a print of unpaid transactions and, secondly, a cash allocation or matching routine.

The purpose of this latter routine is to use cash received to pay invoices. Once an invoice has been paid, and perhaps after it has appeared on the statement, it can be removed from the ledger. However, there are several factors which complicate this procedure. A single cash payment can be received to pay a range of invoices; credit notes may be used as a form of payment. Minor discrepancies in payment could be written-off. A part payment might be received. Settlement discount may be applicable. Invoices may be placed in dispute. For a variety of reasons a debit or credit journal entry may be present. The system must be capable of dealing with all these requirements and allocating cash to certain transactions. Once a series of invoices, i.e. invoice, part-payment or a write-off – all with or without discount – have been allocated against a sum of cash (for a total write-off it could be zero), then an entry is made in the temporary transaction file to this effect. Subsequently, the invoices which have been matched against a particular cash item may be deleted. If only unpaid invoices are kept in the transactions file, the file is sometimes called a live transactions file.

Analysis reports

The analysis reporting system usually relies on the posting of invoices and credit-note analysis details directly to the sales analysis transactions file when the ledger is updated. When an analysis report is prepared, it will utilize details held on the sales analysis transaction file and the analysis descriptions file. The latter holds details of the analysis descriptions and perhaps the budgets. Descriptions are necessary since only analysis codes are maintained on the analysis transactions file in order to reduce the size of the file. Analysis routines include:

Amend analysis descriptions and budgets;
Print analysis descriptions and budgets;
Print sales analysis.

Period end processing

At the month end (or period end if a firm chooses its accounting year to consist of 13 four weekly periods), the operations that are performed are a statement print and maintenance of the ledger. Statements are usually prepared on a standard two-part form, one part of which is a remittance advice. The statement can be prepared on a consolidated basis (i.e. branch, sub-branch and head office levels) or the statement can be prepared on a branch or head office basis.

The month end is also an opportune time for tidying up the content of the ledger. Items which have been paid may be removed after they have appeared on a statement. Deleted accounts will need to be removed from the files.

At a quarter end, the VAT return will be prepared and the quarter date accumulations set to zero. The usual month-end processing is also involved.

At year end, the turnover year-to-date accumulations are set to zero. Another special procedure is to transfer this year's transactions on the analyses to last year. Again, the month-end process is involved.

Other non-routine procedures

There are a number of routines which are essential to the operation of the computerized system but which do not need to be run on a regular basis.

(a) *Sales ledger system maintenance and creation.*
There are a number of routines which are used to create and maintain the ledger system. For example, the various files have to be created to take a certain number of accounts and a certain number of transactions.

(b) *Account details maintenance and creation.*
A number of routines are used to create and amend the 'static' details relating to a customer account and to perform enquiries into the current status of the account. Also provided are certain routines used for the performance of necessary housekeeping procedures in relation to the accounts file. Examples include:

Insert account details;
Amend account details;
Print account details,
Delete account details.

Figure 12.6 showed an example of inserting a new account.
(c) *VAT routines.*

These would include a routine to amend VAT rates and print details for the VAT quarterly return.

Reports

We have talked about the generation of routine reports and those especially able to help management; it is these reports which are the heart of any MIS system. In this system, there are a number of routine reports and management reports. Figure 12.7 shows the typical run diagram. The reports include:

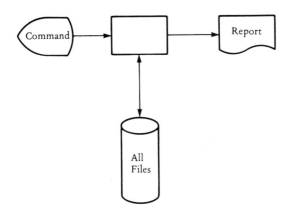

Figure 12.7   *Monthly routine reports*

Print-out of all the customer's accounts;
Print of unpaid transactions;
VAT register;
Age of debtors schedule;
Statements;
Sales analysis print;
Debtors schedule in analysis code sequence;
Labels (for envelopes).

Information regarding the following two control or parameter files may also be required:

Ledger parameter print;
Analysis description print.

On transaction entry, a number of reports will be prepared, they include:

Batch list,
Sales daybook or journal,
Ledger control report.

Management may like to see a more concise report or to highlight certain key features. This is an advantage of a computerized system and we return to this at the end of the chapter.

Operation of system

As with most business systems, the user of this system is led through a number of menus. To begin with, the user of the debtors system types in a command which starts the system running – this could be:

RUN ACCSYS

and the master or system menu for the system is displayed. This is shown in Figure 12.8. By typing 01, the user can get into the major part of the sales ledger; similarly, 03 gives entry to the invoicing routine. Remember that transactions can be initiated without necessarily going through the invoicing routine. After being transferred to the invoice menu, one can select any of the operations on that menu (see Figure 12.9). When finished with whatever invoicing operations were required, by pressing 99 the user can return to the main system menu. Sometimes, in invoicing routines, the price is either authorized or input at some later stage.

Assuming that we are back in the main menu, we shall now press 01 and enter the debtors main menu. The parting routine is the day-end routine which transfers the transactions from the various temporary files (equivalent to the journals or books of prime entry in a manual system) to

99P005   03–Jul–84

DESCRIPTION	FC
DEBTORS	01
STOCK	02
INVOICING	03
CREDITORS	04
NOMINAL LEDGER	05
PAYROLL	06
SYSTEM SHUTDOWN	99

PLEASE ENTER FUNCTION CODE

Figure 12.8   *Master or system menu*

9TP005   03–Jul–84

DESCRIPTION	FC
LOAD DELIVERY ADDR	01
AMEND DELIVERY ADDR	02
ONLINE INVOICING	03
PRINT INVOICES	04
INVOICE RESTART	05
DEBTORS ENQUIRY	06
STOCK ENQUIRY	07
RETURN TO SYSTEM MENU	99

PLEASE ENTER FUNCTION CODE

Figure 12.9   *Invoicing menu*

the transaction and customer/debtors file which makes up the sales ledger.

From the master/system menu we have moved to the next-level menu which is the debtors main menu (see Figure 12.10(a)). If we select any of these operations, then in turn there will be a second-level menu. For example, by selecting the month-end routine (06) a new month-end menu is displayed. This is shown in Figure 12.10(b) where the various operations within that menu are shown. The levels of menus are thus master/system menu, debtors main menu, month-end menu.

Advantages of a computerized system

One particularly useful feature may be the preparation of delinquency or reminder letters; for accounts which are overdue to an extent specified by the user, appropriately worded first and second reminder letters can be printed.

For management who want something short to read yet at the same time require the output to be specific enough to highlight vital areas, the computer is an ideal tool. Examples of typical exception reports include:

1 Aged outstanding debt schedule – which shows all the account details aged over a three-month period including the date of the last sale.
2 Overdue accounts schedule – a concise report of account balances which have been outstanding for two months or more.
3 Credit limit listings – the computer prints those accounts where the credit limit has been exceeded, or where a percentage of the credit limit has been reached.
4 Activity listings – a list of accounts which have remained inactive over a specified period.

All these reports should help to provide better credit control.

ORP005 *Debtors Main Menu*   03–Jul–84

DESCRIPTION	FC
FILE MAINTENANCE	01
CONTROL ENQUIRY	02
ENQUIRIES	03
POSTING	04
SALES ANALYSIS	05
MONTH END	06
UTILITIES	07
RETURN TO SYSTEM MENU	99

PLEASE ENTER FUNCTION CODE

(a) Debtors main menu

DRP030 *Month-end Menu*   03–Jul–84

DESCRIPTION	FC
PRINT STATEMENTS	01
PRINT AGE ANALYSIS	02
VAT ANALYSIS REPORT	03
UPDATE AGE ANALYSIS	04
RETURN TO MAIN MENU	99

PLEASE ENTER FUNCTION CODE

(b) Debtors month-end routines

Figure 12.10   (a) *Debtors' main menu*, (b) *Debtors' month-end routines*

If budget data are also kept on the customer file then budget, actual or variance reports can also be provided, thus improving control over sales. Both managerial and strategic problems can be better tackled by analysis of sales and profitability under a number of heads; for example, by salesman, product group, market equipment, region, customer, type of customer, period and so on. Sometimes complex questions, such as what are the sales for customer X broken down by product group and by period, are the most informative. Supposing total sales are dropping off, it would be useful to isolate which product groups are responsible, are there some principal customers (or industries) responsible, are the sales force slacking, are the firm's prices too high and so on. The ability to extract and analyse information necessary to answer these and other such questions is fundamental and at the heart of the information system. Better decision-making at the operational, managerial and strategic level can be made by the production of better information.

Sometimes *ad hoc* reports are required to help provide information for a specific problem. For example, a list of customers with a high turnover in a certain product group may be required to help plan a sales promotion, or a list of each salesman's customers might be required to re-organize salesmen's territories.

In general, the advantage of a computerized system is that it can use all the data in its files and produce information that is timely, concise and relevant. It should be accurate and complete as well. This ability to scan several files and produce selected information is invaluable. The data base concept takes this flexibility to deal with complicated *ad hoc* queries to its logical conclusion.

Another advantage is that the input of data can be minimized. For example, the account number of a customer is all that is required to flash up on the screen the name of the company and its address. This ability to prevent unnecessary input increases the productivity of the sales-processing section of a company.

Again, as mentioned at the beginning, the centralization of the various data is an advantage. Different people within different functions may be able to access the same data.

Other application areas

The purchase ledger is very similar to the sales ledger. The reverse of the sales analysis is the cost centre and nominal allocation codes for each item of expenditure. As with the sales ledger there would be a supplier's file and a transaction file. Input to the system would comprise cash, invoices, adjustments and standing data amendments. Output reports would consist of a purchase journal, creditors/suppliers' report, expenditure analysis and so on.

Figure 12.11 shows the inputs, files and outputs from a purchase system. The minimal system shown in Figure 12.11(a) has inputs of

Cash;
Adjustments;
Invoices; and
Standing data amendments.

to update two files:

The suppliers master file; and
The purchase transaction file.

The output from the system includes such reports as:

Creditors' balances;
Expenditure analysis;
Master file movements summary;
Standing data amendments; and
Other special reports.

A more complete system is shown in Figure 12.11(b). Additional inputs include orders and goods received notes. Additional files include an orders/goods received note file, a purchase movements file, and a stock master file. Additional reports include outstanding orders, stock receipts, price variances and accruals.

A payroll system again would be similar. Some systems would only maintain one payroll file, though where there are complicated manpower

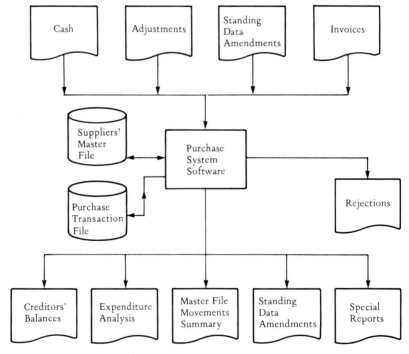

(a) A minimal system

planning or job costing systems, a separate transaction file of number of hours worked by an individual and on what job may be maintained. Similarly, there may be a complicated analysis of allocation of the hours or cost to various cost centres, jobs, processes, or nominal codes.

Figure 12.12 shows a typical computerized payroll system. Static data amendments and the numbers of hours worked are input and are used to update the payroll master file. The output generated includes payroll and

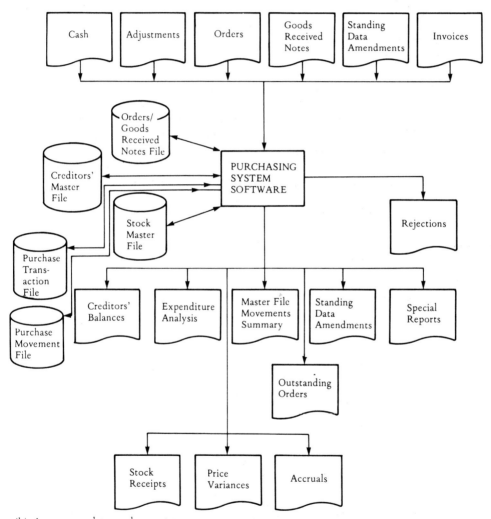

(b) A more complete purchase system

Figure 12.11 *A purchase system (a) A minimal system, (b) A more complete purchase system*
Source: *Modified from course material* Computers and Auditing, *Institute of Chartered Account-ants for England and Wales (1977)*

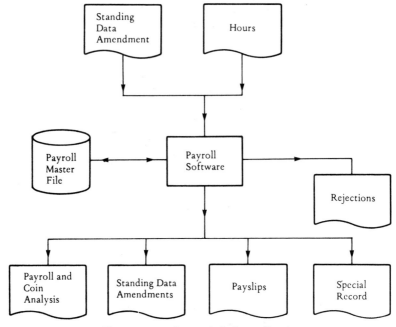

Figure 12.12   *A computerized payroll system*

coin analysis, (how many £5 notes, £1 coins, 50p coins, 10p coins and 1p coins do we need?), lists of static data amendments (for control and auditing reasons), payslips and special reports.

A minimal sales ledger system would simply comprise transaction entry, master files and the minimum of reports. A more sophisticated sales system would incorporate all the areas for receipt of order, order processing, shipping/delivery, finished-goods stock control, credit control, sales analysis, invoicing and a large number of routine structural reports as well as permitting requests for all structural and *ad hoc* reports.

A more complete system has as inputs:

Delivery or despatch notes;
Cash;
Adjustments;
Orders or invoices;
Standing data amendments;

with files covering orders, finished goods stock control and sales analysis. Output reports would include statements, age of debt listing, sales analysis, master file movements, despatch notes/delivery notes, picking lists, despatch notes outstanding, invoices and stock issues.

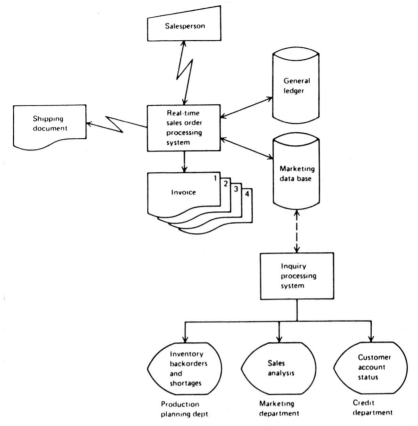

Figure 12.13   (a) *Document flow in a manual system for sales-order processing,* (b) *Document flow in computerized batch processing of sales orders,* (c) *Real-time sales order processing system* Source: *Cushing (1978)*

Sales system flowcharts

In order to give one final summary of the difference between three types of system, we provide document flowcharts (drawn in different but clearly understandable formats) for:

1   A manual system for sales-order processing;
2   A computerized batch-processing system for sales orders;
3   A real-time sales order-processing system.

Figure 12.13(a) shows the complete manual system. Many different documents are raised in different departments. Orders are raised, invoices are produced and statements prepared manually. These manual operations give rise to a vast paper flow with many clerks generating and controlling the paper flow.

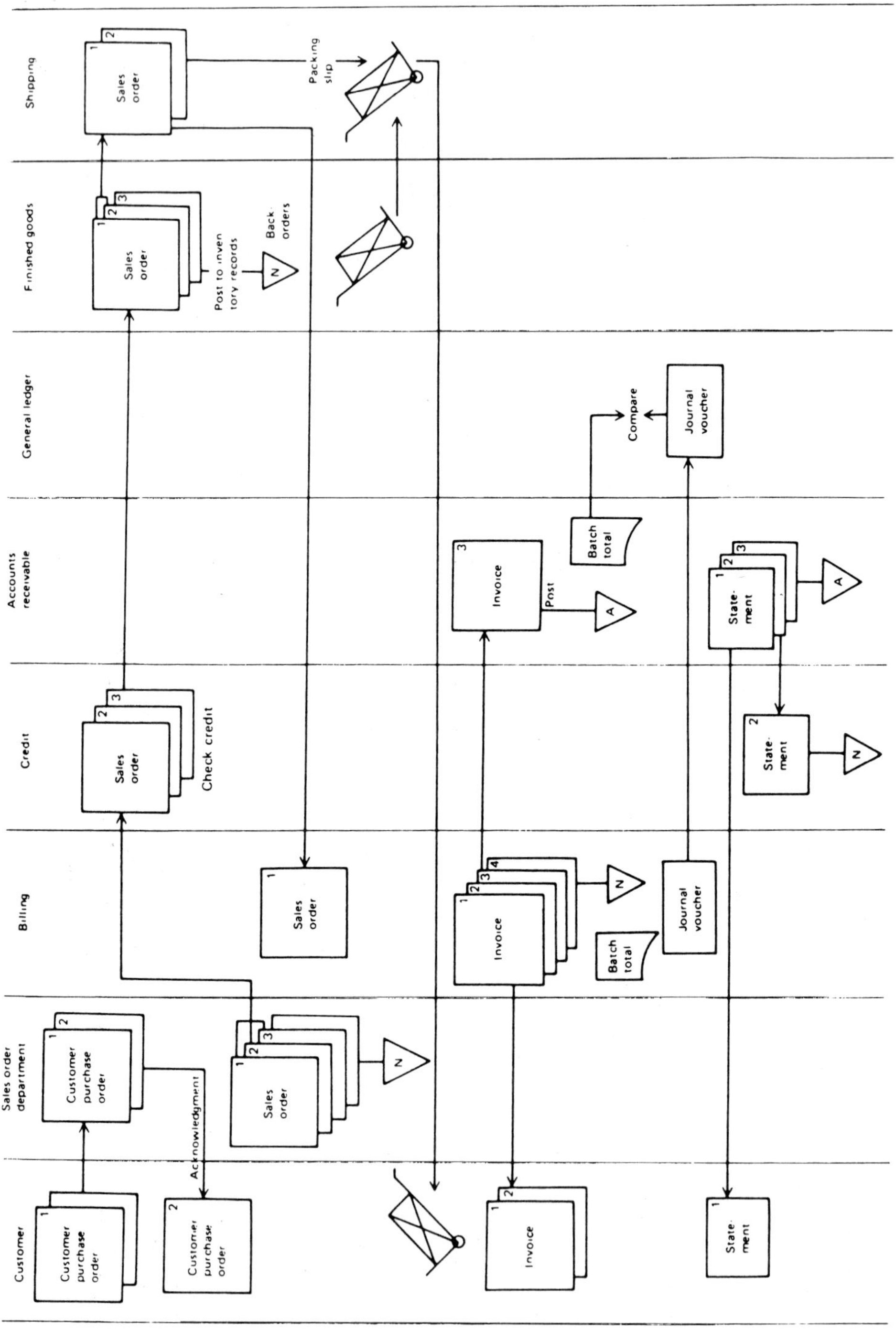
Shipping
Finished goods
General ledger
Accounts receivable
Credit
Billing
Sales order department
Customer
Sales order
Packing slip
Post to inventory records
Back orders
N
Compare
Journal voucher
Batch total
Invoice
Post
A
Statement
Check credit
Customer purchase order
Acknowledgment

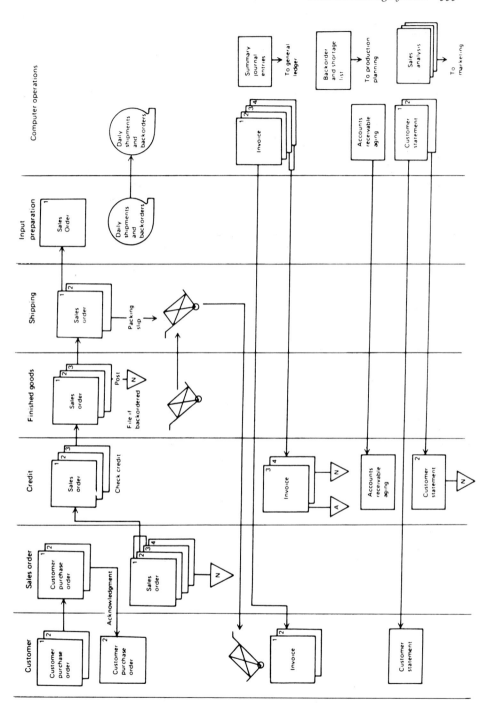

Figure 12.13(b) shows a more streamlined system in a batch computer system. To the extent that the computer has taken over a manual system, the document flow is simplified and reduced. But in the generation of the sales order, an operation which has not been computerized, the document flow and clerical procedures are still significant.

This is further simplified by the introduction of an on-line, real-time system in which all input is entered through on-line terminals by salesmen, by the marketing department or by the stock-room staff. Here, the document flow is minimized with the computer generating all the documentation, which is then fed back to the various departments. This system is one of the most sophisticated in computing terms yet gives rise to the simplest in business organization terms. It does, however, provide some control headaches such as authorization of alterations or input of data.

We shall return to the discussion of fully computerized systems in Chapter 17, where we briefly describe the Japanese approach to computerized business systems.

13 Enhanced management accounting systems

The previous chapter provided an introduction to computerized basic accounting systems. In that introduction the advantages of computerizing such simple systems were discussed. In this chapter, we consider how a computer-based information system can provide information to management across the whole range of activities of the organization. The computer implementation must include a costing system which implements the process of responsibility accounting – the reporting of financial results in accordance with the assignment of managerial responsibilities within a business organization. The heart of a management control system is the budgeting system. This too must be incorporated in the firm's total information and data-processing system. These extensions or enhancements to the basic accounting system are discussed in this chapter.

An MIS has three important implications for the management accountant:

1 It includes extensions to cover all aspects of order processing, inventory records and other fairly routine applications;
2 In addition to the routine data processing normally performed, extensions to the computerized system can provide valuable additional information enabling the management accountant to monitor and assess the company's performance (for example, sales analysis and inventory control subsystems can provide important measures of efficiency);
3 The budgetary control feature of a MIS is of major importance in diagnosing and reporting any deviations from the company's approved plans.

To illustrate some of these features, which are typical of any MIS, we use examples from the MSA (Management Science America, Inc.) system. This system, produced by one of the market leaders in mainframe applications software, is representative of the Management Information systems marketed for IBM and other large mainframe systems.

Enhancing the system

Previously, we have considered only a sub-set of an entire organization. However, management require information concerning all aspects of the business. It is the function of the management accountant, and therefore of the MIS, to provide information pertaining to the whole business.

To illustrate these various areas which have to be incorporated in the MIS, we choose a simplified manufacturing environment. Let us consider the information flows and subsystems which have to be monitored by the MIS.

These various functions can be grouped in certain ways. For example order entry, order processing, invoices and other functions associated with customers are sometimes within the province of the sales department of an organization. One way of viewing all the components in an organization is to group them in the following way:

Sales system;
Production system;
Cash receipts and payments system;
General ledger system.

One such system is shown in Figure 13.1 which provides an overview of the components of a typical, more complete, information system. This is divided into four areas:

1   The general ledger systems, which include the general ledger, budgeting, and responsibility/reporting areas;
2   The cash receipts/payments systems, which include the sales ledger (accounts receivable), payroll, and purchase/bought ledger (accounts payable) systems;
3   The production management systems, which include the materials inventory control, work-in-progress control, cost estimation, and production scheduling systems.
4   The sales systems which include finished goods inventory control, order processing, and sales analysis systems.

We now examine each of these subsystems individually. For the management accountant one of the most significant of the systems is sales analysis. From the point of view of the efficiency of the business and safeguarding the assets of the company, the finished goods inventory control system is equally important.

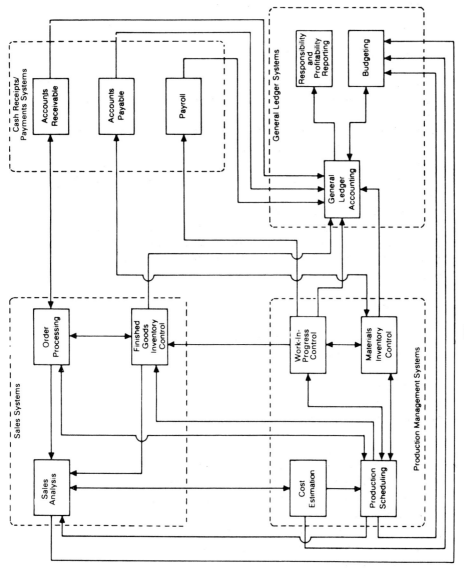

Figure 13.1   *Overview of the accounting information system.*

The flow lines between the various systems in the figure illustrate interfaces between these systems. The arrows on the low lines indicate the direction of the information flow from one system to another
Source: *Hicks and Leininger (1981) (modified)*

The cash receipts/payments system on the other hand is quite routine and was covered in the previous chapter.

Sales system

A broadened sales system has to cope with three distinctive subsystems: order entry and processing, sales analysis, and finished goods inventory control. Within a sales system there are a host of different commercial circumstances each requiring different systems. For example, orders may be standard items or may be expressly designed to fulfil a customer's requirements.

A retailing company selling standard products has an easier task than an engineering company manufacturing products to individual customers' requirements.

In the engineering example, a sales representative submits a customer's job specifications to the cost estimation system (which, unlike the illustration in Figure 13.1 may be within the sales system). Once the cost estimation system has prepared an estimate of production costs and the sales/marketing function has added a profit margin then the estimate can be communicated to the customer. If the bid is accepted the sales representative can place an order in the order-processing system. Certainly, a feature of the engineering company's reporting system must be the state of the various potential orders for which cost estimates have been prepared. Too many lost or outstanding orders may mean that costs or the profit margin are high and that estimates are uncompetitive.

Order processing

Order processing is the point of entry for customer orders. An order-processing system should keep track of and deliver customer's orders in a way which meets the customer's delivery date and product specification. This service should be provided at a minimum cost. From the management accounting viewpoint it is a pure data-processing function with very little important information generated.

Yet an inefficient order-entry system may lose customers or orders and thereby lead to a less efficient system. Figure 13.2 shows the various decision points. Information about stock-outs or situations in which customers do not place orders on receipt of the firm's (uncompetitive) price are extremely important.

Very often once an order has entered a system, there are inadequate controls to ensure that the order is shipped on time or that a back-order to a supplier is adequately followed up. In many systems, an inadequate

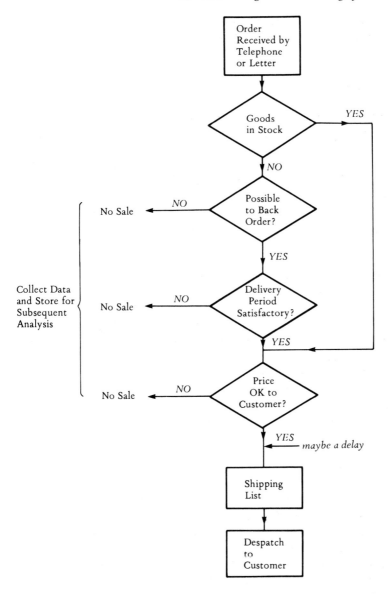

Figure 13.2   *Steps in accepting order*

B+H CO. PLC			Orders Received Report For Month of:		Date: 3–12–84 November 1984	
Order Ref.No.	Customer Name	Sales Representative	Taken from Stock or Production		Est. Date of Shipping	Out on Time
ON121	McDONALD	ROY DWIGHT	Y		19–11–84	Y
ON122	SMITHIES	TOM COLLINS	Y		10–11–84	Y
ON123	KENT-CO	JEAN CROSS		Y	01–02–85	
ON124	FITZROY	BOB SHAW	Y		26–11–84	Y
ON125	BROWNING	PETER ADAMSON	Y		10–04–85	
ON126	BARRY	GEOFF GREEN		Y	07–01–85	
ON127	BOLTON	MICHAEL WALSH		Y	04–01–85	
ON128	WALLACE	BOB SHAW		Y	01–02–85	
ON129	QUIKFIT	ROY DWIGHT	Y		15–07–85	

(a)

B+H CO. PLC		Order Status Report				Date: 3–12–84	
Order Ref.No.	Date Received	Manufacturing		Delay (days)	Shipping		
		Required	On Schedule		Scheduled Date	Date Shipped	
ON101	10–08–84	Y	Y		10–11–84	11–11–84	
ON102	02–06–84	Y	N	30	09–11–84		
ON103	16–07–84	Y	N	20	07–11–84	27–11–84	
ON104	04–11–84				08–11–84	08–11–84	
ON105	10–06–84	Y	Y				
ON106	20–10–84				21–10–84	04–11–84	
ON107	18–11–84				19–11–84	19–11–84	
ON108	08–09–84	Y	Y		05–03–85		
ON109	25–11–84				05–12–84		
ON110	27–11–84				17–12–84		

(b)

Figure 13.3   (a) *Orders received report, (b) Order status report*

follow-through of an order can lead to an inefficient business with a poor service and consequently lost customers. Similarly, it may be management policy not to stock certain items because it is not optimal from the company's point of view. It is quite another for stock-out situations to occur accidentally or because no action has been taken to re-order goods.

The danger with an order-processing system is the possible lack of adequate and routine maintenance of the orders. Sometimes this occurs with the maintenance of standing data. One company in the Midlands installed a computerized order-processing system and all went well initially, with an improved level of service being offered for approximately the same cost as the previous system (but the computerized system had a greater capacity to deal with the volume of orders than the replaced manual system, and at little extra cost). After a few years, the company started losing orders yet a survey showed that its prices were competitive. An analysis of the system showed why. The credit limit checks had not

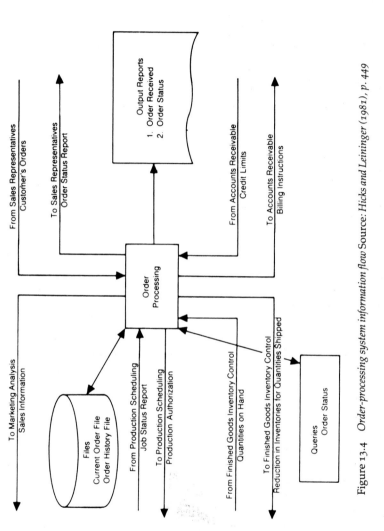

Figure 13.4 *Order-processing system information flow* Source: *Hicks and Leininger (1981), p. 449*

been adjusted to keep in line with inflation. Many of the customers placing orders did so through large purchasing departments. Rather than a purchasing clerk having to raise a letter requesting a change in the buyer's credit rating, it was easier to simply order from another company which had no credit check or who maintained adequate credit limits.

The firm's information system was not properly maintained. Moreover, the order-entry clerks (this job had a high staff turnover) failed to realize the significance of a large number of refusal of orders due to credit limit checks. Management had no way of monitoring what was happening and talks to order entry clerks failed to highlight the problem.

The obvious solution to this problem is routine maintenance and review of standing data items such as the credit limit.

Typical reports produced by the MSA order-processing system are shown in Figure 13.3. Figure 13.4 shows the information flow related to the order-processing subsystem.

Finished-goods inventory control

Inventory control is a generalized concept common to both finished goods and materials inventory. Specialized aspects of inventory control are therefore discussed separately. Within the sales system, the finished-goods inventory system marks the point at which manufactured or bought goods enter the sales system. Within a production environment the objective of a finished-goods inventory control system must be to minimize inventory holding and shortage costs as well as production start-up costs. We shall return to the general concept of inventory control later in this chapter.

Sales analysis

In terms of information on which routine and more strategic decisions can be based, the sales analysis report is the most important. In addition to information about sales it may include an analysis of profitability. There are endless possibilities; a few are described below.

(a) *Product sales report* in which information (current, YTD, previous months/years, and comparative figures) is provided on a product or product group basis. This information should include quantity/volume sold, revenue, cost, gross contribution and gross contribution as a percentage of sales.

(b) *Customer sales report*. This should show similar information but broken down for each customer.

(c) Either (a) or (b) can be run showing either customers sales analysis within product grouping or product groupings within customer sales.

These reports are extremely important in identifying the most profitable products and customers. There are endless ways of reclassifying the details to take account of location of sales, advertising/marketing strategies, packaging, distribution mechanism and so on. Often the type of enquiry or report will require a database structure and a query language. For example, questions such as:

'Breakdown product X by customers with sales of over £1,000 a year in the south-east into monthly sales and produce comparative figures for the last 5 years.'

can provide valuable insight into changing customer trends and purchasing patterns. It may be that sales of product X are declining because a principal customer is experiencing difficulty in this region. Of course, what such a system cannot provide for management is detailed figures about competitors.

A final type of report provides information about sales representatives.

(d) Sales representative reports can show monthly, YTD and comparative figures for sales by representative. The report should include quantity/volume information, revenue, costs, profit contribution on both orders received and actual sales.

(e) Obviously, the sales representative report may then be broken down by customer or product grouping or both.

This leads to the possibility of extremely complicated queries. For example, you may wish to select:

A product group or item or a range of items;
A customer or range of customers (or you may wish to find all the customers or important customers e.g. sales in excess of £x a year);
A particular marketing region;
Data for particular sales representatives;
Data for a particular period.

Alternatively, you may wish to find the most (or least) profitable customers and then try to ascertain the reason for this by analysis of sales by products/sales representative and so on.

A poor performance by a sales representative may be due to the customer or product mix. By asking complex queries more light can be shed on the effectiveness of salesmen. Alternative advertising, pricing, marketing and packaging strategies can be analysed as to their effectiveness by specifying selective enquiries.

The information flow related to sales analysis is shown in Figure 13.5.

Production management

The production management subsystem of our accounting system, as portrayed in Figure 13.1, includes cost estimation, production scheduling, work-in-progress control and materials-inventory control. As before we shall describe each of these subsystems in turn indicating the functional requirements of the computer system that implements them. Information flows are shown in Figures 13.6 and 13.7.

Cost estimation

The cost-estimation system may be critical in gaining orders. The system must be accurate (underestimating costs may lead to reduced profits whilst overestimation may lose orders) and provide a fast service at a

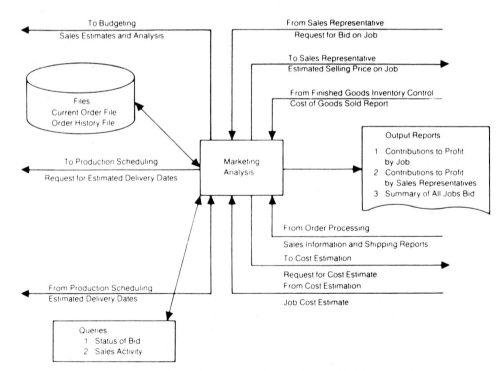

Figure 13.5   *Sales analysis information flow* Source: *Hicks and Leininger (1981), p. 445*

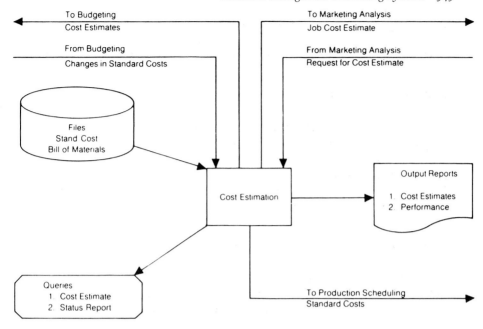

Figure 13.6   *Cost estimation system*

minimum cost. Cost estimates may relate to a standard product or may require a one-off estimate. In the latter case, the quantity/volume of materials and labour hours are required, together with production set-up time and production run quantities. These will then be costed according to standard cost per unit stored on file. Overheads may then be added according to one of several standard mechanisms. Pricing will include a mark-up which should not be an automatic percentage but which should relate to the customer, the product, the competition and general consider-ations of what the market will bear. Product differences and character-istics (e.g. delivery, back-up service) should be taken into account in assessing the competition.

A good MIS can support all of these requirements and provide accurate estimates quickly and at a minimum cost.

Production scheduling

Production scheduling is concerned with monitoring the physical flows through a manufacturing process and, if appropriate, assists the sched-uling of jobs through various production stages.

The order-processing system should authorize the production-sched-uling system to start work on a job. The production scheduling system will provide the sales system with an estimated delivery date. Production scheduling should also inform the materials inventory system of the

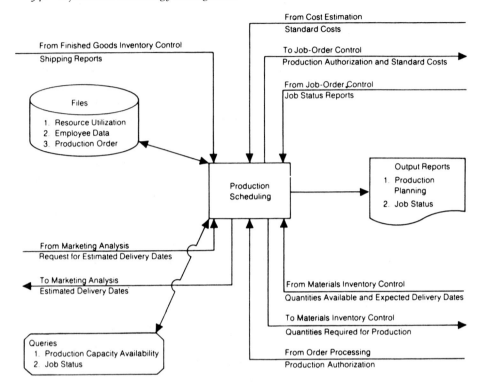

quantity of materials required for production and the timing of these requirements. The cost-estimation system will provide budgeted costs.

As well as these links to other systems, there are two types of major management reports which are vital for production and cost control. One such report aids the production-planning process which shows the available capacity and scheduled utilization of labour and machinery. Such reports indicate where excess capacity exists. If production cannot be re-scheduled to improve capacity utilization then marketing and pricing strategies may be considered to alleviate the problem. Where capacity utilization is high for long periods (or forecast to be high) then new investment to increase production capacity may be necessary. Consequently, this report is extremely important for managerial decision-making.

A more routine report concerns the status of jobs in a production process. Two control criteria are relevant: one is performance and can be gained by comparing actual hours against budgeted hours. The second concerns completion time and may be broken down into materials which may, in turn, be on order. A critical material which has been ordered but not yet received (or even shipped) may delay a whole order. If such a delay is suspected then it is important to record the potential delay.

Materials-inventory control

We shall restrict our consideration of materials inventory control to a few specific details and defer further consideration to the general discussion of inventory control later in this chapter. Specifically, this system needs such information as the timing of purchases, whether materials received have met specifications and have been properly costed, the status of inventory on hand, the status of unfulfilled orders, and anticipated demand.

Examples of typical reports from such a system include the inventory status report which contains the quantity in stock, cost and quantity on order of individual items. An open purchase order report shows information relating to outstanding purchase orders. A good materials-inventory control system will contain information concerning turnover, stock-outs, shrinkages, holding costs and so on. This information is contained in the inventory-performance measurement report.

Work-in-progress control

The function of a work-in-progress system is to monitor the progress of a product or a job as it works its way through various manufacturing processes. It is concerned partly with cost collection and partly with efficiency as with inventory control. Costs are collected by means of recording or having assigned materials, labour, and overhead costs to production jobs, processes or products. In a job-costing system, costs will be assigned to jobs and then to product groupings or departments. In a process-costing system, costs will be assigned to departments (i.e. processes) and then to products.

Consequently, the cost collection system will require the following inputs:

Materials requisitioned for each job or process;
Labour time employed on each job or process;
Overhead costs allocated or directly incurred by each job or process;
The production status of each job or production details of each process.

However, the costing mechanism also supplies the necessary information to assist management with controlling costs and measuring the efficiency and performance of various departments involved in the manufacturing process.

Performance in this context can only be measured by comparison with plans or standards. So a job-costing system produces a report which compares costs incurred to date with the budgeted cost. One other control is necessary, that is whether the job is on time and whether the estimated completion date can be met. Figure 13.8 shows a typical job cost report. Again, since a work-in-progress system falls within the class of problems associated with inventory control which we cover next, no further consideration is given to this here.

Inventory control

The function of an inventory control system is two-fold.

1   The system must monitor all movements of inventory and maintain an up-to-date inventory of items in stock.
2   The system must help the performance of the company. This it can do in two distinct ways.
    (a)   Information can be provided on turnover, stock-outs, shrinkage, holding costs and so on.
    (b)   The system can help to keep the inventory under control so as to prevent stock-outs by automatically re-ordering (or at least drawing it to management's attention) when stock levels fall below a critical point (re-order point). The other side of the coin is to highlight slow-moving stock so that further quantities of this stock are not ordered and the existing stocks may be moved by low-pricing strategies or other marketing policies.

One other concept which is important in inventory systems is to

	Job Cost Report			Date: 3–12–84		
Job Number 3893	Customer J Pardee & Co.			Estimated Completion Date: 4–2–85		
	Standard Cost	%	Actual Cost to date	%	% Standard	
Material						
Steel	£ 6,500	10.6	£ 6,700	15.3	103.0	
Machinery	21,800	35.7	14,900	34.0	68.3	
Total	£28,300	46.3	£21,600	49.3	76.3	
Labour						
Welding	£ 3,840	6.3	£ 4,120	9.4	107.0	
Machining	7,860	12.9	4,780	10.9	60.8	
Electrical	600	1.0			0	
Painting and preparation	800	1.3			0	
Total	£13,100	21.5	£ 8,900	20.3	67.9	
Overhead	£19,650	32.2	£13,350	30.4	67.9	
Total	£61,050	100.0	£43,850	100.0	71.8	

Figure 13.8   *Job cost report* Source: *Hicks and Leininger (1981), (modified)*

record, in addition to the quantity-on-hand, the quantity-on-order and the expected delivery date. Cost details will be maintained and these could be two-fold, standard costs as well as actual costs (on specific identification, FIFO, LIFO or average costing). Sometimes a quantity-on-hand will be sub-divided into allocated and free stock. Allocated stock will be reserved for a specific customer, although in practice allocated stock can sometimes be used to prevent the loss of a sale especially if there is an order with an expected delivery date prior to that when the allocated stock is required by a customer.

Besides keeping an opening balance, movements include transfers, receipts and adjustments. Because an auditor often verifies the accuracy of a system by a stock count, it is important to keep a record of the date of a stock count of a particular item and the amount of any discrepancy. In any case this is important for the efficiency of an organization. If there is a stock loss (i.e. the recorded quantity-on-hand is greater than actual) then it is important to ascertain why and prevent a recurrence or at least to minimize the losses. One reason for a loss may be inaccurate recording of movements. Another may be theft – there is often an element of materials being 'borrowed' by the work force. This may be acceptable with nuts and bolts but not so with precious metals or diamonds. A third reason may be shortages on delivery. Whatever the reason it is up to management to undertake a cost/benefit analysis of whether to prevent further losses.

One interesting stock loss occurred at an oil refinery. Enterprising crooks decided to tap an oil pipe-line by renting a house near an underground line and tapping into it. For years no-one suspected that losses on a particular oil tank were anything else but random. However, as the oil prices rose, it came to management's attention that losses on one tank in particular were out-of-line with the historical experience of other tanks. Some five years later management still could not explain these losses. So, in desperation, they emptied the tank and pipe-line of oil and pumped water under high pressure down the line. Sure enough, one house started gushing water and the source of the stock loss was discovered.

A typical inventory control system would consist of a set of programs designed to perform various functions. Figure 13.9 shows three aspects of the system.

To give an example of a stock status report, the following information may be printed:

item number, item class, item description, pricing unit of measure, volume unit of measure, quantity-on-hand, quantity-on-order, quantity available (on-hand plus on-order), actual quantity-on-hand (= on-hand quantity less spoilt/broken goods), unit standard cost, unit cost, on-hand total cost, quantity sold month-to-date, quantity sold year-to-date, sales-to-date, comparative figures for previous years.

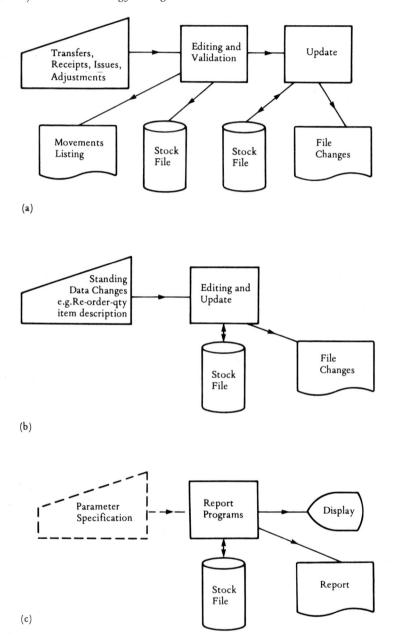

Figure 13.9   *Inventory system: (a) Movement update of stock file, (b) Standing data maintenance of stock file, (c) Report generation of stock file*

In addition, certain exception conditions may be highlighted; for example, where quantity-on-hand is below minimum stock level, where cost change exceeds a certain percentage, or where stocks have not moved for some time.

Other reports may produce the stock file flows of movements or value and ranked in sequence of, for example,

Item number;
Cost-in-hand;
Date of last use;
Month's supply on-hand;
Year-to-date;
Many other criteria.

A sophisticated general ledger system

Although many of the other systems provide important performance reports (e.g. production scheduling and inventory control systems), the key to a financial reporting and cost accounting system is normally contained within a general ledger system. Most of the other systems are based on a transaction processing system with a performance or budgeting system tacked on.

The importance of the general ledger is that most of the other systems pass information on to it. Figure 13.10 shows how the sales, production and cash receipts/payments system feed information into the general ledger system. Apart from these systems there may be a shareholders' register monitoring changes in the ownership of shares and providing details of individual payments. A fixed-asset system may also maintain details of cost, depreciation, sale of assets and new purchases or investments in fixed assets. The fixed-asset system also provides input to the general ledger.

While other systems feed summary information into it, the general ledger system often provides high-level management reports. These reports include the highly summarized financial reports of the company, actual-versus-budget reports, profitability and cost reports and other performance reports.

Conventional general ledger systems provide the ability to take transaction information and, through the chart of accounts, to summarize and aggregate the events that have occurred. A sale of a specific product to a specific customer will be aggregated into a revenue account where only the monthly total figure is maintained. Similarly, oil and electricity costs may be aggregated into a single account called energy costs. If a firm wanted to measure the impact of an oil price rise, it would be difficult if the energy costs account includes all forms of energy. The only way to find out the total of oil costs may be to find the individual transactions. (In this example, it may be easy since only a few suppliers may be involved in

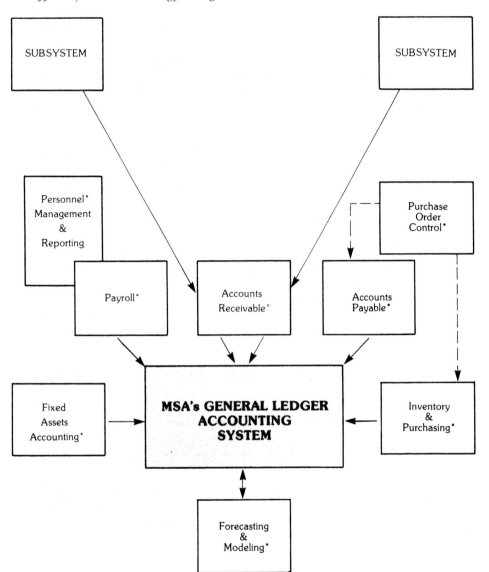

*Other systems also available from MSA

Figure 13.10   *General ledger system overview*

the provision of oil so the details may be available on the purchase ledger.) However, in general the process of aggregation and summarization can lead to a convenient way of viewing the firm (as modelled through the chart of accounts) but it can also mean the loss of information.

One way of overcoming this loss of information is to have an extremely detailed chart of accounts and a sophisticated general ledger system based on a database.

A good general ledger system will attempt to capture and maintain financial and non-financial information relating to all other systems in order to provide information on performance and profitability. Obviously, reports that help to evaluate and provide performance/efficiency information on the position of the company, subsidiaries, divisions, regions, departments, processes and products are important.

Although a budgeting system can be provided as an adjunct to other systems, it is most common to find a budgetary control system being maintained as part of the general ledger system. A good profitability reporting system should be capable of producing reports of actual revenue and expenses directly related to profit/cost centres or products as well as any indirect or allocated revenues and expenses. These should be compared with budgeted amounts and any variances noted. It should be possible to produce such reports for any level of management in the organization structure.

The cost allocation system allocates to profit/cost centres, departments or products, financial data captured by the general ledger system. For example, the cost of administrative or service centres can be allocated to cost centres which are responsible for profits or products.

Inputs to the general ledger system were discussed earlier. Sometimes, one entry can produce multiple entries such as the allocation of fixed costs or the automatic reversal of accruals.* Unlike the example at the beginning of the chapter, a multiple transaction may be generated, when a user enters one side of a transaction (e.g. a debit for an expense account) and the system generates the off-setting entry automatically (e.g. a credit to the bank account).

Other financial transactions include:

1. Normal journal entries which can be manually or automatically input from other systems;
2. Standard or recurring journal entries such as items that must be made at regular intervals involving the same expense (e.g. rents, insurance premiums or depreciation entries): for example, a debit to depreciation expense and a credit to accumulated depreciation can be generated every month/accounting period.

*The automatic reversal of accrual entries can be achieved by the following method. When accruals are made the appropriate reversing entry is generated and held in a pending record at the time the accrual is entered. The system releases all reversals at the beginning of the next period thus reversing the accrued entries.

Automatic journal entries need to be suspended until the entry is due, at which time a journal entry is created for the appropriate amount, input to the system and posted to the general ledger. A good general ledger system will also allow entries to be input in advance of the posting date – the entry being suspended automatically until it is due to be posted. Similarly, entries which are effective to a prior accounting period may be input. Balances of a prior time period may have to be adjusted or corrected after the accounting period has passed.

However, financial data is not the only type of information that may be relevant to management and a good general ledger system will keep non-financial information through a number of non-financial accounts. Examples include the quantity of sales, the volume of purchases, the hours of a service used (e.g. computer).

The MSA general ledger system

The MSA general ledger system is one of the market leaders for information systems. Figure 13.10 shows the overview of the system. There is a single database for the general ledger system, which is essentially hierarchical in format. The system contains four subsections – the budget system, the responsibility-reporting system, the cost allocation system and the profit-reporting system. Standard reports can either be prepared or custom-made reports can be produced by means of a high-level report-generating language.

The MSA general ledger database contains five different logical files. The first is the general ledger file which contains actual balances by accounting period for each general ledger account number for up to 99 years with either 12 (calendar months) or 13 (4-week) accounting periods a year. The general ledger file will also contain each period-budgeted amount for the account and several different budgets or alternative plans may be stored. Different plans may correspond to the original budget, various revisions, an agreed 'control' budget, several current forecasts, various budgets consistent with various long-term plans, and perhaps some tentative attempts at a proposed budget for next year. The general file can also handle multiple charts of accounts. The general ledger file maintains data in disaggregated form by company or division. Each company or division can have its own separate chart of accounts.

The total system is shown in Figure 13.11. In addition to the main database there are four other files used to generate the various reports from the database. The *allocations schedule file* contains the various factors and methods used to allocate indirect costs and overheads to various codes and classifications in the general ledger. Costs which cannot be directly traceable to individual products or production departments can be allocated on a number of bases such as direct labour hours or square footage of space.

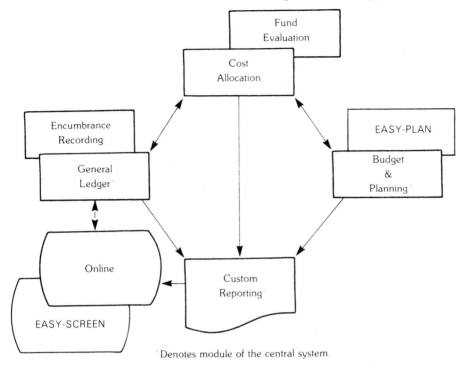

Denotes module of the central system.

Figure 13.11

The *relationship-linkage file* contains (1) pointers that link data in specific general ledger accounts to specific reports, and (2) allocation criteria that link specific accounts to the allocation schedules contained in the allocations schedule file.

The *reporting hierarchies file* defines the organizational hierarchical structure for reporting purposes. This is far superior to conventional general ledger computer systems which used a cost centre code to define the reporting hierarchy. This approach had the disadvantage that a change in the reporting hierarchy required changes in the cost-centre code, which in turn required changes in operating procedures and pre-printed forms. A change in reporting hierarchy tended to produce many errors until the new system settled down. By maintaining a separate file of reporting hierarchies the MSA system can identify where a particular cost centre should report to.

The *report characteristics file* contains the characteristics of individual reports including formatting and report-specification instructions as well as logic dealing with arithmetic and totalling calculations.

The advantage of the MSA system is contained in its database. In a non-database system, program code would have to be written to cover all the information in the five files. MSA's approach emphasizes flexibility

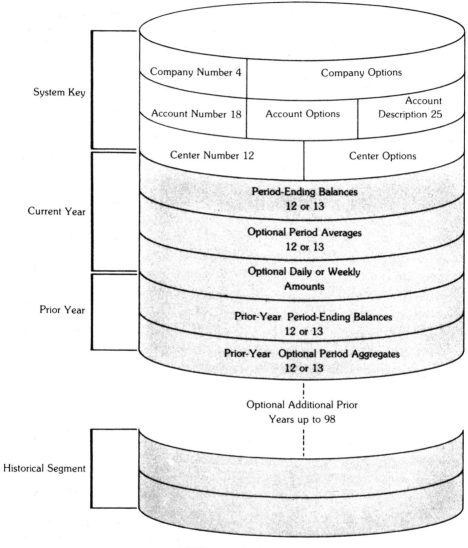

Company Number 4 | Company Options

Account Number 18 | Account Options | Account Description 25

Center Number 12 | Center Options

**Period-Ending Balances
12 or 13**

**Optional Period Averages
12 or 13**

**Optional Daily or Weekly
Amounts**

**Prior-Year Period-Ending Balances
12 or 13**

**Prior-Year Optional Period Aggregates
12 or 13**

Optional Additional Prior
Years up to 98

System Key

Current Year

Prior Year

Historical Segment

(*b*) **The general ledger database**

through the use of a database. By making simple changes in the four
supporting files the user can make fundamental changes to the system.
Hicks and Leininger (1981) comment:

> 'These changes are much faster and can usually be made by users [generally
> accountants] rather than data-processing professionals. This user-oriented
> approach is definitely the trend in information systems. It is flexible enough to
> allow the user to define custom reports without going through data-processing
> professionals for expensive changes in detail program code.' (p. 365)

We agree. Some accountants find that the simple changes required are in reality equivalent to high-level programming. In some organizations, the new generation of accountants react well to this challenge. But not all accountants respond well and many still require the help of a data-processing professional.

The MSA system provides three major categories of reports; control, general financial and operating, the custom reports. Examples of *control reports* include accounting reports such as batch proof, error alert, cost allocation from-to report and cost allocation to-from report. Other control reports are peculiar to a computer-based system and include file-update reports, processing summaries, file-content reports and cross-reference summaries.

General financial and operating reports are pre-programmed and include posting ledgers, journal ledgers, trial balances, individual account analysis, budget markets and so on. The MSA system provides considerable flexibility in the layout and information provided.

Custom reports provide complete flexibility in summarizing data and performing new calculations in order to allow management to highlight or present the information they deem important. Designing a custom report is equivalent to building a financial model (which is discussed in the next chapter) with the exception that most of the input data is drawn from the general ledger.

Budget system

The MSA general ledger system also makes provision for a flexible and powerful budget system which can maintain multiple budgets. The MSA system provides six basic functions:

1 It provides the historical information necessary to formulate a new budget.
2 It provides several short-cut methods for inputting the budget such as:
    (a) The input of an annual amount to be spread automatically pro-rata over twelve months.
    (b) The input of a quarterly amount to be spread automatically pro-rata over the appropriate three months.
    (c) A percentage increase or decrease over the current year's actual cost.
    (d) A repeat of the previous year's plan.
    (e) The direct calculation of one account's budget from another's.
3 The system allows both direct (controllable) and indirect (non-controllable or allocated) items to be budgeted.
4 It captures budget data and produces summary budget reports.

ACTUAL	PLAN	VARIANCE	LAST YEAR		ACTUAL	PLAN	VARIANCE	LAST YEAR
MSA MANUFACTURING COMPANY			PRODUCTION EXPENSE REPORT				PAGE 73	
NORFOLK PLANT		FICS 57002		PERIOD ENDING MARCH 31, 1984			ISSUED 3-4-84	
CENTER NO. 2400								
- - - - CURRENT PERIOD - - - -					- - - - YEAR TO DATE - - - -			
				LABOUR EXPENSE				
23,468	22,750	718	22,741	ADMIN AND OTHER NON-PROD.	71,642	70,009	1,633	68,147
7,562	7,800	238-	7,634	SILK SCREENING	22,141	21,545	596	22,876
3,193	3,133	60	2,982	BLOW MOLDING	10,478	10,789	311-	8,958
11,715	12,250	535-	11,677	MACHINE FAB AND BCMB	29,764	31,436	1,672-*	31,216
32,134	33,059	925-	31,734	ASSEMBLY	102,372	104,809	2,437-	95,838
78,072	78,992	920-	76,768	TOTAL LABOUR EXPENSE	236,397	238,588	2,191-	227,035
				OTHER PRODUCTION EXPENSE				
10,368	11,700	1,332-	11,438	ADMIN AND OTHER NON-PROD.	29,481	33,240	3,759-	34,240
2,144	2,000	144	1,926	SILK SCREENING	6,517	7,000	483-	5,846
4,300	4,133	167	4,472	BLOW MOLDING	11,673	11,270	403	12,813
3,747	2,350	1,397-*	2,369	MACHINE FAB AND BCMB	10,170	6,540	3,630	7,645
5,835	5,283	552	5,716	ASSEMBLY	16,286	15,052	1,234	16,561
26,394	25,466	928	25,921	TOTAL OTHER PROD. EXPENSE	74,127	73,102	1,025	77,105
				OTHER CONTROLLABLE EXPENSE				
1,639	1,700	71-	1,832	ADMIN AND OTHER NON-PROD.	5,316	5,100	216	5,001
879	1,000	121-	988	SILK SCREENING	2,377	3,000	623-	2,846
6,256	5,333	923 *	5,115	BLOW MOLDING	17,522	16,000	1,522	14,733
2,081	1,760	321	1,669	MACHINE FAB AND BCMB	5,478	5,275	203	5,110
3,778	3,550	228	3,410	ASSEMBLY	11,464	10,633	831	9,772
14,633	13,343	1,290	13,014	TOTAL OTHER CONTROLLABLE	42,157	40,008	2,149	37,462
119,099	117,801	1,298	115,703	TOTAL PLANT EXPENSE	352,681	351,698	983	341,602
13,697	13,875	178-	12,889	DIRECT LABOUR HOURS	41,791	42,550	759-	38,847
5.87	5.93	.06-	5.79	AVERAGE HOURLY RATE PROD. EMP.	5.85	5.92	.07-	5.76
21,327	19,500	1,827 *	18,364	NO. OF FINISHED UNITS PRODUCED	62,746	57,600	5,146	56,871
111	123	12-	109	NO. OF PERSONNEL	110	121	11-	107

* VARIANCE EXCEEDS 7 PCT

MSA

Figure 13.12   (a) *Production expense report for a specific plant,* (b) *Expense report for manufacturing and warehousing division,* (c) *Summary expense report*

5   It permits revisions to be made in the plan as often as required.
6   It permits the use of either fixed or variable budgets. Variances that are attributable to volume changes, changes in standard rates, and changes in efficiency can be calculated.

The reports produced by the budget system can produce expense items by month and quantity with actual, actual plus projected, planned and comparative figures for previous years. For example, a production cost-centre report may contain actual, budgeted and variance for controllable (i.e. direct) expenses. For each general ledger expense account, the report may contain the following monthly figures: planned, actual, variance, variance per cent, monthly per cent of annual plan used – this information may be repeated on an accumulative year-to-date basis. A typical production report is shown in Figure 13.12(a) – notice the reporting of non-financial data at the bottom.

The *responsibility reporting system* reports on actual versus budgets for all revenues, expenses, non-financial statistics, assets and liabilities for which a manager is responsible. The system can respond at any level

MSA MANUFACTURING COMPANY				MANUFACTURING EXPENSE REPORT					PAGE 118
MANUFACTURING AND WAREHOUSING				FICS 57003			PERIOD ENDING MARCH 31, 1984		ISSUED 3-4-84
CENTER NO. 3500									

ACTUAL	VARIANCE	CURRENT PERIOD LAST YEAR	% CHANGE/YR		ACTUAL	VARIANCE	YEAR TO DATE LAST YEAR	% CHANGE/YR
				LABOUR EXPENSE				
137,216	2,148 *	131,172	4.60	PITTSBURGH PLANT	407,322	8,549 *	394,716	3.1x
53,829	1,364-	54,617	1.44-	ESSEX PLANT	162,846	7,243 *	159,833	1.88
78,072	920-	76,768	1.69	NORFOLK PLANT	236,397	2,191-	227,035	4.12
27,274	572-	23,862	14.29	BOSTON WAREHOUSE	79,188	3,454	73,519	7.71
296,391	708-	286,419	3.48	TOTAL LABOUR HOURS	885,753	2,569	855,103	3.58
				OTHER PRODUCTION AND WAREHOUSE				
49,723	1,136-	51,468	3.51-	PITTSBURGH PLANT	148,339	5,9.1-	149,844	1.00
16,174	362	15,384	5.13	ESSEX PLANT	50,008	2,173-	46,920	6.58
26,394	928	25,921	1.82	NORFOLK PLANT	74,127	1,025	77,105	3.86
8,466	118-	7,926	6.81	BOSTON WAREHOUSE	21,126	433	20,524	12.67
100,757	136	100,699	.05	TOTAL OTHER PROD. AND WARE.	276,599	6,942 *	294,343	.40
				OTHER CONTROLLABLE EXPENSE				
23,666	372-	24,832	4.69	PITTSBURGH PLANT	71,088	1,121-	70,548	.76
8,048	145	8,224	2.14	ESSEX PLANT	25,349	826-	24,216	4.67
14,633	1,290	13,014	12.44	NORFOLK PLANT	42,157	2,149	37,462	12.53
3,726	217-	3,555	4.81	BOSTON WAREHOUSE	9,566	745	8,240	16.09
50,073	846	59,625	16.02	TOTAL OTHER CONTROLLABLE	148,160	947	140,466	5.47
447,221	274	446,741	.10	TOTAL PLANT AND WARE. EXP.	1,129,512	1,4.9	1,289,362	1,9x
47,939	336	45,111	6.26	DIRECT LABOUR HOURS	143,735	714-	142,318	.99
347	27-	322	7.76	NO. OF PRODUCTION EMPLOYEES	342	2x	320	6.87
1,073	16-	1,054	1.80	AVE. EMPLOYEE COST	1,069	15-	1,050	.81
56	2-	51	9.80	NO. OF ADMIN. PERSONNEL	57	2	52	1.6x
1,379	14	1,313	5.02	AVE. PERSONNEL COST	1,364	13	1,310	4.12

* VARIANCE EXCEEDS $2,000

The % CHANGE/YR Calculation is based on the following:
Actual this year - actual last year
──────────────────────────────────
Actual last year

MSA

specified in the reporting hierarchy. Figure 13.12 illustrates an expense report for three levels within an organization. Figure 13.12(a) is an expense report for a specific plant, whilst Figure 13.12(b) is an expense report for the manufacturing and warehousing division which includes the specific plant. Similarly, Figure 13.12(c) is a summary report which includes the manufacturing and warehousing division. The MSA system can also be used to produce project reports.

Cost-allocation system

The cost-allocation system allocates revenues and expenses as well as assets, liabilities and non-financial information from service or support centres, with which they have been identified for responsibility and control purposes, to other centres or products for profitability and reporting purposes.

The problem arises that costs are collected and controlled through various cost centres, yet management may also require reports on product, process or regional profitability. The cost allocation should be capable of handling one of the schemes below:

MSA MANUFACTURING COMPANY			SUMMARY EXPENSE REPORT				PAGE 14)
			FICS 57004	PERIOD ENDING MARCH 31, 1984			ISSUED 3-4-84

- - - - - - - CURRENT PERIOD - - - - -				- - - - - - - YEAR TO DATE - - - - - - -			
ACTUAL	VARIANCE FROM PLAN	VARIANCE FROM LAST YEAR		ACTUAL	VARIANCE	VARIANCE FROM LAST YEAR	VARIANCE %
			PERSONNEL EXPENSE				
296,391	298-	9,972	MANUFACTURING	885,753	2,569	30,650	3.57
243,672	3,173	7,237	MARKETING	731,443	7,477	24,614	3.36
374,166	2,371	5,644	ADMINISTRATION	1,113,381	1,210-	8,386	.72
169,514	1,115-	917-	CORPORATE FINANCE	506,214	4,633-	783-	.13-
1,083,743	3,311	21,936	TOTAL PERSONNEL EXPENSE	3,236,791	4,203	62,667	.19
			OTHER OPERATING EXPENSE				
100,757	136	58	MANUFACTURING	295,599	6,942	1,206	4.09
461,019	16,421	18,769	MARKETING	1,169,318	18,225	63,115	4.68
237,183	3,268-	1,943	ADMINISTRATION	709,563	6,244-	1,241	1.27
78,316	2,116	1,614	CORPORATE FINANCE	235,181	14,211	21,617	9.08
877,275	15,415	21,098	TOTAL OTHER OPERATING EXP.	2,409,661	39,250	87,889	3.85
			GENERAL AND ADMINISTRATIVE EXP.				
50,073	846	9,552-	MANUFACTURING	118,160	947	7,704	6.72
63,218	1,316-	6,981	MARKETING	163,661	4,244	5,477	2.99
117,426	4,524	11,128	ADMINISTRATION	349,711	5,816	29,200	8.36
32,368	1,434-	357	CORPORATE FINANCE	98,438	1,162	2,388	2.71
263,085	2,620	7,620	TOTAL GEN. AND ADMIN. EXP.	769,972	4,643-	44,759	5.95
2,224,103	21,346	50,654	TOTAL EXPENSES	6,416,424	38,810	200,315	3.12

MSA

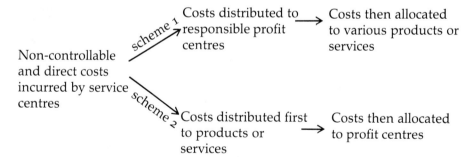

The MSA system also supports the simultaneous method of cost allocation in which a series of simultaneous linear equations are used for allocating to both profit centres and products simultaneously. The system can handle a number of costing systems such as absorption costing (which includes fixed overheads in product costing) or direct costing. The basis of allocation can depend on up to six different methods. These are:

1   Pre-determined fixed expenses (e.g. department A receives 10 per cent of the cost of the computing centre);

2   A statistic is divided by another statistic (e.g. the square footage of department B is divided into the total factory space of plant X and this proportion is used to allocate space-heating costs for plant X);
3   Weighted average (in which the statistic is weighted by another factor prior to determining the percentage by which the allocation is made);
4   Volume statistics for a department are multiplied by a standard cost;
5   A pre-determined amount is allocated to each individual recipient department;
6   A combination of methods 1–5 is used.

Profitability-reporting system

Although the responsibility-reporting system deals with cost control in cost centres for individual managers, the technique can be extended to profit centres – a segment of the business that is responsible for both revenues and costs.

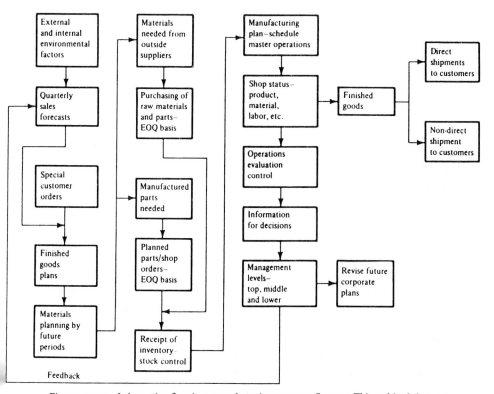

Figure 13.13   *Information flow in a manufacturing company* Source: *Thierauf (1982), p. 39*

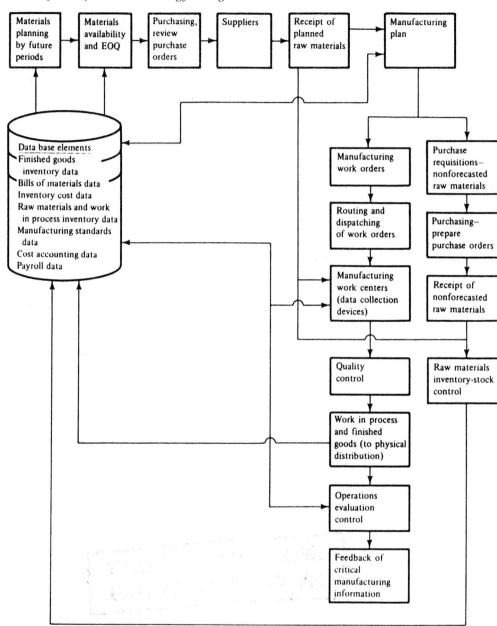

Figure 13.14   *Important functions of the manufacturing, inventory and purchasing subsystems*
Source: *Thierauf (1982), p. 47*

A second-example – MIS in a manufacturing environment

Our next example illustrates a wider concept of an MIS. We shall look briefly at a typical system, in a manufacturing environment, based on a example given by Thierauf (1982). Figure 13.13 shows the information flow in this system from the external and internal environment phase to actual day-to-day operations whereby output from one subsystem becomes input to another subsystem.

The manufacturing subsystem is used for producing regular or special production orders. Its essential components are:

Receiving;
Production scheduling and control;
Manufacturing operations;
(a) Machine shop,
(b) Assembly – major and minor,
(c) Plant and machine maintenance,
Quality control and inspection;
Data collection.

One especially important feature of this system is the interplay between physical activities and data files for operations evaluation, allowing feedback of critical information where it is needed.

Figure 13.14 shows the important functions of the manufacturing, inventory and purchasing subsystems. We shall return to this example in Chapter 15 when we consider decision support systems.

14 Financial models and spreadsheet applications

Introduction

In Chapter 15 we discuss decision support systems. This chapter concentrates on one class of ill-structured problems called financial or corporate models. The concept of a model or mathematical representation of real-world phenomena and the reason for the use of computers has already been discussed. The terms financial or corporate models are often used interchangeably to describe the same concept – in this chapter we standardize by using the term, financial model.

Some readers will have become used to the electronic spreadsheet approach to financial modelling through the use of Lotus 1–2–3 or some similar package. Since this type of package first became popular on microcomputers, we defer a major discussion of this type of technique until Chapter 16 when a full discussion of the impact of microcomputers on MIS is carried out. In the next chapter we will consider the more advanced topics of optimizing, probabilistic and statistical forecasting. However, in this chapter only the basic features of financial models and their uses are discussed. In order to explain the technique of financial modelling, a worked example is provided and a number of different applications are discussed. Finally, this chapter provides a brief case study of a manufacturing company. The reader may find this example a little unrealistic in that it is a much simplified example; nevertheless we feel it is important for the reader to gain a firm understanding of a simpler model rather than to begin with the study of a more complex one.

Put succinctly a financial model is a deterministic simulation of some financial aspect of a company. The model is deterministic because, given the same values, the model will always arrive at the same result. It is only by the accountant changing an assumption, or input value that a change in output will occur. A financial model is a simulation because it only represents the real world. The normal operation of financial markets and systems are defined in terms of rules that the computer can use. The extent to which these rules accurately represent real situations will determine the accuracy and success of a financial model.

A financial model essentially has four ingredients:

1 Some existing data on financial performance, for example, an opening balance on a balance sheet.
2 Assumptions concerning events over time or company data, for example, forecasts of future sales.
3 A mathematical representation relating the data and assumptions to important forecasts, projections or analyses, for example, how increased sales on credit influences cash flow.
4 A series of reports tabulating the input data, assumptions and results in a form which is of use to management, for example, a graph of projected bank balances for different assumed levels of sales.

A more formal way of describing these ingredients of a financial model is shown in Figure 14.2.

The *Data* contains the initial input values, parameter values (e.g. length of time over which model is to run) and assumptions.
The *Model Logic* is the set of equations and relationships which form the mathematical representation of the firm or object to be simulated.
The *Results*: running the model by using the model logic and the data

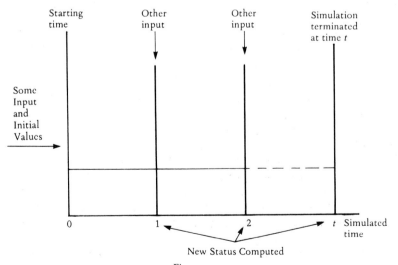

Figure 14.1

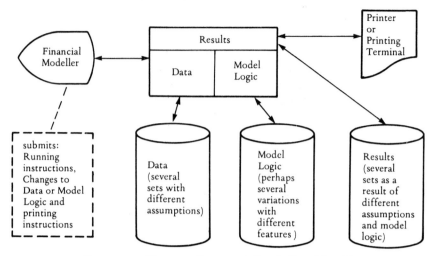

Figure 14.2   *Diagrammatic representation of a financial model*

produces a set of calculated or derived values which together may make up an operating and financial statement of the company's future.

For management accountants, there is an increasing tendency to use microcomputers and spreadsheet packages for financial modelling. Mainframe and large software packages are important but do not represent the bulk of new applications.

The purpose of the financial model – defined as the mathematical representation of the firm – is to simulate the activity of a company over a given period of time (e.g. 12 months in a short-run model or 5 years in a longer-horizon model). By applying certain formulae (often very simple accounting relationships) to the assumptions and data, the model will produce a set of results (forecasts or projections) for each period. Figure 14.1 shows how some input may be required initially (such as the bank opening balance) whilst other information (sales forecasts) will be required for each time period.

Not all models simulate over time. Increasingly, and often at a divisional or departmental level, spreadsheets are being used to provide detailed analysis of existing data, for example, in calculating the time taken for customers to pay invoices. The advanced graphic and presentation capabilities of modern spreadsheets means that the data can be represented in a number of different ways, and this is an important area of development in spreadsheet packages. The delay in invoice payments just mentioned could be represented as a simple average or a graph of frequency against time taken to pay. Figure 14.3 shows a hypothetical graph which provides interesting information on invoice payments and is more useful than a simple average in devising a strategy for debt management.

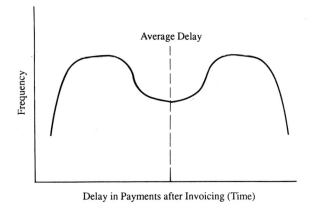

Figure 14.3   *Financial model of customers' delays in paying invoices*

A growth area

In Chapter 1, we identified financial modelling as one of the growth areas in the use of computers to aid in the planning, forecasting and decision-making process. The computer must not just be regarded as a tool for helping to process routine information as described in Chapter 12. The development of spreadsheet applications (particularly in presenting information), the increased power of microcomputers and the growing familiarity with computers makes the computer an important asset. Once the techniques and method of computer-based modelling are developed, the preparation of reports and the production of new models is simple and practical.

One reason why financial modelling is such a growth area is that once the technique is learnt, the use of such models is simple and practical. The financial modelling process can support the planning *and* control functions by making it easy and cheap to produce pro-forma financial statements. By automating the boring, time-consuming and labour-intensive parts of the planning process, financial models have become an important and indispensable part of the planning process.

At this point a word of caution is necessary. In talking about plans we may actually be referring to three concepts with different and distinctive meanings:

budgets, targets and forecasts.

Short-run plans may often become the budget. Yet a budget may be viewed as an acceptable level of performance rather than what may be

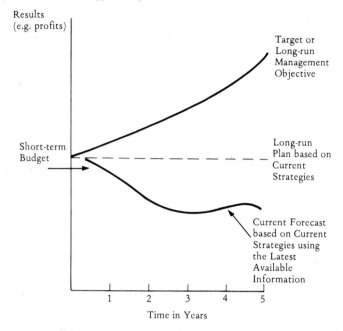

Figure 14.4   *Targets, budgets, plans and forecasts*

desirable. Once a budget has been set for control purposes, new information or changes in the environment may become apparent. This raises the question of the distinction between the following:

1   A *target* (or desired plan) is a desired result or a desired objective. For example, a profit level of £x million may be a long-term goal or aim.
2   A *budget* or current plan is the result of a number of strategies intended to put us on the path to achieve our targets; the plan may not, however, move us the whole way to our target. Nevertheless, a budget is something made regularly in a planning cycle and through which the performance of managers may be judged. It is the variable through which control is exercised. A budget may also be used as a motivational device. Sometimes, the managers involved participate in the creation of a budget.
3   A *forecast* may be made at any time with all the available information at hand. Almost certainly prices and the general macro-economic situation will have changed. Ford, for example, make a forecast monthly (taking care to number each forecast uniquely), whilst the budget is set annually.

The result is that the situation portrayed in Figure 14.4 may occur. (This obviously indicates that there is a substantial gap – between long run objectives and current performance – which must be reduced either by making the target more realistic or by internal and external gap-reducing plans consistent with a corporate strategic approach (see H. I. Ansoff (1965)). The budget/plan has been divided into a short-run budget – covering, say, the next twelve months – whilst the long-run plan covers the next five years. The current forecast assumes that the current plans embodied in the budget/plan are carried out, but uses all the available information to predict the results of those plans. Of course, the situation may become complicated if, as a result of the current forecast, action is taken to change the budgets. Hopefully, this will be the desired result of using current information to highlight what is going wrong with plans at an early stage.

Financial models

Perhaps the easiest way of introducing the reader to financial modelling is by giving examples. There are two examples given here. The first pro-vides a basic insight into financial modelling. While this example could be carried out using an ordinary calculator, there are a number of steps and equations which are ideally suited to computer implementation, especially if values are changed and the whole model needs to be recalcu-lated. The second example shows a simple spreadsheet implementation of a cash-flow forecasting model.

Table 14.1 shows the financial statements for Planning Nightmare Ltd. The results for 1987 are actual (as in the 1986 Balance Sheet values). The reports shown include a Profit-and-Loss account, Balance Sheet and Sources-and-Uses of Funds. The Profit-and-Loss account has a number of cost categories such as materials (cost of goods sold), labour, overheads and depreciation. Depreciation is calculated, on a straight-line basis over a ten-year life and for simplicity is calculated on the opening balance plus half the new investment. For 1987, the interest is 15 per cent on the average debt balance. The average tax rate after allowances and other deductions for tax purposes is 40 per cent. Dividends were fixed at £225,000. Net working capital including cash balances is around 10 per cent of revenue. (Revenue increased by £3m over the year.) There were no new equity issues and debt was increased by £100,000.

Forecast for 1988

Table 14.1 also shows the forecasts for 1988. Suppose that the firm is a one-product firm and the sales department hopes to sell 15,000 units at an average price of around £1,100. Capacity of the plant is expected to be 12,000 units per year. There are 500 people working as direct labour on an

Table 14.1   Financial statements for Planning Nightmare Ltd.

Row number	Profit and loss account		1987 Actual £'000	1988 Forecast £'000
1	Revenue (REV)		10,000	13,000
2	Cost of goods sold (CGS)		3,000	3,828
3	Labour costs (LAB)		3,500	4,100
4	Overheads (OH)		1,000	1,320
5	Depreciation (DEP)		1,050	1,195
6	Profit before interest and tax (PBIT)		1,450	2,757
7	Interest (INTR)		686	990
8	Profit before tax (PBT)		764	1,767
9	Tax at 40% (TAX)		300	706.8
10	Net profit (NET)		464	1,060.2
11	Dividends (DIV)		225	225
12	Addition to revenue reserves (ARR)		239	835.2

	Balance sheet	1986 Actual	1987 Actual	1988 Forecast
	Assets			
13	Net working capital excluding cash (NWC)	700	1,000	1,320
14	Cash (CASH)	203	292	2.2
15	Fixed assets (FA)*	10,000	9,950	12,755
16	(ASSETS)	10,903	11,242	14,077.2
17	Equity (EQUITY)	5,000	5,000	6,000
18	Revenue Reserves (RR)	1,003	1,242	2,077.2
19	Debt (DEBT)	4,900	5,000	6,000
20	(LIAB)	10,903	11,242	14,077.2

	Sources and uses of funds		1987 Actual	1988 Forecast
	Sources			
10	Net profit (NET)		464	1,060.2
5	Depreciation (DEP)		1,050	1,195
21	Operating cash flow (OCF)		1,514	2,255.2
22	New debt (NEW DEBT)		100	6,000
23	Less debt repayments (REPDEBT)		0	5,000
24	Net change in debt ($\triangle$DEBT)		100	1,000
25	Equity issue (EQI)		0	1,000
26	(SOURCES)		1,614	4,255.2
	Uses			
27	Increases in net working capital (INCNWC)		300	320
28	Investment (INVEST)		1,000	4,000
29	Dividends (DIV)		225	225
30	(USES)		1,525	4,545
31	Equals net change in cash ($\triangle$CASH)		89	−289.8

*Net of accumulated depreciation

average wage of £5,000 but it is likely a pay award will be made (backdated to the beginning of 1988) of 20 per cent. There are 100 indirect and salaried employees who will earn an average salary of around £11,000 in 1988. Material costs will be approximately 29 per cent of revenue. General inflation will take place at 10 per cent for all other costs, except that overheads will also incur an additional cost equal to 6.875 per cent of the additional revenue over 1987. In order to overcome the capacity limitation, management have decided to invest £4m worth of fixed assets financed by a £1m stock issue and £1m debt issue.

In order to obtain the extra £1m debt, the entire £5m existing debt was retired and a new £6m loan was made at a higher interest cost of 18 per cent. Although unrealistic in this example we will still retain the 40 per cent tax rate. Dividends for 1988 will remain at £225,000.

The results of the projection are shown in Table 14.1. Profit was substantially up, and the £4m of new investment was financed by retained earnings, depreciation, the increased debt and equity issue. Cash fell by £289,200 during 1988. Part of the increase was due to a relative fall in material costs and part due to an increased volume of sales. One of the conclusions of the current plan is that the amount of finance raised only just makes the expansion feasible. Extra finance may be needed to provide a degree of comfort.

The calculations in Table 14.1 for 1988 are relatively trivial and would only take a few minutes. However, if these calculations were to be performed for 5 separate years and if a number of different assumptions were to be made for the plan then this would involve a significant amount of work. Obviously, building a financial model and letting the computer perform the tedious work has two attractions: (1) the computer toils in your place and (2) it frees the management accountant to concentrate on the more important tasks such as the logic of the model and the realism of the assumptions.

The model

Table 14.2 attempts to write down the systematic calculations. There are **two types** of programming-like statement or equations. One type is the *assignment* such as:

SALES = 15,000,
or   PBIT = REV–CGS–LAB–OH–DEP.

The **actual values** can be substituted for the various variables which have been **given mnemonic** names (see Table 14.1), e.g.:

$$PBIT = 13,200,000 - 3,696,000 - 4,100,000 - 1,320,000 - 1,400,000$$
$$= 2,684,000.$$

Instead of using mnemonics, row or equation numbers (see Table 14.1) may be used:

$$6 = 1 - 2 - 3 - 4 - 5.$$

The second type is the *conditional* statement, which involves a comparison. For example:

$$IF\ SALES > 12000\ THEN\ SALES = 12000.$$

This could be translated into English as follows: If the projected number of sales is greater than 12,000 (the capacity limit) then reduce sales to be equal to the capacity limit otherwise (i.e. if sales are less than or equal to the capacity limit) ignore this statement.

As with any program of instructions for a computer, the operation of the model is to start with the first statement (SALES = 15,000) and proceed downwards, one statement at a time (unless directed otherwise). On the right-hand side of Table 14.2 the calculated (or derived) results are shown.

The Balance Sheet equations make reference to the previous year's values. Hence,

$$FA = FA(-1) + INVEST - DEP$$

means that fixed assets for 1988 are equal to the opening balance (i.e. 1987's value), described as FA(-1), plus new investment less depreciation.

A more general version of the model given in Table 14.2 is provided in Table 14.3. This model could be run for a number of years and has converted constants (i.e. 0.1) into variables which may be altered easily and rerun without changing the model logic.

Additional realism

The construction of any model always balances real-world complexity against simplicity, ease of comprehension and the ability to manipulate. The more complex the model is, the more realistic it may become. Yet a modeller should be able to understand and manipulate the model. The task becomes easier if the model is simpler.

Additional realism could have been incorporated by:

Table 14.2   The specific model for Planning Nightmare Ltd

	Calculated value

Profit and loss account

SALES = 15,000	15,000
IF SALES > 12,000 THEN SALES = 12,000	12,000
REV = SALES × £1,100	13,200,000
CGS = 0.29 × REV	3,828,000
LAB = 500 × £5,000 × 1.2 + 100 × £11,000	4,100,000
OH = 1,000 × 27.1 + (REV − 10,000,000) × .06875	1,320,000
DEP = (£9,950,000 + £4,000,000/2)/10*	1,195,000
PBIT = REV − CGS − LAB − OH − DEP	2,757,000
INTR = .18 × (£6,000,000 − £5,000,000)/2	990,000
PBT = PBIT − INTR	1,767,000
TAX = 0.4 × PBT	706,800
NET = PBT − TAX	1,060,200
DIV = £225,000	225,000
△RR = NET − DIV	835,200

Sources and uses of funds

OCF = NET + DEP	2,255,200
△DEBT = NEWDEBT − REPDEBT	1,000,000
SOURCES = OCF + △DEBT + EQI	4,255,200
NWC = 0.1 × REV	1,320,000
INCNWC = NWC − NWC (−1)	320,000

  Last year's net working capital excluding cash

USES = INCNWC + INVEST + DIV	4,545,000
△CASH = SOURCES − USES	−289,800

Balance sheet

CASH = CASH (−1) + △CASH	2,200

  Last year's cash balance

†FA = FA (−1) + INVEST − DEP	12,755,000

  Last year's fixed assets

ASSETS = NWC + CASH + FA	14,077,200
Equity = EQUITY (−1) + EQI	6,000,000

  Last year's equity

RR = RR (−1) + △RR	2,077,200

  Last year's revenue reserves

DEBT = DEBT (−1) + NEWDEBT − REPDEBT	1,000,000

  Last year's debt

LIAB = Equity + RR + DEBT	14,077,200

*This is an approximation. Straight-line depreciation should be calculated on gross value and not net value.
†FA Fixed assets net of accumulated depreciation.

Table 14.3　A general model for Planning Nightmare Ltd

Assumptions and data

No. of periods to be run
Starting year
Opening balances of
　NWC　　　　　　　　(net working capital)
　CASH　　　　　　　(cash)
　FA　　　　　　　　(fixed assets)
　EQUITY　　　　　　(equity)
　RR　　　　　　　　(revenue reserves)
　DEBT　　　　　　　(debt)
　BASE OH　　　　　(base level of overheads)
Previous year's value of REV
Assumptions for the whole of forecast period for
　SALES　　　　　　(sales in unit)
　CAPACITY　　　　(capacity limit)
　PRICE　　　　　　(price)
　CGSPC　　　　　　(cost of goods sold as a % of revenue)
　WORKERS　　　　(no. of workers)
　AVERAGE　　　　(average wage)
　STAFF　　　　　　(no. of staff)
　SALARY　　　　　(average salary
　INFL　　　　　　　(inflation rate)
　VOHPC　　　　　　(variable overheads as a % of additional revenue)
　INVEST　　　　　(new investment)
　RATE　　　　　　(interest rate)
　TAX RATE　　　　(tax rate)
　DIV　　　　　　　(dividends)
　NEW DEBT　　　　(new debt)
　REP DEBT　　　　(repayments of debt)
　EQUI　　　　　　(equity issues)
　NWCPC　　　　　(net working capital as a % of revenue)

The model logic(* = multiplication)

Profit and loss account
IF SALES > CAPACITY THEN SALES = CAPACITY
REV = SALES * PRICE
CGS = CGSPC * REV
LAB = WORKERS * AVERAGE + STAFF * SALARY
OH = BASE OH (-1) * INFL + (REV − REV(-1)) * VOHPC
DEP = (FA(-1) + INVEST/2)/LIFE
PBIT = REV − CGS − LAB − OH − DEP
INTR = RATE * (DEBT + DEBT(-1))/2
PBT = PBIT − INTR
TAX = TAX RATE * PBT
NET = PBT − TAX
△RR = NET − DIV

Sources and Uses of funds
OCF = NET + DEP
△DEBT = NEW DEBT − REP DEBT
SOURCES = OCF + DEBT + EQI
NWC = NWCPC * REV
INC NWC = NWC − NWC(-1)
USES = INC NWC + INVEST + DIV
△CASH = SOURCES − USES

　　　　　　　　　　　　　　　　　Balance Sheet

CASH = CASH (-1) + CASH
FA = FA(-1) + INVEST − DEP
ASSETS = NWC + CASH + FA
EQUITY = EQUITY (-1) + EQI
RR = RR(-1) + △RR
DEBT = DEBT (-1) + NEW DEBT − REP DEBT
LIAB = EQUITY + RR + DEBT

Note:
Some early modelling systems, such as VISICALC, do not include conditional operations.
Therefore, instructions such as:

　　　　　　　IF SALES > CAPACITY THEN SALES = CAPACITY

cannot be expressed. This is a serious deficiency of such systems.

1   Including separate and detailed current assets and current liability sections;
2   Allowing 100 per cent depreciation for tax purposes and the ability to carry forward tax losses, and the full fixed-assets register with depreciation being calculated on gross fixed assets (less any assets whose value has been written down to zero);
3   Including a more detailed product and cost information process;
4   Including a more comprehensive production process;
5   Including different types of debt and perhaps an overdraft facility;
6   Including a short-term deposit for 'spare' cash;
7   Including separate production and finished goods stock variables.

There are many other types of inclusion which may make the model easier to use. For example, the first year's actual interest may be read in as data and the rate calculated thus:

IF TIME = 1987 THEN INTR = RATE
$$\text{RATE} = \text{INTR}/(\text{DEBT} + \text{DEBT}\ (-1))/2$$
$$\text{ELSE INTR} = \text{RATE} * (\text{DEBT} + \text{DEBT}\ (-1))/2$$

This has the advantage of calculating the exact rate for the whole year, rather than manually calculating this rate. There are, of course, many other extensions and additions which may be incorporated into this model.

Types of model

This example illustrates the basic concept of a model. Remember that a model can always be calculated by hand; the reason for the use of a computer is that the model may be run many more times under different assumptions or may enable greater complexity to be built into the model. The example given above deals with very broad aggregate information, probably run for five-yearly periods. Some management accountants will not be used to planning as far as five years ahead and may be more used to thinking of plans in less global figures. Financial models can be constructed to aid in most areas. The example above was one such illustration.

Changes in model design are also reflected in changed applications. Early models were often designed for a wide range of applications – intended to aid both long- and short-run financial planning, to assist production and marketing decisions, and designed for use by line or middle management. Although models of this type are still being developed, there has been an increase in the use of a simpler model geared to the needs of top management with a much greater emphasis on specific financial considerations. In order to illustrate the range of applications a somewhat arbitrary classification is given below.

1 *Strategic* – to evaluate alternative courses of action (e.g. diversification into different fields, new plants, etc.).
2 *Impact* – to provide a rapid calculation of the impact of changes in the environment (including inflation) on the firm.
3 *Budgeting* – to computerize the short-run budgeting process of a firm and to facilitate the recalculation of those budgets (typically, short-run models vary from six to twenty-four months with the most common models being twelve monthly ones); heavily accounting-oriented.
4 *Planning* – an extension of the budgeting models, but usually simpler and less detailed with a longer-term horizon (5–10 years), less well-equipped to deal with major alternative courses of action, such as diversification (although new products could be analysed in this model).
5 *Cash-flow forecasting* – relatively, a shorter-run model (daily, weekly, monthly) to aid in cash-flow management. (To decide how much finance is needed for a major long-term investment programme, the planning or strategic model should be used.)

A model may obviously span a number of these arbitrary categories; they are given merely as an indication to the reader of the variety of applications. The applications are not mutually exclusive.

It would, however, be difficult to combine the budgeting (3) and the strategic (1) model, although it is common to link models together by using a common database; for example, a budgeting model (3) may budget for twelve months whilst the planning model (4) may plan for ten years – the input for the first period of the planning model may be taken directly from the budgeting model. Another way of combining models is to use a mixed-period model in which, for example, the first year is analysed by months, the second year is analysed by quarterly periods and subsequent periods are analysed at yearly intervals.

To illustrate the differences between variables, Figure 14.5 shows some conclusions as to the observed behaviour in the U.K. Models at the corporate level tend to use the year as the basic time period and deal with global financial variables only. Models developed at the operating or cost-centre level tend to have monthly time periods and deal with more physical relationships such as quantities, production data, machine capacity, material utilization and wastage rates, and so on.

Many management accountants will be concerned with aggregating information (such as budget data) from the detailed cost-centre level to broader aggregate figures. A parallel process involves the splitting up of

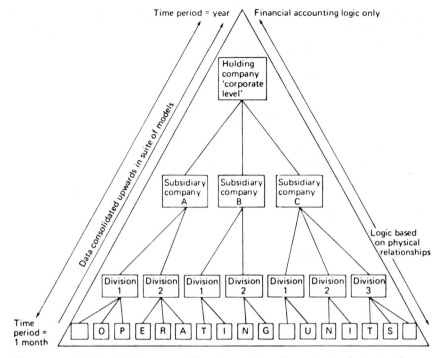

Figure 14.5 *Relationship between variables, time periods and organizational structure* Source: *Peter H. Grinyer and Jeff Wooller (1975)*

the broader aggregate figures and allocating these to various cost centres. Let us look at an actual example of how one medium-sized company uses the techniques of financial modelling.

Example 2

In this example we are going to develop a simple spreadsheet model of cash flow. The method of representing this cash flow is the change in closing cash balances. These changing cash balances are a reflection of the income for the period less any expenditure undertaken in the period. The resulting surplus or deficit can then be matched against any cash brought forward to identify the closing cash balance. The essential elements of the model will therefore be the income, the expenditure, the surplus/deficit, the cash brought forward and the resultant cash position.

Having outlined the basic features of our cashflow model it is necessary to identify and define the variables we need for the calculations. These have to be specified in mathematical terms and can be obtained by:

(a) *Definition.* For example, revenue = volume × unit price;

(b) *Estimation*. A financial modeller can use past behaviour of variables as an estimate (for example, a retailer may observe that the gross margin on sales has, on average, been x per cent of sales value);

(c) *Derivation*. Relationships between variable can be derived using algebra from other combinations of relationships (for example, if the pricing mechanism in an industry is such that a manufacturer's price to a wholesaler is based on cost plus a fixed mark-up, and similarly the wholesaler sells to the retailer on a cost plus basis, it is clearly quite simple to express the retailer's cost of purchases in terms of manufacturing cost and to ignore the wholesaler);

The process of setting up the model is one in which we specify each of the variables and their relationship. With a cash-flow model we would take the following basic steps.

1 Firstly, the closing cash balance may be defined as opening cash balance plus change in cash position for the month.

2 The opening cash balance for any period may be defined as closing cash balance in the previous period. We may express this as being: opening cash balance period T is equal to closing cash balance in period T−1.

3 The income for the month = receipts from debtors + cash sales + interest on deposits + dividends on investment + cash investments for the month + the sale of fixed assets.

4 Expenditure for the month = payments for purchases + wages and salaries paid + expenses + taxation + dividends paid + capital expenditure.

5 Finally the change in cash position for the month is equal to the income for the month minus the expenditure for the month.

However, while this simple outline adequately defines what we have to do, we have to be able to implement this simple model in a spreadsheet.

In order to do this we will sub-divide income and expenditure into the component parts and allocate each a row in our spreadsheet. The columns represent our accounting period and in the example we will use quarters.

A   B..............Z

1 Receipts from debtors
2 Cash sales
3 Interest on deposits
4 Dividends on investments
5 Cash investments

Figure 14.6   (a) *Basic spreadsheet for income and expenditure calculations*

	A	B..............Z
6 Cash sale of fixed assets		
7 Total income	SUM lines 1 to 6	
8 Payments for purchases		
9 Wages and salaries paid		
10 Expenses		
11 Taxation		
12 Dividends paid		
13 Capital expenditure		
14 Total expenditure	SUM lines 8 to 13	
15 Change in cash position	Line 7 MINUS line 14	
16 Opening cash position T	Use line 17 previous column	
17 Closing cash position	Line 16 ADD line 15	

Figure 14.6   (b) *Cash calculations incorporated into the spreadsheet model*

Our spreadsheet needs to incorporate the calculations for the cash position of the company. We can do this by adding a further three rows to our spreadsheet.

Notice that the opening cash balance period T is equal to closing cash balance in period $T-1$. This means that, for the initial period, the opening balance must be defined by the input variable; thereafter it is a dependent variable.

We have now achieved our basic objective of producing a simple cash-flow model. However, this first generation model has some major limitations, which a second generation may seek to overcome. It can also be used to illustrate how a spreadsheet model can be developed further, to incorporate more sophisticated features. For example, 'Receipts from debtors' is shown as an input variable while in fact it is a dependent variable. Receipts from debtors = sales revenue × credit taken. We can incorporate this into our spreadsheet by introducing two new rows and putting an equation in row 1. This is shown in Figure 14.7

	A	B..............Z
1 Receipts from debtors	MULTIPLY lines 18 and 19	
.		
.		
.		
.		
.		
18 Sales Revenue		
19 Credit Taken		

Figure 14.7   *Incorporating more advanced features into our model*

With a spreadsheet, in which the model is also primarily the report format, consideration of reporting formats is important; hence for simplicity a sub-model may be maintained in a separate part of the matrix which may be referred to by the main model in processing. So in the example we have lines 1 to 17 represent the main elements of our model. This would form a cash-flow report. The subsidiary elements, necessary for calculating receipts from debtors, are in rows 18 and 19.

We could continue to add increasingly sophisticated features into our model without having to change the basic format of our first generation model. For example, receipt from debtors may be further developed as follows:

Receipt from debtors = sales revenue × credit taken.
Sales revenue = sales volume + price.

But this may be made up of:

Sales mix: range of products (with multiple products, the sales revenue may be an aggregation of individual products).
Customer/outlet mix: range of products + prices.
Price: Differential prices according to customer, credit taken, special promotional pricing, etc.

These changes would increase the sophistication of the model without altering the basic report received by management. The important criterion of financial modelling, to produce relevant reports for management, is maintained. The model can continue to be developed and more features added. In the spreadsheet model outlined so far, all the variables have been defined. The final model is likely to contain estimates and derived formula, for example, the influence of advertising on sales. If a major promotion is planned it is likely to affect the expenditure before it influences sales. An estimate of sales in one period based on advertising in an earlier period could be incorporated into the model.

Testing the model

Once the management accountant has incorporated all the features that are required into the spreadsheet it is necessary to test that it is behaving correctly. The usual method used is to compare the output produced for some given set of input data against the expected output, probably in the form of actual observations from a previous period. Alternatively, it may be possible to derive estimates of some of the output variables using other modelling techniques, for example statistical regression.

If it is found that the output values indicated by the simulation model are not significantly different from their expected values, the decision maker should be able to proceed to use the model with a fair degree of

confidence. If, however, there appear to be systematic differences between the actual output and the expected output, then the model is
probably mis-specified and steps will have to be taken to improve its
design. This may involve changing the set of variables assumed to be
significant and/or altering the form of one or more of the relationships
between variables.

In many modelling situations, the testing process and any subsequent
model revisions will be an important, continuous exercise. Whenever the
system being modelled contains elements whose natures change over
time, it is important that the changes in relationship are reflected in the
model immediately, otherwise serious mistakes could be made as a result
of taking decisions on the basis of information from a mis-specified
model. Hence the testing process should be regarded by the modeller as a
regular exercise in all except the most stable systems.

Applying the model

Once the model has been validated it can be used to produce answers to
the questions originally identified by the decision maker in the first step.
The behaviour of the endogenous variables which interest the decision
maker may be observed for given sets of input data, as can the effects on
the system of marginal changes in the exogenous variables, thus providing some idea of the sensitivity of the model.

Besides answering 'what if' type questions, it is possible to set up
routines based on the simulation model which automatically test the
values of various items of output data as the input data are changed in
some way, for example to represent various decision choices available to
the manager. By remembering the 'best' value of an objective function
based on values of the output data, it is possible to identify an optimal
action from a set of specified alternatives by re-running the model for each
set of input data. This type of search procedure is sometimes described as
'iterative'.

Modelling choices

In the Planning Nightmare Ltd. example, the type of reports which were
wanted were closely proscribed by the historical information for 1987 in
Table 14.1. Very often a modeller will want to stick fairly closely to the
pro-forma financial statements of his company. But in some circumstances the modeller may wish to branch out. In any case, the modeller
will wish to assess whether to include the sections listed below and in
what detail.

1   A complex *marketing and revenue* section which would split the market-
    ing area into (a) types and location of markets and (b) the number and

specification of products. A further section may deal with market share and the competitor's actions.

2   *Cost structure* has two important attributes: (a) the number and level of detail of cost categories and (b) the number of cost centres, departments or processes over which costs are collected.

3   *Trading* versus *Profit-and-Loss Account* is one question that the modeller may wish to think about. Some companies simply require a build-up into a trading profit level; the reasoning being that the remainder of the Profit-and-Loss account figures are either open to manipulation by management or are very simple. On the other hand, anyone who has built a model of a complicated financial structure such as British Steel Corporation's accounts will know that one reason for not building a full-scale model of the Profit-and-Loss account and Balance Sheet is its extremely complicated make-up and the ever-changing structure of those statements. If a Profit-and-Loss plus a Balance Sheet is required but time is not available to build a full-scale model then one alternative may be to build a much simplified and reduced structure in their place.

4   The level and detail of *operational* data raises similar questions to those concerned with the level of detail in the cost structure. Types of data that could be included are: the volume of materials consumed, number of personnel and hours worked, the physical movement of materials and products and so on. In one instance the inclusion of machine utilization statistics highlighted that a re-arrangement of production would avoid the necessity of buying expensive additional equipment as had hitherto been the case (see the case study later in this chaper).

Other choices include whether to match actual against budgeted figures, the possibility of including a DCF calculation and so on. This however is only one aspect of the choice open to a modeller. Most models will, for example, have a revenue figure. How detailed should this figure be? Revenue could be simply input as data. Alternatively, prices and quantities of various products could be input and the sum of the products prices × quantity would yield the total revenue. A third possibility is to specify a demand relation in which the quantity of a product sold is a function of the price of the product, product characteristics, GDP per capita, level of advertising and so on. The revenue build-up would be calculated as the product price × quantity once both were fixed and the level of advertising and other assumptions determined.

One example of the type of problem which may arise is when a modeller has specified data relating to a price and quantity for each of 100 products. The managing director may walk in and suddenly ask what happens if revenue increases by 10 per cent. The modeller is at a loss since his model was not designed to cope with this type of question. All the prices or all the quantities could be changed by 10 per cent but this is a rather time-consuming task. An easier amendment may be to alter the model logic by the inclusion of the following statement:

REVENUE = REVENUE* ADJUSTMENT FACTOR

where the adjustment factor = 1.1 at the appropriate place in the model. In this instance, care must be taken to reset the adjustment factor to 1 when the modeller returns to the detailed specification of price and quantities for all the products.

This highlights another important choice. The modeller should always attempt to identify his research objectives prior to the designing of any model. In other words what type and level of detail is to be included in various reports? What types of questions are to be asked? What assumptions will be varied? Which are the especially sensitive or uncertain variables? Which strategic or operating variables will the management be interested in varying? The types of questions that are to be examined by the model will determine many of the model choices. Remember that the purpose of a model is to allow many experiments to be conducted before finalizing a budget or plan.

Other model choices include choice of a time period (monthly, quarterly, yearly or mixed); this question is often determined by the type and purpose of the model. Similarly, questions such as whether the firm is modelled at an operating unit, divisional or corporate level, and the number of financial and physical variables, the number of inputs or assumptions and the number of calculated/desired variables are all part of the modelling process of abstracting the important or crucial elements from the real world into a simple set of equations.

Decision rules also form part of the choice open to the modeller in the design of the model logic. Certain rudimentary decision rules can be determined by the model, for example, the raising of new finance by bank overdraft up to a certain level and then the issue of equity. Other rules require the model builder to feed the decisions in externally. Table 14.4 provides a checklist of some of the major choices open to the modeller.

Choosing a financial modelling system

Like most decisions about computer systems it is not simply a matter of buying a package and you are ready to produce a model. There is always an investment in time and resources, and these have to be balanced against the potential benefits of the system. Different systems have different implications for the user. So what are the key considerations in choosing a financial modelling system in terms of both hardware and software?

Table 14.4   A check-list for building financial models

In summarizing, we provide check-lists of possible decisions in building a model.

Key decisions
A list might include:
Level of disaggregation (number of products)
                         (number of plants)
                         (number of cost centres)
Period interval of model (e.g. 1 year)
Time horizon of model (e.g. 10 years).

Cost and revenue structure
The detail, complexity, number of variables and organizational structure to be included in the build-up of costs and revenues.

Variables
The number and type of financial and physical variables. A check-list of physical variables is provided below.
Products
Production (and related variables, e.g. production interruption due to strikes)
Employees
Raw materials
Production processes
Depreciation

Special routines
The check-list should include:
Employee requirements
Stocks
Tax
Dividends
Interest charges
Finance
Production levels
Working capital

Special decisions
These may include such decisions as:
Can production be different from sales?
Can purchases be greater or less than production requirements?
Is the number of employees required calculated endogenously?
Constraints?
Automatic expansion and contraction varying with demand?

Scale of the project

One obvious constraint on the availability of funding for financial modelling is the scale of the project. It is only with the availability of microcomputer systems that cost-effective financial modelling has become feasible for smaller scale projects. If the requirements for modelling are marginal and related more to providing budgetary information then a microcomputer-based spreadsheet system will probably be adequate. A financial model of the economy, however, would require a rather more sophisticated package running on a mainframe computer.

Availability of computer resources

A decision has to be made about whether there is sufficient computing capacity to run a financial model. Clearly, issues of how often the model is run and how long each run takes are of importance. Does the proposed timing of running the model compete with peak loads on the existing computer system, for example, when payrolls or sales figures are being prepared? If resources are not available then investment in a computer system as well as in the modelling program is necessary.

Software compatibility

If computer resources are available then is the modelling package you are intending to use compatible with your computer system? This is not a problem if you are developing a model in-house using a general purpose computer language, but it may be if you are intending to make use of a ready-made modelling package or spreadsheet.

Availability of technical resources

If you are developing a system using a general-purpose computer language do you have the manpower resources, in the accounting, system development and programming fields, or will you need to buy in these skills? Even for a ready-made package you may need to invest in training and development to get the system to do what you want, but you will not need such a high level of technical input.

Facilities available

Most financial modelling systems offer facilities for data handling and storage, file control, and mathematical and logical operations. However, general purpose languages offer the user a greater degree of flexibility, in that modelling facilities and functions can generally be programmed in if they are not already available. A modelling package or spreadsheet will be limited to built in functions. However, the built in functions of any modelling package should make it adequate for most financial modelling tasks. More care, however, should be given to the evaluation of modelling capacities of a spreadsheet program if you have any unusual requirements.

Ease of use: set up

A management accountant wants a financial modelling system that is easy to use. Ease of use needs to be considered in terms of ease of setting up the model and getting sensible output. In setting up a spreadsheet, for example, it may be necessary to set up all the equations and routines in the cells, which a dedicated modelling program might actually prompt for the values it needs.

Ease of use: output

Not a great deal has been achieved if a financial model outputs as much data as that originally entered. The output of any financial modelling system must be meaningful to the user. Does the system you are considering provide templates for different kinds of data presentation, including graphics?

Strategic model

To overcome the limitations of the detailed tactical planning model, which still provides the detailed forecasts and budgetary control mechanism, the company has developed a smaller strategic forecasting model which can be run on the computer in minutes rather than hours and which provides a broad set of results over a 5-year time horizon which can be measured against the current year forecast. Essentially, there are three modules to this strategic model:

> *Module I* concentrates on producing volume information given sales forecasts and opening stock balances.
> *Module II* produces a sales revenue forecast using module I's results.
> *Module III* uses the volume information produced in module I and takes the revenue forecast from module II to produce the following output:

1   Manufacturing, Distribution, Selling and Administration Operating Accounts for 5 years;
2   Company Trading Account for 5 years;
3   Profit and Loss Appropriation Account for 5 years;
4   Cash-Flow Analysis for 5 years;
5   Balance Sheet for 5 years;
6   Statistical Analysis for 5 years giving, e.g.,
>   Return on capital,
>   Sales margin,
>   Manning required,
>   Productivity levels,
>   Energy cost, etc.

Modules I, II and III are run once before inflation is taken into consideration. Modules II and III are then re-run with an inflated sales income and with different inflation factors being applied to various cost items.

Conclusion

Financial modelling is a rapidly growing use of computers – acting as a superior desk calculator – in the decision support area. In the next chapter other decision support systems will be considered. Some financial models will be linked to the firm's existing data files (in an attempt to automatically lift actual data). Other financial models may be stored on stand-alone microcomputers. The conditions for the successful use of financial models include:

1 Identifying a simple and clear-cut area where financial modelling may produce concrete productivity gains or provide increased information quickly; and
2 The full support and co-operation of top management.

15 Decision support systems

Financial modelling, which we have discussed in the previous chapter, is part of the more general range of techniques embodied in decision support systems (DSSs). In their widest sense, DSSs exist to support managers responsible for making and implementing decisions. The lower levels of management generally deal with well-structured problems. Computer aid for such areas is well established. Higher levels of management are concerned with strategic or tactical decisions and rely on aggregated or external data. Until recently, computer-based information processing had little to offer this level of management and their decision-making activities.

There are two broad avenues in a DSS. As with financial modelling, a DSS can contain an explicit model providing structure for particular decisions. A second branch of DSSs helps management by accessing information (normally unavailable) in novel ways. This latter usage is referred to as data extraction or manipulation.

The characteristics of a DSS are to some extent at the other end of the spectrum of applications to those considered in Chapters 12 and 13. DSSs are not designed to process transactions, keep records or report on the routine operations of a business. The usual characteristics of a DSS are as follows:

A DSS is concerned with less well-structured problems (but not so unstructured that only human intuition can tackle them).
Although a DSS can help at any level of management activity it is more usually applied at middle to senior levels.
Some information characteristics were given in Figure 11.11 (on p. 296). In keeping with the middle-senior managerial mix, the characteristics of the DSS information tend towards the strategic level.

These characteristics do not prevent DSSs being used in different ways by different people. Sometimes, they might be used by individuals working more or less in isolation whilst other systems help to facilitate communication and co-ordination.

The computer techniques employed in a DSS include database techniques, interactive graphics, on-line/real-time systems with good man-machine interface and dialogue.

The distinction between the modelling aspect and the data extraction and manipulation aspect of DSSs should not be over-emphasized. Both are concerned with predicting the consequences of a particular course of action. For example, take the consequences of a pay award and/or strike action by a particular group of employees. A good manager may want to examine what has happened in the past as a *predictive* basis for future action. He may also want to build a model, using the historical data as a determinant to assumptions and model logic, to predict the effect on profitability of several alternative consequences (e.g. protracted strike followed by low settlement, short strike with a higher settlement, or no strike with a very high pay award).

Thierauf [1982] has identified the essential characteristics of a DSS as:

Broad-based approach to support decision-making – accent on 'management by perception';
Human/machine interface where human retains control over the decision-making process;
Support decision-making for solving structured, semi-structured, and unstructured problems;
Utilization of appropriate mathematical and statistical models;
Query capabilities to obtain information by request – interactive mode;
Output directed to organization personnel at all levels;
Integrated subsystems;
Comprehensive database;
Easy-to-use approach;
Adaptive system over time.

These characteristics are further explained in Table 15.1.

The range of operations covered by the term DSS include:

Providing a mechanism for ad hoc data analysis; and
Providing prespecified aggregations of data in the form of reports; leading on to
Estimating the consequences of proposed decisions; with some coverage of
Proposing decisions.

All four types of operation are encompassed by the DSS. In order to gain

Table 15.1 Essential characteristics of decision support systems *Source*: Thierauf (1982) p. 78

---

1 *Broad-based approach to supporting decision making – accent on 'management by perception.'* Decision support systems go beyond capabilities of a typical management information system by taking a broad view of the organization in terms of supporting decisions. They utilize 'management by perception', whereby managers are assisted in perceiving important future trends and helped in adapting the organization to upcoming conditions.

2 *Human/machine interface where human retains control over the decision-making process.* The utilization of CRT terminals gives the decision-maker the capability to retrieve, manipulate, present, and store data such that there is a human/machine dialogue during decision-making. Throughout the interface, the decision-maker has complete control over all stages of the decision-making process in solving a problem.

3 *Support decision-making for solving structured, semi-structured, and unstructured problems.* Generally, the focus is on semi-structured and unstructured decisions although well-structured decisions can also be made in a DSS environment. Basically, DSS recognizes the need for bringing together human judgment and computerized information for improving the quality of the final decision.

4 *Utilization of appropriate mathematical and statistical models.* Based on the needs of the problem being solved, one or more mathematical and/or statistical models are employed to assist the decision-maker in evaluating alternative solutions. The real payoff from mathematical and statistical models as well as modeling languages comes from integrating them into the decision support system as decision tools.

5 *Query capabilities to obtain information by request – interactive mode.* In DSS, query capabilities go beyond those of interactive computation and include those of responsiveness. The latter item refers to utilizing the system as an extension of the individual's reasoning process throughout the decision-making process.

6 *Output directed to organization personnel at all levels.* Although DSS has the capability to supply top and middle management with important short- to long-range planning information for decision-making (that was not available with earlier computer systems), it is also capable of providing lower management and their operating personnel with the necessary output for supporting decision on controlling current operations.

7 *Integrated subsystems.* This concept refers to the capability of processing data for use by all subsystems along broader, functional lines rather than the traditional, narrow departmental lines. Integrated subsystems allow managers and their personnel to retrieve and manipulate information of concern to them for supporting decisions.

8 *Comprehensive database.* Contents of the database for DSS must go beyond just providing historical information about current and past operations. It must also contain appropriate external information that is compatible with internal information contained in the database. Generally, it is desirable to utilize a database management system (DBMS) to assist in a human/machine dialogue.

9 *Easy-to-use approach.* The hallmark of effective DSS is that it is easy to use, that is, not only does it assist the decision-maker in supporting decisions via a human/machine interface, but also allows the individual to pursue his or her own natural tendencies to problem-solving. From this view, the individual feels comfortable and 'at home' with the system rather than intimidated by it.

10 *Adaptive system over time.* The main thrust of the adaptive system concept is that the decision-maker is able to confront changing conditions and adapt the system to meet these changes. The time factor for effecting system changes is a few weeks to several months.

---

an understanding of them we discuss the first two together under the heading of data analysis and manipulation; then the last two are considered under the heading of computer models; finally, we consider an example of a DSS in a manufacturing environment.

Data analysis and manipulation

Although some authorities would classify as a DSS a system with the ability to make simple enquiries about operational data items, such access amounts to little more than a mechanized 'file drawer' and does not really constitute a decision support system.

Data analysis is concerned with the *ad hoc* analysis of files of data – usually historical and current data. Examples of such systems occur in budget analysis where the user, instead of examining a detailed print-out comparing budgeted versus actual expenses of a vast number of categories, allows a budget manager to browse or define a range (such as 10 per cent over budget) to highlight the most 'significant' features. (It may, of course, be just as effective for an organization to focus on those items which have met, or performed better than, the budget.)

Another example of data analysis is an on-line data retrieval and manipulation system used by American Airlines to compare, among other things, the recent performance of various airlines and so to develop a better understanding of how each competitor is progressing.

In both the above cases a set of data is analysed in some way. The information can be summarized or aggregated in certain ways, or a subset of the information produced. This is reminiscent of the section in Chapter 6 on Databases. Using the relational format, one can combine flat tables of data in the following way:

Selection of data items according to some criterion;
Joining two tables together;
Projection of certain columns of a table with non-repetition of duplicates.

The selection operation should be capable, by means of decision tables, of item-to-item comparisons, or comparisons with a constant. The possible comparisons of two items should include:

$$<, >, =, <> \quad \text{(not equal)}.$$

As well as relational operations, the data-manipulation functions should allow for a large number of arithmetical operations and the ability to sort and merge data. Totalling and analysis, including the ability to perform statistical analysis, is also useful.

The next type of system moves further away from the concept of an information retrieval system towards a transaction-processing system. In order to aid management, the data are chosen from a decision-oriented point of view; a data-manipulation system should be sufficiently flexible to permit small models to be written.

One example of such a system is a sales analysis DSS which could contain internally generated sales data, purchase information about customers and potential customers, and forecasts concerning the industry from specialized economic consulting agencies. The system may be viewed as a tool-kit of data and simple models for supporting *ad hoc* planning activities. One application could be product planning. This is achieved through the development of growth forecasts by industry segments, and of corresponding forecasts for product sales growth within industry segments and geographical regions. In this example, the relevant data is extracted from the existing data-processing systems and this data is augmented by external data. The actual 'database' (in a non-

```
ACCT. NO.        COMPANY NAME        CODE
  44164          XYZ COMPANY         B12

AVAILABLE
STATEMENT DATES                   OPTIONS
        6/83              E - END
       12/82              S - STATEMENT ENTRY
        6/82              A - STATUS FOR ACCT.
       12/81


ENTER OPTION A
```

(a)

```
ACCT. NO.     COMPANY NAME     STATEMENT DATE      TYPE
  44164       XYZ COMPANY          6/83             I

LINE    OPERATOR
  10       +      CASH
  20       +      ACCT. REC.
  30
  40
  50       S      LIQUID ASSETS
  60       +      INVENTORY
  70
  80       S      CURRENT ASSETS
  90       +      FIXED ASSETS
 100       +      DEFERRED ITEMS
 110
 120
 130
 140       T      TOTAL ASSETS

ENTER 'Y' TO STOP ENTRY
```

(b)

Figure 15.1   *Sample screen layouts for the financial statement analysis (Finstan) system* (a) *Available statement dates,* (b) *Financial data for credit analysis,* (c) *Output of calculated current ratios,* (d) *Current ratios plotted in graphical output* Source: *Thierauf (1982), pp. 522–3*

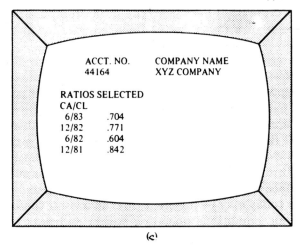

(c)

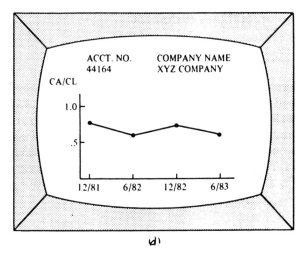

(d)

technical sense) is unencumbered by all the non-relevant transactions-oriented data and is kept for the sole purpose of supporting decisions. The ability to manipulate data, construct simple models, and generate reports is built on top of the bespoke database.

The software and computer systems necessary to run the data analysis and manipulation type of DSS are similar to those required to support databases. The software supporting the database system provides a range of facilities to retrieve information. These query facilities provide a powerful information-retrieval function. In some DSSs, as well as the query facility, calculations to analyse the data are necessary and this is usually not part of the database software.

One other important aspect of a DSS, apart from the modelling capability of the computer, is the ability to display information in clear visual or graphical form (e.g. pie charts). Figure 15.1 shows some typical results of creditor analysis as displayed on a VDU – some external data is required. The particular DSS used here is FINSTAN, a financial statement analysis system. The results shown are:

(a)   The available statement dates of creditors;
(b)   The financial statement data structure and model logic of a much simplified balance sheet for a creditor;
(c)   One possible calculation – the current assets to current liabilities ratios: many other calculations are permitted;
(d)   The information displayed in (c), presented as a graph to facilitate human perception.

Computer models

The second type of DSS is concerned with models. In the previous chapter we saw an example of a deterministic model. However, models can be of several different varieties.

Broadly speaking, models may be defined as representations of all or part of a company's current or prospective operations or of its economic environment. There are many classifications of the different kinds of models, one of which is given below:

Deterministic models (discussed in Chapter 14)
Optimizing models
Probabilistic models
Statistical forecasting models

Deterministic models

Chapter 14 was devoted to a consideration of these models. Examples of applications in financial models are given in Bhaskar [1978], Bhaskar *et al.* [1982], Flower [1974], Naylor [1981], Alter [1980] and Thierauf [1982]. Examples include models of all parts of a company in a variety of industries and specific studies dealing with:

Voyage profitability estimator (dealing with what charter rate should be charged for a ship on a particular voyage);
Preliminary budget analysis;
Monthly budget calculations;
Cash-flow forecasting;
Top-down budgeting model and demand analysis models.

Sometimes, a distinction is made between accounting models and representational models. Clear-cut accounting models deal with accounting relationships that involve mainly addition and subtraction and the computer in such models is thus seen as a glorified calculator. An accounting model involves the clarification of accounting definitions and relationships that are internal to the company. Representational models deal with the underlying economic relationships. Such models are based on the creation of meaningful relationships that describe the connection between actions and outcomes. The more detailed the model is and the more complex the relationships are, the closer the model may become to the real world. However, the more complex the model, the less easy it is to understand and manipulate. All models must achieve a balance between complexity and ease of use.

With purely accounting models, the accuracy of the relationships is well defined and the major focus is on the input values. Representational models have economic functional relationships approximating the real world which roughly describe the links between future actions and future outcomes. In these models, although input values are also important, the main issue is whether the model is a reasonable representation of the organization being modelled. Almost all financial models involve:

1 Some accounting definitions;
2 Some relationships which are known precisely although the input values may not be 100 per cent accurate;
3 Some relationships which attempt to represent how part of the business and economic environment works (though these relationships will not necessarily be good representations).

Statistical forecasting models

Statistical techniques can be used to provide forecasts by operating on historical data. This type of model is often used in conjunction with a deterministic model.

Econometric approach

One type of model which may be constructed attempts to represent the causal relationship in a company or environment. For example, demand for consumer durables may be functionally related to gross national product, per capita real income, credit restrictions and so forth. If the coefficients measuring the effect of these components on demand can be statistically estimated then, by specifying future values for these variables, a forecast for demand can be made, as shown in Figure 15.2. The

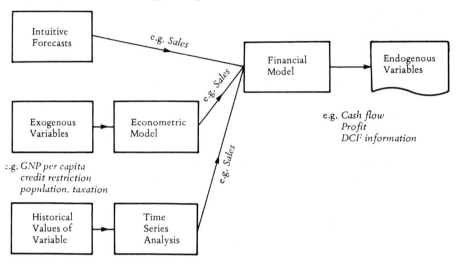

Figure 15.2   *Forecasting methods for determining input data of exogenous variables in a financial model*

disadvantages of this technique are: (1) it requires specialist knowledge to create the model and estimate its coefficients and (2) forecasts of the causal variables must be made in order to determine the future value of the variable in which we are interested. Thus, instead of estimating one variable, the modeller may have to estimate several, intuitively or otherwise. This technique is, theoretically, the most appealing. In order to catch the simultaneous movement of several causal variables, it may be necessary to estimate what is known as a *simultaneous equations* model. Such models require even more specialist skills and the simpler, but theoretically inferior, techniques may be easier for the financial modeller to use.

Time series analysis

The second broad classification of statistical models differs from the superior econometric approach in that only historical values of the variables to be forecast are necessary to derive a value of an input variable to the financial model (as shown in Figure 15.2). The theory assumes that a time series is made up of a number of components: an absolute level, a trend from this level, a seasonal pattern (there may be several, e.g. monthly, summer/winter, business cycles, etc.) and a random disturbance term. Various techniques are used to attempt to decompose these constituents of a time series and, by using the decomposed information, to derive forecasts. Within this broad category of statistical models, there are a variety of distinct techniques, e.g.:

Trend lines and curves;
Moving averages;
Exponential smoothing;
Multiplicative or additive smoothing;
Adaptive methods of exponential smoothing;
Auto-regressive techniques;
Box–Jenkins (a mixture of auto-regressive and moving averages);
Multivariate Box–Jenkins techniques.

Box–Jenkins is probably considered the most sophisticated of these techniques although auto-regressive methods are almost as good and are simpler for the modeller to use.

Time series analysis is less appropriate for forecasting applications such as predicting the rate of inflation. A simple econometric model with an appropriate lag structure of the form, say

inflation rate, $= f(\text{unemployment}_t, \text{consumption}_{t-1}, \text{money supply}_{t-2})$

may be better, whilst purists would argue that nothing less than a full-blown simultaneous equations macro-economic model would be sufficient to forecast the rate of inflation accurately.

Optimizing models

The model in this instance derives an 'optimum' solution of some specified objective using mathematical techniques and analysis. By adjusting the controllable variables, a model builder may be able to research for optimal or best plans. Some models automatically search for such an optimal plan in which case they are said to be *optimizing* models. However, all models, to a certain extent, allow the model builder to search for better alternatives. The distinction between optimizing and non-optimizing models is that an optimizing model, within the confines of a given set of objectives, searches for an optimum automatically. The model builder may, however, only wish to know what is the likely outcome of differing variables given a range of alternatives.

Optimizing models usually use a technique known as mathematical programming in order to make the search for the optimum more efficient. The most common mathematical programming technique in use today is one called Linear Programming (LP) which permits the use of only linear relationships. This technique involves the specification of a linear objective function (e.g. contribution per product) and a number of constraints (e.g. total machine hours and total labour hours available to the firm). The solution to the LP model will then yield an optimal plan (e.g. an optimal product mix) which maximizes the objective function (e.g. the contribution to profit). An example of an LP model will be given to illustrate the concept of an optimizing model using the 'product mix' problem.

The problem is: given that there are limited resources, how much of each product should be produced so as to maximize profits? Apart from price limitations, a firm faces constraints on the volume of output it can produce. Production constraints include shortages of various factors such as labour, raw materials, machines and space. Where there is only one limiting factor, the firm should maximize the contribution margin (i.e. unit sales revenue less unit variable cost) in relation to that factor. An example demonstrates the point.

A company manufacturing two products, product A and product B, aims to maximize its profits. The estimated unit cost and the factor requirements of labour, machine time and raw materials are shown in Table 15.2.

Table 15.2   Costs and input requirements for the manufacture of products A and B

	Product A	Product B
Selling price per unit	3	5
Less variable costs per unit (£)	2	3
Contribution to fixed costs and profit per unit (£)	1	2
Labour time per unit (hours)	2	1
Machine time per unit (hours)	1	1
Raw materials per unit (lbs)	1	3

Initially, it will be assumed there is no shortage of machine capacity or of raw materials, but there is a shortage of skilled labour; we assume that the maximum number of labour hours available for the next production period is 20,000. Using the limiting factor analysis it is necessary to calculate the contribution margin per labour hour (the scarce factor) for each product.

Table 15.3   Calculation of contribution margins for the limiting factor

	Product A	Product B
Labour hours per unit	2	1
Contribution per unit (£)	1	2
Contribution margin per unit of scarce resource (£)	0.50	2.00

The optimal solution is to produce as much of product B as possible since that product has the higher contribution margin (£2/unit) in terms of labour hours. Hence the firm should manufacture 10,000 units of product B which will give rise to a profit contribution of £20,000.

The position may change, however, if constraints are imposed on other factor inputs. For example, suppose that only 8,000 machine hours and

10,000 units of raw materials are available for the half year. The simple limiting-factor optimizing rule will no longer be satisfactory and, instead, a linear programming solution is required.

The objective is to maximize the contribution to fixed overheads and profit, so the objective function may be formulated as

maximize
$$x_A + 2x_B$$
where

x_A is one unit of product A
x_B is one unit of product B
and the parameter values of A and B are the unit contribution margins.

This equation is subject to the limits $x_A \geq 0$ and $x_B \geq 0$ since it is not possible to produce negative quantities of the two products. The constraints may also be expressed algebraically as follows:

$$2x_A + x_B \leq 10,000 \text{ (labour hours)}$$
$$x_A + x_B \leq 8,000 \text{ (machine hours)}$$
$$x_A + 3x_B \leq 10,000 \text{ (raw materials in lbs)}$$

input units per
unit of output.

Although this problem, being a two-dimensional problem (i.e. having only two variables, x_A and x_B) can be solved graphically, normally a computer program would find the solution to the problem using a 'simplex' algorithm. The solution to the problem is given below:

$$x_A = 4,000,$$
$$x_B = 2,000,$$

that is, four thousand units of product A and two thousand units of product B. The total contribution to profits would be £8,000 ($= 1 \times 4,000 + 2 \times 2,000$). The LP solution also provides other valuable information dealing with opportunity costs and shadow prices of the various resources. The computer printout may appear as

LINEAR PROGRAMMING-SOLUTION

NUMBER OF VARIABLES: 2

NUMBER OF CONSTRAINTS: 3
MAXIMISATION PROBLEM

PROBLEM DESCRIPTION: LP PROBLEM SOLUTION FOR KNB
VARIABLE INFORMATION

NUMBER	NAME	VALUE	OPPORTUNITY-COST
1	XA	4000.000	0.00
2	XB	2000.000	0.000

CONSTRAINT INFORMATION

NUMBER	NAME	DUAL	SLACK	TYPE	RHS
1	LABOUR	0.200	0.000	=(	10000.000
2	M. HOURS	0.000	2000.000	=(	8000.000
3	RAW MATS	0.600	0.000	=(	10000.0000

OBJECTIVE VALUE FUNCTION =   8000.000 IN 3 ITERATIONS

Other short-run examples of optimizing models include the raw material-mix problem. Here the objective is to minimize costs subject to certain physical constraints on the composition of the product (usually food or chemical). Price and availability of raw materials will fluctuate throughout the year. The LP model consequently responds to these fluctuations by varying product recipes to meet production requirements at minimum cost.

Another use of LP models is in the area of optimal capital project selection in capital-rationing situations, where money is sufficiently scarce to prohibit the adoption of all worthwhile projects.

Yet another short-run problem involves scheduling. One classic problem in this area is the transportation problem. This involves scheduling a number of, say, lorries transporting goods from a number of warehouses to several locations.

A further example involves investment opportunities and financing alternatives. Such a model will either attempt to maximize the net present value of projects undertaken or the discounted future dividend stream. In situations of capital rationing, firms may be forced to choose between a number of projects all of which at face value have positive net present values. During the early 1980s, the authors have seen investment projects with internal rates of return (i.e. yield) of greater than 70 per cent rejected because of capital shortages. If a company has a number of projects each year, with some projects capable of being undertaken in a particular year or deferred until another year when money is available, the selection of the optimal profit is extremely complex.

Other examples of optimizing models, apart from LP models, include goal programming, integer programming, quadratic programming, non-linear programming, dynamic programming, stochastic programming and chance-constrained programming.

Goal programming and multi-criteria programming are attempts to enter more than one variable in the objective function. Instead, two variables (e.g. growth and profits) can exist simultaneously in the objective function and the optimization technique would make trade-offs between each goal. Hence, this more flexible approach allows multiple and conflicting objectives. A priority structure is specified for these objectives which then permits an optimal solution to be found. By and large, the use of LP models has not been very successful because early models tended to be too complicated (i.e. have too many variables) and users misunderstood the nature of the models. Although an optimal solution is produced by the model, this solution cannot be regarded as optimal for the firm, but optimal only in so far as the input data are correct (a rare occurrence). Alternatively, the model must be run several times, each run yielding more information towards the best plan of action for the firm as a whole.

Integer programming constrains the solutions to integer values, whilst quadratic and other non-linear programming allows quadratic and non-linear terms in the objective function. Dynamic programming is a sort of decision-tree approach to the problem in that optimal decisions in one period may depend on the decisions taken in another period.

Stochastic programming models are an attempt to build a probabilistic simulation model around an LP model with a probability distribution of solutions. Chance-constrained programming allows constraints to be violated some of the time but subject to a level of tolerance that the constraint will be met with a minimum probability (e.g. 50 per cent of the time).

Probabilistic models

Up to now it has been assumed that the values of the input and output variables have been defined in terms of single numbers or point estimates. It is true that within these deterministic models, risk and uncertainty can be considered by means of sensitivity analysis. This technique examines the effects on the output variables of changes in the input variables. Probabilistic models, or as they are sometimes called, Monte Carlo simulation techniques, try to cope with risk in a systematic manner by identifying or estimating the probabilities associated with different uncertain situations in the world. They attempt to broaden an input value from a point estimate to a complete probability distribution. The user is required to specify the probability distribution of a (small) number of initial input variables. The simulation model then randomly selects values from these input probability distributions. This process of randomly selecting is analogous to picking a ticket out of a hat. Suppose we had a simple discrete probability distribution for sales:

good sales of 500	20 per cent
moderate sales of 300	50 per cent
poor sales of 200	30 per cent

(a) Uniform probability distribution

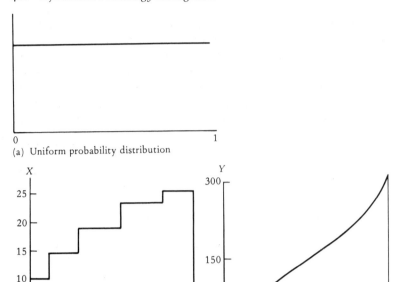

Discrete cumulative distribution   Continuous cumulative distribution

(b) Discrete and continuous cumulative distributions

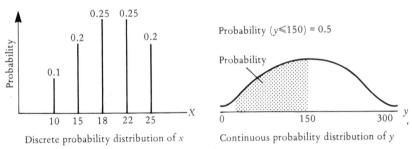

Discrete probability distribution of *x*   Continuous probability distribution of *y*

(c) Discrete and continuous probability distributions

Figure 15.3   (a) *Uniform probability distribution*, (b) *Discrete and continuous cumulative distributions*, (c) *Discrete and continuous probability distributions* Source: *Bhaskar* et al. *(1982)*

If we had 1,000 pieces of paper that were to be placed in the hat, then 200 (i.e. 20 per cent) of the pieces would be marked with the value 500, whilst 500 pieces of paper would have 300 marked on them and 300 pieces would have 200 marked on them. Consequently, if we took out 1,000 pieces of paper (in technical terms equivalent to sampling 1,000 times) we would obtain our original probability distribution. If we sampled only 100 times and took the pieces out in a truly random fashion, we would expect the sample to approximate the original probability distribution.

The computer can perform sampling in a similar way. The 1,000 pieces of paper could be represented by an array of 1,000 storage locations. In these locations would be stored the values written in our pieces of paper. Thus, the first 200 elements in the array each have the value 500, the next 500 elements contain the value 300 and the remaining 300 elements each contain 200.

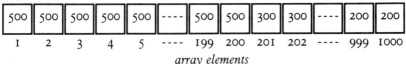

array elements

To sample from this array the following procedure is followed:

1   Generate a random number in the range 0 to 1. For this we normally use a built-in random number generator (part of the system software) to generate a value according to a *uniform distribution*. This means that any value in the range 0 to 1 is equally likely to be generated.
2   Multiply this number by 1,000 to obtain a value in the range 0 to 1000.
3   Discard the fractional part giving an integer in the range 0 to 999, and
4   add 1.

With this procedure, if initial random numbers obtained in step 1 are 0.0006, 0.5214 and 0.9999 then the values yielded are 500 (from array element 1), 200 (from element 522) and 200 (from element 1,000).

You may wonder why we didn't apply the following much simpler and obvious procedure for sampling and distribution:

1   Set r to a uniform random number between 0 to 1.
2   If $r \leqslant 0.2$ then sample value is 500,
    if $r \leqslant 0.7$ then sample value is 300,
    or sample value is 200

The answer, of course, is that the technique using the array has more general applicability. Further treatment of this subject can be found in Flower [1973] (Chapter 5) and Naylor [1971] Chapters 2 and 10.

With discrete distributions some of the elements have identical values. However, a continuous distribution, as shown in Figure 15.3, would have each element separately valued. The probability statement about sales would then have to be changed to: roughly 20 per cent of sales lay in the region 400–600 and so on.

To sample from theoretical distributions, such as the normal or Poisson distribution, a calculation is performed using a formula requiring a uniform random number and parameters as input.

The steps in the process of running a probabilistic model are shown in

Figure 15.4. Assumptions and parameters are input. The probability distributions are set up. There are then two loops in the simulation program.

1 The iteration loop controls the number of times the probability distribution is sampled.
2 The time loop controls the number of periods for which the simulation is to run.

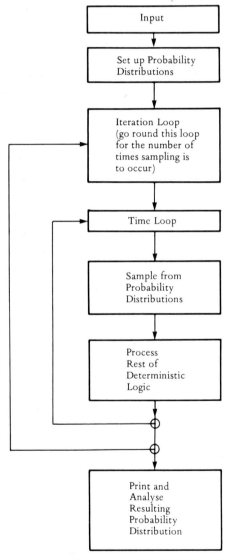

Figure 15.4 *Steps in process of probabilistic model*

Inside these two loops, the sampling process and the rest of the determi-nistic logic is performed.

At the end of the exercise, the result is a series of derived probability distributions. To have a different probability distribution for the profits in each of, say, 10 project periods may not be very informative. So prob-abilistic models usually focus on one or two key variables, for example the net present value or internal rate of return, or even the probability of bankruptcy and so on. Other probability distributions, like the profit in

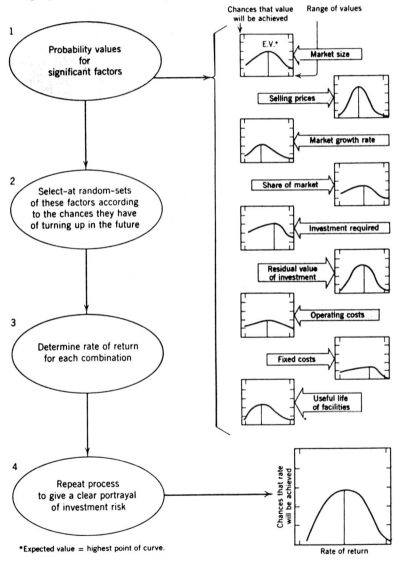

Figure 15.5 *Simulation for investment planning*

projected future years may be summarized or analysed. The mean, median, standard deviation and measure of skewness (third moment) may be printed-out.

Probabilistic models are probably best when there are a small number of very risky variables. Project appraisal is certainly one area where probabilistic simulation can be effectively used. With corporate models, the models are too large to have probability distributions systematically incorporated. In any case, the data requirements for the specification of the probability distributions would not exist.

Figure 15.5 shows an example of several variables with probability distributions being used to produce a probability distribution of the viability of an investment project. The probabilistic variables include:

Market size;
Selling price;
Market growth rate;
Share of market;
Investment required;
Residual value of investment;
Operating costs;
Fixed costs;
Useful life of facilities.

The actual output of such an exercise may appear on a print-out as:

2 FEB 80 11:59.03	RISK	PAGE 1

THORNCROFT MANOR SERVICES, DORKING ROAD, LEATHER–
HEAD KT22 8JB

****

NPV   *

****

       NO. OF SIMULATIONS: 500
       MINIMUM VALUE: −25069.8812
       MAXIMUM VALUE: 45331.9008
       MEAN: 11580.8475   + OR −   1019.4187
                                  195% CONFIDENCE LEVEL)
       STANDARD DEVIATION: 11630.0486
       PROBABILITY OF EXCEEDING VALUE:
          90.0%   −2578.5397
          75.0%   3071.7900
          50.0%   11950.5582
          25.0%   19540.4379
          10.0%   27007.0750

The resulting probability distribution of the net present values can be graphed in either the frequency distribution or the cumulative probability function. As can be seen in Figure 15.6, the example produces a bi-modal distribution. The earlier statistical representations did not adequately describe the peculiar nature of the risk in this project.

Other analytical models

Analytical models are models in which some type of algorithm is used to produce a solution or output. The LP type of model mentioned above is an example of an analytical model. Other analytical models such as DCF (Discounted Cash Flow) techniques and optimal inventory holding models (such as the simple economic recorder point model) may be used within a deterministic simulation model.

Sometimes these models are referred to as suggestion models since they are used to 'suggest' a result or a decision. A model is, at best, an approximation to the system it represents. It can only provide a mathematical solution to this representation. The input data are often very rough, so too much reliance should not be placed on the results. All models should be viewed simply as decision aids.

The current trend in the use of models is towards simple deterministic simulation models with a financial application bias. Neither optimizing nor probabilistic models have found the general acceptance of the former simpler type of model. The growing use of the simpler type of model will lead some modellers (after the learning process concerned with these financial models has been completed) to experiment with optimizing models (e.g. LP models) in order to search for optimum solutions. Similarly, some modellers will want to incorporate probabilistic elements into their deterministic models in order to have a better understanding of the riskiness of their business. However, it is likely that deterministic models will always have a wider appeal. Statistical forecasting models will probably be used increasingly as an extension of deterministic models to aid the derivation of assumptions such as future sales.

Examples of decision support systems

BIS

A case study[*] is now given that concerns an on-line system for planning, budgeting and control at a bank. The system is called BIS (budget information system). BIS is a series of applications including actual budget on an operating division basis, bank-wide planning, profit-and-loss analysis and other applications.

*This is based on the case study in Alter (1980).

```
17 MAR 80   9:57:34              R I S K
      THORNCROFT MANOR SERVICES , DORKING ROAD , LEATHERHEAD KT22 8JD

                              A PROBLEM
=====================================================================

**********
* NPV    * NET-PRESENT-VALUE OF PROJECT
**********

VALUES IN
THOUSANDS     0%      5%      10%      15%      20%      25%
---------   --------------------------------------------------------
 -4.000       .       .       .        .        .        .
            ===<0>    .       .        .        .        .        2%
 -3.000       .       .       .        .        .        .
            =============<=0 >        .        .        .        8%
 -2.000       .       .       .        .        .        .
            ==================<==0   >        .        .        12%
 -1.000       .       .       .        .        .        .
            ==================<==0 >  .        .        .        11%
  0.000       .       .       .        .        .        .
            0         .       .        .        .        .        0%
  1.000       .       .       .        .        .        .
            0         .       .        .        .        .        0%
  2.000       .       .       .        .        .        .
            0         .       .        .        .        .        0%
  3.000       .       .       .        .        .        .
            =======<=0   >    .        .        .        .        5%
  4.000       .       .       .        .        .        .
            ======================================<===0  >  .      22%
  5.000       .       .       .        .        .        .
            ==========================<===0    >     .        .    18%
  6.000       .       .       .        .        .        .
            ==========================<==0   .>      .        .    14%
  7.000       .       .       .        .        .        .
            ============<=0   >     .        .        .        .    7%
  8.000       .       .       .        .        .        .
            ===<0>    .       .        .        .        .        2%
  9.000       .       .       .        .        .        .
            ---------------------------------------------------------
              0%      5%      10%      15%      20%      25%
                       --------------- PROBABILITY --->

        PROBABILITY DISTRIBUTION DERIVED FROM 1000 SIMULATIONS


17 MAR 80   9:57:34              R I S K
      THORNCROFT MANOR SERVICES , DORKING ROAD , LEATHERHEAD KT22 8JD

                              A PROBLEM
=====================================================================

**********
* NPV    * NET-PRESENT-VALUE OF PROJECT
**********

VALUES IN    ----------------- CHANCE OF NOT EXCEEDING ----*>
THOUSANDS     0%     20%     40%     60%     80%    100%
---------   --------------------------------------------------------
 -4.000     100% 0      .       .       .       .       .      0%
            ----  (0)    .       .       .       .       .      ----
 -3.000      98% (0)     .       .       .       .       .      2%
            ----  .(0)    .       .       .       .       .      ----
 -2.000      91%  .   (0)  .       .       .       .       .     9%
            ----  .   (0)). .       .       .       .       .    ----
 -1.000      79%  .    (0)) .       .       .       .       .    21%
            ----  .       . (0)   .       .       .       .      ----
  0.000      68%  .       .  (0)   .       .       .       .     32%
            ----  .       .  (0)   .       .       .       .     ----
  1.000      68%  .       .  (0)   .       .       .       .     32%
            ----  .       .  (0)   .       .       .       .     ----
  2.000      68%  .       .  (0)   .       .       .       .     32%
            ----  .       .  (0)   .       .       .       .     ----
  3.000      68%  .       .  (0)   .       .       .       .     32%
            ----  .       .  (0)) .       .       .       .      ----
  4.000      62%  .       .  ((0))  .       .       .       .    38%
            ----  .       .   . ((0))  .       .       .         ----
  5.000      41%  .       .       . ((0))  .       .       .     59%
            ----  .       .       .  . (0))  .       .           ----
  6.000      23%  .       .       .       . ((0))  .       .     77%
            ----  .       .       .       .  .(0))  .            ----
  7.000       9%  .       .       .       .       . (0       91%
            ----  .       .       .       .       . (0  .        ----
  8.000       2%  .       .       .       .       .  0.         98%
            ----  .       .       .       .       .   0          ----
  9.000       0%  .       .       .       .       .   0        100%
---------   --------------------------------------------------------
             100%    80%     60%     40%     20%     0%
                 <------ CHANCE OF EXCEEDING -------------------->

        PROBABILITY DISTRIBUTION DERIVED FROM 1000 SIMULATIONS
```

Figure 15.6

The typical data structure is as follows:

Cost centre;
Transaction code within cost centre;
Five-year actual history;
This year's revised budget by month;
Current long-range plan for this year and the next five years.

A cost centre could either be a corporate department (e.g. marketing, auditing), a cost centre within the operating group or one of the live divisions (such as trust funds). Within each cost centre there are five transaction types:

1   Direct expenses, broken down further by expense class, such as telephone and stationery;
2   Indirect expenses, such as the allocation of overhead to the charged cost centre, broken down by charging divisions;
3   For charging cost centres, an allocation of expenses on a 100 per cent basis by charged cost centre;
4   Charges for the data-processing services of the Computer Services Division;
5   Miscellaneous data, such as transaction volumes, incomes, and personnel by grade.

It can be seen that the basic budgeting and planning activity of the bank takes place at the cost-centre level. This data can be aggregated in planning or evaluating the performance of large units (e.g. product lines, profit centres, divisions and so on).

To produce profit-and-loss accounts, income data had also to be stored by profit centre. Those cost centres which were not also profit centres had their expense data allocated to appropriate profit centres by a number of formulae. Cost-centre data could be aggregated in a number of different ways (e.g. by region, by product line, by profit centre, by department and by division). The 'actual' data are input monthly by a standard monthly update run from information obtained from the separate accounting system. (This was a previously developed transaction-orientated expense accounting system called RAS – responsibility accounting system – which captures all transactions within each expense class for each cost centre.) The budget and long-range plan figures are entered on-line to files by the cost centre manager.

BIS, whilst using one common set of files, has a number of different applications.

Interactive exception reporting

A cost centre manager can prepare a customized monthly variance report comparing actual with budgeted performance. BIS also allows the divisional managers to select for their attention only those expense classes in each cost centre that merit their attention. This is a considerable improvement on the alternative of looking at all transactions from the detailed RAS batch reports.

The divisional manager specifies absolute amount and percentage criteria for the exception reports. The exceptions are scanned on-line and comments can be added to those exceptions which require note or further investigation or explanation. The report is then passed on to a cost-centre manager who will investigate/explain those variances which were flagged by his superior. The cost-centre manager in explaining these variances may have to refer to the detailed RAS batch report. This is because BIS will only break down a cost class into a monthly total (e.g. month's expense for stationery by cost centre X was £4,182.16) whilst the detailed RAS will have this information broken down by transaction. The cost-centre manager then returns the annotated report to the divisional manager.

Some of the observations made and advantages gained in using the system are described by Alter [1980] pages 253–4.

> 'BIS is designed as a tool for facilitating communication between comptrollers and cost centre managers. Instead of being forced to thumb through the transaction-by-transaction detail of the RAS batch reports, the comptroller can allow BIS to select for his attention only those expense classes in each cost centre that merit his attention. The cost centre manager, who should have a close fix on the detailed expenses, can then refer to RAS output to explain what happened wherever it isn't apparent.
>
> Although exception reports can be generated in batch mode, the on-line nature of BIS permits the customizing and annotation of these reports. The cost centre manager knows that the exception report contains only variances that really require some explanation. In addition, the process of customising exception reports means that both divisional managers and cost centre managers will have given some thought to the exceptions prior to their meeting, thus facilitating communication.'

In smaller divisions where there is little effort in controlling the budget, BIS need not necessarily be useful. In a large division with many cost centres, the amount of effort that is required to control budgets may be great. BIS can provide a valuable aid in these circumstances.

Interactive planning tool

This sub-system is used to develop both long-range plans and the yearly budget. Within this sub-system there are two functions:

1 One function provides a status report by expense type for the manager to review:

2 The second function leads managers through each data item that must be included in the long-term plans and/or the annual budgets and allows them to experiment with various projections for any item and to perform changes and differing projections based on alternative assumptions.

This planning function is embedded in the usual planning process of the firm. Bank managers attend an annual planned-growth conference every May, where they work out the strategy they want to pursue over the next five-year planning period. By mid-July, the financial implications of the new long-range plan are developed. Around September, the budget for the next year is finalized.

When the system was undertaken manually, a great deal of clerical work was carried out at three distinct levels.

Level 1: The cost-centre manager has to develop an adequate one-year budget and five-year plan. Previously, the managers found this task distasteful as it involved extensions of payroll taxes and other payroll items that varied between staff.

Level 2: The divisional manager has to consolidate the individual cost-centre plans to produce a one-year budget and a five-year plan for the division. On compilation of these divisional plans, the totals may seem too high and further pruning of the individual cost-centre plans may be required. Hence, there is iteration of the planning process and each iteration requires more clerical work.

Level 3: The corporate comptroller consolidates all budgets to produce an overall financial plan for the bank. Here, too, revisions in the plans at corporate level (and hence at divisional and consequently cost-centre level) occur and this will require further iterations of the planning work at all three levels.

During the planning process, the system aids the preparation of a budget by providing listings for each expense class of:

Last year's actuals,
This year's budget,
Year-to-date actuals, and
Projected actuals for the remainder of the year.

When constructing a new budget, this information incorporates both the history and the new considerations that have become relevant.

BIS also helps the process of planning by allowing the user to consider several alternative plans before deciding which one to submit. One important feature is the automatic calculation of estimated expenditures for taxes, insurance, and other items. To produce these figures, the cost-centre manager merely inputs the number of people of each grade and the area of work-space.

The following incident demonstrates the power of the systems. A mistake was discovered in one of the assumptions which affected each division and each cost centre. The faulty assumption was that budgeted pay increases occur on the first of January. However, the salary review process was spread evenly across the year. The action that was necessary to correct the error was to reduce all cost centre and all division's budgeted salary increases by one-half. Each individual cost centre's figures were changed and all the consolidations reworked within one hour.

Alter (1980) assesses the usefulness of BIS on page 256.

'By expediting the production of budgets and long-range plans, BIS frees time formerly needed for clerical functions and allows the comptrollers on both levels to consider more alternatives and thus to do more analysis. The assumption is that these improvements in the planning process will lead to "better" plans. Whether "better" plans are being produced is not known with certainty, but it is clear that tighter and more consistent plans are developed, given the assumptions on which the plans are based. The plans are tighter because the calculations are more accurate and because the growth of the plan can be tracked from year to year. The plans are more consistent because it is possible to make comparisons across divisions or cost centres and thereby to spot discrepancies.'

Profit-and-loss statements

Formerly, these statements were prepared by hand and involved a cumbersome clerical process. Expenses had to be allocated manually from cost centres to profit centre, product lines, and products throughout the bank. The computer would automatically produce not only the transfers but also the consolidations. In total, this system saved clerical time and allowed the cost analysts to spend more time analysing the profit-and-loss statements rather than simply preparing them.

Inquiry/report generator

As well as the standard uses of BIS as outlined above, BIS has an *ad hoc* enquiry/report generator facility. This allows a user to structure his own report based on the information already stored. The user can specify the data to be examined, the computations and logical operations that he wants to perform and the output desired.

More complex models

More complicated modelling techniques (such as LP, probabilistic models and so on) have been undertaken but they have not proved successful since the types of data maintained on BIS are not of the kind that would be useful for this type of modelling.

An improved system

So far we have simply described this case study as found in Alter. It is no surprise that the more complex models do not share the same actual data. At the strategic level the information does not need to be so accurate, can be highly aggregated and is often external.

However, the interactive exception reporting could have been taken one step further. It should be possible to explode variances isolated for further analysis down to their more detailed levels as in Figure 11.7 (on p. 286). The divisional manager should also have been able to isolate the individual transactions affecting a particular monthly item at the lowest reporting level. The exception reporting (by absolute amount, percentage variance, a combination of both, or some other suitable formulae) should be able to operate at any level and perhaps there should be different exception criteria at each level. Such a selective search would be a powerful management facility.

It must be remembered, however, that a greater improvement in performance may be achieved by concentrating on the positive variances. Therefore, any exception criteria ought to be capable of working both ways.

As well as exploding the information top-down, a cost-centre manager (at a lower level) may wish to know the consequences of a particular variance if it were replicated across the company (or group or division) on the total profit (or some other suitable measure). The interactive planning tool used the same set of data but provided a different set of facilities: an information system on the history and a projection/modelling facility.

The profit-and-loss statements, in which the tedious allocations of expenses are done, should be possible in a good general ledger system, but do not necessarily form part of a DSS. However, a good general ledger system (e.g. the MSA system discussed in Chapter 13) should have some elements of a DSS.

This case study provides a fascinating insight into the concept of decision support systems. This example allows some data-manipulation facilities and a little modelling. So far as the data are concerned, there are two deficiencies:

The data were split between two systems with BIS having the aggregated data and RAS holding the original transaction data;
The data were stored in a primitive way by a cost centre and aggregated
into a monthly time period.

We really require a much more flexible approach. We ought to be able to
examine the data by cost categories, cost functions, products, or in any
other way *and* by any time period. BIS confines the user to monthly time
intervals and transaction types within cost centres. Once input into a cost
centre, a transaction code and month, no disaggregation of that data is
permissible. In Chapter 17 we will discuss how innovative accounting
ideas along with advanced database techniques can be used to extend the
flexibility of access to a particular set of data.

A manufacturing example

Earlier, in Chapter 13, a MIS within a manufacturing environment was
discussed (based on an example in Thierauf (1982)). We would like now to
widen this to look at a DSS within a manufacturing environment.

It will be assumed that the following data are distributed between two
databases:

Plant databases	*Corporate database*
Daily production data	Weekly production data
Daily production orders	Sales quotas per next period
Weekly maintenance schedule	Maintenance history
Daily machine utilization data	Period machine utilization data
Quality control data	Manufactured parts data
Vendor data	Purchased parts history
Daily payroll data	Weekly payroll data
Manufacturing standards and costs	Manufacturing rates and capacities
Production scheduling and routing	Plant expansion data
Work centre budget data	Capital equipment data
Manpower data	
Machine shop, assembly – major and minor data	
Bills of materials	
Exploded bills of materials	

The plant data collection system uses data collection devices which are
conveniently situated for use by all production personnel and allow data
to be fed directly into the system. Data are transmitted to the computer to
be stored, for example, by job number for cost analysis, by employee
number for payroll analysis, by quantity produced, for updating of production schedules and the inventory system, and so on.

This system of data collection has great implications for cost perform-ance as it can compare the results of labour hours expended against standards, thus throwing light on problem areas and eliminating un-necessary expense. Similarly, staff at every management level have on-line access to manufacturing data, and can thus monitor the progress of individual components through the production process, and take any necessary action when problems or exceptions occur.

Exception reports are produced regularly for a variety of operational problems. Figure 15.7 shows a number of VDUs being used to provide information – on an exception basis – relating to production scheduling.

The DSS, in the same environment, would place greater emphasis on the use of computer models and mathematical techniques and the com-puter's number-crunching capabilities. For example, linear programming may be used to determine production quotas for the next period. Such a program is only one of a range that could be used in a manufacturing environment. A full range of models and applications of mathematical techniques for use within this environment is shown in Figure 15.8.

We shall now examine the use of a DSS for a cost-accounting appli-cation. Once again, this example uses a distributed approach with local files at plant level and some centralized files at corporate level. This example is drawn from Thierauf (1982), Chapter 18, and is illustrated in Figure 15.9.

In this instance the input can take one of two forms: either VDUs which are used to input issues of raw materials and parts, or data collection devices (for example, machine-readable badges) which collect labour-cost data. Both are on-line and record the data in real-time. The costs are recorded at plant level and three cost-centre reports are available:

1   A cost-centre report, produced daily, which shows all the direct and indirect costs by cost centre. This report will also provide information on:
    (a)   Material usage variances;
    (b)   Labour variances; and
    (c)   Overhead or volume variance;
          broken down by a sub-classification such as product costing.
2   A cost-centre report which shows the attendance time of personnel by cost centre on the payroll file: this is generated daily.
3   An exception-conditions report for retrieving information used inter-actively in an on-demand mode. The parameters for altering excep-tions can be changed interactively and the exceptions are based on a comparison of materials and labour costs with standards stored on the plant files.

A program is triggered at the end of each week to transfer summary

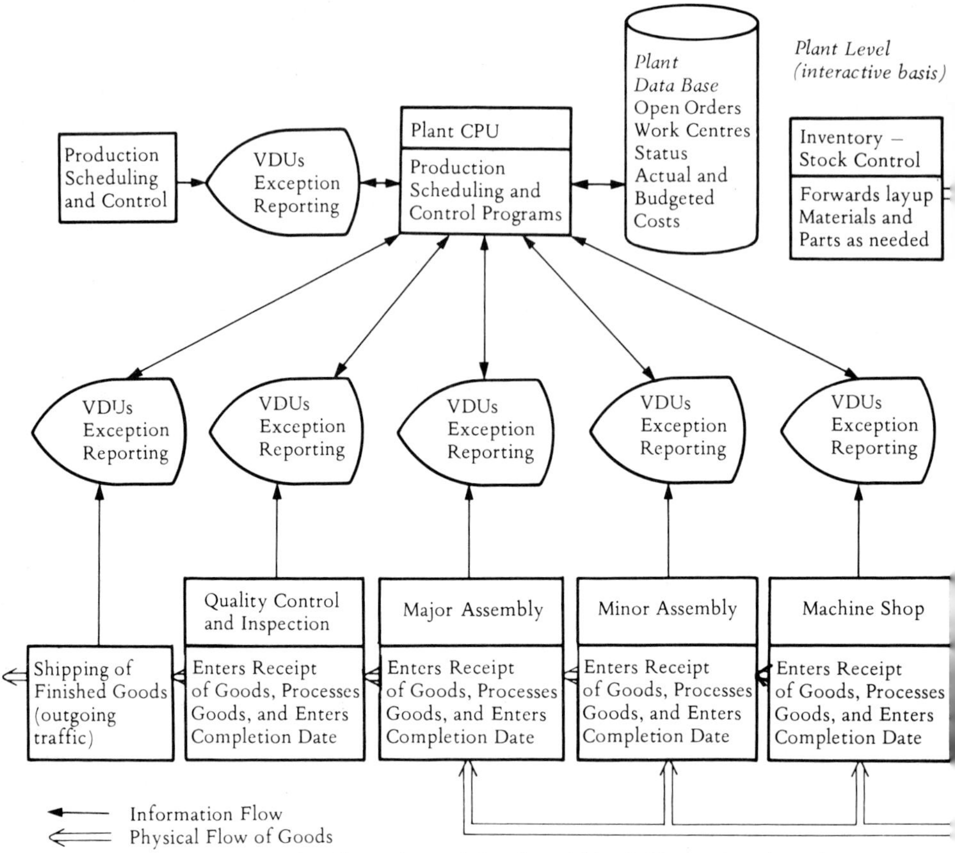

Figure 15.7   *Production scheduling and control data flow within a DSS manufacturing subsystem-emphasis on exception reporting* Source: *Thierauf (1982), p. 426*

cost information from the plant to the central headquarters for longer-term analyses: such as improving the operations of a particular plant – new investment may be needed to improve productivity and eliminate unfavourable labour hours, or a new machine to eradicate unfavourable material variances due to high wastage rates. Alternatively, these figures may be used to compare the operations of one plant with another.

The weekly cost analyses are processed at the corporate level and a variety of variance reports can be routinely produced. The weekly production cost report, one of the reports produced, brings together information generated in other reports and is sent to the manufacturing, inventory and management accounting departments for review on a weekly basis at both plant and corporate level.

Other cost analyses are produced periodically at the corporate level. These include, for example, a monthly listing of materials, labour and overhead costs to be absorbed into the financial statements of that month

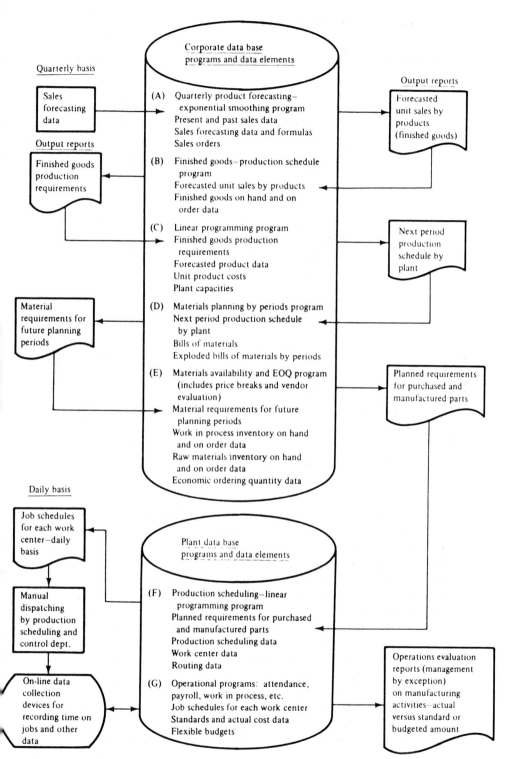

Figure 15.8 *Corporate and plant database programs and data elements that control manufacturing in a DSS environment* Source: *Thierauf (1982), p. 424*

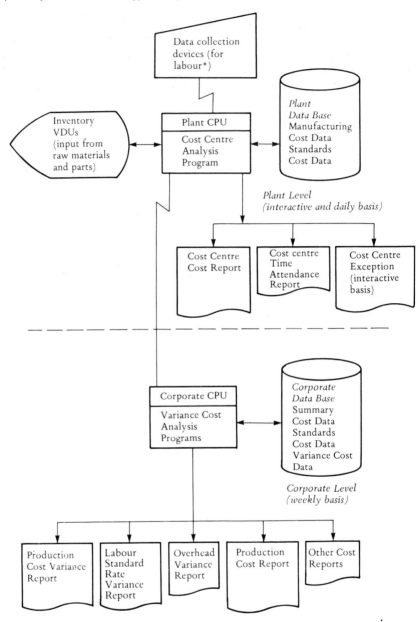

Figure 15.9   *Cost-accounting data flow for a DSS accounting subsystem* Source: *Thierauf (1982),*
p. 525

and a report showing the actual versus standard cost of a particular product at a particular cost centre. Such a report may signal rising costs and the continual need for review by management. This may lead to a change in standard costs to take account of current operations or it may be used to 'explain' a large number of unfavourable material variances.

Conclusion

To date, DSSs have not been widely used. Computers were first introduced into the routine and well-structured operational areas. Gradually, applications have been developed to support higher levels of management. However, the use of computers to support decision-making is not widespread as yet.

In Chapter 17 we shall discuss how innovative accounting ideas, along with advanced database techniques, can be used to extend the flexibility of access to data. Meanwhile, in the next chapter we consider the microprocessor and its range of applications.

16 Office automation

Office automation can be defined as the integration of computerized technologies in a business environment. At the heart of today's automated office is the microcomputer workstation. The microcomputer workstation can not only provide the user with a range of application but can also be viewed as the centre of a communications system. Increasingly, through Local Area Networks (LANs), the microcomputer is being

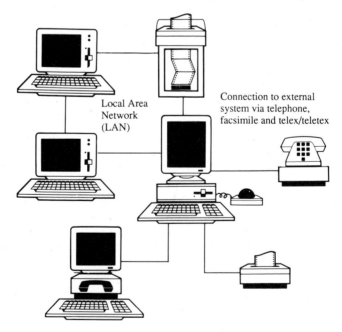

Figure 16.1 *The microcomputer workstation as a central feature of office automation*

connected to other computers and to other equipment to provide other services. This is represented in the diagram above (Figure 16.1). The internal communications are provided through a LAN and external communications can be provided through telephone, telex and facsimile systems.

The microcomputer

One of the most important forces for change in the business world has been the revolution in information technology and information processing. In the last few years the most significant advances have occurred in the field of microtechnology. The microcomputer (also known as the desktop or personal computer) is now an essential office tool, combining a number of functions which make it a highly versatile workstation. Its popularity can be attributed to increasing power and performance coupled with steadily decreasing costs. Additional advantages which have made it attractive to the end user include portability, control of applications by the user, the availability of colour and graphics display, low hardware maintenance and ease of use.

The microcomputer offers extensive storage and processing capabilities. Since the early 1980s, with dramatic increases in speed and power, it has been fully integrated into the world of the mainframe and can provide nearly all the facilities needed to run a modern business. Indeed, some of the current microcomputers offer a capability characteristic of mainframe systems. The current IBM PS/2 range, for example, has performance comparable with earlier IBM mainframe computers.

Since mid-1987 a new generation of micros has emerged with a greatly enhanced overall performance. Depending on the model, the standard memory available now exceeds one million bytes (1MB), expandable to 16MB. Similarly, hard disk storage can now be several hundred MB. However, there are so many different microcomputer systems available on the market and technological developments are taking place at such a staggering rate that there is little point describing any particular configuration or piece of hardware in detail. Suffice it to say that, based on recent developments (particularly increased speed and power), we can expect both wider applications and increased specialization for the micro. The trend now is increasingly towards integration and making use of the speed and power offered by microcomputers. It is worth mentioning that the arrival of the new operating system OS/2, with a memory capacity well beyond the 640K imposed by MS-DOS, will substantially increase the potential of the micro.

Selecting a microcomputer system

Anyone in business will realize that major purchases and major system changes are not made without careful consideration. Making the correct decision is of great importance, particularly when the outlay on a new system can mean the postponement of some other high-priority scheme. It is essential to devise and follow a plan, keeping a careful eye on the end objective. It may be that, after evaluating an application and alternative hardware/software systems, the decision is not to go ahead with the plan.

Before any purchasing decision is made, it is important first of all to determine the functional requirements of the system and the software needed to achieve these. The configuration of microcomputer hardware will depend upon the specific demands of the office environment. As a general guide, the typical system would include the following:

1   A keyboard for inputting data;
2   A display monitor for visual display of information and editing purposes;
3   A central microprocessor (the CPU);
4   Disk drives which read from and store data on disks (either floppy disks or hard disks may be used);
5   A printer (e.g. daisywheel or laser) to produce hard copy output.

Application software

The traditional use of the microcomputer is to run applications software programs. These are designed to perform specific functions and are usually prepackaged but may be purpose-built. Prepackaged software is relatively cheap because development costs are spread over the large number of packages sold. In contrast, purpose-built software can be very expensive. For the business thinking of buying its first computer system a package program is undoubtedly the best choice.

Today's packages are heavily user oriented; that is, they incorporate tools and features designed to provide the best user interface. These will include:

1   Menus which offer a list of options;
2   Forms which provide spaces into which entries can be made by the end user;
3   Windows dividing the screen into a number of rectangular areas where different applications can display information;
4   Mice whose movements on a flat surface are duplicated by cursor movements on a visual display unit;

5   Icons displayed on screen to symbolize a function;
6   Touch-sensitive pads and screens which allow for selections to be made from menus or in applications with only minimal computer interaction;
7   Help facilities providing supplementary or explanatory information during an interaction (in dBase 111+, pressing function key F1 will load the HELP menu on the screen).

Typical applications which the computer workstation is required to perform include: text and graphics processing (word processing, graphics packages and desktop publishing); accounting, information storage and retrieval (databases); numerical and data analysis (statistical, modelling and spreadsheet packages); and management support (electronic diaries).

Text and graphics processing

One of the earliest applications available to the officer worker was the word processing package. Used on a standalone workstation or a network, word processing packages allow the end user to produce high class documents, reports and correspondence. Some of the familiar features include the ability to move sentences and blocks of text, adjust margins, highlight and underline text, justify, and adjust pitch. In recent years, spelling checkers and thesauri have been added, and the tendency is now increasingly towards incorporating some of the features common to desktop publishing applications.

The cost of a word processing package may range from under £100 up to several hundred, depending upon the quality and range of features available.

In the past few years or so desktop publishing (DTP) has made a considerable impact in the computer world, by allowing users to be able to produce high quality printed materials with their computer. In 1986, the only real package available was the Apple Macintosh Pagemaker, but now there is a host of hardware and software products offering desktop publishing facilities, and the buyer is confronted with a difficult choice.

What makes DTP so attractive is that it can provide typesetting-quality publications both quickly and cheaply. It can also integrate graphics, photographs, design and typography on the same page without requiring any sophisticated training. Generally, DTP facilities are suited to smaller volumes of output (under 100 pages). Newsletters, reports and proposals are just some of the more common applications. However, the DTP market is now so large and varied that the buyer should assess his or her needs carefully before a purchase is made. For example, is the best package one that will produce books, or one that will tackle magazine layouts? Are intricate adverts required, or just simple newsletters? Is black and white sufficient or is colour required? Is typesetting necessary or will dot matrix output be sufficient. All these questions need to be addressed before a system is chosen.

A basic desktop publishing system will consist of a good word processor, a graphics application, a page-layout package, a processor with a minimum memory of 512K bytes and a good printer. At the time of writing, prices for software vary from under £100 for a basic package like Fleet Street Editor to several hundred for a more sophisticated package like Ventura.

In the last few years graphics have become an important part of computer systems. As an aid to decision making, pictorial representations are particularly useful since they summarize and present information in an easily comprehensible form. Commonly found on DTP and spreadsheet applications, graphics can produce a wide range of effects including bar and pie charts, time series charts, hierarchy charts, sequence charts, text graphics and scatter charts. These may be used in reports, documents, presentations, or more sophisticated production drawings such as computer aided design (CAD) and computer aided manufacturing (CAM). Taking the production of simple charts and graphs as an example, the process would be as follows:

1   Information is extracted and summarized from a database of some other stored source;
2   The information is viewed on a visual display unit and modified where appropriate;
3   The completed version is printed on a graphics plotter.

Graphical representations are particularly valuable when used to compare items of information, demonstrate trends or highlight relative proportions and distributions. They can be used very effectively as an alternative to figures.

Accounts packages

At the simplest level, accounts packages can be considered as electronic ledgers. The routine transactions are recorded on a computer system, rather than on paper, with the general principles of double entry bookkeeping being incorporated in the software. There are, however, advantages in computerizing an accounts system. For example, Sage Accountant Plus, although a low cost accounts package (under £300), includes sales invoicing, stock control and report generation as well as the basic sales, purchase and nominal ledgers. The format of invoices can be set by the user as preprinted forms. Other features that can be expected from even the simplest packages would include some form of security, and auditing controls. More advanced, and more expensive, packages would be expected to provide such options as payroll, multiple currency accounts, and cheque production facilities.

There are two types of accounts package: complete packages such as Sage Accountant Plus, and modular packages. The complete packages tend to be cheaper single-user systems (£100–£1,000). Modular systems tend to be more expensive by virtue of the fact that a number of modules are needed to produce a complete system. A minimum system would include sales, purchasing and nominal ledgers. With some of the individual modules of more expensive, multi-user systems costing over £1,000, the initial investment in a complete system could be substantial, especially if the hardware is also purchased. However, the modular design of accounts software provides the user with a development path for a growing business. Payroll, financial management, job-costing, sub-contractors, ledger and other modules can be added to the computerized accounts systems as the business develops. However, different systems offer different features, so any decision on purchasing accounts software should take into account the flexibility and expandability of the system, and whether it can be linked to other systems.

Table 16.1 gives an outline of three accounts packages which represent low, medium and high cost systems. The costs are based on a single-user system. The list is by no means exhaustive but rather gives an indication of the range of options available and the hardware requirements. Other packages, of which there are many, have different costs and features.

Data retrieval and storage

Database packages are probably the most heavily promoted but least understood computer applications on the market. Without doubt, a database is one of the most important components of a computer-based business organization, but the problem for the user is selecting the right one for his or her needs from the wide choice available.

A database may be defined as: 'A general, integrated collection of data which is structured on natural data relationships so that it provides all necessary access paths to each individual item of data in order to fulfil the differing needs of all users.' Until recently, there were very few micro-computer packages which could be described as database systems in the full and accepted sense. However, since the early 1980s microcomputer databases have advanced rapidly from somewhat primitive card indexing

Table 16.1

	Sage Accountant Plus	Pegasus Senior	Shortland Imperial
Costs (ex VAT)	(£)	(£)	(£)
Sales ledger	Included	550	1,000
Purchase ledger	in basic	550	1,000
Nominal ledger	price of	550	1,000
Stock control	249 for	550	1,000
Invoicing	packaged	550	1,000
Payroll	149	550	1,000
Total cost	398	3,300	6,000
Multi-user version	500	4,500	9,000
1 year's support	100	Dealer	200
Features			
Other options	Sales processing Purchase processing (options in price)	Sales Processing Job-costing Bill of materials	Cash-book Fixed assets Report writers (Sales, management) Customer order processing
Minimum memory needed	256K	512K	512K
Disk requirements	2 floppy	Hard	Hard
Operating system	MS-DOS	MS-DOS	UNIX/MS-DOS
External links	No	Yes	Yes
Password security	Yes	Yes	Yes
Audit controls	Yes	Yes	Yes
Multiple currency	No	Yes	Yes

packages and systems requiring programming expertise to the sophisticated and powerful tools of today.

In general, current database environments demonstrate greatly improved support facilities which balance power with ease of use. These support facilities may include report writers, query languages, application generators and so on. For the last few years dBase III+ and its precursors have been the *de facto* industry standard, but there is now far greater competition from a range of newer products. However, the makers of dBase, Ashton-Tate, have countered with version IV of their product. Launched in the UK in the summer of 1988, dBase IV is the first Ashton-Tate DBMS to offer a structured query language. In answer to the criticisms levelled against its predecessors, the new version is easier both to learn and to use. Well over 200 new or enhanced commands have been added to the program and there is far more scope for multi-user operation.

Other up-to-date database packages competing strongly with dBase IV include R:Base and Emerald Bay. The latter is a challenging new concept in database design clearly aimed at the multi-user demands of the modern office. What distinguishes this product is the way in which the relationship between program and data is viewed. By applying the concept of surfaces, which establishes an architecture where a common reservoir of information is accessed by numerous surface applications, Emerald Bay promotes the sharing of data. The only real drawback at the time of writing is that the product lacks a structured query language. No doubt this will be included in the future.

Spreadsheets

Features of spreadsheets have been considered in earlier chapters. Chapter 4 gave a basic outline of programming principles behind spreadsheets and Chapter 14 illustrated the development of a simple spreadsheet model of cash flows. This section considers some of the commercial spreadsheet packages available, particularly Lotus 1-2-3.

Following its introduction to the market, Lotus 1-2-3 – an IBM PC/compatible spreadsheet package – quickly became a bestseller amongst microcomputer programs, overtaking its main rivals, such as VisiCalc, SuperCalc and Multiplan. The later release (version 2) added to this popularity and Lotus 1-2-3 further established itself in the business environment as the standard spreadsheet package. As a result, many other packages (not only spreadsheets but also word processing and database applications) have introduced direct links with Lotus 1-2-3 to enable easy transfer of information between the various packages and the Lotus spreadsheet. The most recent version of Lotus 1-2-3 (version 3) is a large program which requires the microcomputer to have a minimum memory of one megabyte (including extended memory). Version 2.2 is still available for those who want to use the program on a 640K byte machine.

The Lotus spreadsheet is divided into almost two million cells arranged as 8,192 rows (numbered 1 to 8,192) and 230 columns (labelled A, B, etc, to Z; AA, AB, etc, to AZ; and so on as far as IU, IV), each of which is initially nine characters wide.

Lotus also offers the user a fairly wide range of formats so that the final spreadsheet can be presented in an attractive way. For instance, if a spreadsheet looks untidy, the user can move cell positions, enter explanatory text, add underlines, and re-format data items (either individually or as a range) so that the data can be presented:

With a fixed number of decimal places;
In scientific format (e.g. 1E+1);
In currency format (e.g. £1.12);
With added comma (e.g. 1,250);
As a percentage (e.g. 12%);
As a date in a variety of formats (e.g. 12/05/89 or 89:05:12).

In addition, it is possible to 'hide' cells so that their values are not displayed or printed but are contained in the spreadsheet. For instance, an adjustment factor may be needed to fine-tune a complex calculation. This would, however, not need to be displayed.

Other features of Lotus include facilities for:

Fixing permanent title areas on the screen which cannot be scrolled off;
Splitting the screen in two so that two windows are displayed which can be scrolled independently;
Changing the width of a cell;
Printing a hard copy of any part or all of the model on a printer;
Inserting new rows and columns;
Deleting existing rows and columns;
Protecting cells to avoid accidental deletion;
Drawing graphs;
Creating 'macros' – these contain a string of Lotus commands (such as 'GOTO', 'Copy', 'Input' and 'Recalculate') which may need to be repeated on several occasions.
A range of statistical (such as data regression), mathematical (such as cosine) and logical (such as 'if . . . then . . . else') functions;
An indexed on-line help facility which briefly describes each of the functions/commands in Lotus;
A range of text-handling functions e.g. @ LOWER, which converts a line of text to lowercase.

We have not attempted to give a full description of Lotus. Only a few of its extensive range of facilities and commands have been described to give the reader a feeling for the nature of spreadsheet software and its possible applications. Other state-of-art spreadsheets from major suppliers include Microsoft Excel and Borland's Quattro.

Management support

Facilities are increasingly available to assist the user to organize workload and make decisions. For example, an electronic diary facility is able to maintain diaries and is usually provided as a supplement or support to some other system. Indeed, most office automation systems make provision somewhere for an electronic diary. These will vary from single versions which hold information for a single user only, to sophisticated multi-user systems which schedule meetings and accommodate priority levels. Some systems also provide decision-making aids which usually involve the user being required to structure a problem in a particular way. By structuring the problem in this way the user is able to gain some insight into the problem and by rearranging the variables may be able to provide some optimum decision.

Integrated packages

With the increasing sophistication and power of computer hardware there is a movement towards larger and larger integrated packages incorporating all the applications outlined above in one package. While Lotus 1-2-3 has many integrated features, the first truly integrated package was Symphony, released in 1984. There are now a number of integrated packages on the market, although features and prices vary greatly. However, in general an integrated package can be expected to provide:

1   Spreadsheeting;
2   Database management;
3   Word processing;
4   Graphics;
5   Communications.

One of the main advantages of integrated packages is that they provide the user with a common interface. Keys allocated to a particular function in one application carry out the same function in the other applications. Another advantage is that there is compatibility between the different applications. For example, merging names and addresses from the database to the word processor is less likely to present a problem with an integrated package than with two applications produced by different suppliers, although some standards do exist. The disadvantage of integrated packages is that they tend to be of uneven quality. You may get an excellent database, spreadsheet or word processor as part of the integrated package but equally another part of the package is weaker.

Communications

The microcomputer is increasingly a focal point for communications, both within a company and with the rest of the business world. Integrated applications will include a communications package as standard. Framework III supports a wide range of automatic log-ons and file transfer protocols. Being able to receive and send information rapidly and in an appropriate form is important in business competitiveness. There is now a range of communication options available to the user of a computer workstation. These include external information sources (databases and viewdata), two-way communications (electronic messaging and electronic data interchange) and interconnection with other communications systems (facsimile, telex and teletex). Communications can operate over the public telephone network using a modem or over dedicated datalines.

External information sources

In addition to database management systems like dBase IV, there is a wide selection of publicly available databases both in the UK and world-wide which can be accessed from a computer terminal in an office. These provide current information on a range of topics such as business, finance and engineering. Some examples of online databases available in the UK are Textline, Datastream and World Textiles. Access to such databases is usually via a terminal connected to a telecommunications network.

Viewdata or videotex describes the transmission of textual or graphical data in page form from a central computer to another terminal using a telephone network. The other terminal is invariably a modified television set which, together with the viewdata retrieval software, provides a low-cost and simple method of displaying information. One of the best examples of a viewdata system is British Telecom's Prestel, developed back in 1978. Although viewdata was initially developed for use by the general public to gain access to data from their homes, the widest application has been for business use. Some of the current business users include travel agents, the Stock Exchange and breweries.

It is likely that viewdata will become a part of most computer systems and contribute to the integration of functions. It should be distinguished from teletext systems, such as Oracle and Ceefax, which are broadcast systems using television stations rather than telephone lines.

Two-way communications

With workstations and the applications that they support operating in-variably in a LAN environment, there is an obvious advantage in trans-mitting documents, memos and messages between locations without using a traditional paperflow. The development of electronic mail and electronic messaging has moved us one stage nearer to the paperless office. Although it is doubtful whether an office can be so automated that there is no requirement for printed material, in recent years we have certainly seen the elimination of much routine paperwork through elec-tronic methods.

Electronic mail describes the computerized transmission of information between two locations. It may be a communication between parties in different countries or between individuals in the same office. Basically the procedure is very simple: a sender specifies the name and electronic address of the party to receive the message and then types the message which is then dispatched automatically. In addition, some systems allow messages to be mailed to several destinations. Those who subscribe to Telecom Gold and similar electronic mail systems are able to leave messages for one another using mailbox facilities. The main benefits of electronic mail are as follows:

1   Immediate and direct contact;
2   The elimination of 'telephone tag' (i.e. the computer stores the message until the recipient is ready for it, thus avoiding the confusion of two parties attempting unsuccessfully to contact each other via the phone);
3   Low costs and the ability to distribute messages to several destinations simultaneously,
4   Obviates the distribution of paper memos, reminders etc.

Another electronic messaging system is voice mail. This stores voice messages digitally and has one very distinct advantage over the conventional telephone in that both parties need not be on the line at the same time.

Electronic data interchange (EDI) refers to the exchange of trade data between the computer systems of trading partners. While this would not normally be associated with a single-user workstation, it is worth mentioning here. Having direct links between two computer systems for regular trading purposes can have advantages for the speed and efficiency of ordering, delivery and payment. Administrative procedures can be reduced because orders, invoices, stock level reports and delivery notes are paperless or are automatically produced.

Connection to other systems

By the use of electronic mailing systems, add-on cards and modems, computers can be made to communicate with other communications systems. For example a computer can send a message to a telex machine anywhere in the world using gateways between mailbox systems and telex.

In the automated office facsimile systems (Fax) provide a means of transmitting electronically a duplicate or 'image copy' of a document between locations which may be local or worldwide. They are particularly useful for sending non-textual information such as diagrams and maps. Faxing information involves the scanning of data and converting it into signal waves which can be transmitted over a telephone network.

Modern facsimile systems belong to one of three groups. Those in group one transmit an A4-sized document in four to six minutes; those in group two take less than three minutes; and those in group three, less than one minute. The first two groups use analogue communication, while group three is for digital devices.

Today, most facsimile machines belong to the third group, some of which are able to transmit a page in less than 20 seconds and include the following advanced features:

1   Resolution and speed selection (allowing the linking of machines from different classes);
2   Automatic dialling and fail-safe transmission;
3   Repeat printing;
4   Automatic answering and paper load;
5   Encryption utilities.

It seems likely that manufacturers will soon be providing facsimile facilities as part of an integrated package together with other applications such as word processing, graphics and spreadsheeting. Links between computers and facsimile equipment can be achieved by using a card which plugs into the expansion slots of the computer.

Both telex and teletex can be considered as forms of electronic mail. Telex has been familiar for many years, while teletex is a far more recent development which may well replace telex altogether.

Dating from the 1930s, the telex system provides users with a fully automated means of communicating via teleprinters. It is still, despite its age, one of the most widely used means of office communication. One of its main advantages is that it possesses a very large worldwide user base and is available 24 hours a day. With add-on software and hardware, it is also possible to generate and send telexes from a PC, thus adding to the integration of workstation functions. The main disadvantage with the telex is its slow transmission rate in comparison with other, more modern, communication technologies.

In contrast, teletex is a high speed international service (approximately 45 times faster than telex) which enables subscribers to exchange correspondence between locations via the telecommunications network. Apart from being faster than telex, the standard of presentation and reproduction is also superior. Unlike telex, it can use both upper and lower case characters. Despite the obvious advantages of teletex, it has proved difficult to implement owing to the problem of agreeing on an international standard. Its real potential therefore remains to be tapped.

Future developments

Office automation and software applications are becoming increasingly sophisticated, integrating communication technology in the business environment to modify and improve traditional work patterns.

The application of the microprocessor to office demands and products, together with the general advances in VLSI (very large-scale integration), have led to the convergence of technologies. As the distinction between data processing, telecommunications and office services becomes increasingly blurred, data, text, image and voice are developing as an integrated information resource.

Widely predicted in the last few years, the multi-function workstation has now become an essential feature of office automation. Word processors have long been sold with the ability to double as personal computers, but the range of functions available on office workstations is now very much wider and will continue to increase with developments in technology. In this respect, one of the most interesting areas for advance is in the developing field of telecommunications. Telephone networks are now being transformed from an analogue to a digital system, thus integrating with the digitally-coded data processing systems found on modern workstations. One implication is that modems will no longer be required. There will be increasing integration of all the present communication services – telex, facsimile, electronic mail, etc – into a single line known as the Integrated Services Digital Network (ISDN).

17 MIS and management accounting, productivity and cost control

Introduction

We looked at management information systems in Chapter 11, prior to a more detailed study of accounting systems. We now carry out a more thorough appraisal of both basic accounting systems and the wider MIS approach to accounting.

The aims of this final chapter are to review and summarize some of the accounting systems dealt with in earlier chapters. In particular, we shall look in greater detail at MIS, at the distinction between MIS and DSS and at some shortcomings in MIS which have been identified. We look briefly at some innovative developments in accounting systems and follow with some illustrative examples of MIS in actual use, including a discussion of its effectiveness as a tool of cost control.

MIS revisited

In Chapter 11, three types of management process were identified: strategic, tactical and operational. The decision types and information characteristics vary between these different types of management. We summarize below the main points in this distinction.

One way of viewing information is to classify it in terms of the type of information provided to different managerial levels. Higher levels of management tend to be planning-oriented and therefore need information relating more to the external environment, as well as internal data of a highly summarized nature. Lower levels of management deal with more detailed reports, generally control-oriented and relating to internal matters.

In reality, though, these categories are not so distinct as this assessment implies; even so, they do need to be borne in mind when designing an MIS.

Operational levels

To remind the reader of the range of procedures and processing which may be relevant at the operational level, Table 17.1 (a) shows the kinds of accounting tasks that need to be performed, and Table 17.1(b) shows a summarized view of business functions. The most usual characteristic of operational processing is that it is repetitive and generally well-structured (if not stable). There has been a relatively high degree of computerization at this level.

Higher levels of management

Middle and strategic levels of management have always been considered less amenable to automation. The shaded area of Figure 17.1 shows the relative extent to which computing has been introduced into the different levels of management.

Middle management are less concerned with detailed control, but nevertheless have a vital role in the management control process of a business. Strategic planning sets objectives and specifies the resources: these two functions help to give management direction. McCosh, Rahman and Earl (1981) argue that there are three other middle and top management functions:

1   *Long-range planning*. Long-range planning is a formal planning process of scanning, forecasting and decision-making which sets the global, and primarily externally-derived premises for subsequent shorter-term control. It also includes continual monitoring of those external variables which the organization cannot influence, but whose impact may be significant, such as competitor innovation or government legislation. McCosh, Rahman and Earl (1982) (page 208)

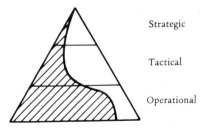

Figure 17.1   *Extent of computerization in differing management levels*

Table 17.1(a)   Some operational tasks in the accounting area (b) A summarized view of business functions and MIS support *Source*: **McCosh, Rahman and Earl (1981) pp. 93 and 95**

(a)

Sales	Purchasing	Overhead
Sales analysis	Receiving	Factory costs
Shipping and delivery	Accounts payable	Non-factory costs
Billing	Cash disbursement	End-period summarizing and closing
Accounts receivable	Timekeeping	Plant and equipment
Credit collection	Payroll	Production control
Cash receipts	Inventory	Tax
Insurance		

(b)

Functions	Documents needed for information generation	Information contexts	Data distribution
Purchase	Requisition; purchase order; receiving report; vouchers	Quantity needed; received; payments; supplier's nature; price; quality; grades; etc.	Accounts payable; inventory record (quantity, price, grades), cash disbursements
Production	Requisition; time ticket; cost distribution; record; for each kind of product	Material consumed for each kind of product; time for each kind of product; work-in-progress; overtime; wastages; factory overhead	Payrolls; cost to process; cost to finished goods; inventory record; overhead distribution
Sales	Sales order; invoice; tickets of shipment, delivery, credit approval	Sales by broker, salesmen, product, price, discounts, customs returns, allowances, date	Accounts receivable; general ledger for total sales; finished goods inventory; salesmen's records; other selling expenses

2 *Short-term planning*. Budgeting and problem-solving demand forecasts from long-range planning, recent trends from the management control and operational control database, and judgements and predictions from managers. The process is thus data processing-intensive, often in iterative, interactive and enquiry mode, requiring considerable co-ordination and frequent revision, so formal MIS, such as cost-accounting systems, are a necessary support. McCosh, Rahman and Earl (1982) (page 209)

3 *Performance-tracking and diagnosis*. Tracking is the measurement of actual performance, whilst diagnosis is the analysis of any deviation from plan, determining how much deviation is controllable, who might be responsible, and what is the cause. Much tracking and diagnosis is shaped by a hierarchical organization structure in the form of responsibility accounting – departmental cost reporting, stan-

dard costing, divisional performance measurement and the like – but can also focus on lateral, global, matrix and other alternative decision and control structures.

McCosh, Rahman and Earl (1982) (page 210)

Figure 17.2 shows the way in which an MIS provides information and feedback. This feedback combines with the organizational structure to form a management control system.

The right amount of information must be available to support the appropriate level of management: too much can be as damaging as too little. In general, the reader is warned against developing a multi-purpose MIS. Data must be distilled in order to produce the right quantity of information for each managerial level.

MIS versus DSS

A distinction has been made between a MIS and a DSS (decision support system) in terms of their usefulness to higher levels of management. Thierauf (1982) argues that a MIS, despite being forward-looking, is centred on operational control (though interactive, i.e. on-line, in its processing mode) and is especially oriented towards lower and middle management levels. McCosh, Rahman and Earl (1981) view the MIS as encompassing the needs of all levels of management and at middle and higher levels including a DSS, whereas Thierauf (1982) regards a MIS system as relevant only to the lower operational levels.

This debate is rather esoteric in nature. Suffice it to say that systems have gradually developed from backward-looking, custodial accounting

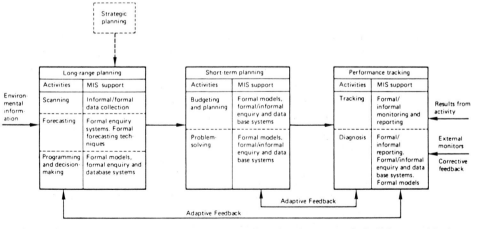

Figure 17.2   *The management control process – MIS support* Source: *McCosh, Rahman and Earl (1981) p. 213.*

systems, through responsibility-reporting systems which were designed to produce relevant information for controlling operations, to integrated data-processing systems in which all the subsystems (including non-financial data systems) are logically inter-related. This evolution has led to the development of the integrated MIS which provides the sort of selected decision-oriented information needed by management to plan, control and evaluate the activities of the business. The ultimate development of the MIS is the on-line, real-time MIS, in which all data are stored on-line and input without delay, and in which the data are processed and fed back to the organization in sufficient time to influence or control that environment.

Thierauf (1982) argues that the classical MIS focuses on well-structured problems. He claims that the reasons for implementing a primarily backward-looking MIS are:

'Better customer service and improved selling efficiency.

More timely and improved management information analysis and reporting at the plant and home office levels.

Improved coordination and control of the overall organisation and its individual parts.

Better opportunity to match demand with production.

On-line information available from a distributed database for management analysis of the organisation's operations and prospective operations.'

Although, other authors may view the concept of a MIS as all-embracing, it is useful for the reader to be aware of the shortcomings of the classical MIS (as defined by Thierauf).

Apart from periodic reports in a static environment, there is a need for individual managers to use the computer directly to aid problem-solving. This combines the individual's knowledge about a subject (subjectivity) with the computer's objectivity.

The ability to cope with less well-structured problems is important. Often the problems with which a MIS is faced are planning-oriented. For example: What happens to profitability if prices are lowered in the short-run, and what type of competitive response will this lead to in the medium- and longer-run? What will be the impact of the installation of robotic technology on profitability, product quality, industrial relations and the morale of the production workforce? How can the company implement productivity improvements that are acceptable to the unions without causing a drop in share prices? Table 17.2 shows a comparison of the important characteristics of the MIS and DSS from Thierauf's view-point.

Examples of the sort of information needed by management are:

(a) Routine reports monitoring the business and tracking current performance;

Table 17.2 Comparison of important characteristics for a typical management information system and a typical decision support system *Source*: Thierauf (1982) p. 79

Important characteristic	*Management information system*	*Decision support system*
Type of system	Forward- and backward-looking control system with integrated subsystems	Forward- and backward-looking planning and control system with integrated subsystems
Reports prepared	Output reports directed mainly to lower and middle management for past, current, and future operations	Information directed to all levels of management and operating personnel in newer work environments for supporting decisions about current and future operations
Exception reporting	Current objectives and plans used for management exception reports	Current objectives and plans are based on 'management by perception' and used for examining exception items
Information orientation	Input/output oriented, with I/O terminals	Input/output oriented, with accent on CRT terminals with graphic capabilities
Processing mode	On-line real-time processing, distributed data processing	Interactive processing mode where human judgment interfaces with computerized information for reaching effective decisions
Data elements	Common (and distributed, if necessary) data base	Comprehensive (and distributed, if necessary) data base
Types of files	Accent on random access on-line storage	Accent on random access on-line file storage for internal data and appropriate data storage for external environment data
Mathematical models	Great use of standard and some custom-made mathematical and statistical models	Great use of all types of simple to complex mathematical and statistical models, whether they be standard or custom made

(b) Budgetary control information which dovetails with (a) above;
(c) The routine accounting information associated with the sales, purchase, wage and general ledgers.

Other questions regarding sales which such a system might answer, are:

What price did we quote this customer last time he ordered?
How long has this item of finished goods remained in stock?

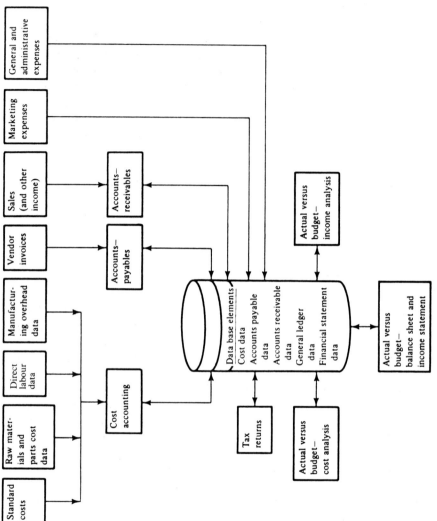

Figure 17.3 *Sales and cost data – essential components of the accounting subsystem* Source: Thierauf (1982), p. 50.

What are its historical and current manufacturing cost, its net realizable value to the wholesaler, and so on?

By and large, computerized accounting systems, as shown in Figure 17.3, focus on the job of recording and reporting sales and costs. In order to produce both general and detailed end-of-period income statements from a general ledger system, data such as revenue, on the one hand, and overheads, on the other, must be recorded, along with all other company expenses. Cash, sales and purchase-ledger data are recorded in the general ledger to produce the balance sheet. The output from this part of the system, in turn, provides input upon which to base analyses of the intermediate – or longer-term. Likewise, information regarding future cash flow and capital expenses can be derived from analyses of income and expenses.

An example is now given of a wider computerized accounting system which is even more extensible.

Computerized accounting systems

Computerized accounting systems very often start life as sales, purchasing and payroll subsystems. Sometimes, businesses are slow to switch the general ledger from a manual to an automated system, because of the desire for flexibility and the relatively small number of transactions. In Chapter 13, a general ledger system was described which included a budgetary control system and allowed some flexibility. However, running such a system would be time-consuming and require significant staff training. Subsequently, in Chapter 16, we examined simpler, though less comprehensive general ledger systems that may be better suited to the needs of the smaller business.

The extent to which a business can be computerized will vary. A sales system may receive only such input items as standing data for the maintenance of a customer file and invoices, payments, and debit and credit entries. A wider system would be concerned in addition with orders, and issues and receipts from finished goods inventory.

Where orders are concerned, there exists a variety of possibilities for subclassification and further processing and storing. Orders that a business has been unable to fulfil may represent valuable information for management. Reasons for an order being unfilled might include:

(a) The customer exceeding his credit limit, or credit facilities not being competitive;

(b) The product being out of stock or the lead time between delivery/manufacturing too great;

(c)   The price being uncompetitive;

(d)   The quality/specification of the product not matching the require-
      ments of the potential customer.

A complete sales subsystem would concentrate on capturing as many
transactions or events as possible. Histories of orders – fulfilled or unfulfilled – would be maintained, along with a comprehensive sales
analysis.

Events accounting

In the previous pages, we looked at a wider MIS view of an accounting
system, which would also function as a DSS in terms of cost accounting.
One innovative technique in accounting is to move away from the conventional approach toward a technique known as *events accounting*. This
technique makes use of modern hardware and software, and utilizes the
sophisticated database approach to files.

Before going any further, it seems appropriate to review briefly the
concept of the database which has become increasingly important in
computing in general, and in the development of the MIS in particular. A
fuller account can be found in Chapter 6.

As a system of structuring computer files, the database has significantly
greater flexibility than conventional systems. The concept of the database
is, however, still in its infancy, and actual databases are very much
inferior to the theoretical models of them produced by computer scientists. One advantage they offer is that, whereas with conventional files,
when one user's view of the data is changed or extended, all files and
programs accessing those files must also be changed, a database system
should be sufficiently flexible to be capable of enhancement for one user
without affecting its use by others. The addition of new fields or respeci-
fication of the structure of data can be done easily and painlessly – or so
the theory goes. In practice, this is not always the case, but it is increasingly becoming so.

In conventional accounting systems, the chart of accounts represents
the basis for the classification of transactions. In the process of posting to
the general ledger, these transactions are measured primarily in monetary terms, and similar transactions are aggregated under broad headings. Thus, the costing process also contains a transformation process
which aggregates transactions across time and by similar groups of transactions – where similar is defined by the chart of accounts. McCarthy
(1979) highlights a number of defects of the conventional accounting
system.

'1   Its dimensions are limited. Most accounting measurements are expressed in monetary terms: a practice that precludes maintenance and use of productivity, performance, reliability and other multi-dimensional data.

2 Its classification schemes are not always appropriate. The chart of accounts for a particular enterprise represents all of the categories into which information concerning economic affairs may be placed. This will often lead to data being left out or classified in a manner that hides its nature from non-accountants.

3 Its aggregation level for stored information is too high. Accounting data is used by a wide variety of decision makers, each needing differing amounts of quantity, aggregation and focus, depending on their personalities, decision styles and conceptual structures. Therefore, information concerning economic events and objects should be kept in as elementary a form as possible to be aggregated by the eventual user.

4 Its degree of integration with the other functional areas of an enterprise is too restricted. Information concerning the same set of phenomena will often be maintained separately by accountants and non-accountants, thus leading to inconsistency and information gaps and overlaps.'

McCarthy (1979), p. 628

There is a good deal of overlap in these shortcomings in the conventional accounting process, as McCarthy points out. The database approach to information systems can offer solutions to all these problems. By taking into account the variety of different needs and viewpoints of data users – accountants and non-accountants alike – the database approach permits an open structure to the information rather than one which is too heavily weighted in favour of one particular user's needs. However, in order to take advantage of such a system, accounting staff must be prepared to adjust their approach to the data they work with. McCarthy continues:

'Most of the work aimed at integrating database ideas with accounting theories has been based on the events accounting concept first advanced by Sorter (1969). What Sorter proposed with his events theory was: (1) that all the relevant variables surrounding an economic event be measured and recorded by accountants and (2) that this information be left in a company's records in atomic (disaggregated) form to be classified and aggregated by the eventual users.'

The concept of events accounting was further developed by McCarthy (1979 and 1982). Here he expounds a new entity-relationship approach to accounting that differs from the earlier approach in that it is based on a less strict definition of an 'event', and uses a more powerful data-modelling tool. Even so, whilst rational accounting systems are relatively easy to follow, not all readers will find it easy or particularly useful to follow the McCarthy approach. However the entity-relationship data-modelling technique does provide a complete methodological alternative to the conventional system of accounting.

Productivity and cost control

One important aspect of the computerization of accounting systems which has not yet been mentioned is its effect on productivity and cost control.

In an accounting department, many people are involved with data processing. All businesses are under pressure to increase productivity and reduce costs; we now examine ways in which this can be done within the accounting department.

1   By extending the sphere of computing: more processes and operations that have traditionally been performed manually can be automated. Japanese companies, for example, usually have highly automated accounting systems.
2   Data collection where possible should be automated. Manual transcription or input has a high error rate associated with it (up to 30 per cent has been found). Automated data collection minimizes correction and re-input functions. Examples of this include mechanized badge reading for payroll, machine-readable documents and turnaround accounting, where, for example, a remittance advice is returned with payment.
3   Simplification of operations and transactions can cut down the complexity of data processing. For example, a 'per day' expense allowance can obviate the necessity for complicated expense claims forms and the internal audit function associated with checking them.

A point-of-sale terminal with an automatic machine-readable device (i.e. bar code or magnetic label) falls into the second category. Documents can be read quickly, automatically and more accurately by a wand or a bar reader. This input can contain the code number which may be self-correcting, and perhaps the price (although this may be obtained from a price file). A description of the goods associated with that label code can be flashed on the terminal for manual verification, to detect cases where a label has been switched. This input can at the same time update both the sales and inventory subsystems. A plastic card for a credit customer can post the sale to a credit account. Thus, one input from an automated data-collection terminal can update the records of several systems.

Another example of a cost-cutting development has been the introduction of distributed computing, i.e. a local computing facility connected to a corporate facility. This practice has been increasing and can offer productivity gains. Increasingly, financial modelling is being carried out (albeit in simplified forms) on micros located in management accountants' offices. However, while distributed computing is used at all levels, the major focus has been at the lower and middle levels of management.

Prior to distributed data processing, substantial delays occurred between the submission of transactions for processing and their eventual processing – thus creating an input bottleneck. A rough rule of thumb is that distributed data processing makes economic sense if 80 per cent of the data generated at a 'down-line' site are used primarily for that site. The break-even point has probably become 70:30 with falling hardware prices and better distributed network facilities. Even if this rule does not hold true, better user involvement and understanding and/or lower error rates strengthen the case for distributed computer processing.

Martin (1982) always manages to have his finger on the pulse of the latest developments. His book *Application Development without Programmers* highlights the high cost of computer programmers. There are two problems. First, the development of new programs takes a fairly long period; each new system has to be analysed, designed, programmed and tested. Secondly, because the demand for new applications is rising faster than DP departments can deliver, there is usually an applications backlog, which can often be measured in years. Sometimes, this backlog is not 'visible', because potential users are aware of the documented backlog and therefore do not even consider making requests for their information requirements. To speed up this process, eliminate the backlog and meet new requirements, there are three possibilities:

1   Users can be given powerful software tools with which to process their own applications (e.g. electronic spreadsheets and modelling systems);
2   Experienced personnel (e.g. consultants, systems analysts or computer-oriented accountants) can use software development tools to create the applications software rather than writing detailed programming specifications for programmers;
3   Standard applications packages can be purchased from software houses, which are amenable to an element of tailoring to a particular firm's requirements.

Table 17.3 shows some of the existing products that are available. Which of these are suitable for end users and which are not is open to debate.

As users, including management accountants, become more computer-experienced, they will become less dependent on the DP professional. In addition, there are now too few programmers to carry out all the applications development and, as their wage rates have risen, it has become too expensive for businesses to employ programmers to carry out all their applications development. Productivity in DP departments can also be increased by the use of structured programming. Some further suggestions are listed in Table 17.4.

Table 17.3 Examples of the types of software for end users and DP professionals. Some of the above products fall into multiple categories *Source*: Martin (1982) p. 19

	Suitable for end users		Suitable for DP professionals	
		Vendor		Vendor
Database query languages	QUERY-BY-EXAMPLE	IBM	SQL	IBM
	SQL	IBM	QWICK QWERY	CACI
	ON-LINE ENGLISH	Cullinane	EASYTRIEVE	Pansophic
	QWICK QWERY	Caci	GIS	IBM
	EASYTRIEVE	Pansophic	MARK IV	Informatics
	ASI/INQUIRY	ASI	DATATRIEVE	DEC
	DATATRIEVE	DEC		
Information retrieval systems	STAIRS	IBM		
	CAFS	ICL		
Report generators	NOMAD	NCSS	NOMAD	NCSS
	QWICK QWERY	CACI	QWICK QWERY	CACI
			GIS	IBM
			IBM SYSTEM 34 UTILITIES	IBM
			RPG II	Various
			RPG III	IBM
			ADRS	IBM
			MARK IV/REPORTER	Informatics
Application generators	MAPPER	Univac	ADF	IBM
	RAMIS II	Mathematica, Inc.	RAMIS II	Mathematica, Inc.
	FOCUS	Information Builders	DMS	IBM
			ADMINS 11	ADMINS
			USER 11	Northcounty Comp., Inc.
			ADS	Cullinane
Very high-level programming languages	APL (simple functions)	Various	APL	Various
			APL-PLUS	STSC
	NOMAD (simple functions)	NCSS	ADRS	IBM
			NOMAD	NCSS
			MANTIS	CINCOM

In terms of its ability to achieve improved productivity, the database system of file storage is perhaps the single most important breakthrough

Table 17.4 Techniques for reducing the cost of software production and maintenance *Source*: Martin (1982) p. 9

* The use of high-level non-procedural languages with which applications can be generated quickly. In other words, application development without conventional programming. A diverse variety of such languages are now in use.
* The use of appropriately designed database systems with high-level database facilities for development of applications software. The databases need better logical design than most that were implemented during the 1970s. Extensive use is then needed of database query languages, report generators and application generators.
* The use of high-level programming languages such as APL or NOMAD, where appropriate.
* Top-down planning of data and procedures to avoid creating redundant programs which exist in profusion in some organizations.
* Conversion of old systems to database operation with high-level generators, where this can lessen the maintenance work load.
* Avoidance of development methods that lead to excessive maintenance.
* Avoidance of slow time-consuming systems analysis methods and a change to fast, database-oriented methods which create the applications software wherever possible without programmers.
* Use of self-documenting techniques to avoid the time-consuming burden of documentation.
* Avoidance, where possible, of the writing of program specifications. Instead, the analyst develops the applications software while interacting with the end users, or prototypes it and adjusts it to what the end users need.

in recent years. If some of the theoretical models proposed by computer scientists come into existence, the database promises even greater efficiency in the years to come.

A comparison between the practice in Japan and the West

It is useful to compare U.K. and U.S.A. systems with those current in Japan. The Japanese are well known for their ability to increase productivity in the manufacturing process. However, Japan has also achieved a high degree of productivity gains in the areas of accounting and data processing.

What follows, then, is a generalization about current Japanese practice. The Japanese publish fairly rudimentary accounts every six months; these accounts are mainly unconsolidated. Internal accounts are usually closed monthly. The primary characteristics of Japanese accounting practice are as follows:

1   The major accounting subsystems (such as sales ledger, purchase ledger, general ledger, fixed-assets accounting, timekeeping and payroll) are all highly automated and mechanized.
2   Responsibility for the major accounting subsystems is assigned to other functional areas. For example, the sales area will be responsible for the sales ledger.
3   The principal areas of involvement for accountants and their support staff are:
    Cost accounting;
    Product costing;
    Preparation of financial statements.

Let us now examine some of the distinctive aspects of the purchase of materials in a manufacturing plant as a representative example.

Purchasing

In Japan, the manufacturer will issue machine-readable delivery documents to suppliers as part of a monthly material-releasing system, whilst in the western world (U.K. and U.S.A.) the normal practice is for supplier, rather than manufacturer, to prepare delivery documents.

We will assume for the purposes of this comparison that there are several functional areas, such as purchasing, receiving and accounting.

The remainder of the differences follow from the tendency towards simplicity, lack of paperwork and high degree of mechanization in Japan. Table 17.5 outlines these differences.

Table 17.5   Purchasing processing compared

Japanese custom	Western custom
Manufacturer issues machine-readable delivery cards as part of monthly material-releasing system	Suppliers prepare delivery order documentation (not machine-readable)
Drivers hand in delivery documentation to receiving areas which is subsequently input (on-line in Japan) to computer system in which the quantity data are priced automatically	
Price file in the above evaluation is maintained by purchasing function	Price file used in the above evaluation is maintained by the accounting function
	Suppliers submit invoices
	Evaluated delivery documentation matched with suppliers invoices
	Where documents match, invoice processed for payment mechanically
	With mismatches (up to 30 per cent), query documentation raised to resolve differences with receiving areas, purchasing and/or suppliers
Monthly listing of shipments (evaluated delivery documents) used to settle supplier accounts.	Suppliers' invoices settled monthly.

The price file kept by the manufacturer for suppliers' goods is maintained by Purchasing. The purchasing function and suppliers agree prices every six months, six months being the normal budgetary period (rather than one year which is usual in the West). Supplier and manufacturer have a close relationship which is not often found in the competitive, profit-oriented approach of the West. There is an atmosphere of trust and a sense of mutual benefit. Thus, prices may not be re-negotiated for a previous period, price increases for future deliveries are always agreed in advance, and the main pricing mechanism is the manufacturer's price file. All remaining transaction data relate to quantities.

In addition, at the end of each month a list of shipments is sent to the supplier in order to agree supplier accounts. This usually contains details of the quantity and prices of deliveries.

With the purchase of bulk production material, standard quantities are agreed and the processing procedure is based on the manufacturer's price file and the machine-readable delivery document which details the amount of each delivery in standard quantities. This procedure is also implemented for non-production materials where delivery documents are issued to suppliers and each month's receipts are priced and summarized by the computer for each supplier. The same system is adopted for

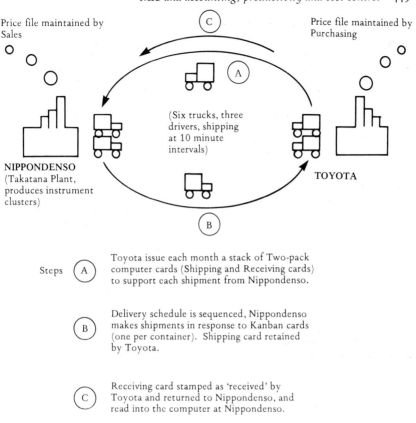

Price file maintained by
Sales

Price file maintained by
Purchasing

(Six trucks, three
drivers, shipping
at 10 minute
intervals)

NIPPONDENSO
(Takatana Plant,
produces instrument
clusters)

TOYOTA

Steps (A) Toyota issue each month a stack of Two-pack computer cards (Shipping and Receiving cards) to support each shipment from Nippondenso.

(B) Delivery schedule is sequenced, Nippondenso makes shipments in response to Kanban cards (one per container). Shipping card retained by Toyota.

(C) Receiving card stamped as 'received' by Toyota and returned to Nippondenso, and read into the computer at Nippondenso.

Each month Nippondenso borrows the Toyota tape and checks its files for accuracy.

Figure 17.4   *Nippondenso/Toyota shipments*

services (e.g. advertising) price files are established for what may be called 'standard condition' purchases.

Figure 17.4 is a diagrammatic representation of the process of purchasing instrument clusters by a manufacturer (in this case, Toyota). Notice the use of the Kanban card, which travels with the goods and is regarded as the necessary authorization for settlement. Another point of interest is that the Japanese try to limit the number of suppliers to a very small number. Because deliveries are kept to schedule and the specification and quality control of goods are excellent and strikes are virtually non-existent, there is no need to double-source.

There are two other fundamental axioms which the Japanese apply:

'just in time' and 'right first time'. Little or no inventory is held, because materials arrive and are delivered literally 'just in time' directly onto the production line. The need for inspection and quality control is reduced since all goods from suppliers and in the production process are of the highest quality.

Time-keeping and payroll

In many installations in Japan, the practice of clocking-in has been abandoned as a contribution to improved productivity. However, where it is still used, it is a highly automated process using mechanical badge readers. All wage payments are made monthly by bank transfer. Overtime returns are made at the department/plant level, and are based on the production schedule. This obviates the need for individual overtime records. Such overtime records and any absenteeism are recorded manually and are passed usually to the industrial relations department. No accounting staff – professional or clerical – are employed in the time-keeping or payroll areas.

Even a brief examination of the Japanese approach to accounting and data processing gives an indication of some of the valuable lessons there remain to be learnt in terms of MIS and productivity. The dependence on computerization and the MIS are very clear.

18 Computer auditing

Internal versus external auditing

As with the computerization of accounting procedures, auditing procedures and controls can also benefit from the ability of the computer to process information rapidly and flexibly. For example, in the same way that other reports can be generated, so too can reports which can aid the auditor. Also, procedures can be built into the software to prevent some abuses of the accounting procedure.

Auditing can be internal or external. An external audit is a legal requirement. It is usually performed by a firm of accountants, in order to conclude whether the financial statements of a company represent a 'true and fair' view of its state of affairs. The external audit, therefore, concentrates on safeguarding the assets of a company and other stewardship functions. Internal auditing, on the other hand, is performed at the instigation, control and direction of the management and is often also concerned with wider issues such as business efficiency, management control and profitability. One other important area for internal auditors is that they should be heavily involved with systems development and be part of, or closely related with, systems development teams.

The dividing line between the internal and external audit can be blurred. It is possible for the internal auditor to do some of the work of the external auditor. The external auditor's role changes to become more of checking and verifying the internal auditor's work. However, the purpose of both internal and external auditing work is to prevent and detect fraud. Internal auditing perhaps acts more as a deterrent, since it performs the role of a constant inspector of the system; an external auditor can only report on fraud after the event. The pre-event/participation auditing of internal auditors means they can act as advisers, consultants or police to the system development team to make sure adequate internal controls are built into the system and operate effectively.

What is computer auditing? The answer to this question is threefold, it can refer to:

1   The auditing of a highly computerized accounting system;
2   The computerization of the various procedures in the audit process and administration of an audit;
3   The use of computers as an audit tool to assist in the audit, for example, in time management and recording actions taken.

This chapter is concerned with basic approaches to the auditing of computerized systems, the techniques used and the procedures which need to be followed. The chapter concentrates on the external audit, although as already mentioned the distinction between internal and external auditing is blurred and some of the methods are valid for both.

Computerized accounting controls

Normal audit principles and procedures apply equally to manual and computerized accounts. Indeed, there are a number of characteristics of a manual system which are built into computerized accounts packages to facilitate auditing. These include double-entry bookkeeping, the audit trail, and control accounts with their own ledger, as well as records of transactions with customers and suppliers. These aspects of the accounting system are included so that errors can be detected in the day-to-day operation of the system, not just at the end of the financial year. The basic manual accounting system characteristics are assumed to be known by the reader.

The implementation of standard auditing procedures in computerized packages is, however, only one aspect of computer auditing. It can also refer to the implementation of audit control by means of specialized computer software, or to the use of a computer to assist in the audit of a system which may or may not use a computer, by logging the amount of time an auditor spends with each member of staff, for example.

Computerized business systems offer the potential for internal checks and controls. These can be in various forms. All transactions could be written to a control log with special logs being taken of particular types of transactions, for example, credit notes, refunds, etc. Authorization limits may be imposed on particular users. Totals may be generated and compared with totals which are input manually to make sure that they coincide. Internal logic may prevent impossible transactions, such as paying a member of staff for working 160 hours in one week. While increasing the security and integrity of the system, these features may actually create additional problems for the auditor. How can the auditor be sure that these controls actually work in practice? The problem is particularly acute for the external auditor who has to understand the particular business system he or she is required to examine. The internal auditor is likely to be a user of the system already and therefore more familiar with its particular features.

Systems-based auditing

This section provides a brief synopsis of systems-based auditing. It is dealt with in more detail later on in the chapter and in Appendix 1 which gives a step-by-step outline of the audit process. The controls built into business and accounting programs, while being of assistance to the auditor, also present him/her with the task of understanding the system. What facilities are available and how do they operate? Attempting to understand the computerized accounts and business systems is part of a systems-based audit.

The first stage in a systems-based audit is the identification of the facilities available. These have to be recorded and their operation clarified. This will give the auditor a degree of understanding and familiarity with the system. The next stage in a systems-based audit is to evaluate and review certain features because in the actual audit the auditor will depend on some of the control features of the system. By identifying and evaluating the internal control features of a program in a systems-based audit, the auditor can be confident of the reliability of the accounts produced by that system. The more satisfied the auditor is with the internal controls, the fewer subsequent checks will need to be implemented.

The next stage of the external audit is to effect further tests. These can be divided into two categories: compliance tests and substantive tests. Compliance tests involve testing that the internal controls have been adhered to. These involve the repetition of some of the procedures practised by the employees, the examination of documents claiming that controls have been implemented, and general observation, checking, and interviewing to ensure that controls are still being implemented.

Substantive tests, on the other hand, examine the actual validity of the contents of the accounting records. They are used to verify the existence of information contained in the financial statements, such as account balances. Again the range of substantive tests required depends greatly on the success of the compliance tests: if the auditor feels satisfied with the results of the compliance tests, fewer substantive tests will need to be implemented.

The two types of test are complementary. A complete audit might check that the relevant program code for a particular check is included (compliance testing) and that on a piece of sample data it performs the task it is supposed to perform (substantive testing). However, such a comprehensive approach to computer auditing is more expensive and involves some duplication of effort. In any audit the onus is on the auditor to satisfy him/herself that the accounts are fair and true. With such a responsibility the final decision on how far to proceed is in the hands of the auditor.

Two approaches to auditing

In attempting to carry out an audit on a computerized system the auditor can use two contrasting approaches. We can relate these different approaches to the simple model of a computer system given in Chapter 2 (Figure 2.1). Here we had an input, an output, a processing unit and a file store. The input and output are available to the user, data can be put into the system and output generated. The auditor can ignore what happens with the processing unit and file store and concentrate on the input and output characteristics of the system. This is known as *auditing around the computer*. The advantage of this approach is that the evaluation of how well the system is operating depends on technical knowledge of accounting and auditing. The auditor will know that for a particular set of inputs a particular output should result. The disadvantage of this approach is that the processing of the system, and therefore of the accounts procedures are not being assessed directly. The alternative approach is to attempt to assess the processing and file store directly. This is known as *auditing through the computer*. However, this approach presents an immediate problem for the auditor, in that the technical expertise required is more that of computer programming than of auditing. Fortunately there are software packages available which can be used in accounting through the computer. We will return to these later.

Auditing around the computer

Auditing around a computer allows the auditor to infer the quality of the processing being carried out by examining *only* the input and output of applications. In so doing, the auditor regards the computer as a 'black box'. But to rely on that 'black box', the auditor must also express an audit opinion of the internal controls around (and in) the computer system. Using this approach, the auditor would therefore carry out vouching, and would perform mainly extended manual substantive tests.

Auditing around the computer depends on the manual auditing techniques which have developed in order to deal with manual accounts. It is a reasonable step to extend these tried and trusted methods to a computer-based accounts and business system. However, we have already seen in Chapter 8 that the computer poses a number of security and control problems not associated with manual systems. Two problems are particularly relevant here:

There is a loss of visible evidence (LOVE), i.e. documentation;
There is a loss of an audit trail.

The difficulties faced by the auditor can be seen in the following example. Suppose an auditor wants to examine the current state of debts owed to a company. Firstly, the auditor must be able to obtain a list of debtors. These can then be approached to verify that they are in fact debtors, and that the stated debts in the company records are correct. In order to obtain a record of debtors the auditor, using an around the computer approach, must depend on the computer printout. There is no way of knowing that the list of debtors is complete. The routines and procedures used to generate the list are transparent to the auditor. If the computer code has been manipulated to exclude certain debtors, for example those who have debts above the credit limits allowed for their accounts, then a false picture of the company's credit control procedures and trading position would be given. Reliance on such a method is therefore risky.

Despite the potential weaknesses of auditing around the computer it is still relied on by smaller accounting practices who do not have the resources and expertise to do the detailed work that could highlight fraudulent use of the computer in accounting. Given the fact that external audits are a legal requirement, and the auditor has a duty to decide that the accounts are fair and true, there has been pressure to develop auditing procedures that take account of the special problems posed by computer-based systems.

Auditing through the computer

Auditing through the computer complements auditing around the computer. In auditing around the computer the central focus is on the accounts themselves, while in auditing through the computer the central focus is on the computer system. This simple assertion offers a working distinction, although in practice it is not that clear cut. For example, physical access to the accounts necessarily implies physical access to the computer, and manual procedures need to be considered whatever method of auditing is used.

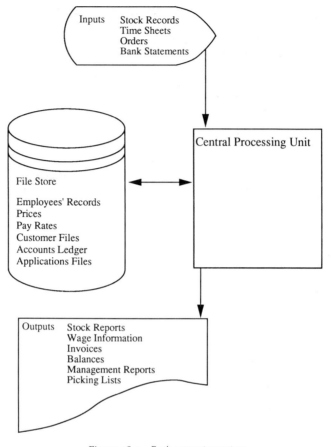

Figure 18.1   *Basic computer system*

Auditing through the computer is concerned with the internal controls of a computer-based system. The auditor needs to examine five main categories of control:

Physical controls;
Integrity controls;
User controls;
Programmed procedures;
Manual procedures and disciplines.

The different kinds of control for auditing through the computer are dealt with in more detail in Chapter 8 and can be illustrated in relation to the simple model of a computer system outlined in Chapter 2. The diagram (Figure 18.1) indicates a basic computerized accounting system. The inputs to the system are entered via a keyboard and include basic infor-

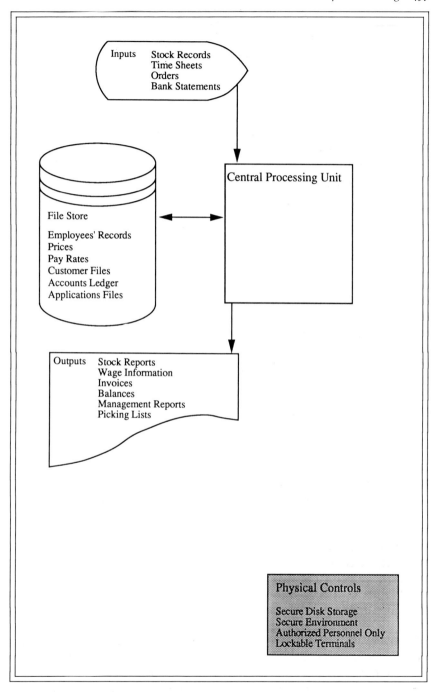

Figure 18.2 *Physical security features*

mation for the running of the company. They may include timesheets, customer orders, payments and stock level reports. The file store contains information on employees, prices, pay rates, stock levels as well as the basic accounts ledgers and customer details. The central processing unit (CPU) processes the information from the inputs and file store and uses these inputs to produce outputs. The outputs include stock reports, wages information, invoices, balances and various management reports.

Physical controls

An audit through the computer cannot ignore the environment of the computer system. The auditor will want to know what are the security arrangements to prevent the physical access to the computer system. The concerns here will be:

The location of terminals and the security of these areas;
Access of personnel to the computers;
Physical access, for example, key-lockable terminals;
Security of disk storage areas.

Physical security is easily represented in our computer system since we can enclose the computer system in a box.

Integrity controls

Integrity controls are controls governing the security of files and programs. These include controls over software as well as physical controls, access controls and controls over the use of information. They are concerned with the functions of the computer system and its implementation, rather than the data itself. Integrity controls should take the form of:

Program development controls;
Cataloguing controls;
Program security controls;
Computer operations controls;
File security controls.

Program development controls govern the procedures required to test the design and implementation of a new system. These controls should include the existence of an outline and description of the system, as well as parallel running of the system when it is tested.

Cataloguing controls concern the testing of a new or revised program which requires the program to be tested outside the live system so as not to disrupt the normal operation of that system.

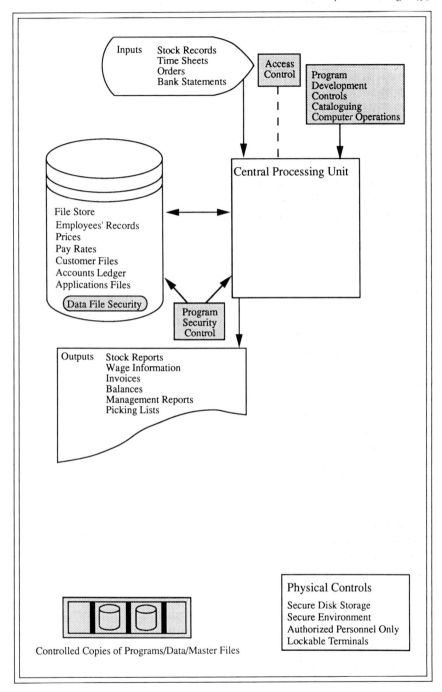

Figure 18.3 *Integrity controls*

Program security controls control access to programs in order to ensure that no unauthorized changes are made to programs which process data. These controls may require the existence of passwords to ensure that no unauthorized access takes place. In addition, any changes which do take place should be approved, checked for appropriateness, and followed up. Comparisons should be made between programs and independently stored copies.

Computer operation controls are used to limit the power and authority of the people actually running the computer. They are also used to check that all proper procedures have been carried out.

File security controls include: access rights and authorization, in the form of locks to control access to terminals; passwords to control access to files and to the system as a whole; various access rights (e.g. read only); access rights governing which files can be used by which programs; and a recording procedure within the system whereby violations (or attempts at violation) can be reported and therefore acted on. For example, the list of employees on a payroll should be recorded and stored separately, and regularly checked against the computer file.

Programmed procedures and user controls

Programmed procedures are additions to computer programs which assist in the control of data being processed. For example, the computer could be equipped to issue a warning message if a member of staff appears on the payroll as having worked more than 160 hours per month.

User controls are manual controls imposed on data before it is processed. An example of such a control would be a check that the same quantity of goods recorded as having been despatched has actually been sent out. The auditor would wish to see a signature on the despatch note as proof that this control has been carried out. These are referred to as external controls in Figure 18.5. Nearer to the computer system some check should be kept on the input to and output from the computer system.

Programmed procedures and user controls can be categorized under the following headings:

Completeness of input and updating;
Accuracy of input and updating;
Accuracy of data processed;
Maintenance of data on files;
Authorization.

Completeness of input and updating

Here the emphasis is on ensuring that no transactions are omitted. These controls, therefore, ensure that all transactions are inputted and re-

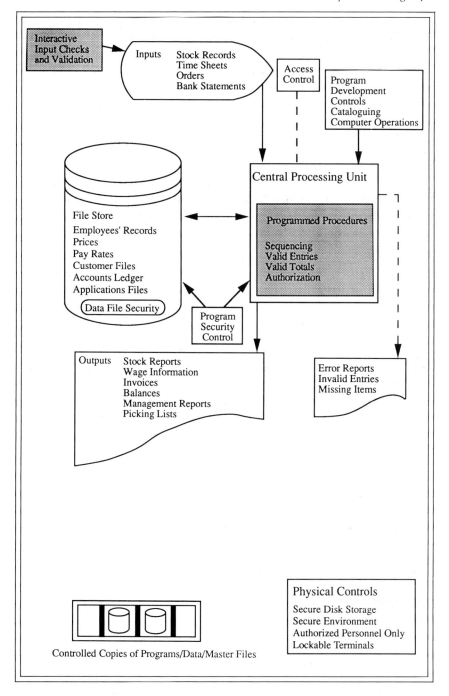

Figure 18.4   *Programmed procedures*

corded, and that masterfiles are updated to include this information. To this end, all original documents should be numbered, and it should be possible to access information stored in the computer in the same sequence so that any omissions can be easily detected. Any omissions must result in the production of an error report.

Information should also be checked against that stored in the master file, with regular controls on the upkeep of the master file. Computer matching is a further control, where items recorded on computer should be matched against original documents, and any non-matching or mismatching investigated.

Following the approval of the input data using the above controls, subsequent updating then undergoes further controls. These controls include: the assembly of control totals, acquired through the sequence checking and computer matching; the transfer of control totals during intermediate processing; the continuous checking of compatibility of accepted totals with accumulated records; and the examination and reconciliation of differences. This investigation and correction should be a continuous process, carried out as and when inaccuracies, incompatibilities and errors are discovered. Any rejections should be corrected and resubmitted as soon as possible, to avoid any possible disappearance of the data.

Accuracy of input and updating

The transference of data from source to record is subject to errors in transcription. These errors can be checked using some of the controls discussed above, as well as a combination of the following controls:

Format checks;
Existence checks;
Check digit verification;
Reasonableness checks;
Dependency checks;
Verification of conversion;
Security of output.

Check digit verification and other checks are discussed in some detail in Chapter 8.

Accuracy of data processing

These controls relate to data produced as a result of the calculations performed by the computer. They must check the accuracy of the command which stimulates the generation of data, as well as ensure that the

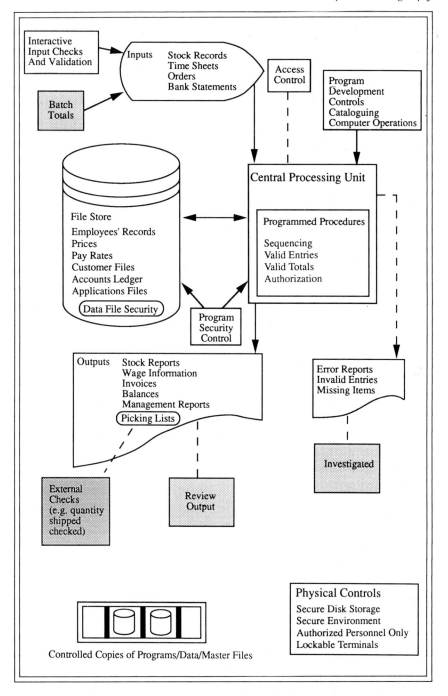

Figure 18.5   *User controls*

process of generating the data is valid. In addition, all data on the master file (including data which has already been checked) must be examined for accuracy and completeness. In addition, the data produced by the computer should be examined manually or by a programmed procedure, for example, a cheque over a certain pre-programmed amount should either be noticed by a warning message or an error report should be generated.

New files are also subject to accuracy controls. This may mean checking the information stored on file against comparable information held on other files (e.g. sales prices, share prices), or the auditor may have to find other ways of checking data by referring to source.

Maintenance of data and updating

Maintenance controls exist in order to check that files have not been corrupted either accidentally or maliciously. This can be achieved by regularly comparing data held on file with the same information recorded independently. For example, a file containing a list of all staff on the payroll should be checked against an independent list to avoid the payment of a salary to a fictional employee. The malicious corruption of data or programs is discussed in detail in Chapter 8.

Authorization

Authorization of data can be performed at any stage of the input – before, during or after. The computer can be programmed to indicate automatically the necessity for manual authorization in the case of, say, a salary claim for double time for working a Saturday. In other cases, the computer is programmed to check selected data according to a standard. In this case, the auditor must check the validity of the selection and of the standard, as well as evidence of the manual authorization itself.

The auditor must also be concerned with three other areas:

1   Any edit, update or modification of data must be properly authorized.
2   All the computer procedures and initiation of program runs (e.g. month-end, year-end procedures and payroll runs) are properly authorized. Apart from batch runs, there may be various online and real-time computer procedures; for example creating a new supplier (perhaps bogus) on a purchase ledger.
3   Access to the company database or computerized records must also be authorized. Information is as much an asset of the company as cash.

Figure 18.4 shows a system which incorporates programmed procedures as part of the functioning of the CPU and which generates a series of error reports as additional outputs. The functions incorporated are the authorization of the user, automatic checking and validation of various inputs, sequencing of inputs and checks against file entries (e.g. client files). Error reports identifying invalid entries and missing items are generated. These error reports have to be acted on. This is another important user control and is shown in Figure 18.5.

In the diagram (Figure 18.5) the outputs are reviewed and the error reports investigated. External checks are also introduced into the diagram. Batch totals are calculated manually prior to input and these totals can be checked against computer generated totals.

Basic disciplines

No computer audit can ignore the implementation of good business practice or disciplines. Such disciplines should include the segregation and intelligent delegation of duties, so that fraud cannot easily be perpetrated by a single person. Hence, the responsibility for handling stock should not be given to the same member of staff who has responsibility for the recording of that stock and for reviewing that it has been entered correctly. Such segregation of duties does not completely rule out the possibility of fraud, but fraud requiring conspiracy is less likely than fraud which can be carried out by a single individual. An auditor, whether internal or external, should consider these manual systems as an integral part of the audit process.

The user controls of segregation and delegation should be accompanied by additional sensible office practice, such as the keeping of records and implementation of similar accounting procedures, the supervision of duties, the authorization of procedures, and the careful consideration of rights of access to records and information. The computer can play an important part here because the sensible use and management of a password security system can be used to regulate and control access to data.

The use of controls with microcomputers

The role of the auditor is to establish that an appropriate level of control is in place. It would be impractical and costly to introduce high levels of control on small microcomputer systems. Large and medium computer systems require thorough auditing and full use of all types of control is justified and desirable. For example, with larger systems there is a greater need to resort to automated programmed controls and to set up integrity procedures and detailed access controls. With larger systems it is also more likely that the computer code is written 'in-house' and this requires the auditor to consider controls relating to this.

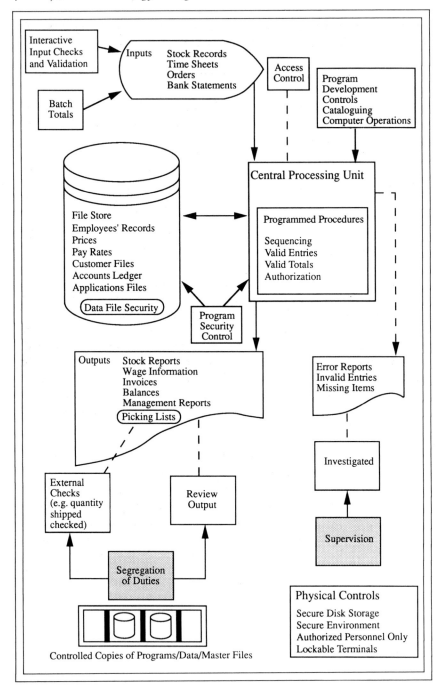

Figure 18.6   *Final computer system with all the controls and procedures illustrated, including user controls*

The auditing of a small business computer system is unlikely to be able to implement all types of control for a number of reasons:

There are less formal controls, particularly in the separation of duties and supervision of staff.

There is no specialized data processing or there are computer programming staff. Controls on programmers, taken for granted in large data processing departments, may be absent.

The system is more likely to be a computer package than a specialist product. While some desirable controls may be built into the software others may not. However, with a tried and tested product the auditor can have a greater degree of confidence in those controls which do exist.

Access control is likely to be limited. The greatest problem for a small business is usually the security of programs and data files.

The auditor will generally be prepared to accept the limitations placed on the controls by the size and nature of a small business, especially as computerized systems will often have advantages over existing manual systems which are even more vulnerable. However, it is important to verify that adequate user controls and physical security are implemented. While formal controls may be absent in small businesses, these may be compensated for by informal controls, for example the greater degree of day-to-day contact between management and staff may compensate for the lack of segregation of duties. Managerial scrutiny of transactions and staff needs to be acceptable, and if it is not, the weaknesses need to be reported.

One final consideration of the auditor is the dependence of the small organization on the computerized system. Large- and medium-sized systems will include extensive backup procedures and strategies for dealing with system failures. The increased efficiency and speed of an integrated business and accounts system for a small business needs to be balanced against whether or not there are manual procedures to compensate for a breakdown in the computer system. The data needed to run a small business tends to become concentrated within computerized systems and the company, usually without realizing it, can become dependent on that system.

Computer assisted auditing techniques (CAATs)

The computer offers the potential for detailed, accurate and rapid auditing. Computer assisted auditing techniques (CAATs) relate to tests of programs and files and are a valuable resource for the auditor. They can be used to make the data stored in large files and databases manageable, test the integrity of accounting programs and verify procedures. However, the development of computer assisted auditing techniques can require high initial set-up costs, a high degree of skill to implement and use, and may be of use with only a limited number of systems.

File analysis

The most widely used CAATs relate to files and data storage. This is not surprising as the information contained in the files is equivalent to the accounts and ledgers of a manual accounting system. It is on the data contained in files and records that the auditor's skills can most effectively be used.

Interrogation

Interrogation software is used to read data on clients' files and to provide information for audit; it is almost a prerequisite for effective auditing of a computerized accounts system. This type of software gives the auditor direct access to the actual records without having to use clients' software and means that a wide variety of audit functions and procedures can be performed.

There are a number of stages in the development of interrogation software. Firstly, it is important to define the aims and objectives of the software and prepare a detailed specification. This can then be used to produce a program which can be used to test files and parameters to generate an output file and a report which resolves the issues outlined in the specification.

Analytical review

Sometimes referred to as modelling, analytical review can provide the auditor with useful information on patterns or trends. This can be used for cost management, financial planning and forecasting. Analytic review involves identifying and collecting key totals, ratios and distributions, for comparison with previous results, with industry-wide performance or with the planned level of activity.

Experimental techniques

The auditor will know what a system should do and can devise experiments which will establish that the system operates as intended. Two techniques can be used: test data, which is the more common, can be used to validate the output from the system; and the rarely used parallel simulation, which reperforms the procedures carried out by the client's program.

Test data

Test data is data where, given legitimate processing, the outcome is known. If a computer system gives a different set of values to those

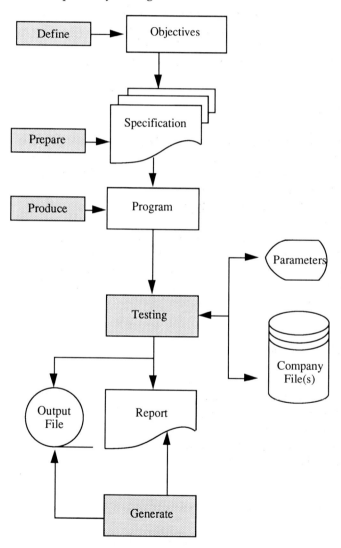

Figure 18.7 *Summary of development of interrogation software*

expected then the system is suspect and more detailed analysis is required. Because of its relative simplicity test data is commonly used. The procedure for using test data is given in Figure 18.8.

One special set of test data can be used to analyse that the system controls over inputs are operating. Most screen layouts will consist of a series of fields into which values, or words are entered. Each field should have restrictions on what can be entered, or edited by the user. For example, the system may not allow values over a certain amount in a particular field. The auditor can devise test data that will try to breach the system's limits and to make sure screen input and editing restrictions are operating.

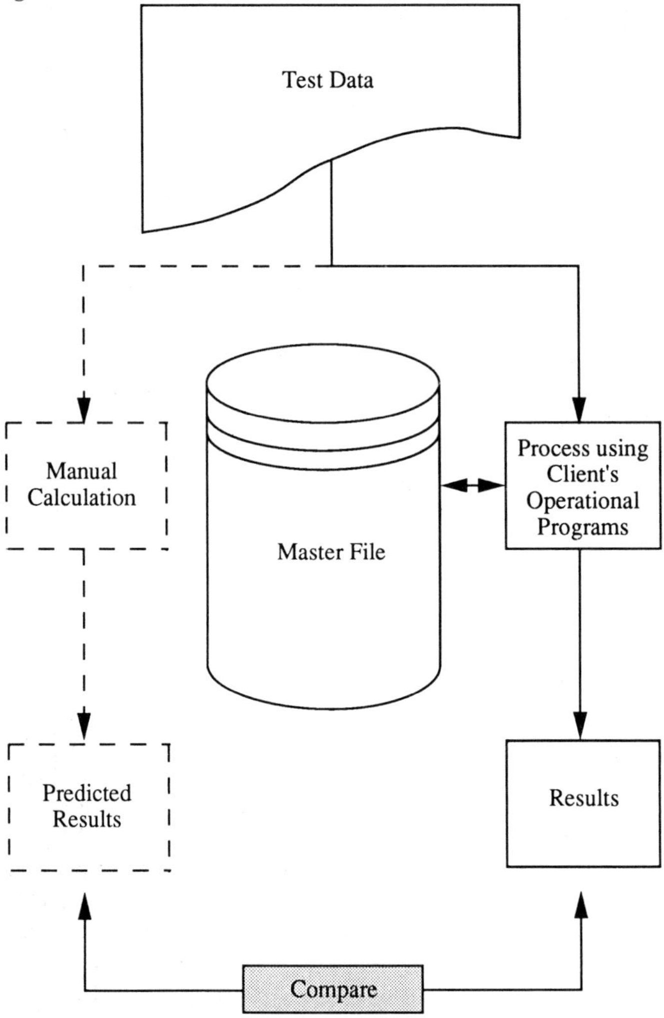

Figure 18.8 *The use of test data*

Parallel simulation

Parallel simulation is an expensive and rarely used technique. It is easier to test that the output, from using test data, corresponds with the expected result than to attempt to replicate the procedures used to generate this outcome. For complex procedures, with a number of different paths that the processing can take, a parallel simulation may provide a better test of the system. However, the fact that the procedure is complex means that the simulation can be developed only with expert knowledge and at some cost.

Code analysis and comparison

Code analysis and comparison aims at checking the integrity and validity of a program or procedure for both the original source code and the resultant compiled code. In the analysis of code the auditor can examine a printout of the source code with a view to following the logic of the program. The auditor can then be satisfied that the program does what it is supposed to do. The analysis of code is rarely carried out because the skills required to use the technique are those of the computer programmer and for 'off the shelf' computer packages the source code will not be available. If code analysis is used it is important to verify that the compiled code in actual use is from the source code.

Another auditing technique is to compare the source code or compiled code of the computer programs in use with a secure master copy. The value of code comparison is in the detection of unauthorized alteration or contamination to a program, including infection from computer viruses. The comparison of code is relatively straightforward with standard packages, but where systems are constantly being modified and updated 'in-house', such a technique is not going to provide useful information. For situations where the program is frequently revised a more appropriate tool is a program library analyser. This can be used to identify unauthorized or abnormal changes to the library of programs used.

Access control analysis

The auditor needs to be able to establish that unauthorized access to the computer does not occur. There are really two situations to be avoided. Firstly, that no one has rights that they should not have and secondly, that unauthorized access has not occurred at any time during the accounting period. An access control analyser allows the auditor to examine the rights associated with terminals and individuals at the time of the audit. Where the accounting system has a large number of users, checking the access privileges is particularly important. A detailed access control

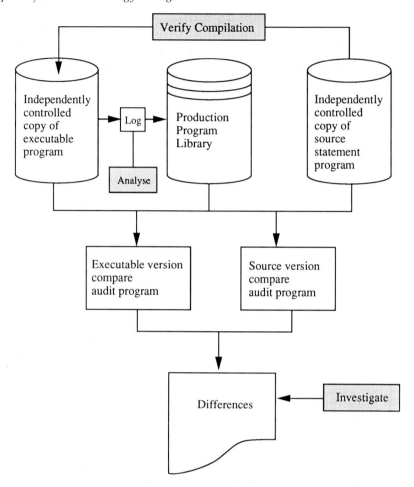

Figure 18.9   *Summary of code analysis and comparison*

matrix should exist to control access to the system. An example of an access control matrix is given in Figure 18.10 below. Each user is allocated a different set of rights (read, write, execute, delete, etc) to the files and controls kept on the computer.

Log analysers can be used to read and analyse records of machine activity and thus used to identify unauthorized access and activity. Logs of computer use generate a large volume of data and so the technique would normally only be used where fraud is suspected and specific analyses can be identified.

Program operation analysis

There are a number of techniques which can be used to analyse the actual

User Identification		Files			Programs			
Code No	Password	R	S	T	1	2	3	4
1 2 3 4 5	ABC	X	O	R –	RW	RW	E	O
1 2 3 4 6	GHJ	O	W	X	O	R	W	O
1 2 3 6 0	KLM	X	O	RW	E	R	O	X
1 2 3 8 9	UVW	E	R	O	W	O	X	RW

O =	No access	E =	Execute
R =	Read	RW =	Read/write
W =	Write	X =	Read/write/execute

Figure 18.10   *An example of an access control matrix*

operation of the system. These tend to be fairly complex in that they demand detailed knowledge of computer systems and programming techniques. As a result they are not widely used.

Mapping, tracing and snapshots

Another computer assisted auditing technique is analysis of the actual operation of the computerized business system at the level of the execution of computer code. For example, if a program contains a worm, which will damage the system at some future date, the code involved will not be implemented during normal operation. A program which monitors the actual code used in normal operation may identify that a section of code is not being implemented. The auditor can then analyse this code in detail and make sure it performs a legitimate, if rarely used, function and is not dangerous. This technique for identifying unused instructions is known as mapping. A similar technique to mapping is tracing. This provides a record of the code used, and in what order, rather than what code is not used.

Embedded code

The availability of source code that can be changed means that the auditor could embed code into the program to assist auditing. This is sometimes referred to as concurrent auditing. The code could examine each transaction as it passes through the system and log unusual transactions. The close cooperation of the client is clearly important in defining the function of the code. What constitutes an unusual transaction will need to be agreed, for example. Subsequent monitoring of the code is necessary to ensure it is not tampered with.

An example of the use of embedded code is the snapshot technique. This involves taking a 'picture' of a transaction as it is processed by the system. By taking a series of snapshots an audit trail for a particular transaction can be established. The software necessary for taking snapshots must be embedded into the program code or operating system.

Computer auditing software

Auditors are making increasing use of microcomputers within the audit process. In some cases the uses are administrative in nature, common examples being the preparation of audit budget or the maintenance of a database of client information. Microcomputers are also used in performing audit work. If it is possible to have software which automates some of the accounting and business procedures, why not have software which automates some of the audit procedures? Not surprisingly, special software has been developed to carry out auditing through the computer. This software is often called a computer audit package.

A computer audit package takes advantage of the same speed and accuracy qualities of computer systems that make computerized accounting packages viable. There are a variety of software auditing tools for microcomputer systems that perform a variety of security, control and auditing tasks. A package like PC Auditor analyses what is on a disk and the state of the disk. The package allows a non-specialist auditor to sample data and write reports on their contents quickly. It will identify and examine hidden or erased files. There are also various tools for spreadsheets which identify errors, examine macros and provide documentation. Other spreadsheet tools can be used to compare two copies of a spreadsheet.

One further use of auditing software is in the administration of the audit process. The reasons for implementation of computerized systems in other businesses are equally valid for an auditing practice. The requirements to maintain lists of contacts, record and analyse the time spent on particular projects, and the production of reports are all tasks that need to be performed by the auditor. The use of the standard computer packages for databases, spreadsheets and wordprocessors can help in the performance of these tasks. Much of the audit software is concerned with the preparation of accounts, the entry of data and the trial balance, and the supporting notes and schedules.

Balance sheet auditing

Up to now we have been concerned with systems-based auditing. This involves understanding and recording all the firm's business systems. An alternative method of auditing is to examine the balance sheet and investigate significant items that could be material. Within a current assets section, the auditors could confirm the debtors by independently check-ing with the debtors; inventories could be checked by physically verifying the stocks or a sample of them. Cash would be verified by reconciling bank accounts and so on.

In this way, the auditors would concentrate on substantive tests with-out a full-side investigation of the system. However, interrogating the relevant files would require some knowledge of the computer systems. So some understanding and recording of parts of the computer system will be necessary.

Summary

The audit approach in a computer system is similar to that in a non-computer system. The auditor should plan and control the approach to the audit so as to ensure that it is performed in the most efficient manner. He or she will need to gain a preliminary understanding of the nature of the client's business, of particular areas of risk and of the accounting system in order to determine audit strategy. Where strategy is to place reliance on internal controls it will be necessary to gain and record a more detailed understanding of the accounting system, evaluate the system of internal control and carry out compliance tests to be satisfied that the controls are working in practice. In a computer system the auditor will have to consider programmed procedures and integrity controls, and in performing compliance tests he or she may need to use computer assisted audit techniques such as audit software or test data.

Part Four: Further reading

Alter, S. L. *Decision Support Systems: Current Practice and Continuing Challenges* (Addison-Wesley, 1980)

Amey, L. R. *Budget Planning and Control Systems* (Pitman Publishing, 1979)

Ansoff, H. I. *Corporate Strategy* (McGraw-Hill, 1965) (Also available in Penguin)

Ashton, F. *Mechanised Accounting: Direct Entry Accounting Machines and Computers* (Macdonald and Evans, 1973)

Bhaskar, K. N. *Building Financial Models: A Simulation Approach* (Associated Business Press, 1978)

Bhaskar, K. N. Cope, P. and Morris R. *Financial Modelling with a Microcomputer: A Guide for Management* (Economist Intelligence Unit, 1982)

Bhaskar, K. N. Williams, B. Cope, P. and Morris R. *Financial Modelling with a Microcomputer: Software Choice and Hardware Selection* (Economist Intelligence Unit, 1984)

Bhaskar, K. N. and Kaye, G. R. *Financial Planning with Personal Computers: 1. Cashflows* (Economist Intelligence Unit, 1985)

Bhaskar, K. N. and Kaye, G. R. *Financial Planning with Personal Computers: 2. Management Accounting Reports* (Economist Intelligence Unit, 1986)

Bhaskar, K. N. and Kate, G. R. *Financial Planning with Personal Computers: 3. Budgeting* (Economist Intelligence Unit, 1986)

Bhaskar, K. N. and Kaye, G. R. *Financial Planning with Personal Computers: 4. Corporate Planning* (Economist Intelligence Unit, 1987)

Bhaskar, K. N. and Shave, M. J. R. *Computer Science Applied to Business Systems* (Addison-Wesley 1986)

Bhaskar, K. N. and Williams, B. C. *The Impact of Microprocessors on the Small Business* (Prentice Hall, 1986)

Bhaskar, K. N., Morris, R. C. and Pope, P. *Financial Modelling with a Computer – A Managerial Revolution* (Economist Intelligence Unit, 1982)

Bodnar, G. H. *Accounting Information Systems* (Allyn & Bacon, 1980)

Bonczek, R. H., Holsapple, C. W. and Whinston, A. B. *Foundations of Decision Support Systems* (Academic Press, 1981)

Bower, J. B. and Welke, W. R. *Financial Information Systems* (Houghton Mifflin, 1968)

Burch, J. G. and Sardinas, J. L. *Computer Control and Audit: A Total Systems Approach* (John Wiley and Sons, 1975)

Chambers, A. D. *Computer Auditing* (Pitman Books, 1981)

Chen, P. P. (ed.) *Entity-Relationship Approach to Systems Analysis and Design* (North-Holland, 1980)

Christ, C. F. *Econometric Models and Methods* (John Wiley & Sons, 1966)

Clifton, H. D. and Lucey, T. *Accounting and Computer Systems* (Business Books Ltd., 1973)

Cushing, B. E. *Accounting Information Systems and Business Organisations* (Addison-Wesley, 1978)

Davis, W. S. *Computers and Business Information Processing* (Addison-Wesley, 1978)

Edwards, C. *Developing Microcomputer-based Business Systems* (Prentice-Hall, 1982)

Eliason, A. L. and Kitts, K. D. *Business Computer Systems and Applications* (Science Research Associates, 1974)

Fick, G. and Sprague, R. H., Jr. (eds.) *Decision Support Systems: Issues and Challenges* (Pergamon Press, 1980)

Flower, J. *Computer Models for Accountants* (Accountancy Age, 1973)

Gessford, J. E. *Modern Information Systems* (Addison-Wesley, 1980)

Ginzberg, M. J., Reitman, W. R. and Stohr, E. A. (eds.) *Decision Support Systems* (North-Holland, 1982)

Grinyer, P. H. and Wooller, J. *Corporate Models Today: a New Tool for Financial Management* (ICAEW, 1975)

Hertz, D. B. 'Risk Analysis in Capital Investment', *Harvard Business Review*, Jan–Feb 1964, 95–106

Hicks, J. O. and Leininger, W. O. *Accounting Information Systems* (West Publishing, 1981)

Hull, J. C. *The Evaluation of Risk in Business Investment* (Pergamon Press, 1980)

ICAEW *Computers and Auditing Course Material* (1977)

Jancura, E. G. and Boos, R. V. *Establishing Control and Auditing the Computerised Accounting System* (Van Nostrand Reinhold, 1981)

Keen, P. G. W. and Scott Morton, M. S. *Decision Support Systems: An Organizational Perspective* (Addison-Wesley, 1978)

Kleijnen, J. P. C. *Computers and Profits: Quantifying Financial Benefits of Information* (Addison-Wesley, 1980)

Mace, R. *Management Information and the Computer* (Haymarket Publishing, 1974)

Mair, W. C., Wood, D. R. and Davis, K. W. *Computer Control for Audit* (Institute of Internal Auditors, 1972)

Martin, J. *Principles of Data-Base Management* (Prentice-Hall, 1976)

Martin, J. *Application Development without Programmers* (Prentice-Hall, 1982)

Mason, R. O. and Swanson, E. B. *Measurement for Management Decision* (Addison-Wesley, 1981)

McCarthy, W. E. 'An Entity-Relationship View of Accounting Models', *The Accounting Review*, October 1979, 667–685

McCoch, A. M. Rahman, M. and Earl, M. J. *Developing Managerial Information Systems* (Macmillan Press, 1981)

McRae, T. W. *The Impact of Computers on Accounting* (John Wiley & Sons, 1964)

McRae, T. W. *Computers and Accounting* (John Wiley & Sons, 1976)

Mepham, M. J. *Accounting Models* (Polytech Publishers Limited, 1980)

MSA *General Ledger System* (Management Science America Inc., 1977)

Murdick, R. G. and Ross, J. E. *Information Systems for Modern Management* (Prentice-Hall, 1971)

Murdick, R. G., Fuller, T. C., Ross, J. E. and Winnermark, F. J. *Accounting Information Systems* (Prentice-Hall, 1978)

Naylor, T. H. *Corporate Planning Models* (Addison-Wesley, 1979)

Page, J. and Hooper, P. *Accounting and Information Systems* (Prentice-Hall International, 1979)

Porter, W. T. and Perry, W. E. *EDP Control and Auditing* (Kent Publishing Co., 1981)

Robinson, L. A., Davis, J. R. and Alderman, C. W. *Accounting Information Systems: A Cycle Approach* (Harper and Row, 1982)

Sardinas, J. L., Burch, J. G. and Asebrook, R. *EDP Auditing: A Primer* (John Wiley and Sons, 1981)

Sorter, G. H. 'An "Events" Approach to Basic Accounting Theory', *The Accounting Review*, Jan 1969, 12–19

Sherman, P. M. *Strategic Planning for Technological Industries* (Addison-Wesley, 1982)

Sprague, R. H., Jr. and Carlson, E. D. *Building Effective Decision Support Systems* (Prentice-Hall, 1982)

Thierauf, R. J. *Systems Analysis and Design of Real-Time Management Information Systems* (Prentice-Hall, 1975)

Thierauf, R. J. and Reynolds, G. W. *Systems Analysis and Design: A Case-Study Approach* (Charles E. Merrill, 1980)

Thierauf, R. J. *Decision Support Systems for Effective Planning and Control: A Case-Study Approach* (Prentice-Hall, 1982)

Tricker, R. I. *Management Information and Control Systems* (John Wiley & Sons, 1976)

Weber, R. *EDP Auditing: Conceptual Foundations and Practice* (McGraw-Hill, 1982)

Wilkinson, J. W. *Accounting and Information Systems* (John Wiley & Sons, 1982)

Appendix: The audit process

This section describes a typical audit approach. It is based on Jenkins, Perry and Cooke (1986). It is systems based and adopts an auditing through the computer approach. This approach is in compliance with the Auditing Standards and Guidelines prepared by the Auditing Practices Committee of the Consultative Committee of Accounting Bodies – this is of relevance to UK audits. The principal steps in the audit process are illustrated in Figure A.1.

The principal steps in the audit process

Determination of an audit strategy

The first stage in the audit approach is for the auditor to determine the most efficient and effective audit strategy for each aspect of the financial statements. In order to determine the audit strategy the auditor will need to gain a preliminary understanding of the nature of the client's business and particular risk areas, of the nature and significance of account balances within the financial statements and of the client's accounting system and related internal controls.

In accordance with this preliminary understanding the auditor will base the audit of each significant account balance or group of account balances in the financial statements principally on one of the following:

1 Compliance tests designed to confirm the consistent and proper operation of accounting systems from which account balances are derived, in combination with limited substantive tests directed to the completeness, validity and accuracy of account balances; or

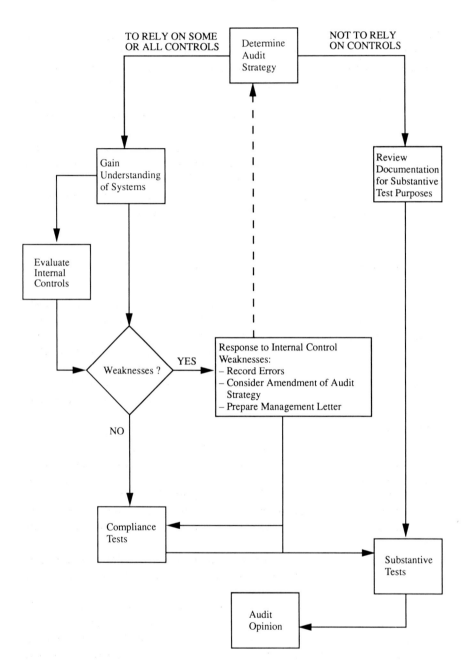

Figure A.1   *Flowchart of audit process*

2   Substantive tests directed to the completeness, validity and accuracy of account balances.

In addition to the manual controls carried out on the data being processed, referred to as user controls, the auditor will be concerned with the other types of procedures and controls which are unique to computer systems, termed programmed procedures and integrity controls.

The particular features of computerized processing may influence the audit strategy decision. For example, the auditor may use computer programs to examine large volumes of processed data thus adopting substantive testing procedures as an alternative to, or to supplement, control reliance. The auditor will also need to be satisfied that significant programmed procedures on which he or she wishes to rely continue to operate properly and this may be done by tests of integrity controls or direct tests of the programmed procedures themselves.

Understanding and recording the system

Where the auditor decides in determining the audit strategy to place reliance on internal controls, it will be necessary to gain and record a more detailed understanding of the procedures and controls comprising a company's accounting system. The auditor normally obtains this understanding by reading systems descriptions and by discussions with company staff. Understanding of the system is usually recorded by use of flowcharts or, in those cases where it is considered to be more efficient, by narrative notes.

The auditor's understanding of the accounting system is ultimately confirmed during the audit by the performance of audit test. However, in order to reduce the risk that time may be wasted in devising and attempting to perform audit procedures on the basis of an incorrect understanding of the accounting system, the auditor may wish to confirm his or her understanding before performing audit tests. This can be done, for example, by inspecting or reviewing transactions records, documents or reports.

Where the audit strategy for an item in the financial statements is to rely principally on substantive tests, the auditor will require a sufficient understanding of the accounting system to enable him to devise and perform these tests. An adequate level of understanding for this purpose may have been obtained at the time of determining the audit strategy. If not, a sufficiently detailed understanding should be obtained and recorded to enable the substantive tests to be designed and carried out.

Evaluation of internal controls

The auditor is concerned with a company's system of internal control because he or she may wish, where possible, to place reliance thereon in order to limit, and phase the timing of, subsequent audit work on the financial statements. A further important purpose is to report to management weaknesses that become apparent, so as to assist management in carrying out its obligations to establish and maintain controls that will ensure, as far as possible, the reliability of the company's records and the safeguarding of its assets.

In assessing the degree of reliance that the auditor can place on the internal controls, it will be necessary to distinguish between what are referred to in this book as 'basic controls', 'disciplines over basic controls' and 'physical controls'. Basic controls are those controls designed to ensure that valid transactions, and only valid transactions, are processed, recorded and maintained completely and accurately in the accounting records. Disciplines over basic controls are those features of the system which are designed to ensure that the basic controls continue to operate properly. They comprise segregation of duties, including separation of the custody of assets from the accounting responsibility for them, and supervision of the results of one person's work by another. Disciplines over basic controls are referred to hereafter for convenience as 'disciplines'. Physical controls are designed to restrict access to assets.

The importance of the distinction between basic controls and disciplines lies in the extent to which the auditor uses them as a means of gaining the audit satisfaction that is necessary to place reliance on the continued and proper operation of the basic controls. Where the disciplines are effective, they will provide assurance that the basic controls continue to operate properly and the auditor can limit work on the basic controls.

Compliance tests

The auditor must carry out suitable tests to provide evidence that the controls on which he or she wishes to place reliance have continued to operate properly throughout the period under review. These tests are referred to as compliance tests in this book. In general the auditor will wish to carry out compliance tests on all those controls which were identified and expected to be relied on.

The auditor will normally carry out compliance tests on the disciplines before those on the basic controls. This is because if the disciplines have operated satisfactorily, the auditor will be able to restrict work on the basic controls. The approach adopted for the basic controls is thus largely dependent on the results of tests on the disciplines.

Compliance testing will for the most part comprise examination of evidence and reperformance. Examination of evidence consists of the inspection of records, documents, reconciliation reports and the like for evidence that a specific control appears to have been properly carried out. An example is the inspection of signatures or initials on a supplier's invoice evidencing that the invoice has been matched with a goods received note. Reperformance consists of the repeating, either in whole or in part, of the same work processes as those performed by the company's employees, for example the actual matching by the auditor of a supplier's invoice with the corresponding goods received note, in order to obtain assurance that the matching process has been carried out. There are some controls that cannot be tested by examination or reperformance, for example the counting and examination of incoming goods or the physical security of stores. In these circumstances the control procedure may need to be tested by observation and enquiry, for example at the relevant location, in order to ascertain whether a specific control appears to be operating. When testing by observation, the auditor should bear in mind the possibility that the observed control may not operate when he or she is not present. The auditor may therefore also wish to see evidence of action taken as a result of the application of the observed control, for example, exception reports produced listing short deliveries of goods.

The audit response to internal control weaknesses

Where the auditor wishes to place reliance on internal controls, it will be necessary to identify all weaknesses and consider the effect which they may have on subsequent audit procedures. Weaknesses may arise from the absence of a required control or the failure to exercise a control, and may come to light when determining the audit strategy or performing compliance or substantive tests.

It is an important feature of the audit approach outlined here that, as regards each weakness, the auditor must decide, taking all the relevant factors into account, whether the weakness could lead to a material error or irregularity appearing in the financial statements.

If, in the auditor's opinion, material error could not arise, change to the audit procedures to take account of the weakness will not normally be made. This is because the auditor is not required to take account of the possibility that an immaterial error exists in the financial statements on which he or she is reporting.

If the auditor decides that, arising from the effects of a weakness, material error could occur, the necessary steps must be taken to ascertain whether or not error has arisen and, if it has, its extent must be determined. In order to obtain this satisfaction, the auditor will need to amend the audit strategy originally adopted by altering or adding to the audit procedures which would otherwise be carried out. Where the audit strategy is to rely on controls, and serious weaknesses are found in the compliance tests, it may be necessary to drop reliance on the relevant controls altogether and instead to perform extended substantive tests of account balances. In those exceptional cases where the effect of a control weakness cannot be ascertained by changes in audit procedures, the auditor will need to consider whether it may be necessary to qualify the audit report.

Substantive tests

Substantive tests represent the final stage of the audit and in conjunction with any compliance tests of internal controls must be adequate to support the audit opinion expressed on the financial statements. Auditors have as their main objective the substantiation of account balances and other information contained in the financial statements. In addition, substantive tests complement compliance tests since they provide further evidence as to whether the internal controls have continued to operate.

Substantive tests comprise direct tests of items making up account balances or of other information in the financial statements, and other procedures of a more general nature such as analytical reviews of financial information or the correlation of account balances with other accounts. Such other procedures provide indirect evidence supporting the completeness, validity and accuracy of the information in the financial statements.

Normally the most important factors governing the nature, timing and extent of substantive tests are the nature and materiality of the account balances, the degree of reliance that can be placed on the company's internal controls, and the risk of error arising from economic or business circumstances. 'Timing' refers to the extent of the opportunity to carry out some or all of the work at a time other than after the year end, if this is of assistance to the client or the auditor. Where the internal controls are satisfactory, the substantive tests can be limited and carried out, to an appropriate extent, before the year end. If the controls are unsatisfactory, the substantive tests must be extended and the opportunity for carrying out much of the work before the year end decreases. Where records supporting balance sheet and income and expenditure accounts are maintained by computer, the objectives of the substantive tests and the relationship between the system of internal control and the substantive tests remain the same. However, because of, first, the opportunity to make use of the computer to assist in substantive testing, and second, the distinctive control features in computer systems, there are often changes in the substantive tests.

The audit use of file interrogation software to examine data held on computer files represents the most common use of the computer to assist in substantive testing. The two most significant features in using computer programs are: first, all relevant items are normally examined, whereas when manual tests are used only a sample is normally examined; and second, additional information of assistance to the auditor can often be produced. The combination of these two factors usually enables the auditor to carry out more effective or more efficient substantive tests than are practicable by manual means.

It is advisable to establish formal procedures to control the use of computer software. This will help ensure that software is used only in cases where the cost can be justified, that the contemplated objectives are appropriate, and that the costs are controlled.

Glossary

The communication of facts and ideas in any field is dependent on a mutual understanding of the words used. In this glossary we present definitions for some of the terms that are often used in the field of data processing.

Absolute address　A machine-language address permanently assigned to a specific location in storage.

Access　See *direct-access, random-access, remote-access, serial-access.*

Access time　The elapsed time between the instant when data are called for from a storage device and the instant when the delivery of the data begins.

Accumulator　A register or storage location in which the result of an arithmetic or logic operation is formed.

Acoustic coupler　A communications device that allows an ordinary telephone handset to be used to connect a computer device to the telephone network for data transmission.

Address　An identification (e.g. a name or number) that designates a register, a particular location in storage, or any other data destination or source. Also, a part of an instruction that specifies the location of an operand for the instruction.

To refer to a device or an item of data by its address.

ALGOL (ALGOrithmic Language)　An algebraic procedure-oriented programming language that is widely used in Europe to perform mathematical computation.

Algorithm　A set of well-defined rules for solving a problem in a finite number of operations.

Alphanumeric　Pertaining to a character set that includes letters, digits, and, usually, other special punctuation character marks.

Analog computer　A device that operates on data represented in the form of continuously variable physical quantities.

ANSI (American National Standards Institute)　An organization for the establishment of industry standards.

Applications software　Programs, routines written for or by a user which apply to particular applications.

Arithmetic unit　The part of a computing system containing the circuitry that does the arithmetic and related operations.

Array An arrangement, in one or more dimensions, of elements of data; the elements are all of the same type and are accessed using index values.

Assembly program or Assembler A computer program that takes symbolic instructions prepared by a programmer and converts them into a form that may be executed by the computer.

Asynchronous data transmission A method of data transmission in which the transmitting and receiving devices are not synchronized. Each sequence of bits transmitted is preceded by a start signal, to 'wake up' the receiver, and is followed by a stop signal.

Attribute Characteristic or property of an entity (e.g. in a database).

Auxiliary storage A storage that supplements the primary (immediate access) storage of a computer, e.g. magnetic tapes and disks.

Background processing The execution of lower-priority computer programs during periods when the system resources are not required to process higher-priority programs.

BASIC (Beginners All-purpose Symbolic Instruction Code) A simple programming language designed primarily for on-line (interactive) use.

Batch processing A method whereby a number of items or transactions to be processed are collected together (batched) for sequential processing during a machine run.

Batch total The sum resulting from the addition of a specified field from each record in a batch of records, which is used for control and checking purposes.

Baud A unit of signalling speed equal to the number of discrete signal events per second.

Binary digit Either of the characters 0 or 1. Abbreviated 'bit'.

Binary number system A number system with a base or radix of two.

Bit Abbreviation for binary digit.

Block Related records, characters, or digits that are grouped and handled as a single entity particularly during input and output.

Boolean Logical data type having value *true* or *false*.

Bubble memory An internal storage device capable of holding large quantities of data in a very small space.

Bucket A logical area of disk storage large enough to store one or more records.

Buffer A storage device used to compensate for the difference in rates of flow of data from one device to another – e.g. from an I/O device to the CPU.

Bug An error or malfunction in a program or a computer system.

Byte A group of adjacent bits representing a character and usually operated upon as a unit.

Cache memory An internal storage device used where extremely fast access is important.

Cathode ray tube (CRT) An electronic tube with a screen upon which information may be displayed.

Central processing unit (CPU) The component of a computer with the circuitry to control the interpretation and execution of instructions.

Channel (1) A path for carrying signals between a source and a destination. (2) A track on magnetic tape or a band on a magnetic drum.

Char Character data type.

Charge-coupled device system A compact form of fast semiconductor memory produced on a chip.

Check digit An extra digit included in identification codes, such as account numbers, for the purpose of checking the validity of the code.

Closed system A system which does not interact with its environment.

COBOL (Common Business-Oriented Language)   A programming language for business data-processing applications.

Code   A set of rules outlining the way in which data may be represented; also, rules used to convert data from one representation to another. To represent a program or routine in a form acceptable to a computer.

Command   A control signal or instruction.

Compiler   A computer program that produces a machine-language program from a user program which is usually written in a high-level language. The compiler is capable of replacing single-source program statements with a functionally equivalent sequence of machine-language instructions or with a subroutine.

Computer network   A processing complex consisting of two or more interconnected computers.

Concentrator   A front-end processor or multiplexor which compresses messages from a number of slow devices to form a compact, smooth stream of data for fast transmission to a central processor.

Conceptual schema   The overall logical structure of a database.

Console   The part of a computer system that enables human operators to communicate with the computer.

Context editor   A computer program which enables a sequence of characters in a given context in a file to be located and changed (edited).

Control total   See *Batch total*.

Control unit   That part of the central processing unit that decodes machine instructions and directs other components of the computer system to perform the task specified in the instruction.

CPU   See *Central processing unit*.

CP/M (Control Program Monitor)   Registered trade mark of Digital Research Inc., an industry-wide standard operating system developed for microcomputer systems.

CRT   See *Cathode ray tube*.

Cursor   A moveable position displayed on the screen of a visual display unit, usually indicating where the next character is to be entered.

Cylinder   The set of all tracks on a disk pack with the same nominal distance from the axis about which the disk pack rotates and which can all be accessed without repositioning the access mechanism.

DASD   Direct-Access Storage Device.

Data   Any representations such as characters to which meaning is, or might be, assigned.

Data administrator   The person responsible for defining, updating and controlling access to a database.

Data bank   See *Database*.

Data communication   The transmission and reception of data. The transmission of computer data is usually over a telephone network without change or processing.

Data description language   A language for describing data; usually for descriptions of the logical data but in some systems for both the logical and the physical data.

Data dictionary   An organized file of all the information pertaining to the data in a system.

Data independence   The concept of separation of the logical definition of data as viewed by the user in his program from the logical definition of the data in the database and from the physical representation of the data.

Data processing   One or more operations performed on data to achieve a desired objective.

Database A collection of data files integrated and organized into a single comprehensive file system. The data is organized to minimize redundant duplication
and to provide convenient access to data within the system to satisfy a wide
variety of user needs.

Database management system The software that builds, manages, and provides
access to a database.

Debug To detect, locate, and remove errors in programs and/or malfunctions in
equipment.

Decision table A table of all the conditions to be considered in the description of a
problem, together with the actions to be taken.

Default An alternative value, attribute, or option that is assumed when none has
been specified.

Digital computer A device that processes discrete data and performs arithmetic
and logic operations on these data. Contrast with *Analog computer*.

Direct access Pertaining to storage devices where the time required to retrieve
data is independent of the physical location of the data.

Distributed processing The use of physically separate computers connected
together so that they can co-operate to execute programs and share data.

Documentation The preparation of documents, during system analysis and subsequent programming, that describe such things as procedures, the computer
programs prepared, and any changes made at later dates.

Downtime The length of time a computer system is inoperative due to a fault.

Dump To write the contents of (part of) a storage, usually from internal to
external storage, as a safeguard against faults or errors.

Duplex In data communication, pertaining to a simultaneous two-way independent transmission in both directions.

Electronic funds transfer (EFT) A computer network which facilitates the movement of funds by electronic means.

Entropy A measure of disorder in a system.

External schema In database systems, a user's view of (a subset of) the data in the
system.

Feedback control The process whereby the output from a system is compared to a
standard and any difference corrected by altering the input.

Feedforward control The process whereby the *predicted* output from a system is
compared to a standard and any difference averted by altering the input.

Field A group of related characters treated as a unit. An item in a record.

File A collection of related records treated as a unit.

Fixed disk A data-storage medium that is a magnetic disk, which is permanently
on-line.

Floppy disk A data-storage medium that is a flexible 5¼-inch or 8-inch disk of
polyester film covered with a magnetic coating.

Flowchart A diagram that uses symbols and interconnecting lines to show (1) a
system of processing to achieve objectives (system flowchart) or (2) the logic
and sequence of specific program operations (program flowchart).

Fold To compact data by combining parts of the data, e.g. to transform a
two-word alphabetic key into a one-word numeric key by adding the numeric
equivalents of the letters.

FORTRAN (FORmula TRANslator) A high-level programming language used to
perform mathematical computations.

Front-end processor A separate communications computer which deals with the
flow of messages between a number of user terminals and the main computer.

Full duplex Synonymous with duplex.

Graceful degradation   A controlled degradation of a computer system following the loss of power or malfunction of some component of the system.

Half duplex   In data communication, pertaining to an alternate, one way at a time, independent transmission of data.

Hardcopy   A printed copy of machine output in a visually readable form. A display image that is recorded on paper.

Hardware   Physical equipment such as electronic, magnetic, and mechanical devices. Contrast with *Software*.

Hash function   An algorithm which given the key value of a record computes the address of a location for the storage of the record on a direct access storage device.

Hash total   A result obtained by applying an algorithm to a set of data for checking purposes.

Hashing   The process of applying a hash function.

Header label   A machine-readable record at the beginning of a file containing data identifying the file and data used in file control.

Hierarchical database   A database in which the logical organization of data is hierarchical, i.e. tree-structured.

Hybrid computer   A data-processing device using both analog and discrete data representation.

Identifier   Character or group of characters used to name an item of data.

Index register   A register or internal storage location where the result of simple integer arithemtic may be formed; used for modification of the address field of a machine instruction.

Indexed sequential file organization (ISAM)   A file organization where records are stored sequentially, yet individual records in the file may be accessed directly through an index of records' addresses.

Information   Meaning assigned to data by humans.

Input/output (I/O)   Pertaining to the techniques, media, and devices used to achieve human/machine communication.

Instruction   A set of characters used to specify an operation and the values or locations of the instruction operands, if any.

Integrated circuits   Refers to miniaturization of electronic circuits such that many thousands of components may be formed on a small chip of silicon.

Interactive   Pertaining to an application in which each command or data entry to the computer system invokes a response from the system; may be conversational, implying a continuous dialogue between system and user.

Interface   A shared boundary, e.g. the boundary between two systems or devices.

Internal schema   In database systems, the definition of physical representations and organization of data in a database.

Internal storage   The addressable storage in a digital computer directly under the control of the central processing unit.

Interpreter   A computer program that translates each source language statement into a sequence of machine instructions and then executes these machine instructions before translating the next source language statement.

Interrupt   A suspension of execution of a program or process, usually caused by an event external to that process, and performed in such a way that the process can be resumed.

Interrupt bit   A binary digit signalling the occurrence and nature of an interrupt.

Interrupt mask   A special register used to determine which interrupt bit is set and hence the cause of the interrupt.

I/O Input/output.

ISAM (Indexed Sequential Access Method) *See Indexed sequential file organization.*

K An abbreviation for kilo or 1,000 in decimal notation. Used to denote 1024 when referring to computer storage.

Key An item that is used to identify a record.

Library routine A tested routine maintained in a library of programs.

Line-oriented editor A computer program which locates a specified (numbered) line of text in a file and allows that text to be altered, or deleted, or additional lines to be inserted.

Line structure A file or data structure in which each record contains the address of the next record in the structure.

Logical record A record seen independently of its environment, i.e. defined in terms of the data it contains and its use, rather than how it is stored.

Loop A sequence of instructions in a program that can be executed repetitively until or while certain specified conditions are satisfied.

Machine language A language executed directly by a computer without any translation.

Macro instruction A source-language instruction that is equivalent to a specified number of machine-language instructions.

Magnetic ink character recognition (MICR) The recognition of characters printed with a special magnetic ink by machines.

Magnetic storage Utilizing the magnetic properties of materials to store data on such devices and media as disks, drums, cores, tapes, and films.

Mainframe A large computer system that typically has over 100 K bytes of primary storage.

Management information system An information system designed to supply managers with the information needed to plan, organize, staff, direct, and control the operations of the organization.

Mass storage Storage having very large capacity.

Memory Same as *Storage.*

Menu A list of alternative actions or processes from which a user may select one at any particular stage in the execution of an application program.

MICR See *Magnetic ink character recognition.*

Microcomputer A very small and inexpensive computer consisting of a microprocessor on a silicon chip, an input/output device and possible low-cost secondary storage such as floppy disks.

Microfilm device A computer output device which produces microimages, arranged sequentially, on a film.

Microprocessor The basic arithmetic, logic, and storage elements of a CPU, generally on one (or a few) integrated circuit chip(s).

Microprogram A sequence of elementary instructions that is translated by a micrologic subsystem residing in the CPU.

Microsecond One-millionth of a second.

Millisecond One-thousandth of a second.

Minicomputer A relatively fast but small and inexpensive computer, usually with somewhat limited input and output capabilities.

MIS See *Management information system.*

Modem (Modulator-demodulator) A functional unit that modulates and demodulates signals. One of its functions is to enable digital computer signals to be transmitted using analog transmission facilities such as the telephone network.

Modularity The extent to which a system or program is composed of modules.

Multi-access Simultaneous access by two or more users or devices.

Multidrop   Refers to a terminal network configuration in which two or more devices share common lines to the central computer.

Multiplex   To simultaneously transmit messages over a single channel or other communications facility.

Multiprocessing   The simultaneous execution of two or more sequences of instructions by separate processors in a single computer configuration.

Multiprocessor   A computer configuration consisting of two or more central processors under a common control.

Multiprogramming   The simultaneous handling of multiple independent programs by interleaving or overlapping their execution.

Nanosecond   One-billionth of a second.

Network   A system of a data communication channels used for the transmission of data from one location to another.

Network database   A database in which the logical data structure allows many-to-many relationships among the nodes in the structure.

Network or plex structure   A data structure which allows many-to-many relationships among the nodes of the structure.

Normalization   In relational database systems, refers to the process of reducing complex relations to a simpler, more regular form.

Number cruncher   A colloquialism for a computer used for numerical computation.

Object program   A fully compiled or assembled program that is ready to be loaded into the computer for execution.

OCR (Optical Character Recognition)   The recognition of printed characters through the use of light-sensitive optical devices.

Off-line   A term describing equipment, or devices, not in direct communication with the central processing unit of a computer.

On-line   A term describing equipment, or devices, that are in direct communication with the central processing unit of a computer.

Open system   A system that interacts with its environment.

Operand   An entity that is operated upon. An operand is usually identified by the address part of an instruction.

Operating system   An organized collection of software that controls the overall operations of a computer including execution of user programs, and may provide scheduling, debugging, input/output control, accounting, compiling, storage management, data management and other related services.

Operation code   The instruction code used to represent the operations a computer is to perform.

Optical reader   A device that reads handwritten or machine-printed characters into a computing system through use of light-sensitive devices.

Page   In a virtual memory system, a fixed-length block that has a virtual address and can be transferred between real primary storage and auxiliary storage.

Parameter   Refers to a data item communicated between a subroutine and the program or subroutine that invokes the subroutine.

Parity bit   A special bit in a group of bits that is used to make the number of ones (or zeros) odd (or even).

Parity check   A check that tests whether the number of ones (or zeros) in a group of binary digits is odd or even.

Peripheral equipment   The input/output devices and auxiliary storage units of a computer system.

Peripheral transfer   A transfer of data between the CPU or primary storage and a peripheral device.

Picosecond   One-thousandth of a nanosecond.

PL/1 (Programming Language 1)   A high-level language designed to process both scientific and file-manipulating applications.

Pointer   A data item in one record that contains the location address of another logically related record.

Pointer chain   A logical sequence of pointers.

Procedure-oriented language   A programming language designed to conveniently express procedures used to solve a particular class of problems.

Program   (1) A set of sequenced instructions to a computer to perform particular operations; (2) to design, write and test one or more routines.

Program library   A collection of programs and routines.

Programmer   One who designs, writes, tests and maintains computer programs.

Programming language   A language used to express programs.

Programming-language translator   A program to translate user programs, expressed in a source language, into equivalent machine-language programs. See also *compiler*.

Progressive linear overflow   Refers to a technique used in direct access storage to resolve problems of overflow: when the algorithm for address computation yields the same address for two or more records, the second and subsequent records are located by a linear search starting from the computed address.

PROM   Programmable read-only memory.

Protected field   On a visual display device, a display field in which the user cannot enter, modify, or erase data from the keyboard.

Protocol   In data transmission, a complete set of rules about the conduct of the communication and the formats of messages which are exchanged.

Query language   A language for expressing user enquiries when interrogating a database.

RAM   Random access memory – see *Random access*.

Random   A type of file organization allowing direct access to any record independently of other records.

Random access   Descriptive of storage devices where the time required to retrieve data is largely independent of the physical location of the data.

Randomizing   A technique by which records may be assigned to specific storage locations by some method of computation applied to the key values.

Real memory   The physical primary storage, cf. virtual memory.

Real-time   Descriptive of on-line computer-processing systems which receive and process data quickly enough to produce output to control, direct, or affect the outcome of an ongoing activity or process.

Record   A collection of related items of data treated as a unit.

Register   A device capable of storing an item of data.

Relation   In database systems, a representation of an entity by means of a table in which the columns correspond to attributes of the entity and the rows represent specific instances of the entity.

Relational algebra   The mathematics applicable to relations.

Relational database   A database system in which the underlying data structure is the relation.

Remote access   Relating to the communication with a computer facility by a station (or stations) that is geographically remote from the computer.

Report program generator (RPG)   Software designed to construct programs that perform predictable report-writing operations.

Ring structure   A linear list structure in which the last record refers to the first record, so forming a ring.

Ring system   Descriptive of a computer network in which all the communicating stations or devices are connected together in a ring.

ROM   Read only memory, pre-written computer memory whose values cannot be changed.

Routine   A subprogram or module of a program.

Secondary storage   See *Auxiliary storage*.

Sector   A subdivision of a track or tracks on a magnetic disk.

Seek area   The set of all tracks that can be accessed on a disk pack without movement of the access device, see *Cylinder*.

Seek time   The time taken to move the disk access device to a particular cylinder position.

Semantic check   In programming language translation, a check for correct use of language constructs.

Semiconductor   An electronic circuit or device which can be reproduced photographically in a miniaturized form on silicon wafers.

Sequential file   A serial file organization in which the records are stored in order of the record key field.

Sequential file processing   A method of file processing in which all the records are processed in sequence, i.e. no record can be processed until all the preceding records have been processed.

Serial access   Descriptive of a storage device or medium where there is a sequential relationship between access time and data location in storage, i.e. the access time is dependent upon the location of the data. No record can be accessed without first accessing all the preceding records. Contrast with *Direct access* and *Random access*.

Serial file   A file in which the records are stored in no particular order other than the order in which they arise.

Software   A set of programs, documents, procedures, and routines that facilitate the use of a computer system. Contrast with *hardware*.

Solid-state   Descriptive of components and devices whose operation depends on the control of electronic or magnetic phenomena in solids, such as transistors.

Source document   An original document (usually prepared manually) from which data are extracted for entry to a computer system.

Source language   A language in which users' programs are expressed, such as FORTRAN, BASIC, COBOL, PL/1 etc.

Source program   A computer program written in a source language.

Spooling (simultaneous peripheral operation on-line)   The use of secondary storage as buffer storage to reduce processing delays during peripheral transfers.

Stand-alone microcomputer   A microcomputer capable of being used independently of other computers.

Star-formation   Descriptive of a computer network in which all devices are connected directly by separate lines to the central (main) computer, cf. *drop formation*.

Statement   A generalized instruction in a source language.

Storage   Descriptive of a device or medium that can accept and hold data, and deliver them on demand at a later time. Synonymous with *Memory*.

Structured programming   A methodology used in the design of computer programs. The approach generally assumes the disciplined use of top-down step-by-step refinement to decompose main functions into lower-level functions for coding purposes.

Subroutine   A routine that can be a part of or invoked by another routine or program.

Synchronous data transmission A method of data transmission in which the receiving and transmitting devices have synchronized oscillators; transmission is at a constant rate with no start and stop signals between characters.

Syntax In programming languages, the set of grammatical rules for forming statements.

Syntactic errors In programs, incorrectly formed statements.

System An organized grouping of people, procedures, machines, and materials collected together to accomplish a set of specific objectives.

System analyst One who studies the activities, methods, procedures, and techniques of organizational systems in order to determine what actions need to be taken and how these actions can best be accomplished.

Text editor A computer program to perform specified amendments to a file of textual data.

Throughput The total amount of useful work performed by a computer system during a given time period.

Timesharing The interleaved use of the time of specific hardware by two or more devices, programs, or people, in such a way as to provide quick response to each of the users and so giving an impression of simultaneous use.

Top-down methodology A disciplined approach to organizing complexity by identifying the top-level functions in a system and then decomposing these functions step by step into a hierarchy of understandable lower-level modules.

Trailer label The last record in a serial or sequential file which contains control information such as a count of the number of records in the file and hash totals.

Transaction file A file of relatively transient data, containing records used to update master files.

Transaction log A transaction file created for the purpose of back-up and audit trail.

Transmission time The time taken to transfer data from one part of storage to another.

Tree structure Descriptive of a hierarchical data structure in which each record may have a one-to-many relationship with records at a lower level.

Utility routine Software used to perform some frequently required process in the operation of a computer system, e.g. sorting, merging, etc.

Variable In a computer program, an identifier whose associated value may be changed or updated during execution of the program.

Variable word length Descriptive of a computer whose instruction set allows manipulation of groups of bits of more than one size (usually multiples of bytes).

Virtual storage Descriptive of the capability to use on-line secondary storage devices and specialized software to divide programs into smaller segments (pages) for transmission to and from internal storage in order to significantly increase the effective size of the available internal storage.

Word A group of bits or characters considered as an entity and capable of being stored in one storage location.

Word length The number of bits in a word.

Workspace An area of storage for data that is needed only for the duration (execution time) of a program or routine.

Index

Access control analysis, 471–2
Access controls, 195, 197–8
Access levels, 178
Access time, 35
Accounting information system (AIS), 274
Accounting packages, 424–5
Ad hoc decision support systems, 296, 297
ADA, 60
Adaptive systems, 217
ALGOL, 60–1
Allocations schedule file, 354
Alter, S. L., *Decision Support Systems: Current Practice and Continuing Challenges*, 394, 410, 412
American Airlines, 391
Amey, L. R. *Budget Planning and Control Systems*, 232
Analog computers, 27
Analytical review, 468
Anderson, J. F. and Berdie, D. R., *Questionnaires: Design and Use*, 260
Ansoff, H. I., *Corporate Strategy*, 369
Apple Macintosh Pagemaker, 423
Apple Talk, 139, 141–2
AppleTalk Link Access Protocol (ALAP), 142
AppleTalk Transaction Protocol (ATP), 142
Application controls, 198 *et seq*
Applications programming, 185
Applications viruses, 179
Arithmetic-logic unit, 28–9

ARPANET, 139–40
Article Numbering Association, 143
Ashton-Tate, 426
AT&T, 148
Audit trail, 150, 173–6, 189, 231, 310, 474
Authorization, 464–5
Automated teller machines (ATMs), 167

Backing store, *see* Secondary store
Balance-brought-froward system, 321
Balance sheet auditing, 474–5
BASIC, 60–8, 72
Batch control system, 18, 127, 205
Batch mode, 18, 79–80, 165
Batch processing, 82, 87, 96–7, 127, 153, 191
Batch totals, 172, 174, 198–9, 308–9
Bauds, 148
Bell System, 145
Berdie, D. R. and Anderson, J. F., *Questionnaires: Design and Use*, 260
Bhaskar, K. N., *Building Financial Models: A Simulation Approach*, 394
Bhaskar, K. N. and Shave, M. J. R., *Computer Science Applied to Business Systems*, 92
Bhaskar, K. N. *et al*, *Financial Modelling with a Computer – A Managerial Revolution*, 394
Binary tree structures, *see* Tree structures
Bit, 31–3

Boot record viruses, 179
Bootleg terminal, 178
Borland, 428
Boundaries 214–16
Box-Jenkins technique, 397
Bridge, 141
British Leyland, 278
British Rail, 278
British Telecom, 142, 145, 148, 430
Bubble memory, 38–9, 78
Budget analysis, 390
Budget control, 5, 8, 182, 186, 335, 353, 441
Budget data, 326
Budget information system (BIS) 407–13
Budgeting *viii*, 13, 335 *et seq*, 367–9, 376
Buffer, 28, 130, 187
Buffer/cache memory, 39
Burroughs Corporation, 21
Bypass procedure, 155
Byte, 31–3

C, 60
Cash-flow forecasting model, 376–81
Cash planning, 230
Cataloguing controls, 458
Ceefax, 430
Central processing unit (CPU), 17, 27–8, 33, 37, 52–3, 89
Chance-constrained programming, 400–1
CIMA, 3, 5
Closed systems, 217–18
COBOL, 20, 59, 61, 68–72
Codd, E. F., 'A Relational Model of Data for Large Shared Data Banks', *Communications of the AGM*, June 1970, 119
Code analysis, 471
Commands, 17–18
Commodore, 21
Compliance tests, 482–3
Computer aided design (CAD), 424
Computer aided manufacturing (CAM), 424
Computer assisted auditing techniques (CAATs), 467–8
Computer auditing, *viii*, 451 *et seq*
Computer networks, *see* Networks
Computer operation controls, 460
Computerized accounting controls, 452–3

Computerized accounting systems, 441–2
Concentrator, 130
Conditional statement, 372
Control accounts, 222
Control Data Corporation, 21
Control totals, *see* Batch totals
Controllers, 27–8, 37
Conversational mode, 18
Conversion system, 237
Corporate models, *see* Financial modelling
Cost collection system, 347
Cost control, 272, 361, 434 *et seq*
Cost cutting, *see* Productivity
Cost estimation system, 338, 344–5
CP/M, 48
Credit control, 229, 311, 325
Cross referencing, 250
Cushing, B. E., *Accounting Information Systems and Business Organizations*, 182, 228
Customer sales report, 342

Data administration, 122–3
Data analysis, 105–10, 390–4
Data collection, 255–62
Data communications, 126 *et seq*
Data control, 186
Data definition language (DDL), 118–19
Data dictionaries, 110
Data entry, 17–18, 174–6, 185–6
Data extraction, 388–9
Data flow diagrams, 245–8, 259
Data independence, 102, 124
Data manipulation, *see* Data extraction
Data manipulation language (DML), 119
Data protection, 123–4
Data Protection Act, 1984, 208
Data reduction, 223–4
Data retrieval, 425–7
Data structures, 234
Data transfer, 138
Data transmission, 128, 145–8
Database, 101–25, 393, 442
Database integrity, 101, 123
Database packages, 425–7
Datagram delivery protocol (DDP), 142
Datastream, 430
Date, C. J., *An Introduction to Database Systems*, 112

Davis, G. B., *Management Information Systems: Conceptual Foundations,Structures and Development*, 220
DB2, 118
DBase III and IV, 76, 426, 430
Debugging, 178
Decision support systems *vii, viii*, 5, 10, 14, 274, 296, 364, 388 *et seq*, 434 *et seq*
Decision tables, 252–5
DECNET, 139, 140–1
Decoupling, 220
Defense Advanced Research Projects Agency (DARPA), 140
Defense, US Department of, 140
Design methodology 236, 241, 243–5
Desktop publishing (DTP), 423–4
Deterministic models, 394–5, 407
Deterministic simulation, 364–6
Deterministic systems, 216–17
Digital computers, 27, 45
Digital Equipment Corporation, 21, 139
Discounted cash flow (DCF), 407
Distributed computing systems, 132, 154
Document flowchart, 289
Documentation, 188, 195–6, 143, 262
Dynamic programming, 400–1

Earl, M. J., McCoch, A. M. and Rahman, M., *Developing Managerial Information Systems*, 280, 435–7
Electronic bulleting boards, 180
Electronic data interchange (EDI), 145, 431
Electronic diary, 428
Electronic funds transfer system (EFTS), 167–8
Electronic invoicing, 166
Electronic ledger, 74, 424–5
Electronic mail, 132, 141, 169, 430–1
Electronic ordering, 167
Electronic payment, 167
Electronic spreadsheet, 364
Electronic trading, 143
Embedded code, 473–4
Emerald Bay, 426–7
Entity analysis, 105–9
Entity models, 248–9
Entity types, 106–8, 115

Entity-function matrix, 250–1
Entropy transfer, 218
Equifinality, Principle of, 227–8
Error log, 204
Events accounting, 442–3
Everest, G. C., 'The Objectives of Database Management' in Tou, J. T. (ed), *Information Systems: COINS IV*, 102
Everest, G. C. and Weber, R., 'A Relational Approach to Accounting Models', *The Accounting Review*, April 1977, 120
Extended entry table, 253
External auditing, 451 *et seq*

Facsimile systems (fax), 431–2
Feasibility study, 262 *et seq*
Feedback, 214, 225, 437
Feedback control systems, 171, 228–9
Feedforward control systems, 171, 229–30
Field, 77, 106
File security controls, 460
File storage, 446
Filestore, 16–17, 27–8, 34
Filtering, 227
Financial modelling, *vii*, 12–13, 364 *et seq*, 388
Finished goods inventory control 337–8, 342
FINSTAN, 394
Fleet Street Editor, 424
Flower, J., *Computer Models for Accountants*, 394, 403
Forecasts, 367–9
FORTRAN, 20, 60–8
Framework III, 429
Front-end processor, 128–30
Full-duplex data transmission, 138, 147
Functional analysis, 109

Gardner, Bert (FCMA), 13
General ledger, 304, 308, 311, 336, 351, *et seq*, 441
Goal programming, 400
Gorry, G. A. and Scott-Morton, M. S., 'A Framework for Management Information Systems', *Sloan Management Review*, 1971
Grandfather, father, son technique 80, 190–4

Graphics, 424

Hackers 177–8
Half duplex data transmission, 138, 147
Harris, 21
Hash function, 89–92
Hewlett-Packard, 21
Hicks, J. O. and Leininger, W. O., *Accounting Information Systems*, 207, 356
Hierarchical archiving, 194
Hierarchical databases, 110–11
Hierarchical structures, 279–80, 284
Honeywell, 21
Hooper, P. and Page, J., *Accounting and Information Systems*, 173
Hosts, 133

IBM, 21–2, 52, 61, 139–40, 195, 336, 421, 427
IBM Mass storage system, 37
IBM System, 20, 360
ICL, 21–2, 143
ICL 1900 range, 20
Indexed sequential files, 91–3
Information flows, 285 *et seq*, 336 *et seq*
Information overload, 8, 14
Information processing system, 16
Ingres, 118
Input controls, 174
Integer programming, 400–1
Integrated circuits, 20
Integrated packages, 429
Integrated services digital network (ISDN), 433
Intel, 21
Interactive exception reporting, 410, 413
Interactive graphics, 389
Interactive planning, 410–12
Interface, 28
Interface message processor (IMP), 133, 135
Internal audit, 229, 451 *et seq*
Internal audit review, 189
Internal control policies, 181 *et seq*
Internal control systems, 272, *see also* Preventive control systems
International Network Services, 143
International Standards Organisation, 137; reference model, 138–9, 141
Interrogation software, 468, 485

Interrupt feature, 19, 50–1
Inventory control, 230, 348–51
Israeli virus, 179
ITT, 21

Job costing system, 347

Kanban card, 449
Key field, 78, 82–3, 120
Key to tape units, *see* Magnetic tape encoders

Large scale integration (LSI), 21
Latency, 35
Law of requisite variety, 227
Lehigh virus, 179
Leininger, W. E. and Hicks, J. O., *Accounting Information Systems*, 207, 356
Library functions, 67, 194–5
Limited entry table, 253
Linear programming, 13, 397–401, 415
Local area networks (LANs), 420–1, 430
Logic bombs, 179
Long range planning, 435
LOTUS 1–2–3, 76, 364, 427–9

McCarthy, W. E., 'An Entity-Relationship View of Accounting Models', *The Accounting Review*, October 1979, 442–3
McCoch, A. M., Rahman, M. and Earl, M. J., *Developing Managerial Information Systems*, 280, 435–7
Magnetic ink character recognition (MICR), 40
Magnetic tape encoders, 40
Magnetic tape systems, 37
Mainframes, 21–2, 37, 52, 131–2, 185, 421
Management Information Systems (MIS), *viii*, 6–14, 101, 214–16, 218, 232, 272 *et seq*, 335 *et seq*, 434 *et seq*; accounting applications, *vii*, 303 *et seq*; development of, *vii*
Management Science America, Inc (MSA), 336, 342, *see also* MSA
Mapping, 473
Martin, J., *Application Development without Programmers*, 445
Martin, J., *Design of Real-time Computer Systems*, 152

Mass production, 282
Materials inventory control, 347
Mathematical programming, 7
Mechanistic systems, 280
Mercury, 142, 145
Microcomputer, 22, 420 *et seq*
Microprocessor, 21–3, 46, 422
Microprogram, 33
Microsoft, 52
Microsoft Excel, 428
Minicomputer, 21–2, 36–7, 52
Mixed entry tables, 254
Model logic, 366
Modems, 145–6, 179
Modularity, 20
Monte Carlo simulation technique,
      401
Motorola, 21
MSA general ledger system, 354–363;
      budget system, 354, 357–9; cost
      allocation system, 354, 359–61;
      profit-reporting system, 354,
      361–2; responsibility reporting
      system, 354, 358–9
MS-DOS, 48, 421
Multi-access, 20, 48, 154
Multidrop formation, 129, 140
Multilevel index, 92
Multiplan, 427
Multiple decision tables, 254
Multiplexor, 130, 146
Multiprocessing, 48–51, 53
Multiprogramming, 20, 48–51
Multitasking, 52

Name-binding protocol (NBP), 142
National Computing Centre, UK
      (NCC), 284
Naylor, T. H., *Corporate Planning
      Models*, 394, 403
NCR, 21
Negative feedback, 225
Network analysis, 13
Network architecture, 137 *et seq*
Network databases, 110–11
Network structures, 100–1, 110–11,
      114, 133–6
Networks, 127 *et seq*
Nodes, 133, 143
Non-linear programming, 400–1
Normalization, 114–22
Notation, 234–5

Object program, 71

Office automation, 420 *et seq*
Off-line, 18
On-line, 18
On-line input, 204–7
On-line storage, *see* Secondary store
On-line systems, 126 *et seq*
Open item ledger system, 321
Open systems, 218–19, 227
Operational planning, 274
Operational processing, 434–5
Optical character recognition (OCR),
      see Optical mark recognition
Optical mark recognition (OMR), 40–1
Optimizing models, 394, 397–401
Oracle, 430
Order processing, 338–42, 345
Organismic systems, 280
Organizational structure, 279–80
OS/2, 48, 52, 119, 421
Output values, 380–1

Page, J. and Hooper, P., *Accounting
      and Information Systems*, 173
Pakistani Brain, 180
Parallel simulation, 471
Parity check, 187
Parkin, A., *COBOL for Students* 71;
      Systems Analysis, 260, 263
PASCAL, 60–8, 75
Payroll system, 328
PC Auditor, 474
PDP, 11, 53
Performance measurement, *viii*, 3, 5,
      10
Performance tracking, 436
Perkins-Elmer (Interdata), 21
Piggybacking, 178
Plex structures, *see* Network
      structures
Poisson distribution, 403
Post Office, 278
Prepackaged software, 422–3
Prestel, 430
Preventive control systems, 171 *et seq*,
      230–1, 482–5
Primary memory, 33
Primary store, 16, 27–9, 45, 53–4, 78,
      88, 92, 150
Prime, 21
Probabilistic models, 394, 401–7
Probabilistic systems, 216–18, 227, 290
Procedural controls, 187 *et seq*
Processing outlines, 251–2

Process production, 282
Processing controls, 207
Production control, 229
Production management, 344
Production scheduling, 345–6
Productivity, 121, 444–7
Program development, 241–3
Program development controls, 458
Program security controls, 460
Programmable read-only memory (PROM), 33
Programmed procedures, 460
Progressive linear overflow, 91
Project appraisal, 405
PROLOG, 60
Prompting, 206
Protocols, 128 137–9, 141–5
Prototyping, 73
Public network systems, 139, 142–3
Public switched telephone networks (PSTNs), 145–8
Purchase ledger, 304
Purpose built software, 422

Quadratic programming, 400–1
Quality control, 272
Quattro, 428
Query language, 426–7

Rahman, M., McCoch, A. M. and Earl, M. J., *Developing Managerial Information Systems*, 280, 435–7
Random access memory (RAM), 33–4
Random files, 88–91
R:Base, 426
Read only memory (ROM), 33
Real memory, 54
Real-time 18, 79–80, 126–7, 148 *et seq*, 187, 331, 389
Records, 77, 106
Redundancy, 199, 221–3
Redundancy check, 187, 202
Relational databases, 111–22; developments in, 118–19
Relationship linkage file, 355
Remington Rand, 20
Responsibility accounting, 229, 285, 335, 409–14, 436
Ricoh, 38
Ring structures, 99–100

Sage Accountant Plus, 424–5

Salami principle, 176
Sales analysis, 313–15, 320–6, 336, 342–4, 391–3
Sales day book, *see* Sales journal
Sales journal, 317, 324
Sales ledger, 304 *et seq*, 328–34
Sanders, D. H., *Computers in Business: An Introduction*, 176
Scott-Morton, M. S. and Gorry, G. A. 'A Framework for Management Information Systems', *Sloan Management Review*, 1971, 296
Secondary store, 16, 53–4, 88
Security controls, 171 *et seq*
Seek area, 34
Seek time, 35
Semantic integrity, 119
Semiconductor memory, 33–4, 38
Semprevivo, P. C., *Systems Analysis: Definition, Process and Design*, 257
Sensitivity analysis, 401
Sequential files, 82–8, 93
Serial files, 81–2
Serial storage, 88
Shave, M. J. R. and Bhaskar, K. N., *Computer Science Applied to Business Systems*, 92
Short-term planning, 436
Sidekick, 33
Simplex data transmission, 138, 147, 399
Simplistic structures, 279
Simultaneous equations model, 396
Snapshot, 473–4
Sorter, G. H., 'An "Events" Approach to Basic Accounting Theory', *The Accounting Review*, January 1969, 443
Span of control, 279, 282
Sperry-Univac, 21
Spoofing, 178
Spooling, 19, 31, 50
Spreadsheets, 73–4, 364 *et seq*, 427–8
Staff organizations, 280
Standard cost systems, 229
Star network, 129
Statistical forecasting models, 394–7
Stochastic programming, 400–1
Stochastic systems, *see* Probabilistic systems
Stock Exchange, 430
Strategic analysis, 5
Strategic model, 376, 386–7

Strategic planning, 273–4, 435
Structured query language (SQL)
    118–19; Informix SQL, 118
Structured systems analysis and
    design methodology (SSADM),
    244–5
Suboptimization, 283
Substantive tests, 484–5
SuperCalc, 427
SWIFT, 139, 164
Switching elements, *see* Nodes
Symphony, 429
System development, 233 *et seq*
Systems activity, 182–3
Systems analysis, 174, 185, 233 *et seq*
Systems-based auditing, 453–4
Systems cost determination, 266–9
Systems flowcharts, 289
Systems network architecture (SNA),
    139–40
Systems proposal, 240
Systime, 53, 311

Tactical planning, 274
Tandem Computers, 187
Tanenbaum, A., *Computer Networks*
    139
Targets, 367–9
Telecom Gold, 431
Telenet, 148
Teletex, 432
Teletext systems, 430
Telex, 432
Temporary transactions file, 18
Terminate and stay resident programs
    (TSR), 33
Texas Instruments, 21
Textline, 430
Thierauf, R. J., *Decision Support
    Systems for Effective Planning and
    Control: A Case Study Approach*,
    363, 389, 394, 414–15, 437–8
Time series analysis, 396–7
Time sharing, 154–5

Toyota, 449
Tracing, 473
Tradacoms, 143
TRADANET, 139, 143–5
Transmission lines, 133
Transmission system, 133, 135
Transmission time, 34
Trap door, 178–9
Tree structures, 98–9, 105, 110–11,
    114, 140
Trojan horse, 178

Unit production, 282
UNIVAC I, 20
Universal product code (UPC), 41
UNIX, 48
User charging system, 186
User controls, 460

Vaccine programs, 181
Variance investigation, *viii*, 226–7
Variance reporting, *viii*
VAX 11/780, 53
Ventura, 424
Very large systems (VLS), 21
Videotex, *see* Viewdata
Viewdata, 430
Vigler III/386–25, 38
Virtual memory, 54
Viruses, 179–81
Visible record computer (VRC), 20–1
VisiCalc, 427
Visual Display Unit (VDU), 16–19
Voice mail, 431

Western Union, 145
Word lengths, 31–2
Word processing package, 423
Work-in-progress system, 347–8
Workstation, 420 *et seq*
World Textiles, 430
Write-one-read-many disks (WORM),
    38

Zilog, 21